# Knowledge processing and applied artificial intelligence

### Soumitra Dutta

Assistant Professor of Information Systems

INSEAD

Fontainebleau
France

BUTTERWORTH
HEINEMANN

Butterworth-Heinemann Ltd
Linacre House, Jordan Hill, Oxford OX2 8DP

⟨R⟩ A member of the Reed Elsevier group

OXFORD LONDON BOSTON
MUNICH NEW DELHI SINGAPORE SYDNEY
TOKYO TORONTO WELLINGTON

First published 1993

© Soumitra Dutta 1993

All rights reserved. No part of this publication may be reproduced in any material form (including photocopying or storing in any medium by electronic means and whether or not transiently or incidentally to some other use of this publication) without the written permission of the copyright holder except in accordance with the provisions of the Copyright, Designs and Patents Act 1988 or under the terms of a licence issued by the Copyright Licensing Agency Ltd, 90 Tottenham Court Road, London, England W1P 9HE. Applications for the copyright holder's written permission to reproduce any part of this publication should be addressed to the publishers

British Library Cataloguing in Publication Data
A catalogue record for this book is available from the British Library
ISBN 0 7506 1612 1

Typeset and produced by Co-publications, Loughborough
Printed and bound in Great Britain

To my mother, Tara Dutta and my father, Raj Kumar Dutta

# Contents

*Preface* xiii
*Acknowledgements* xv
*List of abbreviations* xvii

**Part I** 1

Chapter 1 — Knowledge processing and applied artificial intelligence 3
   The evolution of computing in business 4
   The rise of knowledge processing 5
   The origins of knowledge processing 6
   Philosophy 7
   Mathematics 8
   Computing 9
   The development of the field of artificial intelligence 10
   A shift in focus 11
   The evolving sub-fields 11
   Governmental funding 13
   The nature of intelligence 14
   Applied artificial intelligence 15
   Knowledge processing and applied artificial intelligence 15
   The commercialization of applied artificial intelligence 17
   Consolidation and growth 18
   The commercial market 19
   Moving from data processing to knowledge processing 20
   Structure and organization of book 21
   Summary 23
   Bibliography and suggested readings 24
   Notes 25

**Part II — Acquiring, representing, and reasoning with knowledge** 29

Chapter 2 — Knowledge-based systems and the acquisition of knowledge 31
   Digital Equipment Corporation 32
   American Express 32
   Campbell Soup 33
   Structure of knowledge-based systems 34
   The process of building knowledge-based systems 36
   Expert systems and knowledge-based systems 37

| | |
|---|---|
| Epistemology and knowledge-based systems | 37 |
| The definition of knowledge | 39 |
| The computer configuration problem | 39 |
| The dimensions of knowledge | 40 |
| Stages of knowledge | 42 |
| Knowledge in a knowledge-based system | 43 |
| Knowledge acquisition | 43 |
| Knowledge engineer-guided knowledge acquisition | 44 |
| Planning the knowledge acquisition process | 45 |
| Automated tools for knowledge acquisition | 48 |
| Induction | 48 |
| Steps after knowledge acquisition | 50 |
| Summary | 51 |
| Bibliography and suggested readings | 53 |
| Notes | 54 |

## Chapter 3 — Representing and reasoning with knowledge — 57

| | |
|---|---|
| Knowledge representation using rules | 58 |
| Complex rules and structured rule-based systems | 59 |
| Inference procedures in rule-based systems | 60 |
| Forward chaining | 60 |
| Backward chaining | 62 |
| A comparison of backward and forward chaining | 62 |
| Meta-knowledge in rule-based reasoning | 64 |
| Rule-based reasoning under uncertainty | 65 |
| Prolog: a simple rule-based system | 67 |
| The inference procedure of Prolog | 67 |
| Benefits and limitations of rule-based reasoning | 73 |
| Networked representations of knowledge | 74 |
| Semantic networks | 75 |
| Frame hierarchies | 76 |
| Structure of objects | 77 |
| Behaviors of objects | 80 |
| Communication between objects | 82 |
| Comparing frame hierarchies and rules | 82 |
| Alternative approaches to knowledge representation | 84 |
| Blackboard systems | 84 |
| Case-based reasoning | 86 |
| Summary | 88 |
| Bibliography and suggested readings | 89 |
| Notes | 90 |

## Part III — Implementing strategic knowledge processing applications — 93

## Chapter 4 — Creating knowledge-based systems — 95

| | |
|---|---|
| Creating rule-based systems | 96 |
| Problem description | 96 |
| Problem decomposition | 97 |
| Initial prototype | 98 |
| Incremental evolution | 99 |
| Customization | 102 |
| Structured rule-based systems | 102 |
| Creating hybrid knowledge-based systems | 104 |

|  |  |
|---|---|
| Problem description | 104 |
| Frame hierarchy identification | 105 |
| Structure and behavior identification | 106 |
| Prototyping and incremental evolution | 108 |
| Customization | 111 |
| Customizing the user interface | 111 |
| Interfaces to databases | 114 |
| Tools for building knowledge-based systems | 116 |
| Types of shell tools | 117 |
| Hardware platforms for shell tools | 118 |
| Guidelines for the selection of shell tools | 119 |
| Commercial market for knowledge-based products | 120 |
| The database and knowledge-based product markets | 121 |
| Summary | 123 |
| Bibliography and suggested readings | 125 |
| Notes | 126 |

## Chapter 5 — Strategic and organizational issues in knowledge processing — 129

|  |  |
|---|---|
| Levels of organizational knowledge | 130 |
| Managing knowledge in organizations | 130 |
| Knowledge-based systems and the management of knowledge | 132 |
| Applications of knowledge-based systems in organizations | 135 |
| The task perspective | 135 |
| User support types | 136 |
| The systems perspective | 137 |
| Activity types | 138 |
| Organizational benefits | 141 |
| Organizational hazards | 143 |
| Impact on industry structures | 144 |
| Managing the development process in organizations | 145 |
| Choosing a corporate strategy for knowledge processing | 146 |
| Factors affecting the knowledge processing strategy | 149 |
| Identification of potential knowledge-based applications | 150 |
| Cost-benefit analyses of potential applications | 151 |
| Determining feasibility of applications | 152 |
| Creation of knowledge-based applications | 153 |
| Deployment of applications | 155 |
| Maintenance of applications | 156 |
| Summary | 158 |
| Bibliography and suggested readings | 160 |
| Notes | 161 |

## Part IV — Intelligent interfaces — 163

## Chapter 6 — Natural language processing — 165

|  |  |
|---|---|
| The Securities and Exchange Commission | 165 |
| Siemens-Nixdorf | 166 |
| Components of natural language processing | 167 |
| The nature of understanding | 168 |
| Ambiguity in natural language understanding | 169 |
| Approaches to natural language understanding | 170 |
| Keyword matching | 170 |
| Syntax and semantics | 173 |

| | |
|---|---|
| Syntactic analyses | 173 |
| Semantic analyses | 175 |
| Combining syntax and semantics | 175 |
| Knowledge-based | 176 |
| Conceptual dependency diagrams | 176 |
| Scripts | 177 |
| Understanding multiple sentences and dialogs | 179 |
| Machine translation | 180 |
| Approaches to machine translation | 180 |
| Pattern-based translation | 180 |
| Using syntax and semantics for translation | 181 |
| Knowledge-based translation | 182 |
| Machine translation in industry | 183 |
| Evaluating natural language interfaces | 184 |
| Commercial tools for natural language processing | 185 |
| Applications of natural language processing | 186 |
| The Securities and Exchange Commission | 186 |
| The Intelligent Banking System at Citibank | 187 |
| The Direct Labor Management System at Ford | 188 |
| Content-based indexing of news stories at Reuters | 188 |
| Patient medical records system at Hartford Hospital | 189 |
| Natural language applications at Steelcase | 189 |
| The business impact of natural language processing | 190 |
| Summary | 191 |
| Bibliography and suggested readings | 193 |
| Notes | 194 |

## Chapter 7 — Image and speech processing 197

| | |
|---|---|
| Computer vision | 198 |
| Biological roots | 198 |
| Computational requirements | 199 |
| Problems and ambiguities | 200 |
| Information processing in machine vision | 203 |
| Signal processing | 204 |
| Digitizing and sampling | 204 |
| Thresholding | 205 |
| Smoothing | 206 |
| Edge detection | 207 |
| Image processing | 208 |
| Segmentation | 209 |
| Labelling | 210 |
| Image understanding | 210 |
| Identification | 211 |
| Interpretation | 212 |
| Commercial applications of machine vision | 212 |
| Industrial vision applications | 212 |
| Document image processing | 216 |
| Retirement fund processing | 217 |
| Yellow Pages advertising management | 219 |
| Diagnosing heart imagery | 219 |
| Microfossil identification | 220 |
| Speech processing | 221 |
| Interpretation problems | 221 |

| | |
|---|---|
| Speech recognition | 223 |
| Speech understanding | 224 |
|   Speech processing | 225 |
|   Phonetic analysis | 225 |
|   Phonological analysis | 226 |
|   Morphological analysis | 226 |
| The business impact of image and speech processing | 227 |
| Summary | 228 |
| Bibliography and suggested readings | 229 |
| Notes | 230 |

## Part V — Alternative approaches to knowledge processing — 233

## Chapter 8 — Approximate reasoning using fuzzy logic — 235

| | |
|---|---|
| Hitachi: The Sendai subway control system | 235 |
| Yamaichi Securities: intelligent trading programs | 236 |
| Matshushita: intelligent washing machines | 237 |
| Rockwell: modelling stress on wings | 237 |
| Development of fuzzy logic | 238 |
| Fundamentals of fuzzy logic technology | 239 |
|   Representational concepts | 239 |
|   Representation of vague concepts using fuzzy sets | 240 |
|   Linguistic variables | 241 |
|   Practical implications of fuzzy set representations | 242 |
| Reasoning procedures | 242 |
|   Mathematical operations on fuzzy sets | 243 |
|   Inference with fuzzy rules | 244 |
| Comparing fuzzy and conventional rules | 246 |
| Case studies of fuzzy logic applications | 247 |
|   The inverted pendulum | 247 |
|   Fuzzy rules for balancing an inverted pendulum | 248 |
|   Properties of fuzzy control | 250 |
|   Complex inverted pendulum systems | 251 |
| Sendai subway control | 251 |
| Commercial activities in fuzzy logic | 253 |
| Asia | 254 |
| America | 256 |
| Europe | 257 |
| The business impacts of fuzzy logic applications | 258 |
|   Enhancing knowledge-based technologies | 258 |
|   Embedded intelligence | 259 |
|   Intelligent process control | 259 |
|   New product development strategies | 259 |
| Summary | 261 |
| Bibliography and suggested readings | 262 |
| Notes | 263 |

## Chapter 9 — Connectionist modelling of intelligence — 265

| | |
|---|---|
| The connectionist approach | 266 |
| History of connectionism | 266 |
|   Governmental support | 267 |
| Neural networks | 267 |
| Problem types tackled by neural networks | 268 |

|   |   |
|---|---|
| Classification | 268 |
| Generalization | 269 |
| Clustering | 269 |
| Types of neural networks | 269 |
| Selected neural network architectures | 270 |
| Multi-layer perceptrons | 270 |
| Structure of neurons | 271 |
| Training | 272 |
| Testing | 273 |
| Learning | 273 |
| Decision regions solved by perceptrons | 274 |
| The Hopfield net | 275 |
| Kohonen's self-organizing feature maps | 275 |
| Designing applications using neural networks | 276 |
| Domain and problem characteristics | 276 |
| Designing the network | 277 |
| Training and testing the network | 279 |
| Maintaining and integrating applications | 281 |
| Commercial tools | 282 |
| Case study: using neural networks for bond rating | 282 |
| The problem of bond rating | 284 |
| Use of statistical models for bond rating | 285 |
| Decision region required for bond rating | 285 |
| Selection of variables | 286 |
| Data collection | 286 |
| Neural network | 286 |
| Regression | 287 |
| Results | 287 |
| Applications of neural networks | 288 |
| NETtalk | 289 |
| Determining the secondary structure of proteins | 289 |
| Car navigation | 290 |
| Backgammon | 290 |
| Diagnosis and treatment prescription for hypertension | 290 |
| Strengths and limitations of connectionist models | 291 |
| Limitations | 293 |
| The future of symbolic and connectionist approaches | 293 |
| Summary | 294 |
| Bibliography and suggested readings | 296 |
| Notes | 297 |
| Appendix 1 — Commercial applications of knowledge-based systems | 301 |
| Appendix 2 — Commercial vendors of knowledge-based products | 321 |
| Appendix 3 — Commercial applications of neural networks | 341 |
| *Index* | 350 |

# Preface

Within the short span of a few decades, computers have had a dramatic impact on business by automating storage and access of large amounts of data, and by facilitating configuration of information flows. While the foci of most business computing so far has been on data and information, new advances in artificial intelligence technology are making it possible for computing applications to directly impact storage, processing, and application of knowledge. We are entering the era of knowledge processing, the next phase of the computing revolution.

There are significant implications of such a change in the scope of computing applications. Organizations are constantly in the search for new, sustainable sources of competitive advantage. It is recognized today that the cumulative knowledge of an organization (or its intellectual capital) is a rich and largely untapped source of true competitive advantage. Applied artificial intelligence technology offers the ability to process knowledge and harness the potential of a corporation's intellectual capital for achieving a competitive advantage.

Purpose of this book is to help managers and students understand the competitive potential of knowledge processing and the fundamentals of the different facets of applied artificial intelligence technology. It is my belief that both these aspects go together. It is not very useful to study technology without seeing its business impact, and it is not possible to gauge the competitive potential of knowledge processing without understanding advantages and disadvantages of the underlying technologies.

This effort bridges the gap between applied artificial intelligence technologies and the competitive impact of their business applications. The description of artificial intelligence technologies should be easily accessible to business managers and students. The competitive potential of these technologies is clearly described with examples of real business applications. Guidelines and insights are presented at appropriate places for strategic planning and implementation of knowledge processing applications.

A comprehensive view of different technologies underlying knowledge processing is presented in this book. Besides knowledge-based systems, technologies covered here include natural language processing, image and speech processing, fuzzy logic, and neural networks. It has been my aim to balance the breadth of coverage with depth on individual topics. As the focus is on the applications of knowledge processing, more time is spent on technological aspects which have the maximum relevance for and impact on business applications. Bibliography lists at the end of each chapter direct the reader to other references for more details on specific topics.

This book can be used by managers and students from both business and computing disciplines. Business managers and students can learn about applied artificial intelligence technologies and the strategic impact of their business applications. Computing professionals and students without prior knowledge of artificial intelligence can benefit in much the same manner as their business counterparts. Computing professionals and students with some prior knowledge of artificial intelligence will find the discussions on the business relevance of knowledge processing and its links to a corporation's competitive position very interesting and helpful.

It is possible to use this book as a text for courses in both business and computing departments. It would perhaps be most suitable at the senior undergraduate and graduate (masters) levels. I have used it successfully as a textbook for teaching elective courses to MBA students at INSEAD. Alternatively, it can be read by a reader independently. The book is self-contained and technical concepts are explained in a simple language. Several figures and detailed examples also aid the reader.

I believe that this book is the first to offer a comprehensive view of knowledge processing technologies and the competitive potentials of their business applications. Writing the manuscript was both a challenge and a pleasure for me. I hope that you find the book useful and stimulating!

Soumitra Dutta

Fontainebleau
France

# Acknowledgements

An endeavor such as this book can rarely be successful without the support and encouragement of a number of people. Too numerous to name individually, I would like to mention special thanks to the following groups of individuals who contributed in important ways to the development of this book.

I would like to extend my deepest gratitude to faculty members of the computer science department and the business school at the University of California at Berkeley for first stimulating my interest in artificial intelligence and its business applications.

I would like to thank my colleagues at the European Institute of Business Administration (INSEAD) for providing a stimulating work environment and encouraging my work on the book. Thanks also to MBA students at INSEAD who provided detailed comments on the manuscript.

The production of this book would not be possible without the skilled assistance of the editorial staff at Butterworth-Heinemann. I would like to extend my gratitude to them for their help.

Finally, I would like to specially thank my family for putting up with my late nights and idiosyncrasies during the many months I spent working on the manuscript. Without their patience and understanding this book would not have been possible.

The book is certainly a better book due to the cumulative efforts of the above groups of people. While I have tried hard for accuracy and perfection, I know that I must have failed in some aspects. All responsibility for any errors or shortcomings in the book are entirely mine.

## List of abbreviations

Abbreviations in the following list have been used widely in this book. Abbreviations defined and used only in specific parts of the text are not included in the following list.

| | |
|---|---|
| AI | artificial intelligence |
| DIP | document image processing |
| ES | expert system |
| FL | fuzzy logic |
| KBS | knowledge-based system |
| LISP | list processing language |
| MT | machine translation |
| NLP | natural language processing |
| NN | neural network |
| PC | personal computer |
| XCON | expert configurer |

# Part I

Computers have had a tremendous impact on business and industry within the short period of about four decades. Over the years, the emphasis of business computing has evolved from the storage of data and the retrieval of information to the processing of knowledge. This era of knowledge processing promises to fundamentally alter the manner in which business is structured and conducted.

This introductory part of the book consists of a single chapter titled Knowledge Processing and Applied Artificial Intelligence. Aim of this chapter is to motivate the theme of the book and to provide a background for positioning succeeding chapters.

The chapter begins with a description of the evolution of business computing from data processing to knowledge processing, then reviews the origins of the multi-disciplinary field of artificial intelligence (AI). Developments within AI over the last four decades are traced and the emergence of the different sub-fields of AI are described. Next, the lack of our knowledge about the true nature of intelligence and its impact on business applications of AI are detailed. Overall trends in the commercialization of AI technology are described, and general guidelines are provided for successfully introducing AI in an organization. The chapter ends with a description of the structure and organization of the remainder of the book.

# Chapter 1
# Knowledge processing and applied artificial intelligence

> I think there is a world market for about five computers.
>
> Thomas J. Watson, Sr.
> Chairman of the Board of IBM, 1943[1]

Computers have undeniably had a tremendous influence on both industry and society during the past few decades. Computing has completely transformed entire businesses, and is the lifeblood of industries such as travel, banking and insurance. Given the current importance and far reaching influence of computers, it seems rather surprising to realize that the world's first electronic computer was built only in 1946[2]. Developments in computing technology have long overtaken even the most optimistic projections of yesteryear. Over the years, there have been dramatic reductions in the price/performance ratio of computers. The average end-user cost of 1 MIPS (millions of instructions per second), a standard measure of computer performance, declined from about $250,000 to $25,000 over the five year period, 1980-1985. Over the next five year period, 1985-1990, the average price per MIPS fell to $2500[3]. The progress in computing hardware power continues relentlessly, and these cost figures are projected to fall to dramatically lower numbers over the next decade.

# 4 Knowledge processing and applied artificial intelligence

Progress in computing technology over the last decades has been matched by a steady increase in the appetite for computing power. T.J.Watson's prediction (made with all the wisdom in 1943) seems absurd today when you can find organizations with as many personal computers (PCs) as telephones. Large mainframe computers act as storehouses of information and data critical to industry. It is difficult to imagine how a bank can function today without its central transaction processing system. Personal computers have distributed computing power within the organization, and have helped to increase effectiveness of individual employees. Networks of computers have transcended the boundaries of a single computer, and both facilitate group work within an organization, as well as help forge alliances across organizations. Computers have also entered the lives of individual consumers and have affected their work and leisure. The average per capita consumer spending on computing rose from $90 in 1980 to $180 in 1985 and further to $200 in 1990[4]. The impact of computing technology is compounded by the increasing gap between its cost and the relative cost of other technologies. Over the three decades from 1950 to 1980, the capital equivalency ratio (cost of technology/cost of labor) for computing technology has decreased about 25 times per decade as compared to an improvement of 1.4 times for a composite technology group (consisting of other technologies such as automobiles and cameras) over the same period[5]. Thus, over the years, it has become cheaper for organizations to invest in computing technology as opposed to many other technologies. The cost of computing against the cost of labor has also been decreasing rapidly. It is estimated[6] that the cost of the number of people (of an appropriate skill level) equivalent to the computing power of 1 MIPS decreased from 50 in 1980 to 0.5 in 1990. This number is predicted to decrease to 0.03 by the year 2000. These figures have a tremendous significance for industry. As computers become more 'intelligent' and more decision processes are (partially or fully) automated, the cost of having a computer perform a task becomes dramatically different from having a human do it.

## The evolution of computing in business

The evolution of computing in industry can be analyzed along several dimensions. Figure 1.1 depicts the three waves of the information revolution as measured by the shifting focus of computing. Till the early 1970s, computers were used solely for traditional data processing tasks. There was a strong emphasis on building transaction processing systems. This gave rise to the large mainframe databases which form the core of computer systems in most organizations today. The emphasis then was primarily on building efficient data storage and retrieval systems.

During the 1970s there was a realization that transaction processing systems alone were not very useful for supporting management tasks within an organization. Management information systems needed to be designed to provide the required information to management. While the emphasis in transaction processing systems was (and remains) on the storage and retrieval of raw data, management information systems were supposed to aggregate the raw data (in some sensible manner) and provide the required information (i.e., the packaged and massaged data) to management. Thus the emphasis of computing shifted from data processing to information processing. Accelerating this shifting priority in computing was the development of the personal computer and mini-

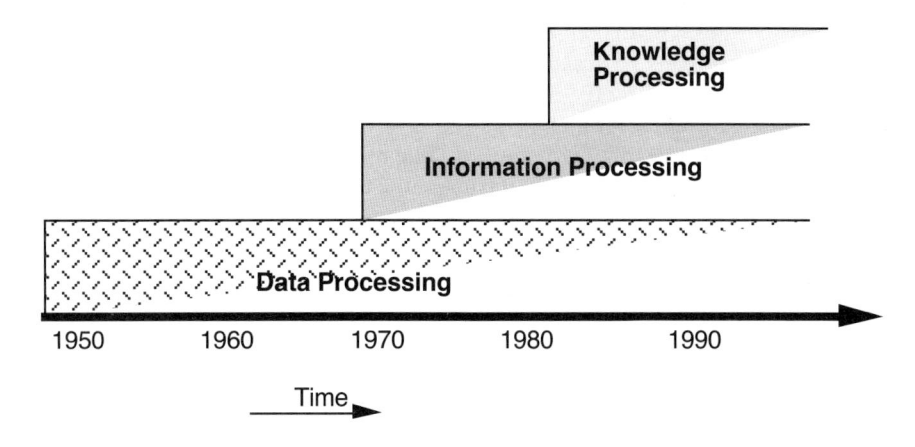

**Figure 1.1** Waves of the computing revolution

computers during the 1970s. The rise of personal computers and mini-computers distributed computing power within the organization and enabled individual managers to have direct access to computing power. Now many of their information needs could be satisfied locally. During the same decade, Gorry and Scott-Morton[7] invented and popularized the concept of decision support systems. Decision support systems took the concept of management information systems one step further. Rather than just package data into information, decision support systems call for incorporating various modelling tools to further analyze the information and make it more relevant for managers. Thus in a way, it calls for enhancing the conceptual level at which information is presented to the end-user. Note that the new emphasis on information processing did not imply a subsequent decline of data processing. Even today, data processing systems form the core of most computer-based systems in organizations and their importance has only increased over time.

## The rise of knowledge processing

The scope of computing has been enlarged since the early 1980s to include knowledge processing. This shift in computing priorities largely reflects the gradual commercialization of the multi-disciplinary field of artificial intelligence. AI, very loosely defined, is concerned with making computers more intelligent in the kind of processing they perform. Knowledge-based systems (KBSs) are a byproduct of research in AI which started being commercialized during the early 1980s. They today constitute AI's most visible commercial successes. Broadly defined, KBSs are computer-based systems which use extensive domain-specific knowledge (typically human expertise) to solve problems and/or automate (usually partially) decision processes. In practical terms, KBSs attempt to move the focus of computing one generation ahead by focussing on knowledge as opposed to information. Knowledge can be seen as being obtained from information by assigning it meaning and interpretation. This interpretation or meaning is typically given by human experts and represents the domain-specific knowledge which a KBS attempts to capture.

# 6 Knowledge processing and applied artificial intelligence

The primary focus of KBSs is on solving problems (as done by human experts) and on the automation of all or parts of decision processes. The potential impact of these systems is very high as they can directly influence the decision making and problem solving processes within an organization.

Figure 1.2 summarizes the evolution of computing and its associated shifts in focus and technology over the decades. The invention of the modern digital computer has been an important milestone in the development of society. Many authors[8] have termed the impact of computers on society as the information revolution or as the second industrial revolution. The first industrial revolution was done with machines which multiplied and leveraged human physical capabilities to produce physical goods. In doing so it brought about dramatic increases in our standards of living. The second industrial revolution is now occurring with computers, machines which extend and leverage our mental skills. The impact on industry and society has already been substantial (over a short period of four decades). AI and its associated technologies have the potential to magnify this impact manyfold over the next decades as they directly impact the extension and leveraging of human intellectual capabilities.

## The origins of knowledge processing

The age of knowledge processing has started. It promises to change many aspects of industry and society. But it also has limitations and shortcomings, some of which are not fully understood. It is important to understand the technology in order to harness its benefits and avoid its pitfalls.

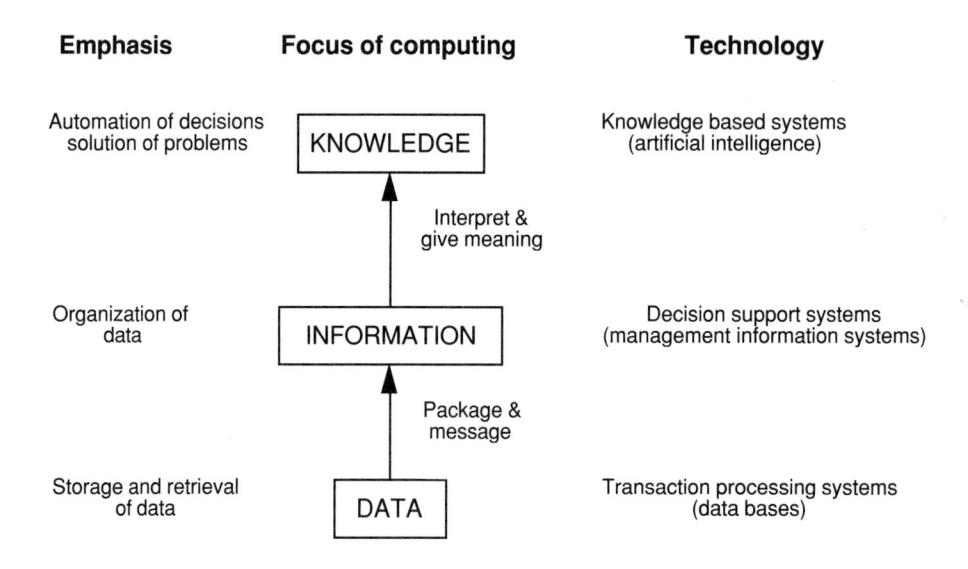

| Emphasis | Focus of computing | Technology |
|---|---|---|
| Automation of decisions solution of problems | KNOWLEDGE | Knowledge based systems (artificial intelligence) |
| | ↑ Interpret & give meaning | |
| Organization of data | INFORMATION | Decision support systems (management information systems) |
| | ↑ Package & message | |
| Storage and retrieval of data | DATA | Transaction processing systems (data bases) |

Figure 1.2 The evolution of computing

# The origins of knowledge processing

Knowledge processing, with its emphasis on the representation, storage, retrieval and processing of knowledge, has its roots in AI. AI is a multi-disciplinary field which has been, and still is, influenced by contributions from philosophy, mathematics, linguistics, biology, psychology and computer science (see Figure 1.3). Although the term artificial intelligence was first used in a computer conference at Dartmouth College in 1956, the origins of the field can be traced back a few decades (and sometimes, centuries) to isolated developments in many of the contributing disciplines. Some important early developments are recounted below.

## Philosophy

The human mind and its relation to machines has been of interest to philosophers since the times of Plato (427-347 BC) and Socrates (469-399 BC). Raymond Kurzweil[9] has noted that over the centuries, philosophers have tended to subscribe to one of two schools of thought. One school termed as mind-as-machine believes that the human mind is a machine (albeit a complex one) and is subject to the same laws of nature as any other physical machine. Thus, in principle, it is possible to build machines with capabilities similar to the human brain. An opposing school of thought, termed as mind-beyond-machine contends that it is not possible to build a rational (and hence machine-like) model of the human brain, as certain aspects of human thought (e.g., feelings and emotion) are beyond these type of logical analyses. The mind-as-machine school of thought treats emotion as any other logical thought process, governed by a complex (and not yet fully understood) set of algorithms and goals. As can be expected, the debate between these two schools of thought still continues (sometimes acrimoniously!). AI is of course, more influenced by the mind-as-machine school of thought. One of the central tenets of AI is that all intelligence can ultimately be reduced to a set of rational procedures.

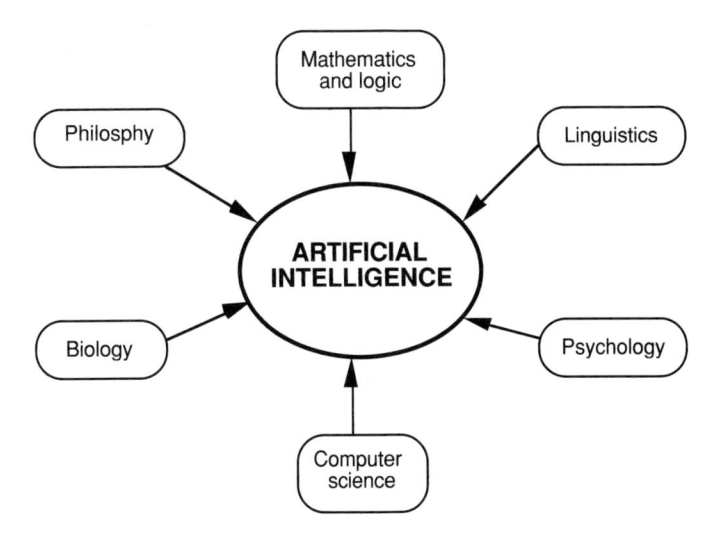

Figure 1.3 Different disciplines influencing artificial intelligence

# 8 Knowledge processing and applied artificial intelligence

## Mathematics

Long before the first (electronic) computers were ever built, the mathematical foundations of computing were being laid by eminent mathematicians such as Bertrand Russell (who established modern set theory), Alan Turing and Alonzo Church (both of whom independently helped establish the modern theory of computation), and Norbert Weiner (who started the field of cybernetics). In 1937 Turing presented a simple abstract computation model (known as the Turing machine), and proved that if any problem could be solved by a machine, it could be solved by his simple abstract computing model. The Turing machine is still today the primary theoretical model for computation. Turing and Church later independently put forward a more fundamental hypothesis (known today as the Church-Turing hypothesis) which asserted that if any problem could not be solved by a Turing machine, it could not be solved by human thought either. The Church-Turing hypothesis is yet to be conclusively proven or disproven, but it represents the core thrust of AI: if a human can solve a particular activity then a machine should also (in principle) be able to do it.

In 1950, the first computers had been built, and though the field of AI was yet to be formally born, Turing started speculating about the ultimate potential of computers — the simulation of intelligence. In an influential article[10] he suggested a test (known now as the Turing test) to determine whether a machine is intelligent. The essence of his test is to have an independent (shielded) observer carry on conversations via a computer terminal separately with a human and a computer (as shown in Figure 1.4).

The independent observer is expected to correctly distinguish between the computer and the human. If the computer can fool the observer into believing it is human, then the computer can be said to be intelligent.

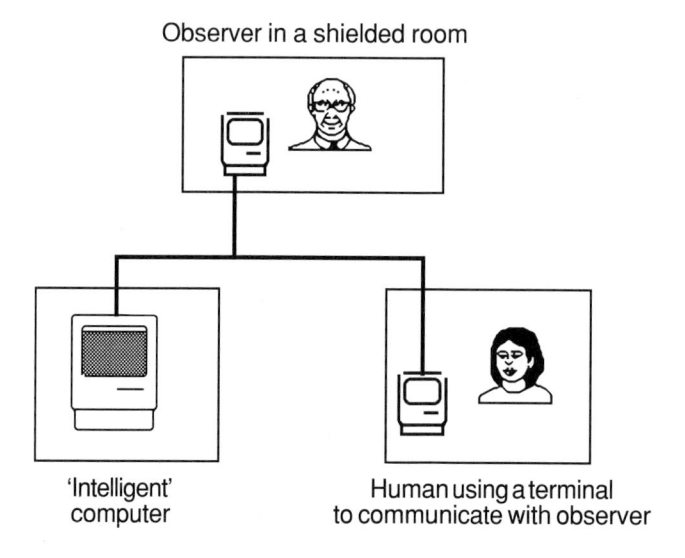

**Figure 1.4** Turing's test: can the computer on the left deceive the observer?

The Turing test has had an important influence on AI research, and has provoked a series of debates about its validity and usefulness. It has also forced a more serious consideration of the determination of the exact nature of intelligence.

Weiner introduced three important concepts in his seminal book, Cybernetics[11]. First, he treated information as the fundamental reality as opposed to energy. Second, he predicted a move towards digital measurement and representation away from the then prevalent analog systems. Third, he argued it is necessary to consider time as irreversible[12]. Taken together, these three concepts have had a profound effect on computation since the 1940s.

The value of products today and the economy as a whole is increasingly dominated by information (the cost of and reliance on energy has decreased dramatically). Digital technology has long overtaken analog technology as exemplified by the digital computer and modern electronics[13]. The irreversibility of time is fundamental to the concepts of computation, communication and intelligence. Intelligence can be alternatively looked upon as the process of selective extraction (or conversely, selective destruction) of information from a large amount of information in the external world. Information destroyed cannot be retrieved due to the irreversibility of time.

## Computing

An important aim of AI is to actually build intelligent machines. The modern digital computer is central to these efforts, as it represents the best-known machine to simulate complex reasoning and to solve problems. Though Charles Babbage is credited with having designed[14] the world's first programmable computer (termed the Analytical Engine) in 1835, the first operational computers were built in the early 1940s[15] by independent teams in Germany (the Z-3 invented by Konrad Zuse), England (the Robinson by Alan Turing and his associates), and the USA (the ABC by John Atanasoff). Successive computers such as the ENIAC (Electronic Numerical Integrator and Computer — the first electronic programmable computer) and the EDSAC (Electronic Delay Storage Automatic Computer — the first stored program computer) introduced progressive improvements in computing technology. The first commercially successful computer, the IBM 701 was designed only in 1952. The fundamental computational structure supported by modern digital computers is not much different from those of the early computers. The dramatic improvements in computing performance over the last four decades is largely due to the invention of the integrated circuit chip in 1958-59, and rapid advances in semiconductor chip design and manufacturing technology. AI systems typically require vast amounts of resources and computing power. But for the rapid development of computing technology, it would have been impossible to build even the simplest of AI systems.

An ordinary computer is a serial machine i.e., it executes one instruction at a time. Today, new computers based on parallel architectures are being designed and built. Parallel computers allow the execution of several tasks in parallel, and allow newer and more complex types of problems to be solved. Part of the motivation for building parallel computers comes from our knowledge of neuro-biology. The human brain consists of millions of densely interconnected simple processing elements (called neurons) operating in parallel.

# 10 Knowledge processing and applied artificial intelligence

By inching closer to the structure of the brain, massive parallel computers (consisting today of a few hundred interconnected simple computers) hope to transcend some of the limitations of serial computing, and provide a new hardware architecture for intelligent systems. They hold the potential for dramatically expanding the range and kind of problems tackled by AI systems. However, the development of parallel computers today is at a stage comparable to what computers were in the 1950s and it will be a few more years before they are used widely. Further evolution of computing hardware and software will significantly influence future developments in AI.

## The development of the field of artificial intelligence

Isolated developments (described partially above) in the various contributing disciplines (Figure 1.3) started being consolidated into what we know today as AI during the 1950s. Early pioneering research was done by Allen Newell, JC Shaw and Herbert Simon at Carnegie Mellon University, and John McCarthy and Marvin Minsky at MIT. Newell, Shaw and Simon created programs called the Logic Theorist in 1956[16] and the General Problem Solver in 1957[17]. The Logic Theorist used algorithmic techniques to solve mathematical problems, and was able to reproduce proofs for many theorems in Whitehead and Russell's Principia Mathematica[18] and, more impressively, find one completely original proof for a previously unpublished theorem. The General Problem Solver (as evident from its name) attempted to generalize the Logic Theorist to solve general problems in a variety of domains. Its basic solution technique (termed as means-end analysis) was to determine the difference between the current state and the desired state (the goal), and take some appropriate actions to reduce that difference. McCarthy invented (in 1959) a powerful new programming language called LISP (list processing language) which made it easier to write the complex algorithms necessary for solving AI problems. It is interesting to note that LISP (with many improvements) still remains the prime choice for the development of AI systems today. The primary emphasis during this early development of AI was on building algorithms for general problem solving. A lot of effort also went into development of programs to play games such as chess and checkers. The ability to play such games successfully was seen as a reasonable intelligence task, and had been clearly identified as having high priority in the research agenda of the future by early computing pioneers such as Turing.

Early successes were relatively easy to achieve and deceived researchers into making unrealistic claims about the future of AI. Buoyed by the success of their Logic Theorist and General Problem Solver programs, Simon and Newell wrote[19] in 1958:

> There are now in the world machines that think, that learn and that create. Moreover their ability to do these things is going to increase rapidly until — in a visible future — the range of problems they can handle will be coextensive with the range to which the human mind has been applied.

They even predicted that by 1968, a digital computer would be the world chess champion. In retrospect, these predictions were overly optimistic. However, progress has been made over the years. Today chess programs can play with the expertise of a grandmaster, while the world champion in checkers is a computer program.

## A shift in focus

Around the late 1960s and early 1970s a fundamental shift took place within the AI community. The early optimism of researchers (such as that of Simon and Newell above) proved to be short-lived, as algorithmic general problem-solving techniques were stumped by some relatively simple and mundane tasks. General-purpose algorithms just seemed unable to cope with the peculiarities of different domains. Increasingly, there was a realization that extensive domain-specific knowledge is required to solve real world problems. The skills and dexterity of humans were seen to be emanating less from the use of general problem-solving algorithms, and more from an enormous store of knowledge, both about the world at large (common-sense knowledge) and about specific domains and problems (expertise). Thus the emphasis within AI shifted from finding general-purpose algorithms to finding methods for encoding and using domain-specific knowledge. This has again proven to be a harder than expected problem. For example, it is very difficult to represent vast amounts of knowledge in a manner such that it is possible to easily and efficiently determine what knowledge is relevant (to a particular problem) and retrieve only the relevant parts. Another hard problem associated with knowledge representation and manipulation is the problem of 'knowing what you know'.

KBSs and expert systems (ESs) arose as a result of this shift in emphasis, and continue to dominate AI efforts today. KBSs tend to emphasize the utilization of domain-specific knowledge for the solution of problems. ESs are a subset of KBSs and are concerned with the solution of narrow bounded problems typically solved by human experts. Most of the early pioneering research in KBSs was done at Stanford University by Edward A Feigenbaum, who lead the efforts to build the DENDRAL (an ES in the chemical domain) and MYCIN (an ES in the medical domain) KBSs. Other early ESs include the INTERNIST system (developed at the University of Pittsburgh for the diagnosis of internal diseases) and PROSPECTOR (developed at the SRI in Palo Alto for the location of geological deposits). Many other KBSs and ESs were developed in both industry and universities during the late 1970s and the 1980s. Today, KBSs and ESs represent some of the most commercially successful parts of AI.

## The evolving sub-fields

As the complexity of their task gradually become apparent to researchers in AI, several new specialized sub-fields of interest started emerging. The understanding of written text came to be studied under natural language understanding, while machine translation dealt with the translation of text between languages and appeared as a subset of work in natural language understanding. The sub-areas of speech recognition and speech synthesis dealt with the specific problems of recognizing spoken words and generating coherent speech. Analogous to speech recognition, computer vision dealt with the recognition and processing of visual images. Robotics arose from the concerns of building autonomous agents, and utilized results from other sub-areas such as machine vision, speech recognition and KBSs. Machine learning developed from a desire to enable a KBS to learn and adapt to its environments. Fuzzy logic became focussed on reasoning with uncertain and imprecise information.

## 12 Knowledge processing and applied artificial intelligence

The multiplicity of the number of sub-areas within AI may give an impression of a fragmented field, but they are a natural response to the complexity and enormity of the task of automating intelligence. There are strong links between the various sub-fields, and results in one sub-area have a strong influence on developments in other sub-areas. The above list of distinct sub-fields of AI is incomplete. New streams of interest are appearing even today. For example, case-based reasoning is one sub-field which has gained in importance recently. Case-based reasoning is concerned with the utilization of prior experiences for problem solving.

Since the mid 1980s the range of AI research and development has enlarged to include a new focus, termed as connectionism. Connectionism is different from the traditional knowledge-based focus of AI by its emphasis on highly parallel computer architectures (as opposed to serial computers on which most of conventional AI is based), and software models (such as neural networks) which attempt to directly simulate the structure and functions of the human brain. Connectionism has been gaining in popularity because it has powerful pattern recognition abilities, and demonstrates the potential to overcome some important limitations of conventional AI systems.

Figure 1.5 illustrates the evolving foci of AI over the past 35 years, and indicates some of the important sub-fields of AI. It is difficult to predict the future at this stage. Certainly, AI will continue to grow, and there will be some flux in the sub-fields of interest within AI.

Some sub-areas will mature, and will be commercialized and exploited, while newer areas of interest will emerge and take center-stage in the research arena. For example, significant parts of KBS technology have today matured to the point at which it is feasible to commercially exploit them effectively.

In contrast, there is considerable excitement about the potential of newer areas such as neural networks and case-based reasoning, and many researchers are actively researching them. The connectionist approach is also gaining commercial importance today with

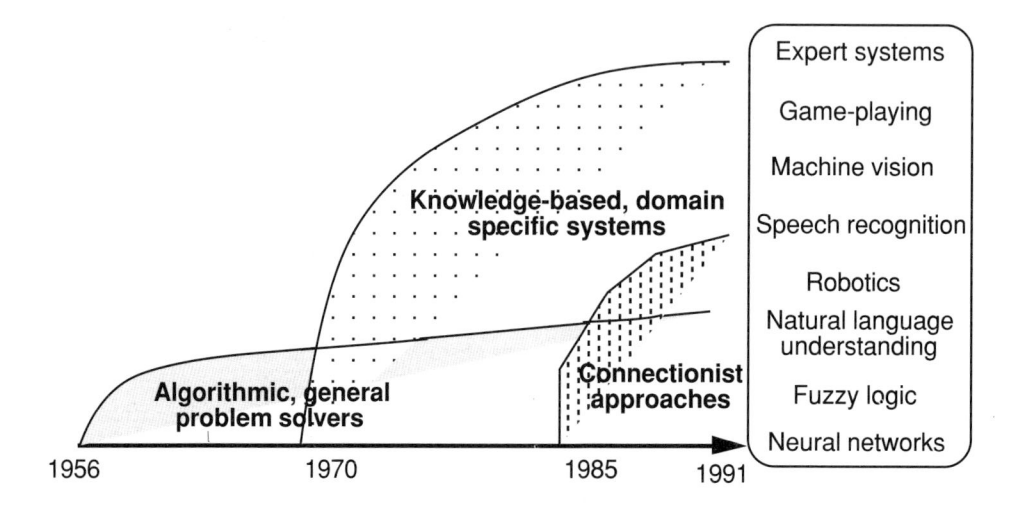

Figure 1.5 The evolution of artificial intelligence technology

advances in parallel hardware architectures and neural software models. Some synergy between the different primary approaches (such as KBSs and connectionism) will also occur. However, it does not look likely that a unifying theory of intelligence will emerge any time soon.

## Governmental funding

Over the years, AI has received strong governmental support in the USA, Japan and Europe. This stems from a belief that AI is one of the critical technologies of the future, and that achieving a distinctive competence in it is of strategic importance for nations.

The US Department of Defense has been particularly committed to its funding of AI projects. During the 1970s ARPA, the Advanced Research Projects Agency (formerly known as the Defense Advanced Research Projects Agency — DARPA) funded two major initiatives in the pattern recognition area: SUR (speech understanding research) and IUP (image understanding program). These projects, while not directly leading to commercial systems, pushed the limits of knowledge in pattern recognition and laid the foundations for future commercial systems.

During the late 1970s and early 1980s, ARPA funded major initiatives in knowledge-based systems which lead to the rapid development and commercialization of the field of expert systems. More recently, ARPA has been actively funding connectionist and case-based reasoning research in AI. The active support of ARPA for AI research and development has helped assure the USA's leading position in AI.

The Japanese government entered the arena of AI with much fanfare by launching the much talked about[20] fifth generation project in 1982 with the aim of building the next generation computer based on AI and parallel processing. The ten year initial time frame of the fifth generation project has come to a close today and there are few successful commercial results to show. This has prompted some to call the project a failure, but others caution that the results from the project are yet to come. They point to the fact that the fifth generation project was the successor of an earlier project called the fourth generation project which aimed at creating the technology to create semiconductor chips. When the fourth generation project was launched in the 1970s, US firms controlled the world semiconductor market. Today, Japanese firms have captured more than 70% of key sectors of the US semiconductor market[21]. The most important success of the fifth generation project has been the production of thousands of engineers from industry trained in the methods of AI. The project has significantly increased the level of awareness and cooperation in AI within Japanese industry and universities. True commercial benefits may yet flow from this project[22].

The launch of the Japanese fifth generation project caused deep concern within European governments about Europe's lagging competitiveness in a key area of information technology. Since the early 1980s, European governments have also been actively funding AI research, primarily through a number of EC (European Community) supported research programs, most notably the ESPRIT ( European Strategic Program for Research in Information Technology) program. ESPRIT is a ten year program launched in 1984 with the general goal of increasing the competitiveness of European industry in information technology. Within ESPRIT, the advanced information processing (AIP) sector has been setup to create conditions for the commercial exploitation of AI technologies by European industry.

# 14 Knowledge processing and applied artificial intelligence

The AIP sector has three sub-divisions: the knowledge engineering area dealing with core technologies derived from AI, the advanced architecture area which includes special computer architectures for AI systems, and the advanced systems interfaces where knowledge engineering techniques are applied to speech, image and multi-sensor applications.

Total funding for AI projects is over $100M in the ESPRIT program. Some individual governments have also developed programs specifically tailored to support AI research. For example, the British government has supported a couple of major initiatives: the Alvey program and the Intelligent Knowledge Based Systems project.

## The nature of intelligence

AI is earlier defined as being concerned with the building of intelligent machines. The catch in the above definition is in deciding what exactly is meant by the term intelligence. Defining intelligence is both controversial and difficult. The best of human minds for many centuries have worked on this question, and a definitive answer is still lacking. Even Turing's test (Figure 1.4) is not very useful from a practical point of view. For example, intelligence can be exhibited in many different ways, and is not limited to the ability of carrying on an intelligent conversation. Also, it has been seen that is possible to carry on seemingly intelligent conversations without actually possessing real intelligence.

Programs such as PARRY[23] (a program which simulated a paranoid patient and fooled some psychiatrists) claimed to pass the Turing test, but a close analysis of PARRY (and other similar conversational programs) reveals a poor level of understanding of the topic of conversation.

While challenging from a philosophical point of view, this disagreement about the true nature of intelligence has had, at times, some unfortunate consequences for the field of AI. First, lacking a precise definition of what intelligence is, people often tend to have unrealistic expectations about what AI is supposed to do. Beau Sheil[24] has described this aptly:

> Many of these problems with "intelligent" programs actually reflect a deep level of confusion in our own thinking about thinking. Marvin Minsky, one of the pioneers of artificial intelligence, once commented that intelligence is "an attribute people ascribe to mental behavior that they admire but do not understand". In other words, about the only thing that "intelligent" skills have in common is our ignorance about how they are done.

Second, AI is handicapped to a certain extent by the fact that the range of topics tackled by AI are poorly understood. Beau Sheil[25] has described this as:

> ...describing something as intelligent means that we don't fully understand it, and any technology that attempts to capture and automate something that we don't fully understand is inherently weak.

Third, improvements in our understanding of a particular topic tend to shift that subject out of the domain of AI into an arena where, often, conventional solution techniques can be applied fruitfully. Marvin Minsky[26] has described one such example. SAINT, an AI program to solve calculus programs was first constructed in 1960 by James Slagle at MIT.

The program, though limited in many ways, surpassed the performance of average MIT students. It also forced a more thorough examination of the basic nature of these calculus problems. As the knowledge of the domain increased, the trial and error search processes in SAINT were replaced by conventional solution techniques and resulted in a highly successful commercial product called MACSYMA, now included under the field of symbolic applied mathematics.

As another example, consider expert systems. Design of expert systems is intimately connected to the extraction of knowledge from an expert. Once this knowledge is extracted (using expert-system building tools), the knowledge-base is often converted into a conventional programming language such as C, because it leads to more efficient systems.

## Applied artificial intelligence

Confusion about the true nature of intelligence lead to some initial unrealistic coverage about the objectives and capabilities of AI in the popular press. During the early 1980s, when the commercialization of AI technology first started, the media (partly lead on by naive and overly optimistic AI researchers) described the potential of AI in wildly exaggerated terms. Newsweek[27] wrote in 1980: "A new generation of electronic servants has been spawned — and they will change the way we all live" Fortune[28] claimed: "Computers can now see, speak, and diagnose diseases". The reality was of course far from this. Even simple real-life problems proved exceedingly hard to solve, and progress was slow. Thus the initial high expectations of industry were dampened considerably during the mid 1980's, leading to a general disenchantment with AI. Overstatements about the potential of AI in automating the tasks of knowledge workers often created fear and resistance among workers. Moreover, most AI systems dealt with poorly understood areas, which made it difficult to guarantee the correctness of their results.

The above issues complicated the initial adoption of commercial AI technology, and even caused some software developers to explicitly avoid using the term artificial intelligence in the description of their AI products. More recently, from a practical application perspective, there has been a shift in priority from software that thinks to software that knows[29]. The emphasis is less on devising software that 'thinks' and is 'intelligent', and more on building software that 'knows' enough about a certain problem or domain to take certain certain decisions by itself. This approach is termed as applied artificial intelligence, and occupies a middle ground between the theoretical work within AI on building machines that think, and today's conventional computer programs which are powerful, but dumb.

## Knowledge processing and applied artificial intelligence

Much of the early emphasis within AI was on the building of general-purpose problem solvers (Figure 1.5). During this initial period, the usual domains considered were games (such as chess and checkers), and other simplified toy domains (such as the blocks world

# 16 Knowledge processing and applied artificial intelligence

— which consisted of simple building blocks much as infants play with). These domains were of little commercial interest, and did not excite industry. Besides, general-purpose problem solvers were producing only modest results.

The commercial potential of AI became clearer with the shift towards knowledge-based domain-specific systems during the 1970s. The realization that extensive domain-specific knowledge was required for solving specific real-life problems struck a sympathetic cord in industry. This was partly due to a growing frustration with general-purpose mathematical models derived from operations research. These models, while mathematically very sophisticated, typically did not take domain-specific peculiarities into account. For example, a complex scheduling algorithm would assume that there were no machine failures, or that all failures could be predicted according to some particular pattern. In real life, machine failures often tend to occur in unexpected, unpredictable patterns. Engineers on the shop-floor have to deal with these unanticipated events. Typically, they use some domain-specific knowledge and heuristics for deciding how to handle such situations. AI and knowledge processing offered a possibility to encode such knowledge, and partially automate the process of exception handling and real-time scheduling. Today, knowledge-based techniques are used extensively in scheduling and planning problems and there are many commercial software packages[30] that provide the means to do such knowledge-based scheduling.

KBSs also offered to organizations a means to capture, disseminate, and preserve parts of the body of knowledge, on which their success was dependent. Consider the example of the XCON (expert coffigurer) KBS built by Digital[31]. Digital, unlike many other computer companies, has a vast range of products (both hardware and software). These products evolve rapidly and can be configured in many different ways. During the 1970s, computer systems ordered by customers were configured by human experts known as technical editors. During the process of configuration, technical editors made sure that each computer system on order had all the necessary components (and no extras), and made diagrams showing how to assemble the system.

After manufacturing, the different components were actually physically connected together (to ensure that everything works) at a Digital test facility in Westminster, Massachusetts, before being disassembled and shipped to the customer. In 1973, the product line of Digital was expanding, and both domestic and international sales were growing. The former factor implied that the task of configuring computers was getting increasingly complex, and the latter meant that the company probably had to spend millions of dollars in building additional test and assembly sites, some in international locations. Digital turned to AI for help in building a KBS which captured the knowledge of its expert technical editors, and performed the task of configuring Digital's broad range of computers. The result was XCON, a KBS that checks sales orders and designs the layout of each computer order it analyzes. XCON was one of the first commercial expert systems ever built. It is still in commercial use in Digital facilities world-wide (it handles 90% of the dollar volume of sales orders), and saves Digital 25 Million dollars (as it enables Digital to ship components directly to the customer site and eliminates the need for assembly sites).

## The commercialization of applied artificial intelligence

The building of XCON during the early 1980s marks the start of the commercialization of AI. This first decade of the transfer of AI technology to industry has not been without its problems. The decade started with the 'overselling' of AI, both by the media and by some over-enthusiastic AI researchers, to industry. This over-selling created a certain sense of confusion and mistrust about AI when results did not live up to promises. Certain quarters of industry looked to AI as a panacea for all its problems, while others were turned-off and ignored the technology.

The actual problems arose when it became clear that the real potential of AI technology (available in the early 1980s) was much less than what it had been sold as. AI programs were not really intelligent. They could not learn and adapt to different scenarios, and often made stupid, simple mistakes, reminiscent of the traditional follies of computers. Their rigidity and often foolish responses seemed opposed to the notion of intelligence which users had been deceived (by the accompanying hype) into expecting.

Moreover, an irritating feature of most early AI systems was that they typically had been developed in isolation, without any links to popular commercial software. As an example, consider PlanPower, a KBS (to assist in the creation of financial plans) sold by Applied Expert Systems (APEX) of Cambridge, Massachusetts.

When Financial Design[32] (a small financial planning company) started using PlanPower in 1985, they were disappointed to learn that there was no interface in PlanPower to popular spreadsheet packages such as Lotus 1-2-3. This necessitated the manual reentry of data from spreadsheets (where the data resided) into the PlanPower system, a process which was not only tedious and frustrating, but also wasteful.

An additional factor impeding early commercialization of AI was the use of special AI computers. Most early AI programs were written in LISP. One of the disadvantages of LISP is that it requires a lot of resources (memory space and computing speed). Special computers (called LISP machines) were used for executing AI programs as they could run LISP programs more efficiently[33].

The problems of LISP machines were twofold: connectivity and cost. Due to the special nature of its hardware, it was difficult to connect them to conventional large mainframe computers (on which corporate data usually resided). Also, each individual LISP machine cost anything between $70,000–$100,000 (during the early 1980s). This high cost made it difficult for most companies to afford more than one or two LISP machines, thus impeding the spread and use of AI systems.

Cumulatively, the above factors had a negative effect on the commercialization of AI during the mid 1980s. Having got burnt by naively dabbling in AI, many companies started adopting a much more cautious and hands-off attitude towards AI. Much of the early enthusiasm concerning AI also cooled rapidly. This shift in the commercial acceptance of the technology had a disastrous effect on dozens of small AI companies which had mushroomed during the early 1980s. While they could earlier demand and get premium prices for their products and services, they were suddenly left grasping for customers. Their stock prices plummeted, and many AI software developers went bankrupt. By believing too much in the (partly self-propagated) hype around AI, they had forgotten the harsh realities of the market-place. An additional relevant factor was that most of these early AI software companies were started by AI researchers with little business experience and possessing limited knowledge about the information demands of organizations. In retrospect, actions like not providing software hook-ups to common spreadsheet packages seem outright foolish.

## Consolidation and growth

The latter half of the 1980s was a period of consolidation for the AI industry. Progress was made slowly on all fronts. Expectations about the potential and capabilities of AI came down to a more realistic level. The media and proponents of AI reduced the hype about AI. At the same time, there was real progress in AI technology, and new methods were discovered for building more powerful AI systems. There was an increased focus on integrating AI systems into the existing information architectures of organizations. Today, almost all AI systems and tools offer links to other commercial spreadsheets and database packages. On a different front, there was also dramatic progress in computing hardware. More powerful PCs to run AI software became available. This prompted a (much welcomed) shift from the use of special LISP computers to ordinary PCs for running AI applications.

The above factors have rejuvenated commercial interest in AI. Today, AI technology is more accessible, and commercial interest in the field is genuine. Most companies have ongoing efforts in building AI applications. Many companies have reaped real benefits from AI. Digital is a good example of a company which has systematically exploited AI technology. Not only did it pioneer the commercial use of KBSs with its XCON system, but it also has about 40 other KBSs covering nearly every facet of its operations. DuPont is another notable example which has adopted a different route to using AI. Rather than build big KBSs, it has instead opted for encouraging the use of KBSs as software tools to increase personal productivity, much like spreadsheets. It has more than 500 small operational KBSs yielding a total savings of $75M annually[34].

Even IBM is actively looking into the potential of AI applications. Herbert Schorr[35], a senior IBM executive, notes that IBM regards AI as the next wave in the computing revolution. Besides providing a practical means to manage information, AI is helping corporations improve productivity, enhance employee effectiveness and attain strategic objectives. For example, the XCON system enables Digital to achieve one of its strategic objectives: to give the customer the maximum possible flexibility while ordering computers. Similarly, the hundreds of small KBSs within DuPont help in attaining one of DuPont's key objectives: to foster innovation.

Figure 1.6 gives a pictorial summary of the above described changes in the commercialization of AI over the last decade. The prospect for the future is, in short, steady growth. AI is being actively researched in research laboratories and universities all over the world, and the technology of AI is improving continuously. Technical developments within AI are also yielding new commercial products. A good example is the dramatic commercialization of fuzzy logic over the past few years. Till about 1987, fuzzy logic was a relatively obscure mathematical part of AI.

However, since 1989, fuzzy logic has exploded onto the commercial arena by being incorporated into a variety of consumer electronic products (primarily manufactured by

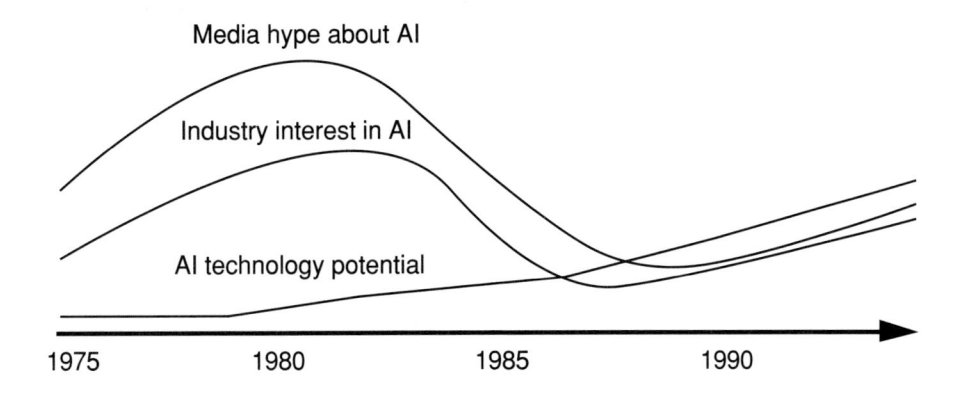

**Figure 1.6** Waves in the commercialization of AI technology

Japanese companies) ranging from cameras and video recorders, to washing machines and toasters. Details about the commercialization of specific sub-fields with AI (such as fuzzy logic, machine vision, natural language understanding, and neural networks) are provided in the following chapters.

## The commercial market

The total AI market has grown significantly over the last decade and is poised for further growth over the next decade. According to International Data Corp, US computer and software companies sold about $200M worth of AI software packages (not including the hundreds of millions of dollars in related consulting and customized programming services)[36]. The worldwide AI market (including software, hardware, and services) is estimated by most market research companies to be in the order of a few billions of dollars. Note that it is not always easy to estimate the AI market, as AI has many different sub-fields, some of which (such as robotics and fuzzy logic) have developed into distinct fields of their own. Different sub-fields of AI are included in different market studies, thus leading to varying estimates of the size of the entire AI market.

Raymond Kurzweil[37] notes that many market analysts predict the bulk of the several-hundred-billion dollar computer and information processing market will be intelligent by 1999, at least by today's standards of intelligence. This is due to the impact of developments within AI on other sectors of the information processing industry. As an example, consider the database industry. Databases represent one of the most mature and commercially important segments of the information processing industry. Most organizations are critically dependent on the information stored in their central databases. Conventional databases store data and provide a platform for running various MIS application programs to generate useful information from the stored data. Looking at the hierarchy in Figure 1.2, it's only natural that databases try and move one step upwards with the storage of knowledge in addition to simple data and information. This is possible by incorporating parts of

# 20 Knowledge processing and applied artificial intelligence

AI technology into conventional database technology. Leading commercial database products such as Oracle, Adabas, and Ingres are moving in this direction. Slowly, AI concepts of knowledge representation, storage and retrieval are being incorporated into these products. By the end of this decade, it is very likely that a substantial part of current KBS technology will be incorporated into commercial databases. The business impact of AI will then be magnified many times.

## Moving from data processing to knowledge processing

There is an increased realization today about competitive benefits of effectively managing knowledge assets within industry and business[38]. Knowledge processing and applied AI can play an important role in managing knowledge assets. KBSs can leverage organizational knowledge by providing a real and practical approach for capturing, preserving, and distributing critical knowledge. For example, the XCON KBS gives Digital a competitive edge by helping it to manage effectively the knowledge required for performing the key tasks of configuring and assembling computers.

Making the transition from data and information processing to knowledge processing in organizations is not always easy. Confusion about true goals and objectives of AI, and memories of bloated promises and poor results, often handicaps the spread and use of AI technology within organizations. Merely shying away from AI is not a good solution for most companies today because:

● Many firms are achieving significant competitive benefits from strategic applications of applied AI technology. If competitors successfully apply AI technology first, a firm might later find itself in a disadvantaged position.

● Applied AI is today a mature and commercially viable technology. Advances in both computing hardware and AI technology have made it feasible to build cost-effective AI systems.

● Knowledge processing is intimately related to management of knowledge within organizations. AI offers a practical and tested approach for creating knowledge assets and leveraging core organizational knowledge.

Tim McCullogh[39] of the 3M company has proposed the following general guidelines to help organizations make the transition from data processing to knowledge processing:

**Build awareness** — it is necessary first to build a certain level of awareness about applied AI and its potential within the organization. This can be done by communicating the benefits of knowledge processing in the language of the organization (and avoiding technical jargon of any kind). The goal at this stage is to simply plant some seeds, and not to either impress (with lofty claims about AI) or seek firm commitments for funding of AI projects. Even small details can help. For example, at the 3M company, the AI task force printed note pads with the heading 3M Artificial Intelligence: Harvesting Tomorrow's Technology and distributed it to appropriate people in the company. This often increased curiosity about AI and generated queries for further information about it.

**Understand corporate strategy** — to be able to get the attention of top management of a company, it is important to understand how exactly does AI fit into corporate strategy and satisfy corporate needs. The best way to do this is usually to ask appropriate managers several questions. What does the company do and how does it use technology to do that? What new business developments could occur over the next five years? What are the real needs of the company?

**Explain benefits in terms of need** — after understanding corporate strategic needs, it is important to decide whether knowledge processing and applied AI can address any important corporate need. If the answer is yes, then all attempts should be made to explain the potential benefits of AI technology to appropriate managers. If the technology can address fundamental corporate needs, then top managers are usually willing listeners. Particular attention should be paid to avoid overselling (or making undeliverable promises), and to use specific corporate problems or situations to explain the application of AI technology.

**Focus on an important and 'do-able' project** — while acquiring funding for AI projects, it is important to seek modest (but adequate) funds and focus on an important and 'do-able' project. It is impossible and dangerous to attempt all or many projects at once, specially if AI technology is new to the organization. The chosen project must also be do-able because the first project has to succeed. Failure in a first project or a large amount of overspending can lead to a negative bias in top management towards future AI applications. An adequate study of corporate needs in the previous stage can help in choosing the right first project.

**Spread the 'gospel'** — after a first success with applied AI, it is necessary to continue reaching out to others in the organization who might potentially benefit from the technology. It is important to focus on increasing the credibility of AI technology within the organization (by successfully building other strategically useful applications), and avoid simply increasing size of the AI development group (as size always begets more scrutiny). All future applications should also be targeted at satisfying real corporate needs.

More details on the process of creating and implementing strategically important AI applications in industry and business are described in Chapters 4 and 5.

## Structure and organization of book

The remainder of this book comprises eight chapters and three appendices. The structure and organization of these components can be best explained with the help of Figure 1.7.

Chapter 1 provides an introductory base for all other chapters by presenting the evolution of knowledge processing and the emergence of its various sub-fields. Chapters 2 and 3 describe fundamental knowledge technologies concerned with acquiring, representing, and reasoning with knowledge. Appendix I is related to Chapter 2 and provides information on commercial applications of KBSs.

Chapters 4 and 5 describe the process of creating and implementing KBS applications in organizations. While Chapter 4 details the relevant technological issues for creating KBS applications, Chapter 5 focuses on the strategic impact of KBS applications and

## 22 Knowledge processing and applied artificial intelligence

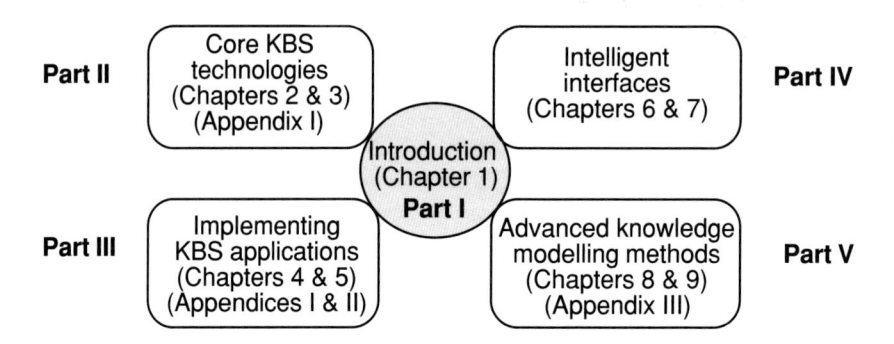

**Figure 1.7** Structure and organization of this book

describes techniques for analyzing and enhancing their competitive potentials. Concepts and techniques described in these chapters are equally applicable to all applied AI technologies (and thus are relevant for Chapters 6 through 9 also). Appendix II is linked to Chapter 4 and describes selected vendors of commercial KBS products. Appendix I also provides useful additional information to complement Chapter 5.

Chapters 6, 7, 8, and 9 cover advanced AI technologies. Chapters 6 and 7 describe natural language processing, and image and speech processing respectively. Thus they are concerned with the impact of applied AI technology on man-machine interfaces. Chapters 8 and 9 focus on alternative approaches to knowledge representation and reasoning and describe fuzzy logic and neural networks respectively. Appendix III is related to Chapter 9 and describes selected commercial applications of neural networks. While each of these chapters is self-contained in its description of the underlying technology and its business applications, they use (or refer to) concepts of knowledge representation and reasoning presented in Chapters 2 and 3. Thus it is recommended that the reader to be familiar with Chapters 2 and 3 prior to reading Chapters 6 through 9.

Reflecting on the book's contents, the remaining eight chapters of this book are seen as organized into four additional parts. Part II consists of Chapters 2 and 3 and presents essential knowledge about the fundamentals of KBS technologies. Chapters 4 and 5 make up Part III and describe the process of creating and implementing competitively advantageous KBS applications in organizations. Chapters 6 and 7 focus on intelligent interfaces and constitute Part IV. Part V contains Chapters 8 and 9 and describes advanced technologies for knowledge modelling and reasoning.

It's possible to read this book in several different ways. It is recommended, however, that all readers read Chapters 1, 2, 3, and 5. Readers with computing backgrounds and with interest in the implementation of KBSs should also read Chapter 4.

Chapters 6 through 9 are optional in the sense that readers may selectively read these chapters (either partially or wholly) depending upon the available time and their inclinations. The summaries of chapters can aid the reader in making these decisions judiciously.

## Summary

This chapter sets the stage for the following chapters by describing the history of AI and trends in its commercialization. The primary points made in this chapter include the following:

- The scope of business computing has moved over the past decades from data and information processing to knowledge processing.

- Combined with the dramatic reductions in computer cost/performance ratios, this change in the scope of impact of computing applications has important ramifications for organizations.

- AI is a multi-disciplinary field with roots in philosophy, mathematics, computer science, and biology. Though the field of AI officially originated in the 1950s, its roots in the contributing disciplines can be traced back many centuries.

- While early focus within AI (1960s) was on building general problem solvers, a shift towards using domain knowledge for problem solving and KBSs occurred during the late 1970s and early 1980s.

- AI is today a vast field with many different sub-fields. New sub-fields within AI are still emerging. This reflects the complexity of the task facing AI — of simulating and modelling intelligence.

- There is general disagreement about the meaning of the term intelligence. This has caused some unfortunate misconceptions about AI and hampered initial implementation of AI technologies in industry.

- The emphasis today in applied AI applications has moved from building software that thinks to software that knows. This is a welcome change and is enhancing the applicability and acceptability of applied AI technologies in business.

- After some initial problems during the 1980s, the commercial market for applied AI technologies is developing rapidly and is well poised for active growth over the coming decades.

- Companies have to adopt conscious strategies for moving into the era of knowledge processing from the earlier eras of data and information processing.

- There are eight additional chapters in this book, organized into four parts. Different options are available to readers for using this book.

After this introductory chapter, it's recommended the reader turns to Part II of the book which covers the fundamental knowledge technologies used for acquiring, representing, and reasoning with knowledge.

# 24 Knowledge processing and applied artificial intelligence

## Bibliography and suggested readings

Best suggestions for additional reading on early developments which influenced and shaped AI are books by Raymond Kurzweil (Kurzweil 90) and Pamela McCorduck (McCorduck 79). Both books are extremely well written, and provide lucid and easily comprehensible (non-technical) descriptions of many issues covered in this chapter. A recent survey of AI in the Economist magazine (Economist 92) presents clear and easily comprehensible summaries of several important issues in AI research and applications. Feigenbaum and McCorduck (Feigenbaum & McCorduck 83) have described Japan's initiative in AI (the fifth generation project) and its impact relative to the USA and Europe. Good management-oriented introductions to AI and knowledge based systems can be found in articles by Sheil (Sheil 87), Leonard-Barton and Sviokla (Leonard-Barton & Sviokla 88), and Schwartz and Treece (Schwartz & Treece 92). The book The Corporation of the 1990s (Scott-Morton 91) provides good background reading on the impact of information technology (in general) on management and corporations during the 1990's.

Economist, A survey of artificial intelligence, March 14, 1992.

Feigenbaum, E. A., and P. McCorduck, The fifth generation: artificial intelligence and japan's computer challenge to the world, Addison Wesley, Reading, Mass., 1983.

Kurzweil, R., The age of intelligent machines, MIT Press, 1990.

Leonard-Barton, D. & J. J. Sviokla, Putting expert systems to work, Harvard Business Review, pp. 91-98, March-April 1988.

McCorduck, P., Machines who think, W.H. Freeman and Co., San Francisco, 1979.

Schwartz, E.I. and J.B. Treece, Smart programs go to work, Business Week, pp. 47-51, March 2, 1992.

Scott-Morton, M.S., The corporation of the 1990s, Oxford University Press, 1991.

Sheil, B., Thinking about artificial intelligence, Harvard Business Review, pp. 91-97, July-August, 1987.

## Notes

1 As quoted in: R. R. Weitz, *Technology, Work, and the organization: The Impact of Expert Systems*, AI Magazine, Vol. 11, No. 2, pp. 50-60, Summer 1990.

2 The world's first fully electronic general purpose digital computer (called the ENIAC) was built in 1946 by J. P. Eckert and J.W. Mauchley at the University of Pennsylvania. It was used for calculating ballistic-firing tables for the US Army.

3 Rappaport, A. S., and S. Halevi, *The Computerless Computer Company*, Harvard Business Review, July-August, pp. 69-80, 1991.

4 Rappaport, A. S., and S. Halevi, *The Computerless Computer Company*, Harvard Business Review, July-Aug., pp. 69-80, 1991.

5 Yates, J., and R. I. Benjamin, *The Past and Present as a Window on the Future, in The Corporation of the 1990s*, M. S. Scott Morton (Ed.), Oxford University Press, pp. 61-92, 1991.

6 Calculated based on data presented in: *The Corporation of the 1990s*, M.S. Scott-Morton, Ed., Oxford University Press, pp. 9-10, 1991.

7 Gorry, G.A., and M.S. Scott Morton, *A Framework for Management Information Systems*, Sloan Management Review, pp. 55-70, Fall 1971.

8 Kurzweil, R., *The Age of Intelligent Machines*, MIT Press, 1990.

9 Kurzweil, R., *The Age of Intelligent Machines*, MIT Press, 1990.

10 Turing, A.M., *Computing Machinery and Intelligence*, Mind, 59, 1950.

11 Weiner, N., *Cybernetics*, MIT Press, Cambridge, 1943.

12 The directionality of time is of no significance while considering a typical high school Newtonian physics problem. Newton's laws would still be satisfied if the Newtonian world were run backward in time. Thus time here can be considered as "reversible".

13 It must be mentioned here that analog computational models are sometimes used today for performing certain AI tasks involving pattern recognition (for example, vision).

14 He died before the analytical engine could be built.

15 Kurzweil, R., *Electronic Roots* in The Age of Intelligent Machines, MIT Press, pp. 174-213, 1990.

16 Newell, A., J.C. Shaw and H.A. Simon, *Programming the Logic Theory Machine*, Proceedings of the Western Joint Computer Conference, pp. 230-240, 1957.

17 Newell, A., J.C. Shaw and H.A. Simon, *Report on a General Problem-Solving Program*, in *Computers and Thought*, E. Feigenbaum and J. Feldman (Eds.), New York, McGraw Hill, 1963.

18 Whitehead, A.N., and B. Russell, *Principia Mathematica*, 3 Vols, 2nd Ed., Cambridge University Press, Cambridge, 1925-27. This book is widely regarded as one of the most important developments in modern mathematics.

19 Newell, A., and H.A. Simon, *Heuristic Problem Solving: The Next Advance* in *Operations Research, Journal of the Operations Research Society of America*, Vol 6, no. 1, 1958.

20 Feigenbaum, E. A., and P. McCorduck, *The Fifth Generation: Artificial Intelligence and Japan's Computer Challenge to the World*, Addison Wesley, Reading, Mass., 1983.

21 Wood, R.C., *The Real Challenge of Japan's Fifth Generation Project*, Technology Review, pp. 67-73, Jan 1988.

22 Gross, N., *A Japanese "Flop" that became a Launching Pad*, Business Week, pp. 75, June 8, 1992.

23 Colby, K., *Modeling a Paranoid Mind*, Behavioral and Brain Sciences, 4, no. 4, pp. 515-560, 1981.

24 Sheil, B., *Thinking about artificial intelligence*, Harvard Business Review, pp. 91-97, July-August, 1987.

25 Sheil, B., *Thinking about artificial intelligence*, Harvard Business Review, pp. 91-97, July-August, 1987.

26 Minsky, M., *Thoughts about artificial intelligence*, in: R. Kurzweil, *The Age of Intelligent Machines*, MIT Press, pp. 214-219, 1990.

27 *And Man Created the Chip*, Newsweek, June 30, 1980.

28 Alexander, T., *Practical uses for a "useless" science*, Fortune, pp. 139-145, May 31, 1982.

29 Schwartz, E.I. and J.B. Treece, *Smart Programs go to work*, Business Week, pp. 47-51, March 2, 1992.

30 For example, consider the SIMKIT system marketed by Intellicorp Inc., Palo Alto, CA.

31 Leonard-Barton, D., & J. J. Sviokla, Putting Expert Systems to Work, Harvard Business Review, pp. 91-98, March-April 1988.

32 *PlanPower: The Financial Planning Expert System*, Harvard Business School case study, No. 9-186-293, 1986.

33 The PCs of the early 1980s were simply not powerful enough to run LISP efficiently.

34 Meador, C.L., and E.G. Mahler, *Choosing an Expert Systems Game Plan*, Datamation, August 1, 1990.

35 Kehler, T. P., *AI or "knowledge processing" will be a boon to MIS*, Information Week, Jan. 26, 1987.

36 Schwartz, E.I. and J.B. Treece, *Smart Programs go to work*, Businessweek, pp. 50, March 2, 1992.

37 Kurzweil, R., *The Age of Intelligent Machines*, MIT Press, pp. 212, 1990.

38 Steward, T.A., *Brainpower*, Fortune, pp. 42-60, June 3, 1991.

39 McCullough, T., *Six Steps for Introducing AI Technology*, Intellicorp Reprint, Palo Alto, California, 1987.

# Part II

## Acquiring, representing, and reasoning with knowledge

Techniques for acquiring, representing, and reasoning with knowledge are of fundamental importance in knowledge processing. These concepts are described in the two chapters (2 and 3) constituting this second part of the book. As the emphasis on representing and reasoning with knowledge permeates through all technologies and applications described in this book, the contents of these two chapters are relevant for all succeeding chapters also.

Chapter 2 introduces knowledge-based systems (KBSs) and presents a few commercial applications of KBSs. These example descriptions are brief and motivational in intent. Additional details on commercial KBS applications are given in Appendix 1. The focus of the chapter then turns to an exploration about the true nature of 'knowledge' and its different dimensions and stages. This is important for understanding the nature and limitations of knowledge in a KBS. The chapter ends with an extended discussion of different methods (both automated and manual) for acquiring knowledge. Problems and challenges in acquiring knowledge are emphasized and guidelines are presented for effective management of the knowledge acquisition process.

The next chapter focuses on issues related to representing and reasoning with knowledge. This is a natural continuation of the discussion of Chapter 2, as the most important issue after knowledge acquisition is use of the acquired knowledge. There are several different methods for representing and reasoning with knowledge. Rules and frame hierarchies are the two most important and common techniques for knowledge representation and reasoning. Chapter 3 describes them in detail and lists their relative advantages and disadvantages. The chapter ends with brief descriptions of two alternative approaches to knowledge representation: blackboard systems and case-based reasoning.

# Chapter 2
# *Knowledge-based systems and the acquisition of knowledge*

Knowledge-based systems (KBSs) can be simply defined as computer systems which rely primarily on extensive domain-specific knowledge for problem solution. It was realized during the early 1970s that it's not possible to replicate the problem-solving behavior of experts with general-purpose algorithms (like those incorporated in the General Problem Solver program[1]). This is because human experts typically tend to rely on their specialized knowledge (accumulated from years of on-the-job experience) about a particular domain to solve problems. It also became apparent that a surprisingly large amount of 'common-sense' knowledge is necessary for solving common, everyday problems such as deciding where to park a car, or how to plan a vacation. These realizations caused a fundamental shift within artificial intelligence (AI), away from general problem solvers towards systems incorporating extensive domain knowledge.

KBSs have been the dominant emphasis within applied AI for much of the 1970s and the 1980s. They also account for most visible commercial successes of applied AI. Today, there are thousands of KBSs performing many different functions, and in actual commercial use all over the world. KBSs have provided companies with significant competitive benefits, such as an ability to manage complex knowledge-intensive tasks, decentralize knowledge to improve consistency, accuracy, and speed of decision making, and a practical means to capture and preserve vital corporate knowledge. Some examples of the application of KBSs are briefly mentioned below[2].

## 32 Knowledge-based systems and knowledge acquisition

### Digital Equipment Corporation

Digital, the second largest computer manufacturer in the USA, has been one of the pioneers in the commercialization of KBSs. Digital's XCON[3] system was the world's first commercial KBS in 1980. XCON is a KBS which solves the computer configuration problem at Digital: it checks sales orders and designs the layout of the corresponding computer orders. Configuring computers is a very complex and difficult problem, when one takes into consideration the many different types and generations of products manufactured by Digital. The release of new generations of products does not mean that knowledge about old products can be discarded, because customers do not discard old computers with equal rapidity. It is estimated conservatively that at least 30,000 different software and hardware options are possible for Digital computers sold worldwide. Note that options can differ from country to country (e.g., electrical sockets are different in most European countries). An overwhelming majority (more than 90%) of all computer orders are also different from each other. The complexity of the knowledge required to configure computers is indeed mind-boggling. It's impossible for any one person to be knowledgeable about all different configuration possibilities. The XCON KBS not only manages this enormous complexity, but also saves money by removing the need for assembly sites (where computer orders were physically hooked-up and checked for accuracy — prior to XCON — before being shipped to customers). Today the XCON system is used worldwide to process about 90% of Digital's dollar volume of orders. It generates real dollar savings (about $25M annually), and performs the configuration task better than any human expert. It also plays a crucial role in helping Digital meet one of its strategic objectives: to give customers the maximum flexibility while ordering.

Besides XCON, Digital has more than 40 other major KBSs performing different functions within the company. Some examples are[4]: XSEL (a KBS which helps Digital's computer salesmen to order the right combination of components), and XFL (a KBS to lay out the site for a computer installation). The annual cumulative savings from these various KBSs is in the order of many tens of millions of dollars.

### American Express

One of the key differentiating features of American Express in the highly competitive credit card market is the absence of a preset spending limit. This feature also complicates the process of authorizing a certain credit purchase. Typically every credit purchase request is passed through a statistical program which checks for aberrations of the request relative to the card-holder's usual spending patterns. In case an aberration is detected, the request is forwarded to a human agent who has to make the final yes/no decision. There are about 300 such authorizers at American Express, handling over a million transactions a month. The agents have to determine the authenticity of the card-holder making the credit request, and also assess the likelihood that the card-holder will pay the amount later. To aid the decision process, agents may have to retrieve information from as many as 13 different databases, and look at possibly 16 different screenfulls of data. Agents also have to include their subjective analyses about the particular credit request (for example, jewellery items are usually favoured by card thieves). Pressures on the agent while making a decision are tremendous. Large amounts of data have to be sifted through rapidly. The final decision is crucial to American Express. Denying credit to an honest card-holder would have a damaging effect on customer relations. At the same time detection of fraud is crucial, because millions of dollars are lost each year to fraud charges. Agents also differ in their decision-making capability, as there are no fixed formal decision procedures.

Since 1987, American Express has been using a KBS called Authorizer's Assistant (AA) for helping agents arrive at a yes/no decision. The AA system embodies the reasoning expertise of one of the most experienced agents at American Express. When faced with a certain credit request, it performs the requisite analyses and gives a yes/no recommendation within 90 seconds. The agent can then accept the AA system's recommendation, or ask for explanation about how the particular recommendation was reached, or override it. The AA system has cut the time of transaction by 20% to 30%, and has helped reduce bad judgements by about 75%[5]. As a result, the AA system is reported to save American Express millions of dollars annually. It has also increased the level of consistency of decision-making among different agents, and helped improve customer satisfaction. From a global perspective, the AA system is playing a critical role in supporting American Express' strategy of differentiating itself from other credit cards by offering individualized credit limits.

There are other KBSs in operation (or under development) at American Express. For example, at IDS Financial Services, the financial planning subsidiary of American Express, a KBS called Insight captures the expertise of its best account managers. According to its chairman Harvey Golub, the Insight KBS has helped even the worst of their 6500 planners to be better than the average planner (before the introduction of Insight)[6]. As a result, within the last four years that the system has been in use, the percentage of clients who leave has dropped by half.

## Campbell Soup

During 1984, Campbell Soup realized that it had a small, but significant problem[7]. One of their employees, Aldo Camino, was about to retire within three years, and take with him a large amount of expertise developed over the years. Aldo was Campbell's resident expert on hydrostatic and rotary cookers (which are used to kill bacteria), and had spent the last several years flying from one plant to the next, repairing broken cookers. The knowledge and experience of Aldo was a valuable 'knowledge asset' to the company.

Faced with the prospect of losing an important knowledge asset with Aldo's imminent retirement, Campbell decided to build a KBS which captured his experience and knowledge. Over a period of 8 months (during 1984-85), Aldo participated in the building of a KBS which was meant to replace him after his departure. The resulting KBS, called Campbell Soup's Cooker (or alternatively as 'Aldo on a Disk'), makes a diagnosis about broken cookers in different plants by asking local plant employees to answer a set of questions about the disabled cooker. Today, Aldo Camino is happily retired and Campbell Soup is content with 'Aldo on a Disk'.

# 34 Knowledge-based systems and knowledge acquisition

## Structure of knowledge-based systems

Several different architectures are possible for KBSs. The most common structure of a generic KBS consists of the following three components (as shown in Figure 2.1): a knowledge base, an inference engine, and a user interface.

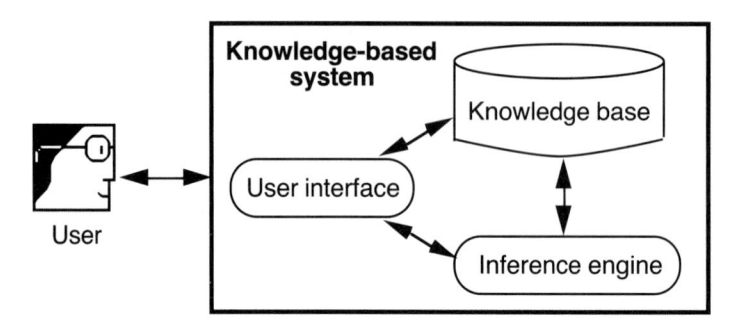

**Figure 2.1** Structure of a generic knowledge-based system

The knowledge base serves as the repository of domain-specific knowledge, and contains all knowledge necessary for problem solution. Conceptually, a knowledge base can be thought of simply as a database augmented with rules specifying how to interpret the data in the database. Consider the simple knowledge base shown in Figure 2.2. The database component of the knowledge base consists of two elementary tables specifying 'father' and 'mother' relations. There are several ways in which we can interpret this simple data. Two rules of interpretation are illustrated in Figure 2.2. Rule 1 specifies how we can interpret the data about fathers and mothers to determine siblings. Rule 2 specifies how the same data can be used to determine husband-wife relations. The father and mother relation data, together with the rules for interpreting data, constitute the knowledge base. Note that the knowledge base is extremely domain-specific. Rules 1 and 2 are only useful for determining specific family relationships. Representing knowledge has its complications. Even in this simple example, while rule 1 is always true[8], rule 2 is usually, but not always true. This is because knowledge is often heuristic[9] and uncertain in nature. There are different possible schemes for representing knowledge in knowledge bases, and two important approaches (rules and frame hierarchies) are described in Chapter 3. The knowledge base is the most important determinant of the power and capabilities of a KBS. Most of the effort in the design of a KBS is usually spent in constructing the knowledge base.

The knowledge base contains knowledge about a specific domain, but not about how to use the domain knowledge for solving particular problems. The inference engine of the KBS is responsible for controlling and directing the use of knowledge for problem solution. The simple knowledge base of Figure 2.2 has two tables of data and two rules. A more realistic knowledge base for a real world problem would contain much more data, and at least a few hundred rules. When faced with a particular problem, the inference engine of the KBS decides the different pieces of knowledge (data and rules) to be used, and the order in which they are to be combined to yield the solution. The task of the inference engine can be conceptualized as a search procedure (Figure 2.3): a combination of

## Structure of knowledge-based systems 35

**Knowledge base**

=

**Database** and **Rules for interpretating data**

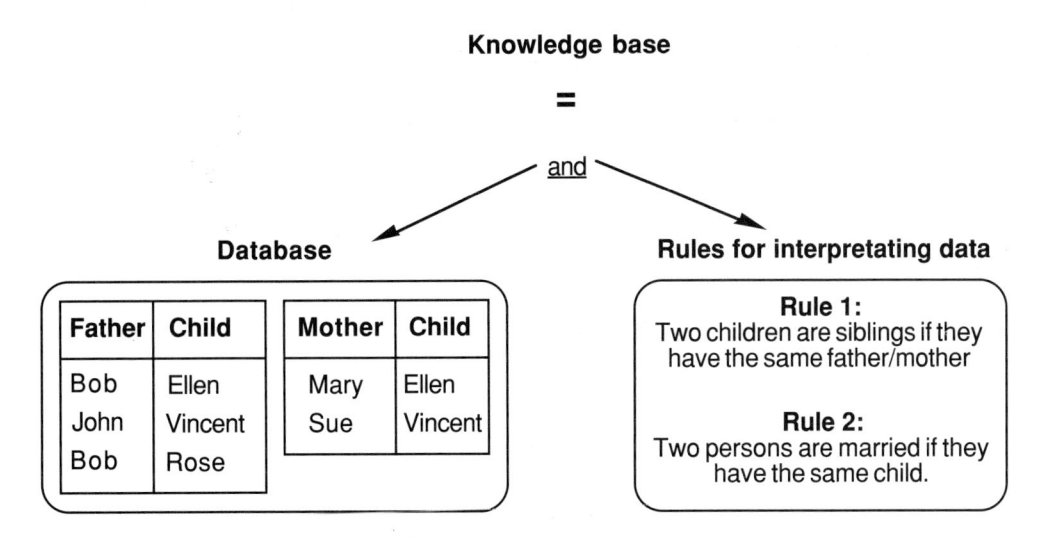

| Father | Child |
|--------|-------|
| Bob | Ellen |
| John | Vincent |
| Bob | Rose |

| Mother | Child |
|--------|-------|
| Mary | Ellen |
| Sue | Vincent |

**Rule 1:**
Two children are siblings if they have the same father/mother

**Rule 2:**
Two persons are married if they have the same child.

**Figure 2.2** Viewing a knowledge base as a database augmented with rules for interpreting data

searching for data to satisfy certain goals, and determining which goals are satisfied by available data. The inference engine is largely domain independent, and contains inferencing techniques which can be used in different domains. The next chapter describes inferencing techniques with rule-based and frame-based knowledge representation schemes.

The user interface module is domain independent, and serves as the interface between the user and the KBS. It has to interact with the knowledge base and inference engine modules of the KBS, and display the appropriate (or requested) information to the user. Two important functions performed by the user interface module are (1) helping the user to access or modify the knowledge stored in the knowledge base, and (2) explaining the reasoning procedure adopted by the inference engine while obtaining a particular solution. The user interface component of most commercial KBSs includes sophisticated graphics for effective communication with the user. More details on the user interface module are given in Chapter 4. Chapters 5 and 6 describe applied AI technologies which help to create 'intelligent interfaces'".

**Data** — Searching for goals satisfied by available data → **Knowledge** ← Searching for data to satisfy specified goals — **Goals**

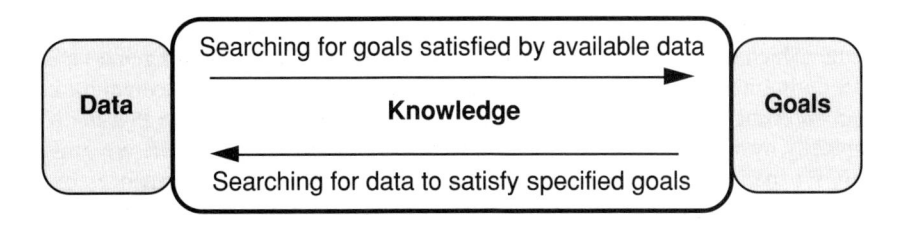

**Figure 2.3** Conceptualizing the task of the inference engine as a search procedure

# 36 Knowledge-based systems and knowledge acquisition

## The process of building knowledge-based systems

Due to the domain independence of the inference engine and user interface modules, several commercial KBS vendors have started selling KBS shell tools which can be used to build KBSs quickly and cheaply. A KBS shell tool is, in simple terms, a bundled package containing an inference engine and a user interface. It is therefore possible, in principle, to buy a KBS shell tool off-the-shelf in the market, add a domain-specific component (the knowledge base) and produce a KBS (as depicted in Figure 2.4). This simplicity in the process of building a KBS has been instrumental in enhancing the commercial acceptance and success of KBSs. A variety of KBS shell tools are available in the market, and range in cost from around $50 to $20,000[10].

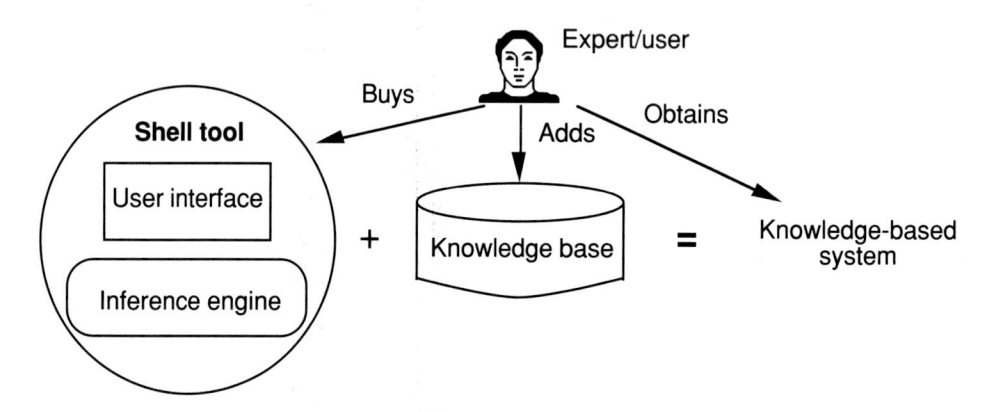

**Figure 2.4** Building a knowledge-based system with a shell tool

With the increasing user-friendliness of KBS shell tools, adding the knowledge base module is becoming easier for the end-user. But trained professionals called knowledge engineers are commonly used for building commercial KBSs. Knowledge engineers are specially trained in design, development and application of KBSs, and can help the user in gaining the maximum benefit from the deployment of the KBS. The process of developing KBSs with the help of a knowledge engineer is depicted in Figure 2.5. The knowledge engineer extracts knowledge (typically via interviews) from the domain expert, and uses the KBS shell tool to build, refine, and test the KBS. The domain expert provides the knowledge which is incorporated into the KBS, and also helps in extending and validating the KBS during its intermediate stages of development. The process of extracting knowledge and encoding it in a KBS is termed as knowledge engineering. Note that the KBS is used typically by someone else other than the expert. Usually, the end users are junior and relatively inexperienced persons, who can expect to improve their performances by using the expert knowledge contained in the KBS. Besides helping in the actual process of constructing a KBS, knowledge engineers can also play an important role in the identification, selection, and field implementation of strategic applications of KBSs within the organization.

# The process of building knowledge-based systems

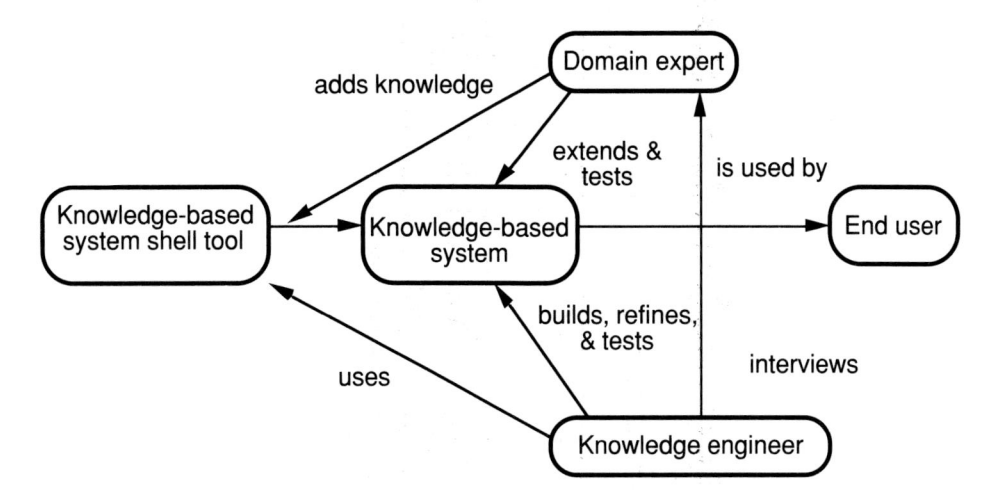

**Figure 2.5** Process of building a knowledge-based system with a knowledge engineer

## Expert systems and knowledge-based systems

It is perhaps useful to clarify the distinction between the terms expert systems and knowledge-based systems. The term expert system is applied to KBSs in which the dominant source of knowledge comes from the experience and expertise of human experts. A good example of an expert system is the Authorizer's Assistant system of American Express (described earlier).

The term knowledge-based system, on the other hand, is more general, and is applicable to systems which incorporate knowledge from human experts and from other sources (such as documents, manuals, and procedures).

While the term expert system has been fashionable in associated literature during the 1980s, there is an increased shift towards using the (more realistic, and less mystical) term of knowledge-based system. This shift has been caused by the realization that usually many different sources of knowledge have to be integrated for solving real life problems. For this reason this book also favours the use of the term knowledge-based system, and we shall stick to it from now on.

## Epistemology and knowledge-based systems

Due to the importance and key role of knowledge in KBSs, it is important to explore the meaning of the term knowledge. To begin this exploration, it is useful to review historical developments within epistemology[11], the field of philosophy that has been concerned with the study of knowledge for many centuries.

# 38 Knowledge-based systems and knowledge acquisition

Several fields such as mathematics, logic, psychology, philosophy of the mind, and the natural sciences have contributed, over the centuries, to epistemology. Epistemologists since Plato and Aristotle (4th and 3rd century B.C.) have been concerned with issues like:

- sources of knowledge — the determination of adequate bases for claims to knowledge;
- justification — the determination of the truth of a particular piece of knowledge;
- certainty — the determination of knowledge which is true beyond any doubt; and
- representation — exploring the stored representation of knowledge in the mind and its links to the physical world.

The classical approach in epistemology (advocated by Plato, Aristotle, and others) was to view knowledge as justified true beliefs. This required attention to the tasks of (a) characterizing how beliefs are acquired and represented, and (b) determining which beliefs qualify as knowledge and which do not. The epistemologists of the 17th century applied new scientific constructs to this traditional view, and this lead to the development of two streams of thought. Rationalists, such as Rene Descartes (1596-1650) believed that beliefs were acquired from mental constructs (pure understanding), and that all justification must be strictly based on the principles of logic. In contrast, empiricists, such as Bishop Berkeley (1685-1753) and David Hume (1711-1776), propounded the view that all knowledge was ultimately based on sensory information alone. The early 20th century saw the emergence of two new approaches. Typified by the work of Edmund Husserl (1859-1938), one approach tried to take a more systematic view to the work of earlier rationalists by focusing on the structure of mental components which lead to the formation of beliefs. An alternative approach, expounded by G E Moore, H H Price and others, formulated the earlier empiricist's view in terms of sense data units, which were viewed as the ultimate components of knowledge.

The dual tasks of determining the sources and components of knowledge formed the focus of most epistemologists until the middle of the 20th century, when attention started to be focused on what it meant to possess knowledge. Several questions were raised about the applicability of prior approaches in epistemology. Godel's Incompleteness Theorem[12] showed that formal logical techniques were inadequate for solving all arithmetic questions, and thus questioned the applicability of logic as a general justification procedure. These investigations were further spurred by the birth of the field of AI. AI research demonstrated the importance of procedural ('know-how') knowledge (ignored previously by epistemologists) in addition to the widely studied declarative ('know-that') knowledge, and the importance of being able to extend judgements and justifications in areas of incomplete knowledge (for which traditional logic was clearly inadequate). Research within AI also focused attention on pragmatic concerns related to the representation of knowledge.

Epistemological issues are unavoidable while dealing with KBSs because the notion of intelligence is closely related to the concept of knowledge. One frequently raised question in this context is whether KBSs (a) produce simulations of intelligent behavior, or (b) contain models of intelligence, or (c) represent actual synthetic intelligence. If KBSs simply produce simulations of intelligent behavior, the emphasis is only on the actual output (does the system behave in an intelligent manner?), and not on how the system produces the output. If KBSs are seen as containing models of intelligence, then they must not only produce seemingly intelligent behavior, but must also contain knowledge and procedures which mirror those found in intelligent beings. If a KBS is actual synthetic intelligence, then there should be no difference (except for history) between a KBS and a real human expert. While the epistemological status of KBSs can be debated, most KBSs are largely perceived as belonging to the second category, where they are seen as containing models of intelligence.

## The definition of knowledge

The field of epistemology is many centuries old, and it has yet to produce a complete and accurate definition of the concept of knowledge. We all have an intuitive feel for what it means to 'know something', but have difficulty in articulating what it exactly means. The Webster's dictionary defines knowledge as:

> ...the fact or condition of possessing within mental grasp through instruction, study, research, or experience one or more truths, facts, principles, or other objects of perception.

Several definitions of the term knowledge can be found in AI literature:

> ...someone's ability to behave with intelligence..[13]

> ...the body of facts and principles accumulated by humankind or the act, fact, or state of knowing[14]

> ...the information a computer program needs before it can behave intelligently..[15]

Rather than try and propose yet another definition, let's try to understand the nature of knowledge by considering one task in more detail: the problem of configuring computers.

## The computer configuration problem

Computer configuration can be seen as consisting of the following three tasks[16]: (a) translating customer requirements into products offered by the computer vendor, (b) verifying completeness and accuracy of the sales order, and (c) designing physical placement and connections of all components of the order. The configuration problem is important because it is the primary means used to process and verify accuracy of sales orders. There are several possible sources of complexity in the configuration process. For a large computer vendor, such as Digital, there are more than 30,000 different hardware and software components, which can be combined together in millions of different ways. To add to the complexity, new components (such as new computers) are introduced rapidly, marketing strategies are modified periodically, and government regulations are changed often. All these factors dramatically increase the complexity of the problem. Customer needs are highly variable, and cannot be predicted in advance. Thus each order has to be configured dynamically as it is being processed. Even slight differences in configurations may dictate large variations in scheduled activities, due to complex interactions between components and constraints.

Given the complexity and importance of the configuration problem, computer vendors have to develop special procedures and skills for performing this task. Prior to application of KBSs for the configuration task, vendors such as Digital had experts performing a technical edit of the configuration at three different points in the order flow process: initial technical edit (done prior to the acceptance of the order), manufacturing technical edit (done before scheduling manufacturing), and final assembly and test (done before delivery to the customer). These experts relied extensively on technical manuals and personal experience for performing their tasks. The manuals provided elaborate descriptions of various hardware/software options and their associated constraints — detail and knowledge necessary for the configuration task. Due to the large number of different possible options, each expert also relied on prior experience to determine workable combinations of different options. There was no unique solution to a particular configuration task, and the normal cycle time to complete the technical editing process varied from 1 to 2 days.

## The dimensions of knowledge

Where does the knowledge lie in the configuration problem described above? It is clearly in the skills of the experts who perform the technical edits, and in their ability to communicate and coordinate the three different technical edits. How can we characterize their knowledge? At one level, we note that the knowledge required is both explicit and tacit[17]. Explicit knowledge refers to the formal systematic knowledge, such as those contained in the technical manuals, necessary for successfully configuring computers. But pure explicit knowledge is not enough for dealing with the complexity of the configuration task. Each expert has developed tacit knowledge, based on his/her own experience and intuition, about configurations which 'work best'. This tacit knowledge, consisting partly of heuristics and partly of intuition, helps the expert to avoid considering all different possible combinations (which would make computer configuration a hopeless problem) each time. This ability of an expert to be able to decide upon the 'correct' configuration without systematically trying out all possible options lies at the core of his/her knowledge and expertise. A major challenge in building KBSs is acquiring and capturing this tacit knowledge.

Related to the ideas of tacit and explicit knowledge, are the concepts of surface knowledge, and deep knowledge. With repeated on-the-job experience, configuration experts typically develop heuristics about specific solutions which work for particular combinations of computer components (input conditions). These heuristics represent simple mappings from input conditions to (output) solutions, and cumulatively represent superficial surface knowledge about the task. When faced with a new problem for which no heuristic mapping to a 'canned' solution (surface knowledge) exists, the human expert has to use deep knowledge about the domain (such as constraints on the connectivity of different components) to devise a solution from scratch. While surface knowledge is generally tacit in nature, deep knowledge can comprise of both explicit and tacit knowledge. Note also that while surface knowledge is (apparently) superficial in quality, it is usually the result of repeated applications of deep knowledge to the same (or similar) task(s).

Another useful distinction is between domain knowledge and common-sense knowledge. Domain knowledge refers to the specialized knowledge required to perform a particular task. For example, all knowledge (explicit or tacit) related to the configuration problem is domain-specific knowledge. At the same time, a configuration expert has a body of knowledge (commonly referred to as 'common-sense'), which though not directly related to computer configuration, is nevertheless essential for effective task performance. For example, a configuration expert knows from common-sense that one should use the telephone to consult with a colleague in a remote location. Such knowledge is vital for effective job performance, but is not (usually) explicitly stated anywhere in manuals. Surprisingly, it has been observed that specialized domain knowledge is often much easier to capture and represent in a KBS. This is because it is difficult to define (what knowledge constitutes common-sense?) and delimit (how much of common-sense knowledge is enough?) common-sense knowledge. Dealing effectively with common-sense knowledge is still a hard problem for KBSs. This often limits the range of applicability of KBSs to narrow and specific problem domains.

Associated literature has also classified knowledge as being either declarative or procedural. Declarative knowledge refers to the information that an expert knows of (from sources such as manuals or from experience), and procedural knowledge refers to the knowledge required to actually perform some tasks (such as procedures for physically connecting together hardware/software components). Thus declarative knowledge can be thought of as 'know-of' knowledge, and procedural knowledge can be viewed as 'know-how' knowledge. Procedural knowledge is closely related to processes, and the notion of competence. Note that knowledge required to co-ordinate the three different technical edits in the configuration task is procedural in nature.

A configuration expert also knows what is known, and when to seek help from other sources. This knowledge about what is known is termed as meta-knowledge[18]. Meta-knowledge is particularly useful when the amount of knowledge in the knowledge base is large, as it can be used by the inference engine of the KBS to navigate through relevant knowledge in an efficient and effective manner. Incorporating meta-knowledge in a KBS is more challenging than adding ordinary domain knowledge because, like common-sense knowledge, it is also difficult to define and delimit meta-knowledge precisely.

Figure 2.6 summarizes the different dimensions of knowledge described here.

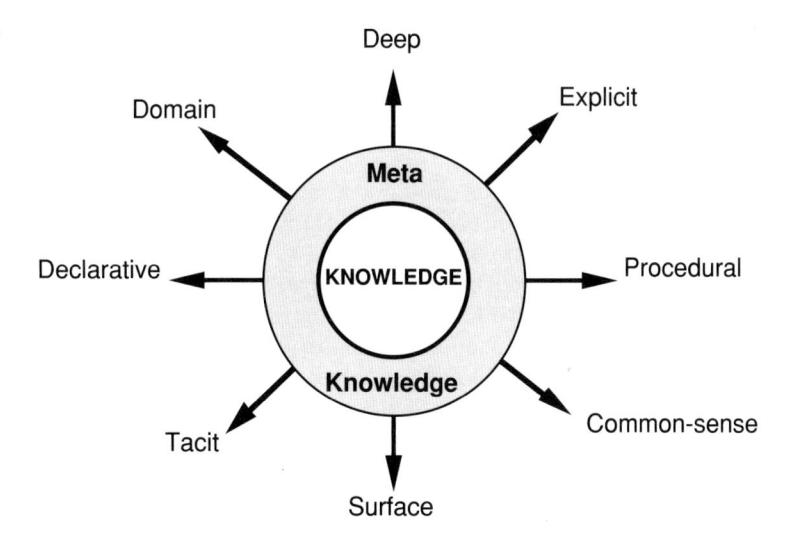

**Figure 2.6** Different dimensions of knowledge

## 42 Knowledge-based systems and knowledge acquisition

### Stages of knowledge

Knowledge is a complex phenomenon, and can be described along several dimensions (as just specified) for a particular task. Along each dimension, knowledge may exist in one of the following different stages[19]:

1 Ignorance — there is complete ignorance about the task.

2 Variable identification — it is possible to identify some of the important variables affecting the task.

3 Pattern identification — it is possible to partially characterize the task in terms of patterns of certain variables.

4 Model formulation and exception identification — it is possible to formulate an initial model, and identify some exception conditions.

5 Model formulation and validation — a reasonably complete model is formulated and tested.

6 Complete knowledge — there is complete (and near-certain) knowledge about the task.

7 Expertise — a complete mastery of the task is achieved, such that solution is usually possible on intuitive knowledge about solution patterns without actual model solution.

The usual movement of task specific knowledge is from stage 1 towards the higher stages. However, it is not necessary that all stages of knowledge are achieved sequentially. For example, it is possible to develop a certain expertise (from repeated task performance) for the task (stage 7) without formulating a domain model for the task (stages 5 and 6). It is also possible for different parts of the knowledge about a particular task to be at different stages in the above hierarchy. Depending upon the task and its knowledge requirements, the highest stage of knowledge (stage 7) may or may not be attained. Note that the above framework of knowledge stages does not imply that a higher stage of knowledge is superior. For certain open-ended tasks (such as creative art design), it may be desirable to leave the task knowledge at a lower stage (such as at stages 3 or 4). In contrast, for other tasks (such as rigid, automated assembly lines), it is necessary to have complete knowledge about the task (stage 6).

A proper understanding of the current stage of task knowledge, and the desired stage of knowledge (typically, different tasks have different desired stages of knowledge) affects the applicability of KBSs to that particular task. It is of little use to try and build KBSs for the lower stages (1 through 3) of knowledge. At stage 6, it may be possible to completely automate the task with a KBS. In the intermediate stages (4 and 5), a KBS can perhaps be employed in the role of supporting a human operator. At stage 7, the expert has to specify the accumulated expertise to a knowledge engineer, so that the expert's knowledge can be captured and represented in a KBS. This process of acquiring an expert's knowledge is non-trivial, and is described in more detail in the following section on knowledge acquisition.

These stages of knowledge also imply that knowledge is dynamic. Knowledge moves across stages. Such movements are caused by factors, both internal (such as knowledge enhancements from repeated task performance), and external (such as changes in the composition and nature of the task). For the computer configuration task, as each new product line is introduced, or as government regulations change, the knowledge required to configure computers changes.

Human experts learn and expand their knowledge continuously. For KBSs to be effective, it's also necessary that their knowledge bases are continuously updated (either by explicit programming, or via autonomous learning methods).

## Knowledge in a knowledge-based system

The knowledge of a KBS is contained in its knowledge base, and can be described along the different dimensions of knowledge shown in Figure 2.6. The knowledge in most KBSs is a combination of both explicit and tacit knowledge about a particular domain (with little common-sense knowledge). Depending upon the domain characteristics, varying amounts of both declarative and procedural knowledge can be present. While surface knowledge is dominant in most rule-based KBSs, there is a trend towards incorporating more deep knowledge in KBSs.

As an example, consider the nature of knowledge in the XCON KBS. The knowledge of XCON lies in its ability to solve the (particular) problem of computer configuration for a wide variety of Digital computer hardware and software options. Similar to human experts, XCON knows about the different option possibilities, and their related constraints (explicit knowledge). In addition, it also contains a large body of the tacit knowledge (comprising heuristics and intuition) used by human experts. All this knowledge has been extracted (from experts and other sources), and represented within the system over a period of many years. XCON is able to reason with this knowledge, and draw conclusions about specific configuration problems.

As the knowledge about 30,000+ different options is horrendously large, the reasoning process is potentially complicated, time consuming, and inefficient. To better manage the reasoning process, some meta-knowledge is used to steer the reasoning process in useful directions. Finally, to keep XCON useful over the years[20], all relevant changes in domain knowledge (such as introduction of a new computer line) are systematically reflected in the system's knowledge base.

## Knowledge acquisition

Unlike epistemologists, AI researchers are faced with the task of both deciding what knowledge is, and capturing it in an actual computer implementation. The latter constraint has often forced AI researchers to take a more pragmatic approach to the concept of knowledge. Any knowledge in a KBS must be acquired first. Knowledge acquisition is a sub-field of AI that is concerned with acquisition of knowledge required for building a KBS. Study and practice of knowledge acquisition is rapidly gaining in importance because acquisition of knowledge is widely recognized today as the bottle-neck, and the most critical part, in the development of KBSs.

## 44 Knowledge-based systems and knowledge acquisition

In a typical organizational setting, there are usually several different sources of knowledge:

- books — handbooks, manuals and brochures often contain a wealth of knowledge;
- historical records — most organizations store information about problems/cases encountered before;
- experts — human experts are potentially the best source of specialized knowledge about a particular task; and
- human contacts — most tasks have other human contacts (such as suppliers, customers, and users), who can all be valuable sources of knowledge.

Books, manuals, and historical records are relatively easy to obtain, and often contain valuable information. But they are also usually outdated, and are frequently difficult to use. Knowledge acquired from these sources is generally explicit in nature. Experts and other human contacts are the primary sources of tacit knowledge. Tacit knowledge is crucial for building effective KBSs, but is often difficult to obtain. Knowledge acquisition techniques can be divided into two broad categories (as shown in Figure 2.7):

- knowledge engineer guided — these techniques are designed to structure and guide the process of knowledge elicitation (usually from experts) by knowledge engineers. These methods can consist of interview-like sessions, and experimental runs on partially completed versions of KBSs.
- automated — these methods deal with development of tools for automating, fully or partially, the process of acquiring knowledge. These knowledge acquisition tools operate autonomously, or are designed to support a knowledge engineer during the knowledge elicitation process.

### Knowledge engineer-guided knowledge acquisition

As human experts are the most valuable sources of knowledge for building KBSs, most of the effort in the field of knowledge acquisition has gone into the design of formal procedures for eliciting knowledge from experts. These procedures are necessary, because experience shows that most experts are unable to explain clearly why and how they do their particular tasks so expertly. Consider the experience[21] of Coopers and Lybrand while

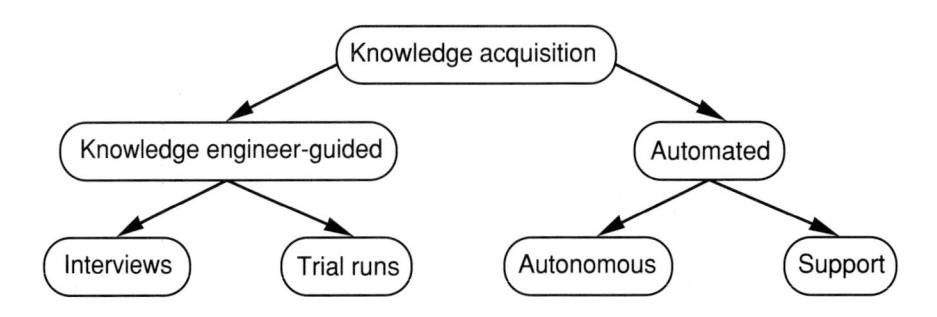

Figure 2.7 Types of knowledge acquisition methods

building a large, sophisticated KBS called ExperTax for helping with the tax accrual process. The developers of ExperTax were repeatedly stumped in the process of acquiring knowledge, as senior tax partners seemed unable to explain clearly how they made their expert judgements during the tax planning process. Numerous techniques, such as interviews and mock problems were tried, but all failed. Finally in desperation, the ExperTax development team decided upon a novel technique: a group of senior tax experts and a novice tax accountant were seated on opposite sides of a room partitioned by a curtain. The junior accountant was given a particular tax problem to solve, and allowed to ask questions to the senior partners. By videotaping the ensuing question response patterns, the development team were finally able to obtain an initial core of knowledge for the ExperTax system. While this solution may not work in all situations, it aptly describes the frustrations faced by knowledge engineers during knowledge acquisition, and emphasizes the need to be open to new ideas and approaches in acquiring knowledge.

There are several reasons why experts usually fail to explain the foundations of their expertise clearly to a knowledge engineer. An expert's knowledge can be characterized as belonging to stage 7 of the knowledge stage hierarchy described earlier. At this stage of knowledge, the expert has formed an intuitive feel for the task. This intuitive feel is usually obtained after years of problem-solving, a time consuming and repetitive process, which leads to the expert storing familiar patterns of solutions in memory. As experts typically solve problems by using a lot of intuition, they have a hard time explaining bases of their intuition to a knowledge engineer. Usually they are only able to specify partial patterns of solutions, which leaves the knowledge engineer with the arduous task of determining which important parts have been left out. At other times, some important domain characteristics are so obvious to the expert, that he/she may not even think of mentioning them explicitly to the knowledge engineer. For example, the developers of a KBS in the medical domain were once surprised to see the KBS declare that a certain male patient was pregnant! On a more careful analysis, they found that the KBS never asked about the sex of the patient, because the expert (the medical doctor) had forgotten to mention it as a question to be asked explicitly.

Other reasons have also been mentioned in the literature to explain the difficulty of knowledge elicitation from experts. Some experts either view KBSs with skepticism (can a computer program do what I do?), or see KBSs as decreasing their power (now a computer will replace my skills), or are simply not comfortable with computers. In such cases, they can be uncooperative, withhold important details, show lack of interest, and in some extreme cases, even sabotage the project. All these factors point to the importance of carefully planning the knowledge acquisition phase, and applying some formal techniques during the process.

## Planning the knowledge acquisition process[22]

The basic challenge facing the knowledge engineer is to sort through the divergent, heterogeneous, and partially complete information available from the expert (and other sources), and determine what is important, and what is not relevant. The knowledge engineer has to be aware of the frustrating and demoralizing effect that a lack of planning can have on the KBS development project, and on the expert. As the domain of the KBS is

## 46 Knowledge-based systems and knowledge acquisition

typically new for the knowledge engineer, good background preparation (from books, libraries, and other sources) is vital to help plan the process of acquiring knowledge, and to appear interested and knowledgeable while dealing with the expert. The knowledge engineer also has to study the organization (in which the KBS will be deployed) with the aim of identifying the key characteristics of the different interest groups in the domain. Some common interest groups to consider, and relevant questions to be asked are:

- experts — who is the expert? Is the expert knowledgeable, articulate, available, and cooperative? Is there more than one expert? If there are multiple experts, is there unanimity between them about the problem solution ?

- users — who will be the users of the KBS? What is their level of sophistication? What are their expectations from the KBS? How will the KBS affect the job responsibilities of the users? What is the relation between the expert and the users?

- stakeholders — which other groups (such as customers and suppliers) are stakeholders in the project? What is the relation between them and the experts and the users?

Attention has to also be focused on the nature of the task to be performed by the KBS. Specific concerns related to this issue are:

- suitability — is a KBS suitable for solving the task? What kind of skills are required for performing the task? Are these skills amenable for capture and representation in a KBS?

- knowledge — where can knowledge required for performing the task be obtained? Is this knowledge unique? Is there agreement upon the knowledge? Is the knowledge static or dynamic? Is it complete? What is the level of uncertainty in the knowledge?

- decomposition — can the task be decomposed into smaller units? What are the interactions between the decomposed units?

- layering — how can knowledge about the task (or its decomposed units) be layered (from general issues to specific details)? What are the interactions between layers?

Interviewing the expert (and other interest groups) is the next task of the knowledge engineer. The interview process can be structured around the identified layers of knowledge in the task, or its decomposed units (this makes the acquisition of knowledge easier).

Three commonly used types of interviewing techniques are:

- outline interviews — these interviews focus on obtaining a high level description of the domain (the outer layers of knowledge). At this stage, the knowledge engineer is still obtaining an initial understanding of the domain.

- structured interviews — aim in these interviews is to elicit details about specific tasks or sub-tasks in the domain. This is useful after the knowledge engineer has sufficient knowledge of the domain to ask relevant probing questions.

- think aloud interviews — during these interviews the expert is asked to solve aloud a particular problem from the domain. The knowledge engineer uses the orally expressed thought processes of the expert to validate the currently known knowledge about the domain.

Because the available time of experts is expensive and scarce, each interview session has to be carefully planned to obtain maximum benefits. Planning an interview consists of the following phases:

● pre-interview planning — prior to each interview, the knowledge engineer has to decide the exact aims, expected outputs, and general approach of the interview.

● elicitation — this is the actual conduct of the interview to elicit the desired outputs. Keeping a transcript of the conversation is useful for following phases.

● analysis — immediately after the interview, the knowledge engineer must analyze the session (usually via the transcript), and consolidate lessons learnt during the session. Any doubts or problems must be noted explicitly, and be clarified in future interview sessions.

● review — before the next interview, the knowledge engineer must review the session in the light of previous sessions, and the overall progress and expectations of the knowledge acquisition process.

While think-aloud interviews allow for a mental or hand simulation of problem solution, another important tool for the knowledge engineer is to use prototypes of the KBS to aid the knowledge acquisition process. A prototype is a partially completed KBS[23], that represents an intermediate stage in the development of the KBS. These prototypes can be used to run experimental runs with (parts of) the problem. The expert can observe results produced by the prototype, and suggest appropriate changes in the knowledge and reasoning procedures. The knowledge engineer can use the expert's comments to validate knowledge contained in the partially completed KBS, and make enhancements to the KBS. These trial runs have the added advantage of actually presenting a concrete example of a functioning KBS to the expert (who may have never seen a KBS before). If utilized wisely, trial runs on prototypes can increase level of commitment and buy-in of the expert, help the knowledge engineer to incrementally increase the knowledge base of the KBS, and provide a better structure to the knowledge acquisition process.

Knowledge acquisition is a time consuming and arduous process. It is often the bottleneck due to the paucity of experts (who are usually few in number), unavailability of experts (who are often hard pressed to find the time for elaborate interviews), and the difficulty of having experts explain their expertise clearly to the knowledge engineer. It is also an expensive, and continuous process. To give an idea about costs, Coopers and Lybrand spent[24] about $1 million, and 7000 hours of expert's time on developing the ExperTax KBS. Assuming conservatively that the cost of one hour of a senior tax partner's time is $200, we see that the cost of the expert's time is well in excess of $ 1 million. As the knowledge contained in a KBS has to be continually updated to reflect changes, the process of acquiring knowledge never really terminates. Even after the first version of a KBS is deployed, some expert has to assume partial responsibility for keeping the knowledge of the KBS updated. This obviously puts enormous constraints on experts. It is therefore necessary to ensure that time required for the knowledge acquisition activities is made a formal part of the responsibilities of the expert, and appropriate incentives are provided to the expert for cooperating at all stages of the project. Due to the importance and scarcity of experts within an organization, such steps can only be taken by senior management, who have to be made well aware of the benefits accruing from the KBS.

# 48 Knowledge-based systems and knowledge acquisition

## Automated tools for knowledge acquisition

Automated knowledge acquisition tools hold the promise of preventing the process of acquiring knowledge from becoming the bottleneck in the development of KBSs. Automating knowledge acquisition is useful because valuable knowledge is often resident in historical records, books, and manuals within an organization. Consider for example a hospital. Most hospitals keep detailed records of patients containing descriptions of symptoms, diagnoses, prescribed medicines, and observed changes over time. Cumulatively, these records contain a wealth of knowledge about medical diagnosis and treatment. The knowledge acquisition process would be significantly simplified if an automated system could look at these records, and extract valuable pieces of knowledge. Doctors would only need to verify the output of these knowledge acquisition tools, rather than sit through hours of interviews with knowledge engineers.

Tools for automated knowledge acquisition can be grouped into two categories: autonomous tools, and tools supporting a knowledge engineer during the knowledge acquisition task. Autonomous tools attempt to learn relevant knowledge from domain sources (such as historical records) independently, with little or no supervision from a knowledge engineer. For doing so, they utilize different techniques from the sub-field of AI called machine learning. Inductive learning is an example of a popular machine learning technique utilized in autonomous knowledge acquisition tools. Inductive learning is described in more detail below. Support tools are generally KBSs designed for a particular domain, for the specific purpose of aiding the knowledge acquisition process in that domain. To be effective, these tools need to possess knowledge about the domain under consideration and meta-knowledge about how to structure domain knowledge and the kind of questions to be asked for eliciting knowledge. These systems are still in the research stage[25], and though they have potential for the future, it will be a few more years before they are commercialized successfully.

## Induction

Inductive learning is the process of hypothesizing general rules from specific examples or instances. Inductive learning is extremely common in human cognition. When we hypothesize that birds fly after seeing a few flying birds, or that Indians are multi-lingual after meeting a few Indians, or that the summers in Fontainebleau are cool after observing a few summers, we are effectively using induction to generalize from a few specific examples. Because induction involves generalization from a set of instances to the entire domain, it is often uncertain in nature. There are birds which do not fly, Indians who are mono-lingual, and summers in Fontainebleau which are warm. However, the heuristic rules resulting from induction play an important role in the remarkable human ability to reason and solve problems in many situations. Induction is also complicated by the fact that only certain aspects of specific instances can be generalized. For example, while it may be reasonable to generalize that all Indians are multi-lingual after observing a small number of Indians, it is not possible to make any generalizations about their heights on the basis of the observed sample.

# Induction 49

| Name | Age (yrs) | Nationality | Height (cm) | Mother tongue |
|------|-----------|-------------|-------------|---------------|
| John | 24 | UK | 181 | English |
| Marcos | 38 | Spain | 175 | Spanish |
| Bob | 22 | UK | 186 | English |
| Carlos | 30 | Spain | 172 | Spanish |
| George | 25 | UK | 184 | English |

Table 2.1 Data about a set of fictional persons

Let us consider a simple, but concrete example to illustrate the process of using inductive learning for knowledge acquisition. Imagine that Table 2.1 represents data about a set of fictional persons. Each row of the table represents an example for the purposes of induction. If we input the data of Table 2.1 to an inductive learning program, we would typically get the following rules as output (determined by observing similarities between different examples):

[1] If nationality is English then mother tongue is English.

[2] If nationality is Spanish then mother tongue is Spanish.

[3] If nationality is English then height is greater than 180 cm.

[4] If nationality is Spanish then height is less than 176 cm.

[5] If nationality is English then age is less than 26 yrs.

[6] If nationality is Spanish then age is more than 29 yrs.

If we act as the expert, we would probably accept rules 1 and 2 as correct, dismiss rules 5 and 6 as incorrect (because we know from common-sense knowledge that age cannot be generalized on the basis of nationality), and perhaps modify rules 3 and 4 as:

[3] If nationality is English then height is generally tall.

[4] If nationality is Spanish then height is generally short.

Even in this simple example, the acquisition of rules has been simplified with the help of inductive learning. For organizations with large stores of prior examples (such as hospitals with patient records, or companies with customer sales records), induction can prove to be a very valuable technique for assisting the process of knowledge acquisition. Automated induction tools alone are rarely sufficient for the entire process of knowledge acquisition, because expert domain knowledge is often required (as in this example) for discerning the output of the induction program. However, a major limitation in the applicability of induction programs is that information about useful prior examples is rarely organized and stored formally in most organizations. Frequently, significant effort has to be expended to even organize the data for use by a inductive program.

## Steps after knowledge acquisition

After acquiring knowledge, some of the important issues facing the knowledge engineer include:

- representation — how to store the acquired knowledge in the knowledge-base of the KBS?
- reasoning — how to reason with the stored knowledge to solve particular problems?
- retrieval — how to retrieve the relevant parts of stored knowledge for reasoning? This is particularly important if the knowledge-base is very large.
- updates — how to continually enhance the knowledge in the knowledge-base?

Developments within epistemology have had a strong influence on the design of knowledge representation and reasoning techniques within AI. Due to the importance of logic in epistemological studies, it should not be surprising to learn that mathematical logic was one of the earliest proposed knowledge representation and reasoning formalisms. Logic has proven to be successful for many applications, and it continues to form the basis for a large part of developments within AI today. However, pure logical techniques have been criticized often as being inadequate for representing and reasoning with knowledge about complex situations. Networked knowledge representation schemes incorporating ideas from object oriented programming, have proven to be much more useful and well adapted for solving complex real world problems. The next chapter describes two important and popular knowledge representation and reasoning schemes: rules and frame hierarchies.

## Summary

This chapter has introduced some basic concepts related to knowledge and KBSs, and has detailed the process of acquiring knowledge. Important issues discussed in this chapter include the following:

● KBSs are computer systems which use extensive domain-specific knowledge to aid problem solution. KBSs have been used for a variety of tasks in business and industry.

● Structure of a generic KBS consists of three components: a knowledge base, an inference engine, and a user interface. The knowledge base stores important domain-specific knowledge and the inference engine controls the use of this knowledge for making useful inferences. The user interface emphasizes an ability to explain inferences to users.

● A KBS shell tool is a bundled package of the inference engine and user interface components. It is possible to obtain a KBS by purchasing a KBS shell tool and adding domain-specific knowledge to it.

● KBSs are usually built by specially trained professionals called knowledge engineers who interact with domain experts and use a KBS shell tool.

● Epistemological issues are important for KBSs. Generally, KBSs are seen as containing models of intelligence.

● It is difficult to define the term knowledge precisely. However knowledge has several dimensions: explicit versus tacit, deep versus surface, commonsense versus domain-specific, procedural versus declarative, and meta-knowledge versus knowledge. Knowledge contained in a KBS can also be analyzed along these dimensions.

● Knowledge exists in many different stages. The stage of knowledge about a particular task has important implications for the feasibility of building a KBS for that task and the manner in which the KBS can be used to support or automate the task.

● Knowledge is dynamic and continually evolving. For a KBS to be effective, it is important to continuously update the knowledge in the knowledge base.

● Knowledge acquisition is a critical component of the process of building a KBS. Acquisition of knowledge is time consuming, expensive, and often a bottle-neck in the development process.

● While the most common method for acquiring knowledge is to use knowledge engineers, automated tools utilizing techniques from machine learning can also be useful under certain conditions.

● There are several different sources of knowledge in an organization: books, historical records, and experts. While human experts are the most important and common sources for knowledge, they can be extremely difficult to find and use. Experts often have inadequate time, can be uncooperative, and more commonly be unable to explain the reasoning behind their expertise in clear terms.

## 52 Knowledge-based systems and knowledge acquisition

● There are several possible pitfalls in knowledge acquisition. The entire process of acquiring knowledge needs to be planned thoroughly. A certain degree of openness to new ideas and flexibility is desirable.

● Inductive learning is a popular machine learning technique, used in automated tools to aid the knowledge acquisition process.

Acquiring knowledge is the first important step in knowledge processing. The next natural step in the process is to consider techniques for representing and reasoning with knowledge. These issues are covered in the next chapter.

## Bibliography and suggested readings

Introductory descriptions of KBSs can be found in many books and articles. Some good sources are books by Waterman (Waterman 86), Mockler (Mockler 89), Turban (Turban 90), and Harmon and Sawyer (Harmon & Sawyer 90). There are several general references on epistemology and the concept of knowledge, such as books by Edwards (Edwards 67), Pappas and Swain (Pappas & Swain 78), Shope (Shope 82), and Pylyshyn (Pylyshyn 84). A good overview of developments with epistemology, and their relation to AI is available in an article by Nutter (Nutter 92). Other useful articles on epistemological concerns within AI are by McCarthy and Hayes (McCarthy & Hayes 69), McCarthy (McCarthy 77), Brachman (Brachman 79), and Newell (Newell 81). References (Hart 86), (Boose 86), (Boose and Gaines 88), and (Firlej and Hellens 91) provide more details on the knowledge acquisition process.

Boose, J.H., Expertise Transfer for Expert System Design, Elsevier, NY, 1986.

Boose, J.H., and B. Gaines, Knowledge Acquisition Tools for Expert Systems, Academic Press, NY, 1988.

Brachman, R.J., On the Epistemological Status of Semantic Networks, in N.V. Findler (Ed.), Associative Networks: Representation and Use of Knowledge by Computers, pp. 3-50, Academic Press, New York, 1979.

Edwards, P., (Ed.), The Encyclopedia of Philosophy, MacMillan, New York, 1967.

Firlej, M., and D. Hellens, Knowledge Elicitation: A Practical Handbook, Prentice Hall, 1991.

Harmon, P., and B. Sawyer, Creating Expert Systems for Business and Industry, John Wiley, 1990.

Hart, A., Knowledge Acquisition for Expert Systems, McGraw Hill, NY, 1986.

McCarthy, J., and P. Hayes, Some Philosophical Problems from the Standpoint of Artificial Intelligence, in Machine Intelligence 4, pp. 463-502, B. Meltzer and D. Michie (Eds.), Edinburgh University Press, 1969.

McCarthy, J., Epistemological Problems of Artificial Intelligence, in the Proceedings of the 5th International Joint Conference on Artificial Intelligence, pp. 1038-1044, 1977.

Mockler, R.J., Knowledge-Based Systems for Management Decisions, Prentice Hall, 1989.

Newell, A., The Knowledge Level, AI Magazine, 2, pp. 1-20, 1981.

Nutter, J.T., Epistemology, Encyclopedia of Artificial Intelligence, Vol. 1, S.C. Shapiro (Ed.), pp.460–468, John Wiley, 1992.

Pappas, G.S., and M. Swain, (Eds.), Essays on Knowledge and Justification, Cornell University Press, Ithaca, 1978.

Pylyshyn, Z.W., Computation and Cognition, MIT Press, Cambridge, MA, 1984.

Shope, R.K., The Analysis of Knowing, Princeton University Press, Princeton, NJ, 1982.

Turban, E., Decision Support and Expert Systems, MacMillan, NY, 1990.

Waterman, D.A., A Guide to Expert Systems, Addison Wesley, MA, 1986.

## Notes

1  Newell, A., J.C. Shaw and H.A. Simon, *Report on a General Problem Solving Program*, in *Computers and Thought* (E. Feigenbaum and J. Feldman Eds.), New York, McGraw Hill, 1963. (Also see section The Development of Artificial Intelligence in Chapter 1.)

2  Appendix 1 lists many representative commercial applications of knowledge-based systems. Issues related to the application of knowledge-based systems within organizations are covered in more detail in Chapter 5.

3  There are many descriptions of the XCON system in associated literature. Two recent articles of interest on XCON are: (a) Sviokla, J.J., *An Examination of the Impact of Expert Systems on the Firm: The Case of XCON*, MIS Quarterly, pp. 127–140, June 1990; and (b) Barker, V.E. & D. E. O'Connor, *Expert Systems for Configuration at Digital: XCON and Beyond*, Communications of the ACM, Vol. 32, No. 3, pp. 298–318, March 1989.

4  Kupfer, A., *Now, Live Experts on a Floppy Disk*, Fortune, pp. 48, Oct. 12, 1987.

5  Kupfer, A., *Now, Live Experts on a Floppy Disk*, Fortune, pp. 49, Oct. 12, 1987.

6  Steward, T. A., *Brainpower,* Fortune, pp. 42, June 3, 1991.

7  Kupfer, A., *Now, Live Experts on a Floppy Disk*, Fortune, pp. 48, Oct. 12, 1987.

8  Assuming that the data in Figure 2 represent true (by virtue of blood) "father" and "mother" relations (and thus exclude adopted relations).

9  A heuristic is a rule which is usually, but not always, true.

10  More details on KBS shell tools are given in Chapter 4 and in Appendix 2.

11  A good review of developments within epistemology, and their relation to artificial intelligence is given in: Nutter, J.T., *Epistemology*, Encyclopedia of Artificial Intelligence, Vol. 1, S.C. Shapiro (Ed.), pp. 280–287, John Wiley, 1990.

12  Godel, K., *Some MetaMathematical Results on Completeness and Consistency*, in J. Van Heijenoort (Ed.), From Frege to Godel, *A Source Book in Mathematical Logic 1879–1931*, Harvard University Press, Cambridge, MA, pp. 592–617, 1967.

13  Barr, A. and E.A. Feigenbaum, *The Handbook of Artificial Intelligence*, Vol. 1, pp. 143, Pitman Books, London, 1981.

14  Patterson, D.W., *Introduction to Artificial Intelligence and Expert Systems*, Prentice-Hall, pp. 10, 1990.

15  Waterman, D.A., *A Guide to Expert Systems*, pp. 16, Addison-Wesley, 1986.

16  Sviokla, J.J., *An Examination of the Impact of Expert Systems on the Firm: The Case of XCON*, MIS Quarterly, pp. 127–140, June 1990.

17  Nonaka, I., *The Knowledge-Creating Company*, Harvard Business Review, pp. 96–104, Nov–Dec. 1991.

18  To illustrate the concept of meta-knowledge rather easily, imagine if someone asked you for the 'phone number of President Clinton (or choose your favorite personality!). You know immediately whether you have the answer or not, i.e., you know what you know, and what you don't.

19  Adapted from: Bohn, R., *An Informal Note on Knowledge and How to Manage it*, Harvard Business School Teaching Note, 9-686-132, 1986.

20  The XCON KBS has been in actual commercial use within Digital for more than a decade.

21  Kneale, D., *How Coopers & Lybrand Put Expertise Into Its Computers*, Wall Street Journal, pp. 33, Friday, Nov. 14, 1986.

22  Some of the guidelines mentioned in this section are based on the KADS methodology described in : (a) Brueker, J.L. and B.J. Wielenga, *Knowledge Acquisition as Modelling Expertise: The KADS Methodology*, Proceedings of the 1st European Workshop on Knowledge Acquisition for Knowledge-Based Systems, Reading, UK, 2–3 Sep, 1987, Reading: Reading University, section B1; and (b) Firlej, M. and D. Hellens, *Knowledge Elicitation: A Practical Handbook*, Prentice Hall, 1991.

23  More details on prototypes, and the process of actually constructing KBSs are given in Chapter 4.

24  Kneale, D., *How Coopers & Lybrand Put Expertise Into Its Computers*, Wall Street Journal, pp. 33, Friday, Nov. 14, 1986.

25  See for example: Davis, R., *Interactive Transfer of Expertise*, in Proceedings of the 5th International Joint Conference on Artificial Intelligence, IJCAI, Cambridge, MA, Aug., 1977.

# Chapter 3
# Representing and reasoning with knowledge

It should be clear by now that a large and reasonably complete body of knowledge lies at the core of every successful knowledge-based system (KBS). Due to the strong emphasis within artificial intelligence (AI) on the actual construction of systems embodying knowledge, AI researchers have been forced to study practical means of supplying AI programs with appropriate knowledge. Knowledge representation is the term used for the sub-field of AI concerned with representing and reasoning with knowledge.

The specification of any knowledge representation scheme consists of two components: a description of the mechanisms used to represent knowledge; and a description of the operations (inference procedures) which can be performed on the knowledge. Due to the strong influence of logic in epistemology, earliest approaches to knowledge representation were based on logic. Consider a simple knowledge base consisting of the following two pieces of knowledge:

> All men are mortal. (1)

> Socrates is a man. (2)

Using logic, we can represent the above two statements as:

$$(\forall x)(\text{man}(x) \rightarrow \text{mortal}(x))$$

$$\text{man}(\text{Socrates})$$

where the first statement reads 'for all x, if x is a man, then it implies that x is mortal'. Using the deductive principles of logic[1], we can conclude from the above knowledge that Socrates is also mortal. This is a simple example of representing knowledge, and reasoning with it to infer a valid conclusion.

# 58 Representing and reasoning with knowledge

Knowledge representation has proven to be a fairly difficult subject to master. Conventional database management systems are clearly inadequate for representing knowledge, as they do not provide any meaningful facilities to represent the 'interpretation of data'. Different knowledge representation schemes (such as the simple logic based scheme described above) have been proposed in related literature. However, no one knowledge representation technique is best suited for all problems, and each approach has its own advantages and disadvantages. This chapter describes rules and frame hierarchies, two popular and important techniques for representing and reasoning with knowledge. Rule and frame hierarchy based knowledge representation schemes are used in nearly all commercial KBSs.

## Knowledge representation using rules

Rules are one of the earliest and most popular approaches to knowledge representation in KBSs. The generic structure of a simple rule is:

IF antecedent_1 AND antecedent_2 AND...AND antecedent_n

THEN conclusion

which is to be interpreted to mean that if all of the antecedent conditions (antecedent_1 AND antecedent_2 AND..AND antecedent_n) are true, then the conclusion can be asserted to be true. Depending upon the nature of the antecedents and conclusion, rules can be used to express:

● heuristic knowledge — rules are particularly useful for representing surface knowledge about relations between different input and output variables. For example, the rule 'IF persons A and B have the same nationality THEN their native languages are the same' expresses a heuristic relating the native languages of persons to their nationalities.

● domain models — rules can be used to represent known relations between different components/objects in the domain. For example, the rule, 'IF country_code = 91 THEN country_name = India', expresses a simple fixed relation between international country codes and country names. A set of such rules can cumulatively define the model of a particular domain.

● action sequences —rather than simply express relations between variables or domain components, rules can also be used to represent actual action sequences, such as 'IF the pressure lever is raised upwards THEN lower the temperature'.

The knowledge base in rule-based systems consists of a specification of facts (or data items), and rules specifying relationships for interpreting the data items. For example, the simple knowledge base of Figure 2.2 can be expressed using rules (in a pseudo-English style) as shown in Figure 3.1.

Note that rules are very easy to read and understand. Also, experts often find it convenient to express their intuitive expertise using rules, which describe mappings from input conditions or patterns (the rule antecedents) to output solutions (the rule conclusion). These factors have contributed to the popularity of rules for knowledge representation

> Facts:
> Bob is the father of Ellen.
> John is the father of Vincent.
> Bob is the father of Rose.
> Mary is the mother of Ellen.
> Sue is the mother of Vincent.
>
> Rules:
> IF X and Y are children AND (X and Y have the same father OR
>     X and Y have the same mother)
>     THEN X and Y are siblings.
>
> IF X and Y have the same child THEN X and Y are married.

**Figure 3.1** A rule-based representation of the knowledge base of Figure 2.1

## Complex rules and structured rule-based systems

The structure of individual rules can be described as either simple or complex. Simple rules have a form similar to that mentioned above:

    IF antecedents THEN conclusion_1 ELSE conclusion_2

where the ELSE part is optional (it was omitted earlier), and specifies the condition (conclusion_2) which is true when the antecedents are false. Complex rules augment simple rules with additional features such as contexts and certainty factors. An example of a complex rule is:

    GIVEN CONTEXT

    IF antecedents THEN conclusion (Certainty = 0.8)

Here, the context gives the conditions under which the IF..THEN rule is to be activated. The context is usually specified by a set of conditions, similar to the antecedent part of a simple rule. Contexts are useful for controlling the activation of rules during the inference process. By specifying the same context for a set of rules, the knowledge engineer can differentiate between sets of rules which are applicable under different conditions. The certainty value of 0.8 attached to the complex rule means the following: upon activation (when the context conditions are satisfied), if the rule antecedents are true, then the conclusion can be asserted as true with a certainty of 0.8 only. The use of such certainty factors is useful for expressing the heuristic nature of rules (which are true usually, but not always). A later section of this chapter elaborates further on rule-based reasoning under uncertainty.

Rule-based KBSs can be broadly classified into two categories: simple rule-based systems and structured rule-based systems. In simple rule-based systems, all rules are kept at the same level within a file. There is no distinction between, or grouping of rules. Generally, simple rules are used in simple rule-based systems. Structured rule-based

# 60 Representing and reasoning with knowledge

systems provide some structure to the rules in the knowledge base. Usually, this structure is in the form of grouping of rules into categories (based on certain conditions — usually the rule contexts), and arranging different categories of rules in a tree-like hierarchy. Complex rules with contexts are commonly used in structured rule-based systems. There are two major benefits of structured rule-based systems: inferencing efficiency and ease of comprehension. A rule-based KBS for a real-life problem would usually have many thousands of rules. If all rules were kept at the same level (with no imposed structure), the reasoning procedure has to typically adopt an inefficient sequential search through all the rules each time. It is also difficult to easily comprehend the complex interactions between so many rules. Structuring the rules into a hierarchical arrangement of rule groups can help to substantially alleviate both problems. More details on creating KBSs with structured rules are given in Chapter 4.

## Inference procedures in rule-based systems

The knowledge base in a rule-based system consists of a set of rules and facts. Different rules are usually interconnected (via the rule conclusions and antecedents) to form chains of possible reasoning patterns. Consider the simple rule-based knowledge base represented graphically in Figure 3.2. There are five rules in the knowledge base. Propositions A, D, and F, can be viewed as initial data items, and E, and F as the final goals solvable by the rules. B, C, and G are intermediate results produced during the rule-based inference procedure (as explained below).

## Forward chaining

There are two fundamental reasoning procedures which can be performed with the simple knowledge base of Figure 3.2. First, it is possible to assert a certain set of data items as 'true', and then determine which goals can be inferred as being 'true'. For example, by asserting that data items A and F are true, the rule-based inference procedure can determine that goal H is true. The entire rule-based inference process can be viewed as a set of match-execute cycles. During each cycle, the rule-based inference engine matches the known ('true') facts with the antecedents of rules in the knowledge base. This leads to the determination of a set of rules whose antecedent conditions are satisfied. Such rules are said to have been triggered. Next, the inference engine executes one or all of the set of triggered rules. The execution of the triggered rules causes some new facts (conclusions) to be asserted as 'true'. These changes are reflected in the knowledge base of known facts, and the process is repeated till either the goal condition is reached or there are no additional rules to be triggered. Figure 3.3 gives a graphical representation of the above inference procedure, with A and F as the initial data items. As the above inference procedure involves a movement from data towards goals, it is commonly termed as forward chaining.

A distinction is often made in KBSs between the knowledge base and the working memory. The working memory refers to a storage space where the intermediate results of the inference procedure are stored temporarily. For the example inference process

# Forward chaining

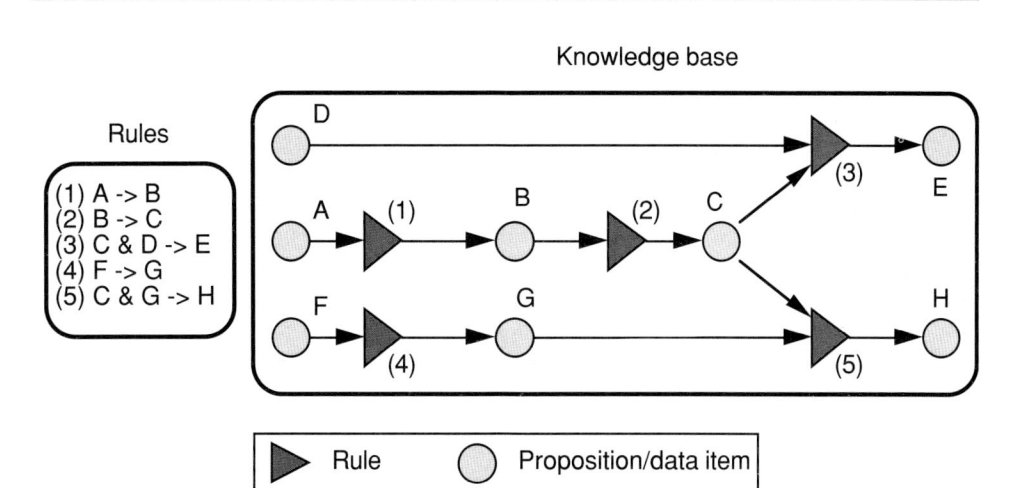

**Figure 3.2** A graphical representation of the structure of a simple rule-based knowledge base

depicted in Figure 3.3, the knowledge base contains facts, A and F, which are stored permanently as 'true'. The working memory stores facts, such as B, G, and C, which are produced as intermediate results during the inference procedure. Only selected contents of the working memory (perhaps, the final goal) are stored permanently in the knowledge base. The distinction between the knowledge base and the working memory mirrors the

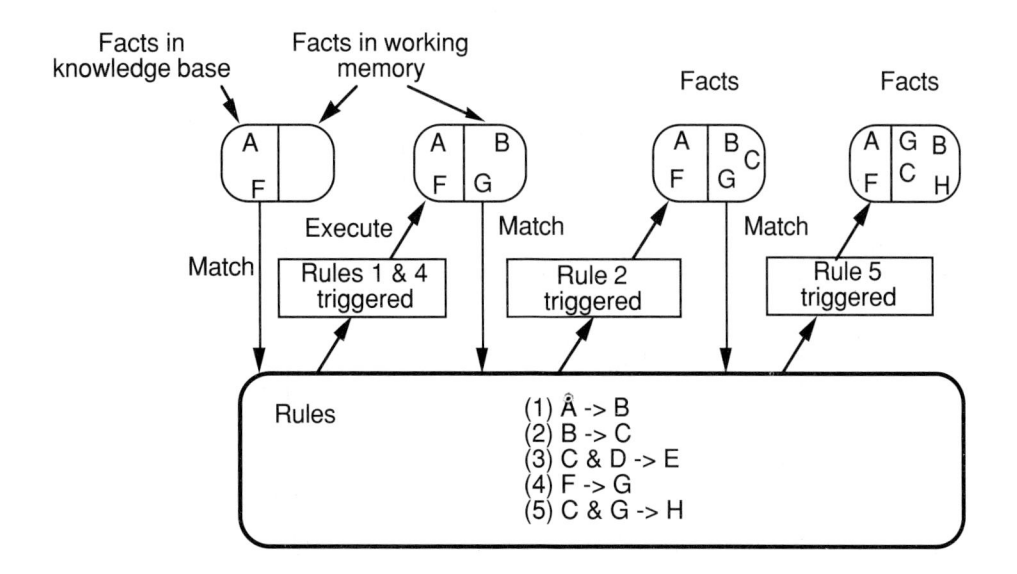

**Figure 3.3** An example of forward chaining in rule-based inference

difference between long term and short term memory in humans[2]. Long term memory refers to the large body of knowledge learnt over the years, and stored in the brain. To solve a particular problem, certain selected parts of this long term memory are brought into the short term memory, where local inferencing takes place. Most of the results stored in the short term memory are discarded after problem solution.

## Backward chaining

The other possible inference procedure with rules is to begin with a goal to be proven, and then try to determine if there are data (propositions known to be true) in the knowledge base to prove the truth of the goal. For example, considering the knowledge base of Figure 3.2, one can begin with the proposition E (the final goal), and try to determine whether the known facts in the knowledge base allow us to prove the truth of the proposition E. Assuming that the facts, A, and D, are known as 'true', the inference procedure would in this example lead to the conclusion that the goal conclusion E is true. The rule-based inference process in such situations can be seen as a sequence of backward goal-proving cycles. During each cycle, the inference engine maintains a list of goals which are yet to be proven to be true, for the initial goal to be proven true. The system begins with the list of goals to be proven being initialized to the initial goal. For each goal in the current goal list, the system first matches the goal with the known facts in the knowledge base. If the goal is known as a true fact, the inference engine marks this goal as proven true, and tries to prove the rest of the goals on the goal list as true. If the goal is not known as a true fact, it matches the goal with the conclusions (right-hand sides) of rules in the knowledge base. If no matching rule is found, the inference process terminates with a 'false' answer regarding the truth of the goal under consideration. If a matching rule is found, the inference engine adds the antecedents of the matching rule to the list of goals to be proven. If all goals in the goal list can be proven as true in this manner, then the system produces a positive response for the original input goal. Figure 3.4 illustrates this inference procedure for the example mentioned above. Such an inference procedure is also termed as backward chaining due to its emphasis on the movement from goals towards data.

## A comparison of backward and forward chaining

Both backward and forward chaining (see Figure 3.5) can be related to reasoning techniques in human information processing[3]. Backward chaining is related to goal directed behavior in humans. When we have a certain goal to solve (such as 'eat out in a restaurant'), we often try to achieve the overall goal by breaking the goal into sub-goals ('obtain money', 'select restaurant', and so on), and then trying to solve each sub-goal separately. Forward chaining can be related to stimuli directed behavior. When we are presented with stimuli (new data), such as the realization that 'an assignment is due tomorrow', we react to the stimulus, and take certain actions, such as 'make free time to do assignment'. Such stimuli directed behaviors are a central notion of behaviorist theories which focus strongly on importance of external stimuli[4].

# A comparison of backward and forward chaining 63

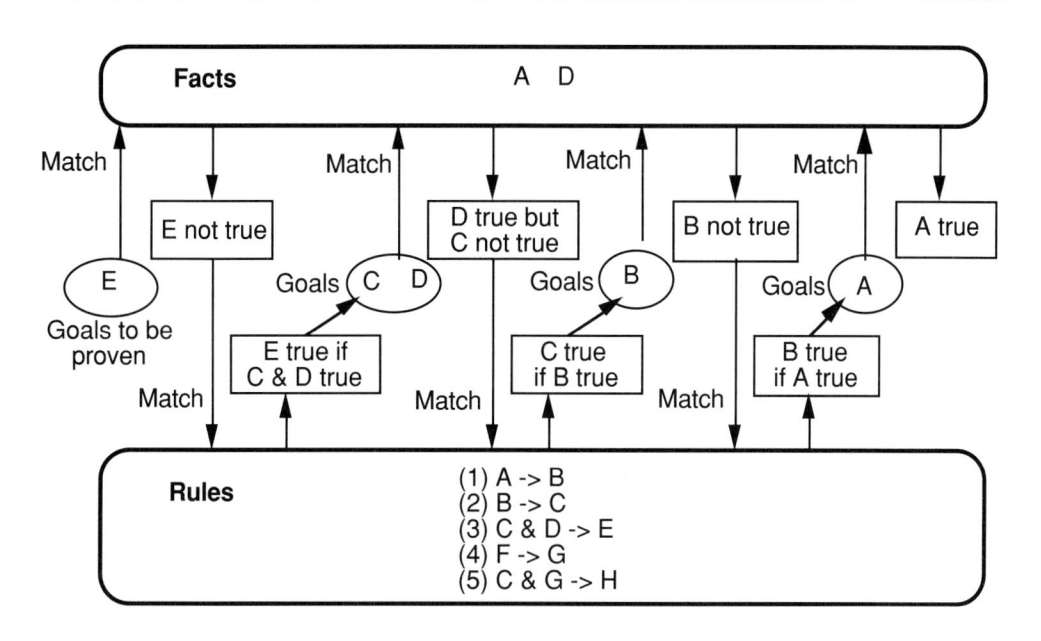

**Figure 3.4** An example of backward chaining in rule-based inference

Backward and forward chaining are the two basic reasoning procedures employed in rule-based KBSs. No one approach is inherently superior. The choice between backward and forward chaining is decided primarily by two factors. The first, and perhaps the more important factor, is the degree of suitability of the particular inference mode to reasoning in the domain under consideration. The knowledge of the domain gained during the

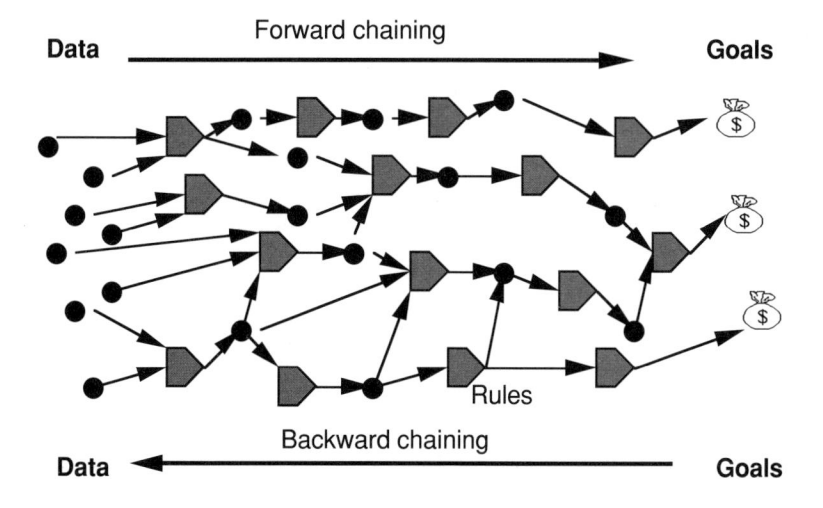

**Figure 3.5** Backward and forward chaining

knowledge acquisition process is important for determining the appropriate mode for problem-solving. If experts are used to solve problems in a backward mode of problem decomposition, then it may be unwise to adopt forward chaining as the inferencing technique in the KBS, and vice versa. Also, note that KBSs are typically used by less experienced workers. A high degree of match between the chosen inference mode and the natural problem-solving behavior, facilitates the process of explaining the answers of the KBS to the users in a simple and understandable manner. The second factor affecting choice of the appropriate inference technique is related to efficiency considerations. If there is a larger number of input data (as compared to goals) then it is more efficient to consider backward chaining, and vice versa.

The choice between backward and forward chaining is also affected by the power of the available KBS tool. Many simple rule-based KBS tools support either forward or backward chaining only. More advanced tools support both backward and forward chaining, and give the user flexibility in choosing the appropriate mode of inferencing. In such tools, it is possible to adopt a mixed mode of reasoning in which the inference process alternates between backward and forward chaining. In mixed mode reasoning systems, the inference engine searches forward from the available data and backward from the goals to be proven until suitable inference paths are identified from the data to the goals. The conditions under which the inference modes are switched are usually domain dependent and have to be decided by the designer of the KBS.

## Meta-knowledge in rule-based reasoning

A KBS for solving a complex real-life problem usually contains many thousands of rules and facts. A simple backward or forward chaining strategy has to search all the rules and facts in a sequential manner during each cycle to determine appropriate matches. This results in a very inefficient search procedure, and slow response times. The incorporation of appropriate meta-knowledge can significantly improve efficiency of the inference process. Meta-knowledge can help the inference process of the KBS by explicitly:

● stating the conditions under which certain rules are preferred over others. For example, instead of simply searching the knowledge-base of rules sequentially, the search can be directed to specific rules (or rule sets) under certain conditions;

● giving any special sequences of rules which are useful for solving a particular problem. This requires some knowledge about the predicted effects of rules in the domain, and the interactions between different rules;

● specifying particular orders in which to solve goals and sub-goals. For example, asking the system to first attempt to solve critical goals and sub-goals can help the inference processes conserve resources, and possibly save time. Determination of the degree of criticality of goals requires meta-knowledge.

Meta-knowledge can also aid the process of providing more meaningful explanations of answers to be provided to users. For example, a KBS can use its meta-knowledge about the relative importance of rules and goals to explain to the user why certain reasoning paths were preferred over others.

## Rule-based reasoning under uncertainty

Simple rules are limited by the fact that they do not allow for any imprecision or uncertainty. For example the simple rule:

'IF it is cloudy THEN it will rain'

does not really represent what we typically mean by such a statement, which is, 'if it is cloudy, then it will rain most probably'. Complex rules offer the facility to represent, and perform inferences under uncertainty. For example, consider the two rules:

IF it is cloudy THEN it will rain (CF = 0.8)

IF it will rain THEN the traffic will be slow (CF = 0.9)

where the certainty factors (CFs) of the rules are mentioned in brackets. The CF of a rule can be interpreted as defining the certainty with which the conclusion of the rule can be inferred when the antecedents are true. Note that these certainty factors are not the same as probabilities. In general, probabilities represent frequencies of occurrence as opposed to certainty factors representing degrees of belief. For these two rules, if we are given the input fact (again with an attached CF):

it is cloudy (CF = 0.7)

we can infer that it will rain with a certainty, CF = 0.8*0.7 =0.56, and that the traffic will be slow with a certainty, CF = 0.56*0.9 = 0.504. Such a conclusion is more realistic than simply concluding (with full certainty) that it will rain, and that the traffic will be slow.

Though the above approach to handling uncertainty may seem simple and ad hoc, many commercial systems do offer similar mechanisms for handling uncertainty. One of the earliest formal approaches to handling uncertainty was implemented in Mycin[5], a rule-based KBS for medical diagnosis. Mycin used the following definition for rules with uncertainty:

IF evidence e THEN hypothesis h (MB[h,e], MD[h,e])

Each rule had two associated measures of uncertainty. MB[h,e] is a number between 0 and 1, which measured the extent to which the evidence 'e' supported the hypothesis 'h'. Similarly, MD[h,e] is a number between 0 and 1, which measured the extent to which the evidence 'e' supported the negation of the hypothesis 'h'. Different rules were defined to specify how to combine these numbers during the inference process. For example, the measures of belief and disbelief in a hypothesis, h, given two pieces of evidence, e1 and e2, was given by:

MB[h,e1 & e2]  = 0   (if MD[h,e1 & e2] = 1)

= MB[h,e1] + MB[h,e2](1- MB[h,e1])   otherwise

MD[h,e1 & e2]  = 0   (if MB[h,e1 & e2] = 1)

= MD[h,e1] + MD[h,e2](1- MD[h,e1])   otherwise

The uncertainty representation and inference strategies of Mycin (and other systems employing similar uncertainty schemes) is based on Bayesian statistics[6]. It however diverges from pure Bayesian statistics in assuming the independence of different rules. To appreciate the importance of this assumption, note that Bayes rule specifies the probability of hypothesis, $H_i$, given evidence E as:

$$P(H_i|E) = \frac{P(E|H_i)P(H_i)}{\sum_{j=1}^{k} P(E|H_j)P(H_j)}$$

where: there are k different possible hypotheses, $H_1,...H_k$, $P(H_i)$ is the a priori probability that $H_i$ is true, $P(E|H_i)$ is the probability that evidence E is observed if $H_i$ is true, and $P(H_i|E)$ is the probability that $H_i$ is true given evidence E.

If two non-independent pieces of evidence, $E_1$, and $E_2$, are given, then the probability of a hypothesis H can be stated as:

$$P(H|E_1 \& E_2) = P(H|E_1)\frac{P(E_2|E_1,H)}{P(E_2|E_1)}$$

This requires the determination of the joint probabilities of E1 and E2. In case there are 'n' different non-independent pieces of evidence, then $2^n$ different joint probabilities are required. This can be a very large number for even small values of 'n'. Not only are these large numbers of probabilities intractable for processing and storage, they are virtually impossible to obtain and keep updated (there is experimental evidence suggesting that humans are poor estimators of probabilities[7]). The problem is considerably simplified if each piece of evidence is considered as independent of the others (which obviates the need for joint probabilities).

In a rule-based system such as Mycin, each rule can be considered as a piece of evidence contributing to the final hypothesis (the result of the rule-based system). Thus, the assumption of independence of rules eliminates the need for determining the joint probabilities of all rules (pieces of evidence), and makes the inference process tractable. However, for the inference process to be justified, the system designer has to ensure that all rules are independent; or else the validity of the conclusions is suspect.

There are other complex and sophisticated approaches to dealing with uncertainty, such as Bayesian networks[8], Dempster Shafer[9], fuzzy logic[10], non-monotonic logics[11], and truth maintenance[12]. Each approach has its own advantages and disadvantages, and a reasonable description of all these techniques is beyond the scope of this book.

Though several of these uncertainty handling approaches are slowly finding their way into commercial KBS tools, only fuzzy logic has had a major impact on commercial applications thus far. The technology and commercial impact of fuzzy logic is described in more detail in Chapter 8.

## Prolog: a simple rule-based system

Prolog (*programming in logic*) is a special purpose AI language invented by Alain Colmerauer and his colleagues at the University of Marseille around 1970[13]. It is based on the notion of using (a subset of) logic as a programming language. It has gained in popularity during the last decade because it is powerful, simple, and easy to learn. It is interesting to note that the Japanese fifth generation project adopted Prolog as its primary AI development language[14].

Prolog is a simple rule-based system. It only allows backward chaining with simple rules. It provides an easy and insightful introduction to rule-based reasoning. The best way to explain Prolog is to start with an example. Consider the simple Prolog program shown in Figure 3.6 containing 22 facts and 3 rules. The meaning of each fact and rule is explained by the comments after the semi-colons, and should need no further explanation. Note the simplicity of the Prolog program. There are of course, a few peculiarities forced by the language, such as requiring all variables to start with a capital letter, and all facts and rules to be terminated with a '.'. However, these are minor restrictions in comparison to most other computer programming languages. This simplicity of structure is partly responsible for the popularity of Prolog.

The representation of facts and rules in Prolog is a (subset of) first order predicate logic[15]. Each fact is a predicate with zero or more arguments, and expresses knowledge about some state of the world. For example, the predicate 'father' has two arguments, and expresses the knowledge that the first argument is the father of the second argument. Each rule (which may contain variables), expresses relations between different predicates. For example, Rule 1 expresses a certain relation between the predicates 'parent', 'father', and 'mother'.

## The inference procedure of Prolog[16]

To understand the inference process of Prolog, assume that the following query is given to the Prolog program of Figure 3.6:

parent(A, rose)?

This query asks the system to determine the parents of 'rose' (note that 'A' represents a variable). Prolog would use backward chaining to provide the following two answers to the above query (corresponding to the two parents of 'rose'):

A = bob

A = mary

It is instructive to hand-simulate the solution procedure adopted by Prolog for answering this simple query:

[1] First, the program is scanned sequentially from the top to search for a match with the query predicate: 'parent(A, rose)'. This query predicate is the overall 'goal' for the system to solve.

## 68 Representing and reasoning with knowledge

[2] A match is obtained with rule 1. Prolog has a rather complex process (termed as unification[17]) to determine matches between predicates. In this case, the variables X and Y of rule 1 are respectively matched (bound) to the variable A and the constant 'rose' of the query.

---

male(bob).                    ; bob is a male
male(john).
male(vincent).
male(marcos).

female(mary).                 ; mary is a female
female(sue).
female(ellen).
female(rose).
female(julie).

father(bob, ellen).           ; bob is the father of ellen
father(bob, rose).
father(john, vincent).
father(john, marcos).

mother(mary, ellen).          ; mary is the mother of ellen
mother(mary, rose).
mother(mary, julie).
mother(sue, vincent).
mother(sue, marcos).

school(ellen, school_1).      ; ellen goes to school_1
school(rose, school_2).
school(vincent, school_1).
school(marcos, school_2).

; RULE 1
parent(X, Y) if father(X,Y) or mother(X,Y).
                ; X is the parent of Y if either X is the father of Y or X is
                ;the mother of Y

;RULE 2
sister(X,Y) if female(X) and parent(Z,X) and parent(Z,Y) and  X ≠ Y.
                ;X is the sister of Y if X is a female ,and X and Y have
                ;the same parent Z and X and Y are different persons.

;RULE 3
schoolmates(X,Y) if school(X, Z) and school(Y,Z) and  X ≠ Y.
                ;X and Y are schoolmates if they both go the same
                ;school Z and they are different persons

---

**Figure 3.6** A simple Prolog program

# The inference procedure of Prolog 69

[3] Prolog then notes that rule 1 is only satisfied if either of the two predicates in the condition of the rule are satisfied. Thus the system generates two additional sub-goals to be solved by the system:

father(X, rose) OR mother(X, rose)

Note that the variable Y (of Rule 1) has been replaced by the constant 'rose' during the unification procedure (step 2). Rule 1 is satisfied if either one of the above two sub-goals is satisfied.

[4] To solve the first (sub) goal of 'father(X,rose)', the system again scans the program sequentially from the top (it always starts at the first predicate while attempting to solve a goal for the first time). It finds the first matching predicate 'father(bob, ellen)', but the unification procedure with the goal fails, because the second arguments of the predicates are different.

[5] Next, Prolog continues searching the program to solve the (sub) goal of 'father(X,rose)'. As this is not the first attempt at solving this sub-goal, it starts searching from the point of its previous failure (and not at the top as in step [4]) i.e., at the predicate 'father(bob, ellen)'. Luckily, it finds a match with the immediate next predicate 'father(bob, rose)'. The unification procedure succeeds and the variable X is replaced by the constant 'bob'. This value is passed up and the system outputs the answer:

A = bob

Note that the variable A had been bound to the variable X in step [2]. Some Prolog systems would stop at this point because Rule 1 (and thus the original goal) has been satisfied at this stage (note the OR condition in the two sub-goals of step [3]). However, Prolog can be asked by the user to find all solutions (some systems would do this automatically) to the input goal. This would lead to step [6] for the current query.

[6] Analogous to steps [4] and [5], the Prolog system solves the second sub-goal of 'mother(X, rose)' to give the second answer:

A = mary

The above inference procedure is illustrated in Figure 3.7. Such a representation is also called a proof tree, as it depicts the procedure used by Prolog to prove that the input goal is true. Note that Prolog 'proves' that the goal (input query) is true by finding values for all variables (if any) in the goal, such that the goal predicate is true. For the sake of clarity in representation, only the successful steps of the above inference procedure are shown in the proof tree of Figure 3.7. Upper and lower semi-circles depict goals and matching predicates respectively. The various bindings during the matching process are shown between the two semi-circles.

If the original query is modified as:

parent(X,Y)?

to ask for any person X, who is a parent of some person Y (note that X and Y are variables), then Prolog would provide the following first response:

X = bob Y = ellen

## 70 Representing and reasoning with knowledge

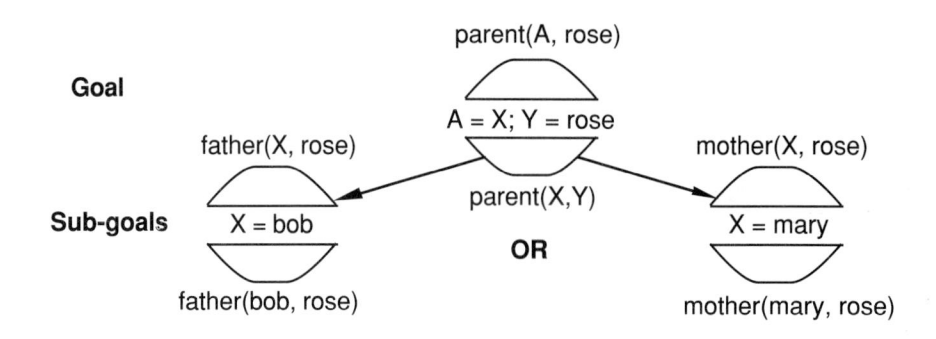

**Figure 3.7** Pictorial representation of a simple inference in Prolog

If prompted for all solutions to the query, Prolog would provide the following additional answers:

X = bob Y = rose
X = john Y = vincent
X = john Y = marcos
X = mary Y = ellen
X = mary Y = rose
X = mary Y = julie
X = sue Y = vincent
X = sue Y = marcos

The order of the above solutions is important because it reflects the order (from left to right) in which the Prolog inference engine solves goals and sub-goals (all 'fathers' are listed first), and searches (from top to bottom) the program database (listing of fathers and mothers corresponds to that given in the program). This will become clear if the reader tries to hand-simulate the solution procedure to the above query.

Consider another slightly more complex query:

sister(rose, X)?

This query asks the system to determine whether 'rose' is the sister of someone (represented by the variable X). From the program of Figure 3.6, we know that the two answers for this query are: X = ellen, and X = julie. Figure 3.8 illustrates the solution procedure adopted by Prolog to produce the first answer for this query. For convenience, the various goals and matching predicates are numbered as 'Gxy' and 'Pxy' respectively, where x denotes the level of the goal/predicate (1 being the top level) in the proof tree, and y is a unique identifier for that goal/predicate.

Rule 2 provides the first initial match to the overall goal posed by the input query. Note that rule 2 generates four additional sub-goals, which are to be proven true (from left to right) for the top level goal to be solved. The first three sub-goals are represented as G21, G22, and G23 in Figure 3.8, and the last sub-goal is the mathematical operation of inequality testing. It is interesting to note the change in bindings as the various sub-goals

## The inference procedure of Prolog 71

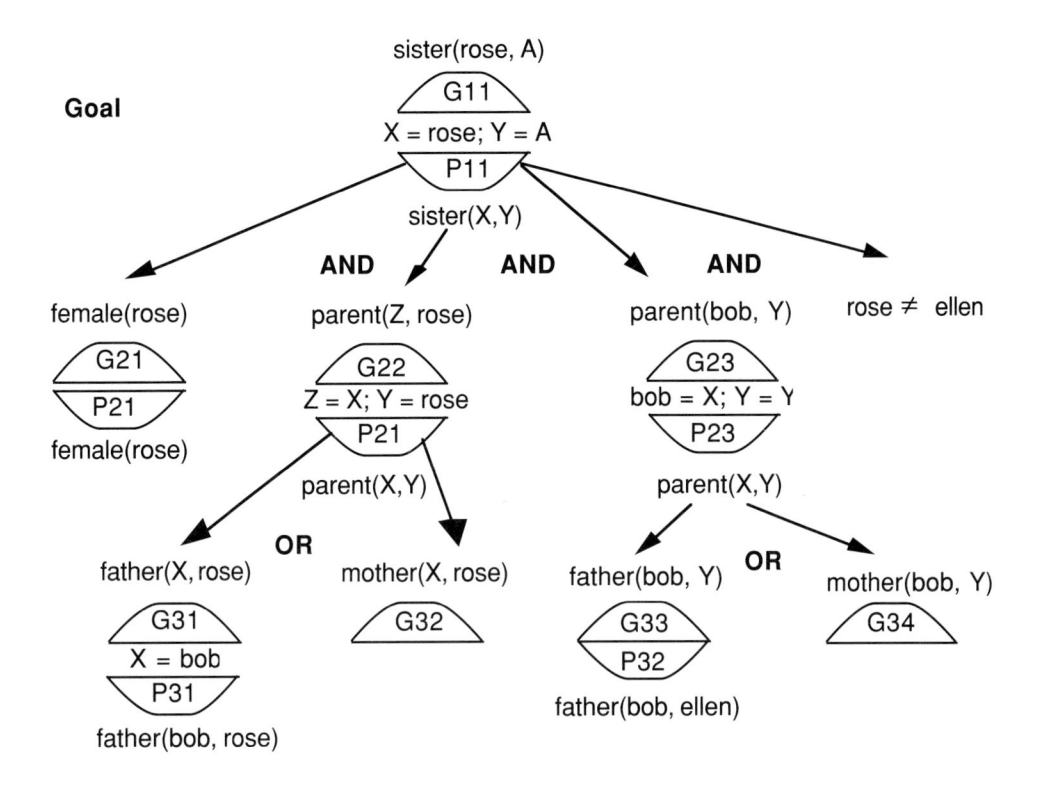

**Figure 3.8** Proof tree generated by Prolog to produce the first answer for the query 'sister(rose,X)?'

generated by rule 2 are satisfied. The solution of G22 yields the result, Z=bob. This value of Z is substituted in G23 before Prolog attempts to solve it. The solution of G23 yields the result, Y = ellen. This value of Y is used for testing the last sub-goal of inequality (which is satisfied in this case). Note that the Prolog system keeps the scope of variable declarations limited to the rules in which they are used. For example, it differentiates between the variable Y in goal G23 and predicate P23. Also, observe that Prolog does not attempt to solve goals G32 and G34, because the satisfaction of goals G31 and G33 solves goals G22 and G23 respectively (due to the OR condition in the sub-goals generated by goals G22 and G23). This meets the conditions for the generation of the first answer.

Note that according to the data of Figure 3.6, Rose has one more sister, 'julie'. This can be obtained by asking Prolog to produce all possible answers to the query: sister(rose, X)?. Figure 3.9 depicts the proof tree generated while producing the second answer, X = julie. A comparison of Figures 3.8 and 3.9 yields further insights into the inference engine of Prolog. Note that goal G31 fails to be satisfied now as rose has only one father, 'bob'. The solution of goal G32 yields Z = mary, which is reflected in G23. Goal G33 fails due to a lack of a matching predicate in the program database ('mary' is not the father of anyone in Figure 3.6). The solution of goal G23 yields, Y = julie, which is produced as the second answer as it satisfies the last inequality. In reality, the solution of G23 would first

## 72 Representing and reasoning with knowledge

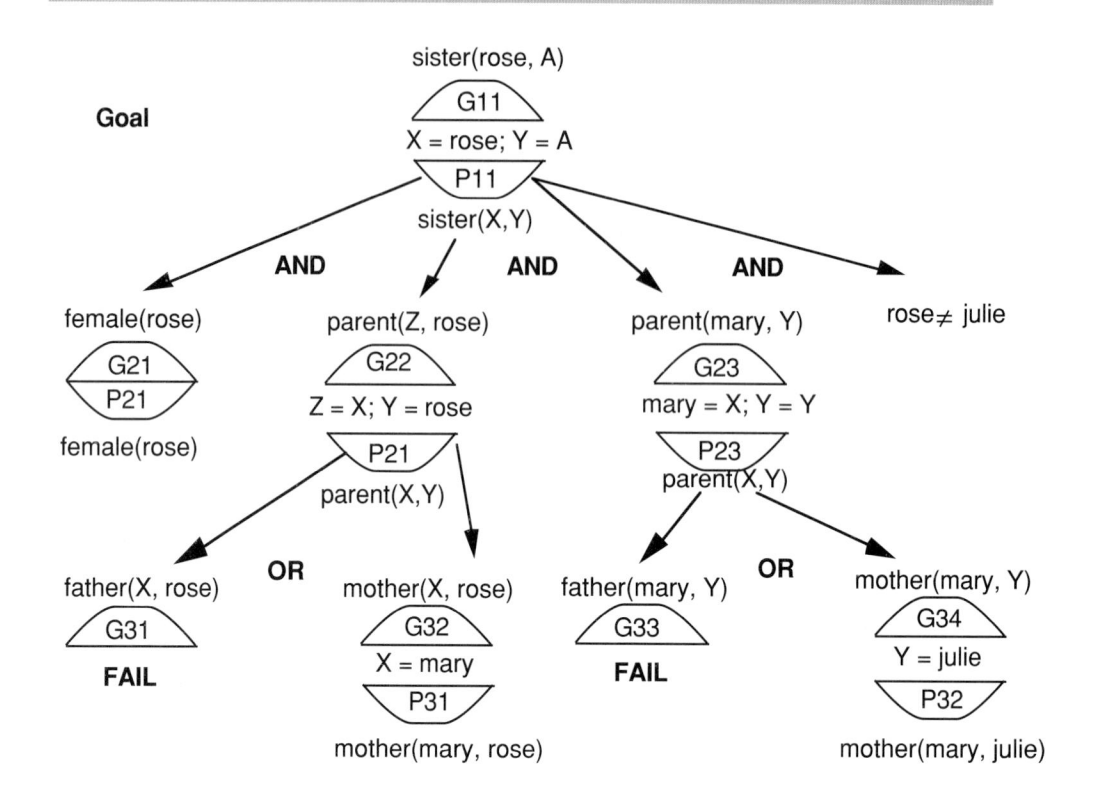

**Figure 3.9** Proof tree generated by Prolog to produce additional answers for the query 'sister(rose,X)?'

yield the answers, Y = ellen, and then Y = rose (due to the particular sequential order in which the Prolog inference engine searches the program database). The first of these values, Y = ellen, is the same answer as produced before (and would be output by the Prolog system). The second of these values, Y = rose, would fail the last inequality test, and thus not be produced as an output answer. These facts are not shown in Figure 3.9.

The inference procedure of Prolog can be characterized as a depth-first, left-to-right backward chaining search of the AND-OR graph characterizing the solution space. The various facts and rules of a Prolog program can be depicted by an AND-OR graph (similar to those given in Figures 3.7, 3.8, and 3.9), showing the relations between different predicates. Given a goal, the Prolog inference engine backward chains by breaking the goal into sub-goals (decomposition), and solving each sub-goal sequentially. For example in Figure 3.8, it first solves goal G22 completely (which requires the solution of goal G31), before it attempts to solve the next goal (G23) at the same level as G22. Backward chaining is the default inference procedure used by Prolog. Forward chaining is not possible in conventional Prolog systems.

Prolog is a good introduction to the fundamental concepts of rule-based reasoning. More advanced rule-based tools offer additional features, such as a choice between backward and forward chaining, the possibility of triggering more than one rule simultaneously (note that Prolog only triggers the first matching rule during each cycle), and the possibility of using meta-knowledge to control the inference process (it is difficult to modify the default inference procedure of Prolog).

## Benefits and limitations of rule-based reasoning

Rules were the first knowledge representation technique to be incorporated in commercial KBSs. Rules are very useful for representing heuristics (an important component of tacit knowledge), and 'situation-action' pairs (a feature common in human problem-solving behavior). When restricted to a small number, rules can express domain knowledge in a modular fashion. One rule can (often) be changed with minimal impact on the entire system. The resulting modularity of the system facilitates changes, and enhances the maintainability of the KBS. It is also easy to explain the results of rule-based systems to users.

Explanations of the results of rule-based inference procedures can be generated by simply back-tracking along the (forward or backward) inference path. These explanations are usually easy to understand and follow, because they directly correspond to the way humans reason and solve problems.

While rules remain a popular choice today for building KBSs, it is important to recognize that rule-based reasoning has the following limitations:

● representation — rules are often inadequate to represent complex real-life data. They are poor at modelling intricate relationships between many domain objects. A good example is the inability of rule-based systems to perform effective pattern recognition

● brittleness — rule-based systems are 'brittle' in the sense they are unable to respond effectively to variations in input data and problems. Thus they usually display a high degree of expertise for narrow domains and crash disgracefully when a related but slightly different problem is presented

● learning — rule-based systems have no inherent learning mechanisms. Thus they are unable to learn from domain examples and improve their own knowledge

● comprehension — a large rule-based knowledge base is difficult to 'read' and 'understand'. Imagine the level of comprehension possible in a KBS containing 5000 rules[18] and 10,000 facts, all expressed sequentially as in Figure 3.6

● efficiency — the inference engines of many rule-based systems search the knowledge base of rules in a sequential 'top-down' manner. The resulting inference process can be slow, and inefficient for a large rule-based KBS

● maintenance — maintenance of large rule-based knowledge-bases is hampered by the fact it is difficult to note all interactions between rules. If a rule is changed, determining the impact of that change on other rules is difficult. This also retards the process of updating the knowledge base to reflect changes in domain knowledge.

Many of these limitations can be eliminated by combining rules with more complex networked knowledge representation schemes, and utilizing object-oriented programming techniques. These concepts are described in the following sections.

## Networked representations of knowledge

The primary motivation for adopting networked representations of knowledge is cognitive evidence which suggests that much of long-term human memory is stored in terms of inter-linked chunks of information[19]. Think for a moment about the concept 'vacation'. What kind of ideas come to your mind? Probably some concepts like: beaches, fun, Hawaii, planes, luggage, and so on. Why did you not instinctively think of other concepts such as: mathematics, library, or dogs? Cognitive scientists would explain this on the basis of the particular 'chunking' of information in your mind (Figure 3.10): concepts such as 'mathematics', 'library', and 'dog' are not 'near' the concept of 'vacation' in your mind. There is experimental evidence to demonstrate that time taken to recall connections between two concepts is proportional to the 'distance' between them[20]. So given the chunking of information shown in Figure 3.10, it will take more time to recall a link between 'library' and 'vacation', as compared to that between 'vacation' and 'hotel'. This is the reason why the concept of 'library' does not come to the mind immediately when the concept 'vacation' is mentioned.

The expertise developed by an expert can also be explained in terms of this phenomenon of 'chunking'. From long experience at a given task, experts tend to learn patterns of problem solutions which are stored as interconnected chunks of knowledge. When an expert views a problem, a particular chunk (in the stored expert knowledge) is activated. This in turn triggers other relevant pieces of knowledge (due to the 'closeness' of chunks). Irrelevant information is not retrieved, and the expert is able to solve the problem with a seemingly adept combination of skill and intuition. The process of chunking for an expert is quite elaborate. It is reported in related literature[21] that a chess grandmaster is able to recognize and recall approximately 50,000 chunks, within a factor of 2. Acquiring all these chunks of knowledge consumes time — at least 10,000 hours of chess for a chess grandmaster. The large number of chunks of expert knowledge, and the complex linking patterns between them, explains why knowledge acquisition is a time-consuming and arduous process.

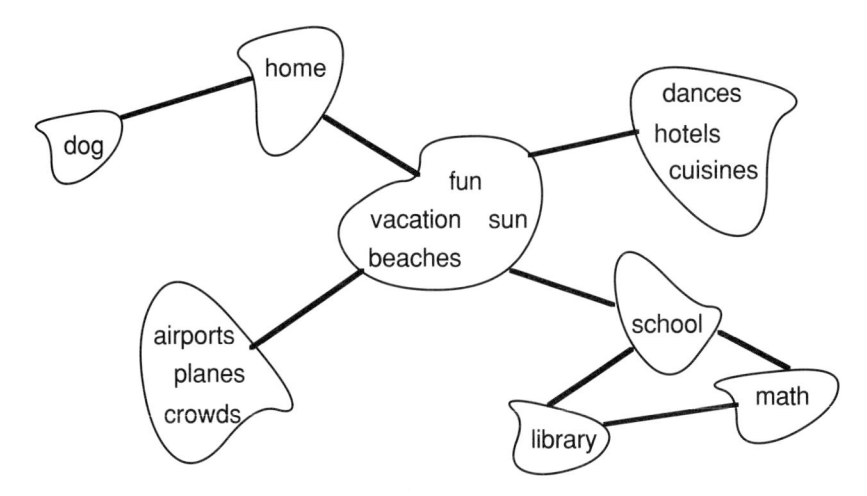

**Figure 3.10** Chunking of knowledge

## Semantic networks

Semantic networks[22] refer to a broad category of networked schemes for representing knowledge. There are many different variations of semantic networks, but they all consist of a collection of nodes, and arcs (or links) interconnecting the nodes. Both nodes and arcs can be labelled. Nodes usually represent objects, concepts, events, and attributes of objects in the domain. Arcs represent relations which hold between different nodes.

Figure 3.11 depicts a simple semantic network partially based on the data of Figure 3.6. An attractive feature of semantic networks is that they are easy to read and understand. It is also possible to incorporate the notion of property inheritance in semantic networks. For example, in Figure 3.11, the property 'likes football' is linked to the node for the object 'male'. By traversing the arcs 'upwards' from any particular male (such as Vincent, or Bob), it is possible to deduce that the property of 'liking football' is also valid for that particular male. This traversal of arcs is an example of a simple inference procedure possible with semantic networks. The most common inference procedure used in semantic networks is to match network fragments. Figure 3.12 depicts a simple network fragment corresponding to query 'find all mother-daughter pairs', which can be 'matched' against the semantic network of Figure 3.11 to generate the appropriate solutions.

Semantic networks are easy to understand, and provide an appealing visual depiction of knowledge (which was not possible with Prolog). However, a semantic network can quickly degenerate into a crowd of nodes and links, when a complex situation is modelled. There is a need to add more structure to both the nodes and the links. These concerns are satisfied in frame hierarchies as described now.

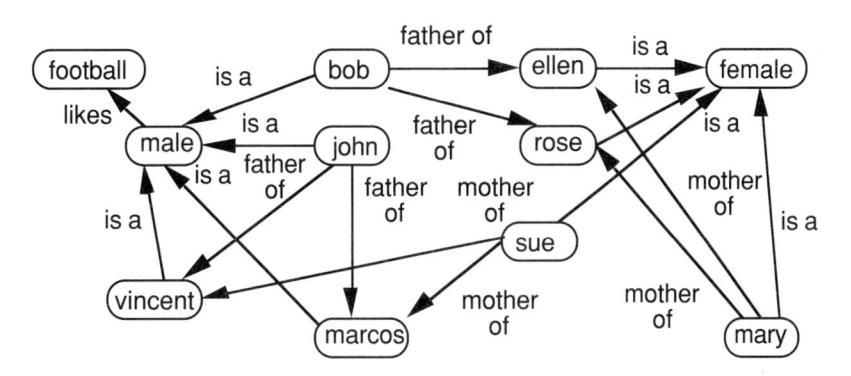

**Figure 3.11** A semantic network

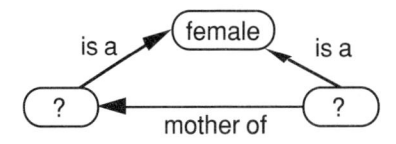

**Figure 3.12** Network fragment of a query for the semantic network of Figure 3.11

## 76 Representing and reasoning with knowledge

### Frame hierarchies

Frame hierarchies form a popular choice for knowledge representation in commercial KBSs. A frame is, in simple terms, a collection of attributes (called 'slots' in AI terminology), and their associated values that describe an entity/object in the domain. Frames are linked together in a special manner called an inheritance-specialization hierarchy. To illustrate a simple example of a frame hierarchy, we consider Kappa[23], a state-of-the-art KBS shell tool marketed by Intellicorp of Palo Alto. Kappa integrates different knowledge representation techniques such as rules, frame hierarchies, and object-oriented programming[24], and provides a comprehensive platform for building real-life complex KBSs. It is important to note that the concepts described below are not limited to Kappa and can be found in other commercial KBS tools also (see Appendix 2). Kappa only serves as a representative tool to support the following discussion of frame hierarchies.

Figure 3.13 depicts a screen dump from the Kappa system. The window on the top depicts the various tools available in Kappa: an Object Browser (to build frame hierarchies), a set of Knowledge Tools (to add various knowledge items), a KAL Interpreter (for typing commands to, and interacting with Kappa), a Session tool (for building the user interface for the KBS application), a Rule Relation tool (for graphically depicting the rule graph), a Rule Tracing tool (for tracing the inference process with rules), and an Inference Browser (for browsing through a trace of the solution of a particular goal). The last three tools are concerned with rule-based reasoning. Kappa provides the facility to combine forward and backward chaining. Only the facilities within Kappa for representing and reasoning with frame hierarchies are described below.

The Object Browser in Figure 3.13 depicts a simple frame hierarchy partially based on the data of Figure 3.6. Each string (such as 'People' and 'Male') represents the name of a particular frame. There are two types of frames:

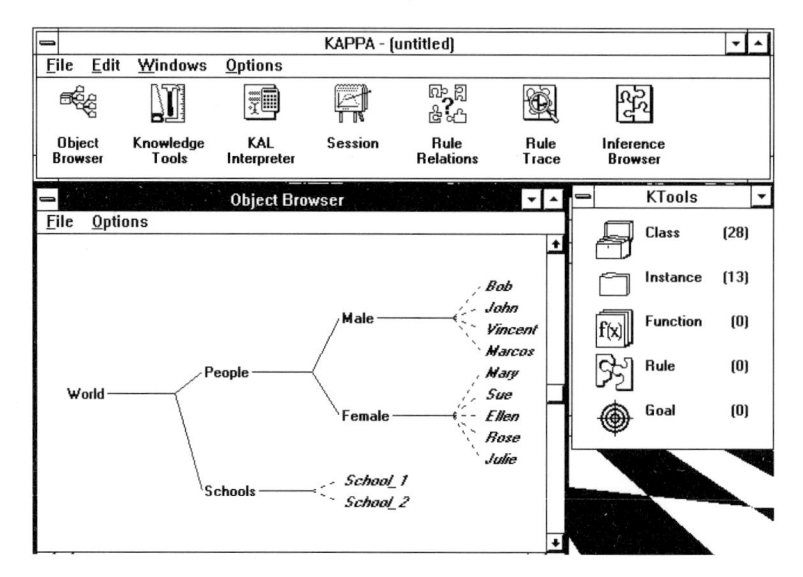

**Figure 3.13** Simple frame hierarchy

- classes and sub-classes — classes are general categories of domain entities. For example, the frames 'Schools' and 'People', are classes referring respectively to the set of all schools and persons in the domain under consideration. Classes are linked to each other by solid links as shown in Figure 3.13. Classes such as 'Male' and 'Female' are sub-classes of the class 'People'. A sub-class can be alternatively termed as a child of the parent class

- instances — specific examples of a certain class of domain entities. For example, the frames 'Bob' and 'John' are instances, because they are specific examples of the class 'Male'. Similarly, the frames 'Mary' and 'Sue' are instances of the class 'Female'. Instances are linked to their parent class by broken lines as shown in Figure 3.13. An instance cannot have any child frames.

Each frame represents an object[25], and can be described by its structure and behavior. The structure of objects is composed of a set of attributes (slots). Two key notions related to the structure of objects in frame hierarchies are inheritance and specialization. Inheritance refers to sub-classes and instances inheriting attributes and values from their parent classes. This ensures the transfer of general properties of a domain (category) to all objects in (members of) that domain (category). Specialization refers to the definition of specific properties of sub-classes and instances which are not present in their parent classes. This allows for distinctions between specific sub-classes and instances.

The behavior component of the definitions of objects describes how the objects behave in reaction to different stimuli. Special programs called methods are used to specify the behaviors of objects. The structures and behaviors of objects in a frame hierarchy are described in more detail below.

## Structure of objects

Figures 3.14 and 3.15 depict the partial structures of the frames representing the classes 'Male' and 'Bob' respectively. The 'Slots' window (towards the left) in Figures 3.14 and 3.15, contain the list of attributes (such as 'age', 'father_name', and so on) describing the classes 'Male' and 'Bob' respectively. Slots inherited from parents are marked with an asterisk (*) on the left. Thus in Figure 3.14, all slots beginning with an * are inherited from the parent class 'People'. Note that though slots are inherited from the parent classes, it is possible to define new slots at any level in the frame hierarchy. For example, the slot 'wife_name' is defined only for the class 'Male' (and not for the parent class 'People'), and is inherited by all children of 'Male'.

It is desirable to define slots at the highest class of abstraction i.e., in the class where the attribute represented by the slot is applicable to all members of that class. Thus, while the attribute 'wife_name' can be attributed to all males, it cannot be used as a valid descriptor for the parent class 'People' (the slot 'wife_name' is not a valid attribute for the class 'Female', a sub-class of 'People').

Note that the inheritance of slots works down the frame hierarchy[26]. Parent classes do not inherit any slots from their children. Also, not all slots of a particular class need to be inherited by the children of that class. It is possible to define slots for a class, and to initialize them as 'local'. Such local slots are not inherited down the hierarchy. The ability

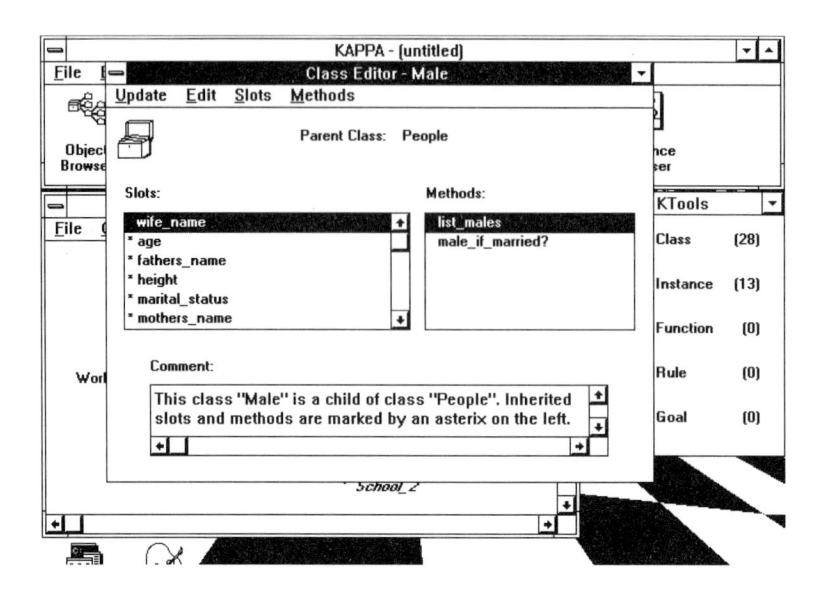

**Figure 3.14** Structure of the object 'male'

to add new slots at any level of the hierarchy leads to specialization down the hierarchy. For example, the class 'Male' is specialized (relative to its parent class 'People'), by the definition of new slots (such as 'wife_name').

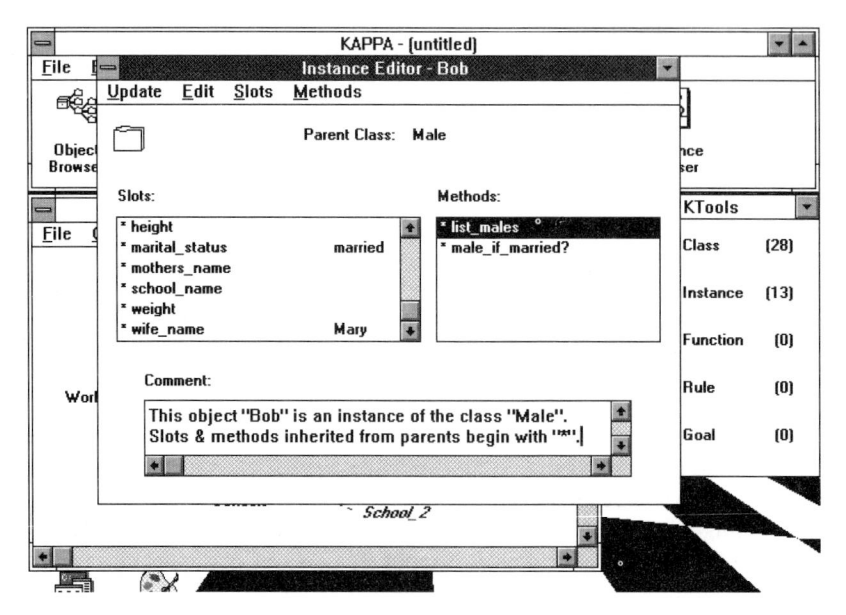

**Figure 3.15** Structure of the object 'Bob'

## Structure of objects 79

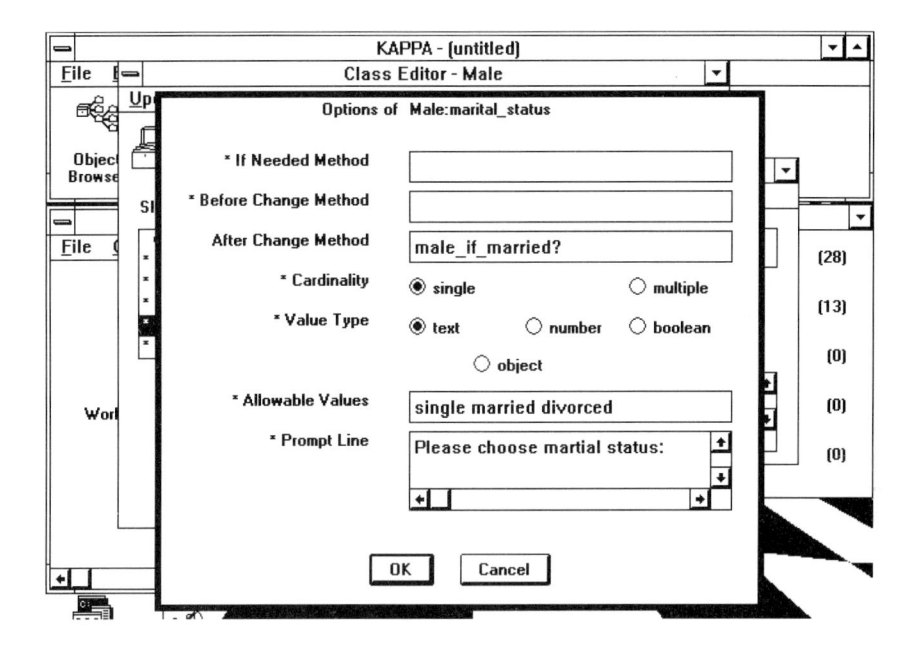

**Figure 3.16** Structure of slots in the object 'male'

Slots are more complex in structure than simple placeholders for values. Slots can be themselves described by a set of characteristic features. Figure 3.16 depicts the partial structure of the slot 'marital_status' in the class 'Male'. Some important features in the structure of the slot are:

● if needed method — this is a placeholder for the name of a certain method, which is invoked when the value of this slot is needed (for some purpose), and there is no value currently stored for the slot. This facility is useful for providing a procedure to compute default values of slots

● before change method — this descriptor contains the name of a method, specifying actions which need to be taken before the value of the slot is changed

● after change method — this is a placeholder for the name of a method which carries out certain actions each time the value of the slot is changed. Note that Figure 3.16 contains a method 'male_if_married?' in this position. The structure and use of this method is explained later

● cardinality — this specifies whether the slot can have single or multiple values (a list)

● value type — this specifies the kind of value (such as text or Boolean) which can be assigned to the slot. The value type 'object' is of special interest. By choosing this type, another frame can be assigned as a value to this slot. This is used under special circumstances, and can aid in building complex knowledge representation schemes

● allowable values — this is a list of allowable values if the value type is 'text'.

There is no one unique way to structure the frame hierarchy and to define the slots in the various frames. The knowledge engineer in consultation with the domain expert, has to decide upon the definitions of individual frames, and their inter-relationships. A major consideration in the design of frame hierarchies is the degree to which the hierarchy reflects the structure of knowledge in the domain. The frame hierarchy provides for a visual representation of domain knowledge, and it is important that this matches the perception of the expert (and users) about the domain knowledge.

## Behaviors of objects

The behaviors of individual objects in frame hierarchies are defined by methods. A method can be simply viewed as a procedure (or program) defining how that particular object reacts to a specific situation, or stimulus. Note that in Figure 3.14, two methods are defined for the class 'Male'. The concepts of specialization and inheritance also apply to methods. Methods inherited from parent objects are represented with an asterisk (*) at the start.

For example, the methods 'list_males' and 'male_if_married?' are used to specialize the class 'Male' (in contrast to its parent class 'People'). These two methods are also inherited down the hierarchy to the children frames (such as 'Bob' shown in Figure 3.15). Analogous to slots, methods can be made local, and not be passed down to the children objects. Methods should also be defined at the highest level of abstraction i.e., in the class where the behavior represented by the method is applicable to all members of that class.

Figure 3.17 depicts the structure of the method 'male_if_married?'. It is a very simple method, and specifies a part of the behavior of the class ('Male') in which it is defined. Ignoring peculiarities of the Kappa syntax, the statement contained in the method means the following (special Kappa functions and keywords are italicized):

*If* my (*Self*) slot 'marital_status' has the value 'married', *Then*

Action 1:

I ask the user (*AskValue*) for the name of my wife, and initialize (*SetValue*) my slot 'wife_name' with this value; and

Action 2:

I get (*GetValue*) the name of my wife (from the slot 'wife_name'), and send a message (*SendMessage*) to (the object representing) my wife, with my name (*Self*) as an argument, to activate her 'set_husband_name' method. (this method initializes her slot 'husband_name' with my name (*Self*)).

The method 'set_husband_name' takes one argument, and is defined for the class 'Female' and (is inherited by) its children. It has the effect of initializing the slot 'husband_name' in the object in which it is activated with the name of the supplied argument. Note that the keyword Self in Figure 3.17 is a special variable, which refers to the particular object in which the method is resident. Thus, Self in the method 'male_if_married?' in Figures 3.14 and 3.15, refer to the objects 'Male' and 'Bob' respectively.

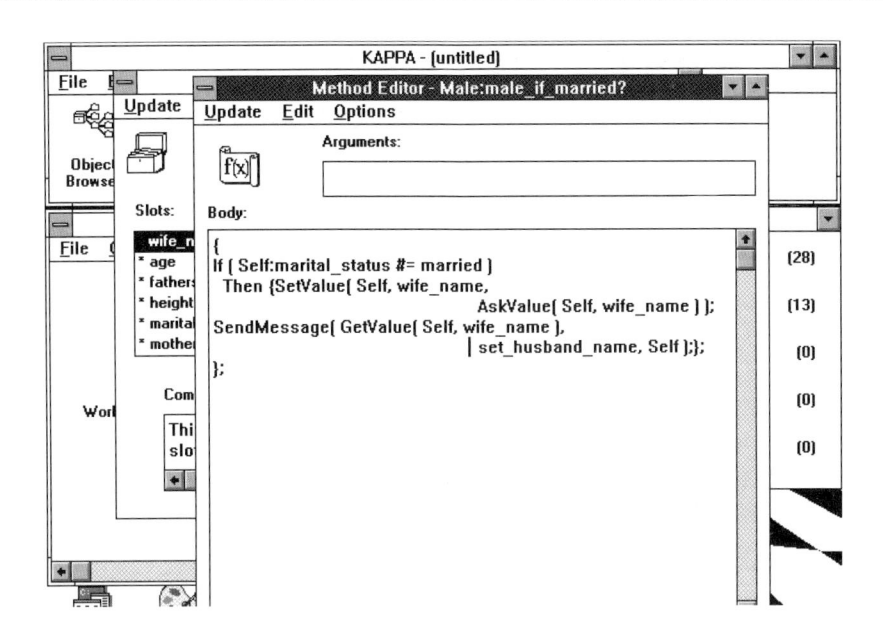

**Figure 3.17** Structure of the method 'male_if_married'

The conditions under which the two actions specified in the method 'male_if_married?' are executed, have to be defined by the system designer while specifying the behavior of domain objects. Recall from Figure 3.16, that this method is specified as the 'after change method' for the slot 'marital_status' in the class 'Male'. This link of the method 'male_if_married?' to the slot 'marital_status' is inherited by all male instances. Whenever the value of the slot 'marital_status' is changed for any male instance, this method is activated automatically after the value is changed. Upon activation the method executes the two actions listed in the body of the method. Figure 3.18 partially illustrates execution of this method. Assuming the user has used the KAL interpreter to change (SetValue) the value of the slot 'marital_status' for the instance 'Bob' to the value 'married' (bottom window in Figure 3.18), the method 'male_if_married' in the instance 'Bob' is automatically activated. As the IF condition of the first statement is satisfied, the user is prompted for the name of the Bob's wife (Figure 3.18); the value of the slot 'wife_name' in the object 'Bob' is initialized to the input value 'Mary'; and a message is sent to the object 'Mary' to activate the method 'set_husband_name' (which sets the value of the slot 'husband_name' in the object 'Mary' to the value 'Bob').

Methods can be more complex in structure than that shown in Figure 3.17. Though not described here, Kappa allows the definition and use of complex rules. Backward or forward chaining with these rules can be activated at specific points within methods. Though it is possible to build arbitrarily complex methods, it is generally desirable to keep methods small and simple. This is because methods aim to describe the behaviors of objects in small, modular components. If a method is large and complex, a second look usually yields smaller, and more sensible solutions.

# 82 Representing and reasoning with knowledge

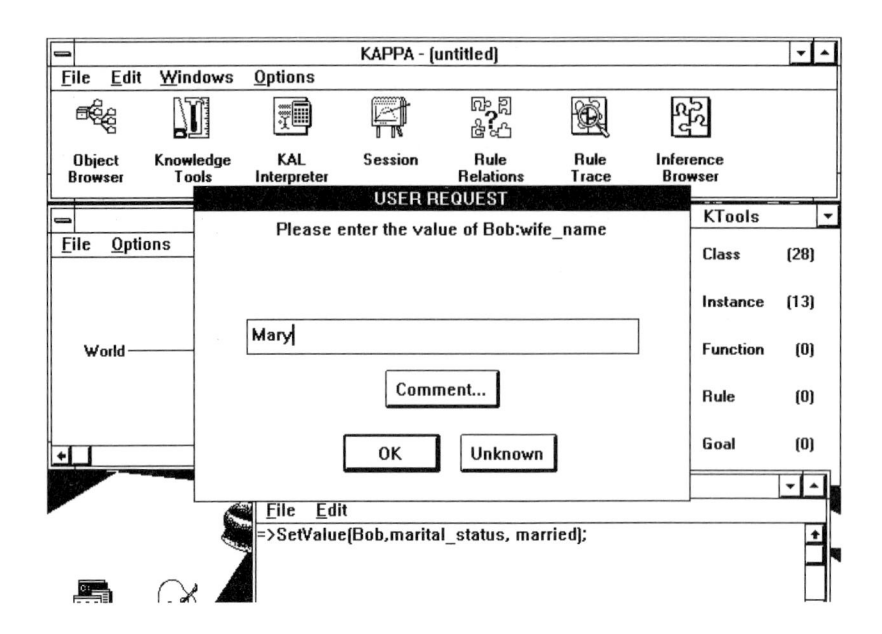

**Figure 3.18** Steps in execution of the method 'male_if_married'

## Communication between objects

Though objects in a frame hierarchy are related by the inheritance of structure and behaviors, all communication between individual objects is done by message passing. Message passing refers to an object communicating with other objects by using the 'SendMessage' function (Figure 3.17). There is no explicit global order or protocol governing these message transfers. Each object is to be viewed as an independent entity, with its own structure (slots) and behavior (methods). Certain actions or stimuli may require the object to communicate with other objects, and this communication is achieved solely by the sending of messages. Messages can affect other objects in different ways. More commonly, they activate certain behaviors (methods) in the recipient objects (as in the example method of Figure 3.17). To give a useful analogy, a collection of objects can be compared to a group of persons. Each person (object) is relatively autonomous, and unique in structure (slots) and behavior (methods). When essential, a person communicates with others by sending messages. Such messages trigger particular responses from the recipients of the messages. Objects can be visualized to be behaving in a similar manner. The behavior of the entire system is defined by the cumulative sum of the behaviors of the individual objects, and the patterns of communication between them.

## Comparing frame hierarchies and rules

Rules and frame hierarchies are the two most common approaches to representing and reasoning with knowledge in KBSs. The relative advantages and disadvantages of these two schemes can be analyzed along the following dimensions:

- comprehensibility — frame hierarchies provide a rich visual representation of knowledge. Thus, they are much easier to comprehend and structure, as compared to the textual representations of simple rule-based systems. Complex rule-based systems do provide the opportunity to graphically represent hierarchies of rule groups, but they lack the notions of inheritance and specialization as seen in frame hierarchies

- modularity — rule-based systems tend to quickly lose their modularity as the number of rules increase beyond a few hundred (due to the increased difficulty of isolating interrelationships between rules). Objects in frame hierarchies have a natural tendency to encapsulate their own structures and behaviors, and are 'responsible' for their own actions. This preserves the modularity of the system, even in complex domains.

- representational richness — frame hierarchies provide a richer environment for representing knowledge as compared to rules. This is due to the ease of defining complex structures and behaviors for objects, and the ability to introduce inheritance patterns between objects. Frame hierarchies are more suitable for representing deep knowledge about the domain, and capturing complex relationships between domain objects

- inferential variety — many frame hierarchical systems (such as Kappa) integrate rule-based reasoning with object-oriented inference techniques (such as message passing). They thus provide for a richer mix of inference techniques, and offer more reasoning possibilities than rule-based systems

- development time — frame hierarchies are more suited for rapid development of systems, because most slots and methods are inherited from parents. Thus, only local (specialized) properties have to be defined for an object. It takes one mouse operation to add a new male instance in the sample knowledge base of Figure 3.13, while it would take many lines of new code to make the same change in Prolog

- maintainability — the ease of repair and maintenance of KBSs is directly related to the modularity of the system. Rule-based systems lose their modularity with increasing size. Hence, it is difficult to effectively maintain large rule-based systems. In contrast, frame hierarchies maintain their modularity much better in the face of complexity and increasing scale. Due to the inherent modularity of objects in frame hierarchies, problems can be quickly isolated, and repaired

- reusability — as each object represents an autonomous piece of domain knowledge, parts of frame hierarchies can be reused for building other systems in similar domains. For example, the definition of the object 'People' (Figure 3.13) can be reused for another problem in which other classes of persons (such as engineers and doctors) are defined. Such an ease of reusability is not possible with rules.

While frame hierarchies do offer a powerful technique for representing and reasoning with knowledge, they suffer too from some of the limitations of rule-based systems mentioned earlier: poor pattern recognition capabilities, an inability to learn, and brittleness. The ability to recognize complex patterns — such as distinguishing between human faces —

seems to be an inherent characteristic of human intelligence. Both frame hierarchies and rules are poor at performing such pattern recognition tasks. Chapter 7 describes how frame hierarchies can be used to provide the domain knowledge for pattern recognition in image processing. Chapter 9 describes an alternative technology — neural networks — with powerful, inherent pattern recognition capabilities. Neural networks also have the additional attractive property of being able to learn from domain examples and evolve continuously. Such abilities are lacking in both frame hierarchies and rule-based systems. Although approaches for incorporating learning into frame hierarchical and rule-based systems exist and are being researched actively, most learning in current systems occurs by the system designer programming in the new knowledge. The brittleness of systems using frame hierarchies and rules is closely related to their inabilities to learn and accept input variations. Neural networks are less brittle due to their capacity to learn. Another applied AI technology — fuzzy logic — described in Chapter 8 avoids the problem of brittleness by accommodating variations in the input data.

Rules and frames are not mutually exclusive knowledge representation techniques. It is possible to incorporate rules into a frame hierarchy by defining rules as objects and incorporating calls for backward or forward chaining within the method definitions. An object representing a rule has slots to store the context, antecedents, conclusions, and other rule parts (such as certainty factors). A call to backward chain would typically be a simple statement of the form 'BackwardChain(goal_name)', which is inserted in the method definition. Based on the results of the backward chaining procedure (i.e., whether the goal 'goal_name' is true or false) certain actions can be invoked by the method. A typical call to forward chain would be the statement, 'ForwardChain(data_items)'. Goals proven true based on the data 'data_items' can further determine actions within the method.

As most advanced frame hierarchical systems (such as Kappa) integrate the benefits of object-oriented programming with rule-based reasoning, they are the usual favorites for commercial KBS development. However, it is important to match the knowledge needs of the domain with the adopted knowledge representation scheme. Simple rule-based systems are often adequate for some domains, and it is recommended a simple rule-based KBS tool is used in such domains.

## Alternative approaches to knowledge representation

Though frame hierarchies and rule-based reasoning are the most common techniques for representing and reasoning with knowledge, alternative approaches such as scripts, blackboard systems, and case-based reasoning are gaining in importance and popularity. Blackboard architectures and case-based reasoners are briefly explained below. Scripts are described in Chapter 6 (see Figure 6.13).

## Blackboard systems

Blackboard architectures[27] were designed to account for the fact that different types of knowledge are sometimes required for solving problems. The architecture of a blackboard system consists of three major components (as shown in Figure 3.19): a blackboard, multiple knowledge sources, and a scheduler.

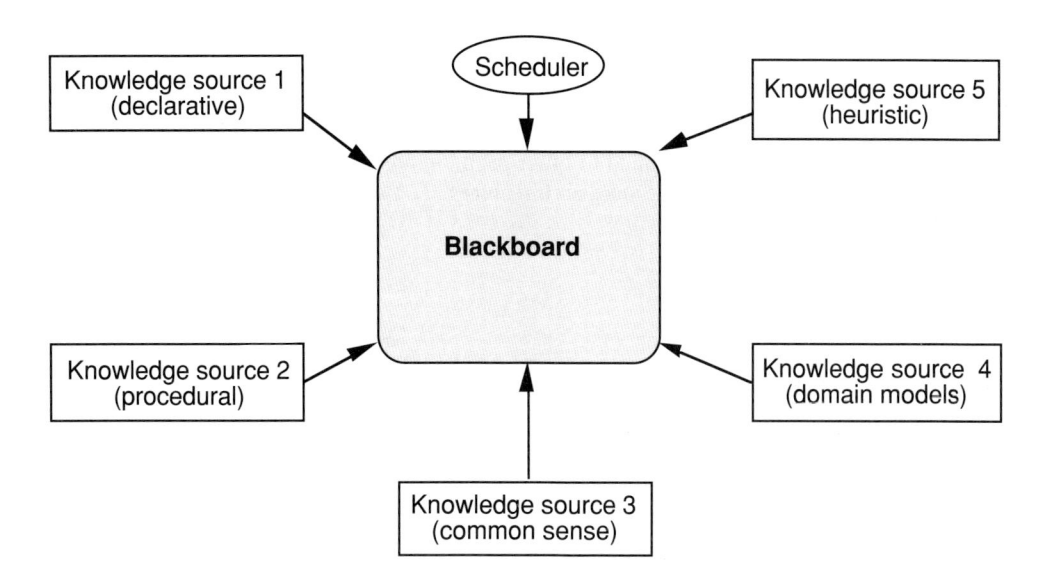

**Figure 3.19** Architecture of a blackboard system

The blackboard contains information about the domain problem, and the different stages of partial problem solution. Upon termination, the complete solution is available in the blackboard. Each knowledge source can be considered as a specialist in a specific type of knowledge. For example, in Figure 3.19, the five knowledge sources contain declarative (know-of), procedural (know-how), heuristic (surface), domain model (deep), and common-sense knowledge. These different types of knowledge are used to solve the problem under consideration. All knowledge sources are independent, but cooperate for problem solution. Each knowledge source acts opportunistically to determine when it can contribute to the solution of the problem under consideration. The various knowledge sources do not communicate directly with each other, but influence each other by their actions on the common solution in the blackboard. As multiple knowledge sources can possibly contribute to problem solution at any stage, a scheduler is required to plan the order in which the knowledge sources act on the solution in the blackboard. Typically, only one knowledge source can work on the blackboard at any time. The complete solution is built progressively with the incremental contributions of the various knowledge sources.

A useful analogy[28] to the functioning of a blackboard system is to imagine a room in which several experts are putting together a huge jigsaw puzzle (the blackboard). Each expert has some pieces of the puzzle, and special knowledge about how the pieces relate to the entire puzzle. The solution evolves incrementally by each expert examining the puzzle solved thus far, deciding whether he or she has something to contribute to the solution at this stage, and if some contribution can be made, moving to the central puzzle, and placing specific pieces.

Blackboard architectures have the advantage of easily integrating different types of knowledge in a single problem-solving system. Because each knowledge source is

## 86 Representing and reasoning with knowledge

independent, the resulting system is modular. This facilitates system modification and evolution. However, care is required for the design of the scheduler, because it manages the order in which different pieces of knowledge are applied for problem solution. Blackboard architectures were first successfully used for the problem of speech understanding[29], but are today being applied to other problem areas also. Appendix 1 lists some KBS applications employing blackboard architectures.

## Case-based reasoning

Case-based reasoning, though common and extremely important in human cognition, has only recently emerged as a major reasoning methodology in KBSs[30]. Case-based reasoning involves solving new problems by identifying and adapting solutions of similar problems stored in a library of prior problem-solving experiences. The reasoning architecture of case-based reasoning consists of a case library (stored representations of solutions of problems encountered before), and an inference cycle. The important steps in the inference cycle are to find and retrieve cases from the case library which are most relevant to the problem under consideration, and to adapt the retrieved cases to the current problem. This is illustrated in Figure 3.20.

Two major classes of case-based reasoning can be identified[31]: problem-solving and precedent-based reasoning. In problem-solving with cases, the emphasis is on adapting the retrieved cases to find a plan, or a course of action to solve the current problem (such as in design and planning problems[32]). In contrast, the focus in precedent-based reasoning is to

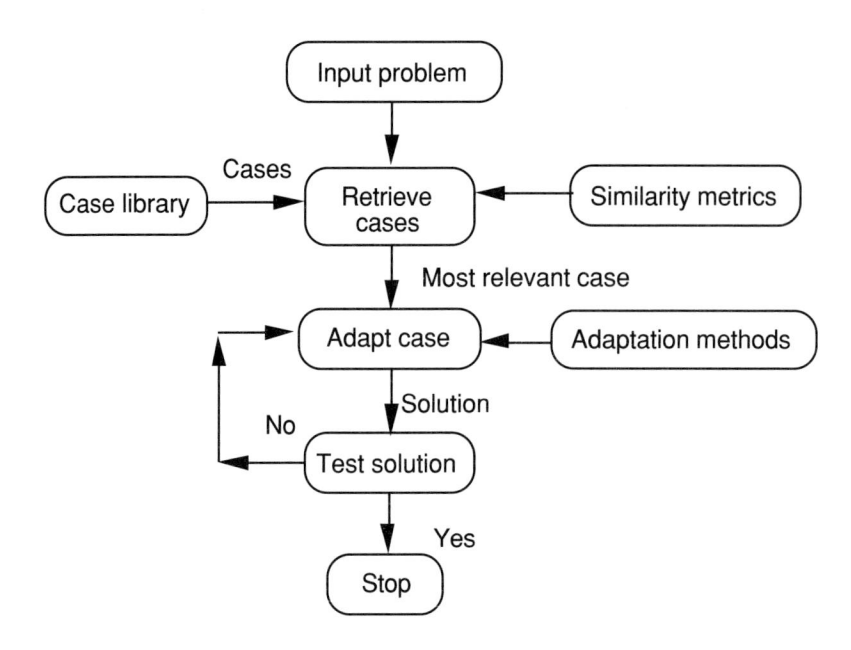

**Figure 3.20** The solution structure in case-based reasoning

use the retrieved cases to justify/explain an action/solution (common in legal reasoning[33]). Cases are generally represented in the case library by a networked knowledge representation scheme. Unlike other reasoning architectures where the solution is generated incrementally, case-based reasoning typically generates a complete solution (the selected case from the case library) first, and then progressively adapts it to solve the current problem. Case adaptation is a difficult and domain-dependent process. There are no well defined general procedures for adapting prior cases to yield solutions to current problems.

Case-based reasoning is being increasingly used in commercial KBSs. Apache III is an example of a commercial KBS incorporating case-based reasoning. Apache III is being used in certain hospitals in the USA to help doctors rate the chances of survival of critically ill patients[34]. Twenty seven different pieces of data (such as the initial diagnosis, vital signs, and the level of consciousness) about a certain patient are collected by doctors and technicians, and fed into the Apache program. These data items are then compared against the records of 17,448 patients who were treated at 40 US hospitals in 1989. The program uses its knowledge about these prior cases to rate the chances of survival of the patient. Studies have shown the program to predict more accurately and more optimistically than the best doctors[35]. Some other examples of KBSs using case-based reasoning are given in Appendix 1.

# 88 Representing and reasoning with knowledge

## Summary

Techniques for representing and reasoning with knowledge are of fundamental importance in knowledge-based applications. This chapter has described two important and common knowledge representation methods: rules and frame hierarchies. The highlights of this chapter can be summarized as follows:

- Knowledge representation is the sub-field of AI which is concerned with representing and reasoning with knowledge.

- A simple rule is of the form: IF antecedents THEN conclusion_1 Else conclusion_2. Complex rules augment simple rules with additional features such as contexts and certainty factors. Rules are useful for representing heuristic knowledge, domain models, and action sequences.

- Simple rule-based systems contain simple rules organized in a flat structure. Structured rule-based systems contain complex rules organized in groups and hierarchies. The two major benefits of structured rule-based systems are increased inferencing efficiency and easier comprehension.

- Forward and backward chaining are two important reasoning procedures with rules. Forward chaining entails moving from data to goals. The backward chaining inferencing procedure moves from goals towards data. Each inferencing mechanism has its own advantages. It is possible to combine backward and forward chaining in some systems. Meta-knowledge can increase the efficiency of inferencing with rules.

- Prolog is a popular logic-based programming language which allows backward chaining with simple rules.

- Rule-based reasoning is simple and useful, but it also has several limitations which get magnified with an increase in the number of rules.

- Networked representations of knowledge do not suffer from many of the disadvantages of rules and are supported by substantial cognitive evidence. Semantic networks and frame hierarchies are two common networked knowledge representation schemes.

- Frame hierarchies consist of objects arranged in an inheritance-specialization hierarchy. The structure of objects is defined by slots and their associated values. Methods are used to define object behaviors. Both slots and methods can be inherited and specialized down the hierarchy. All communications between objects is by the passing of messages.

- Frame hierarchies offer more powerful knowledge representation abilities than rules. It is possible to combine rules and frame hierarchies. It is important to match domain needs with the power of the knowledge representation scheme being used.

- Blackboard architectures and case-based reasoning are two examples of alternative and recent approaches to representing and reasoning with knowledge.

Knowledge representation is a vast field and this chapter has described some of the fundamental ideas of two common approaches to representing and reasoning with knowledge. It is necessary to know more about rules and frame hierarchies to be able to explore or evaluate their applicability for building KBSs. This is the focus of the next chapter. Chapter 4 describes the process of using rules and frame hierarchies for building KBS applications in detail.

## Bibliography and suggested readings

Descriptions of fundamental knowledge representation techniques can be found in virtually every book on expert systems and artificial intelligence. Good non-technical descriptions of rules and frame hierarchies are available in books by Waterman (Waterman 86), and Harmon and King (Harmon & King 85). More thorough and technical descriptions of different knowledge representation techniques (including those not covered in this chapter) are present in references (Patterson 90), and (Rich & Knight 91). Overviews of general issues related to knowledge representation can be found in references (Barr & Feigenbaum 81), and (Kramer & Mylopoulous 92). Extensive descriptions of Prolog are available in books by Clocksin and Mellish (Clocksin & Mellish 81), Clark and McCabe (Clark & McCabe 84), and Bratko (Bratko 86). Case-based reasoning is described in detail in reference (Riesbeck & Schank 89). It may be also interesting to consult books by Newell and Simon (Newell & Simon 72), Lindsay and Norman (Lindsay & Norman 72), and Sternberg (Sternberg 82) for some excellent and varied discussions of general concepts related to human information processing.

Barr, A., and E.A. Feigenbaum, *The Handbook of Artificial Intelligence*, Vol 1, pp 141–222, Pitman Books, London, 1981.

Bratko, I., *Programming in Prolog for Artificial Intelligence*, Addison Wesley, Reading, MA, 1986.

Clark, K.L. and F.G. McCabe, *Micro-Prolog: Programming in Logic*, Prentice Hall, Englewood Cliffs, NJ, 1984.

Clocksin, W.F. and C.S. Mellish, *Programming in Prolog*, Springer-Verlag, Berlin/New-York, 1981.

Harmon, P., and D. King, *Expert Systems*, John Wiley, 1985.

Kramer, B.M., and J. Mylopoulos, *Knowledge Representation, in Encyclopedia of Artificial Intelligence*, Vol. 1, S.C. Shapiro (Ed.), pp. 743–759, John Wiley, 1992.

Lindsay, P.H., and D.A. Norman, *Human Information Processing: An Introduction to Psychology*, Academic Press, NY, 1972.

Newell, A., and H. Simon, *Human Problem-solving*, Prentice-Hall, NJ, 1972.

Patterson, D.W., *Introduction to Artificial Intelligence and Expert Systems*, Prentice-Hall, 1990.

Rich, E., and K. Knight, *Artificial Intelligence*, Mc-Graw Hill, 1991.

Riesbeck, C.K., & R.C. Schank, *Inside Case-based Reasoning*, Lawrence Erlbaum Associates Inc., NJ, 1989.

Sternberg, R.J., Ed., *Handbook of Human Intelligence*, Cambridge University Press, NY, 1982.

Waterman, D.A., *A Guide to Expert Systems*, Addison-Wesley, 1985.

## Notes

1 The deductive principle of logic being used here is called Modus Ponens. Modus Ponens allows us to conclude that a proportion 'q' is true, given the knowledge that proposition 'p' is true, and that the rule 'p → q' is true.

2 Newell, A., and H. Simon, *Human Problem Solving*, Englewood Cliffs, Prentice-Hall, NJ, 1972.

3 Newell, A., and H. Simon, *Human Problem Solving*, Englewood Cliffs, Prentice-Hall, NJ, 1972.

4 Harmon. P. and D. King, *Expert Systems*, pp. 26, John Wiley, 1985.

5 Shortliffe, E.H., *Computer-Based Medical Consultations: MYCIN*, New York, Elsevier, 1976.

6 Bayes, T., *An Essay Towards Solving a Problem in the Doctrine of Chances*, Philos. Trans. R. Soc. London, 53, pp. 370-418, 1763. Reprinted in: Biometrika, 45, pp. 293-315, 1958.

7 Kahneman, D., P. Slovic, and A. Tversky, Eds., *Judgement under Uncertainty: Heuristics and Biases*, Cambridge University Press, New York, 1982.

8 Pearl, J., *Probabilistic Reasoning in Intelligent Systems*, Morgan Kaufmann, Palo Alto, 1988.

9 Shafer, G., *A Mathematical Theory of Evidence*, Princeton Univ. Press, Princeton, NJ, 1976.

10 Zadeh, L.A., *Fuzzy Sets, Information Control*, Vol. 8, pp. 338-353, 1965.

11 McDermott, D., and J. Doyle, *Non-monotonic logic-I*, Artificial Intelligence, 13(1-2), 1980.

12 Doyle, J., *A truth maintenance system*, Artificial Intelligence, 12(3), 1979.

13 Colmerauer, A., H. Kanoui, R. Pasero and P. Roussel, *Un systeme de communication homme-machine en francais*, Groupe d'Intelligence Artificielle, U.E.R. de Luminy, Universite d'Aix-Marseille, Luminy, 1972.

14 Feigenbaum, E. A., and P. McCorduck, *The Fifth Generation: Artificial Intelligence and Japan's Computer Challenge to the World*, Addison Wesley, Reading, Mass., 1983.

15 Descriptions of first order predicate logic can be found in many books giving details on the technical aspects of AI. A good example is: Rich, E., & K. Knight, *Artificial Intelligence*, Mc-Graw Hill, 1991.

16 This section is slightly technical. Some readers may want to skip it (or skim through it) without a significant loss of continuity in the text.

17 A thorough technical description of the unification procedure, and other important concepts of logic programming can be found in: Lloyd, J.W., *Foundations of Logic Programming*, Springer-Verlag, New York-Berlin, 1984.

18 Note that many real life rule based KBSs have many thousands of rules. For example, the XCON KBS of Digital has more than 10,000 rules currently.

19 Quillian, M.R., *Semantic Memory, in Semantic Information Processing*, M. Minsky, (Ed.), Chapter 4, MIT Press, CA, MA, 1968.

20 Collins, A. and M.R. Quillian, *Retrieval Time from Semantic Memory*, Journal of Verbal Learning and Verbal Behavior, 8, pp. 240-247, 1969.

21 Prietula, M.J. and H.A. Simon, *The Experts in your Midst*, Harvard Business Review, pp. 121, Jan-Feb., 1989.

22 Barr, A., and E.A. Feigenbaum, *The Handbook of Artificial Intelligence*, Vol. I, pp. 180-189, Pitman Books, London, 1981.

23 KAPPA is a registered trademark of Intellicorp,Palo Alto, CA.

24 *Software Made Simple*, Business Week, pp. 58-63, Sep. 30, 1991.

25 Each frame in a frame hierarchy represents a class, or a sub-class, or an instance in the domain, and is modelled as an object. We use the term "object" and "frame" (in the context of a frame hierarchy) synonymously.

26 The most common form of inheritance is "down the object hierarchy" as described in the above example. However, in some special cases inheritance "up the hierarchy" may be useful. Such a feature is available only in some advanced KBS tools.

27 An useful survey and description of blackboard architectures, and their applications is available in two papers by H.P. Nii: (a) Nii, H.P., *Blackboard Systems: The Blackboard Model of Problem Solving and the Evolution of Blackboard Architectures*, AI Magazine, 7, 2, 1986; and (b) Nii, H.P., *Blackboard Systems: Blackboard Applications Systems, Blackboard Systems from a Knowledge Engineering Perspective*, AI Magazine, 7, 3, 1986.

28 Nii, H.P., *Blackboard Systems: The Blackboard Model of Problem Solving and the Evolution of Blackboard Architectures*, AI Magazine, 7, 2, 1986.

29 Erman, L.D., F. Hayes-Roth, V.R. Lesser, and D.R. Reddy, *The Hearsay-II Speech Understanding System: Integrating Knowledge to Resolve Uncertainty*, Computing Surveys, 12, pp. 213-253, 1980.

30 Riesbeck, C.K., and R. C. Schank, *Inside Case-Based Reasoning*, Lawrence Erlbaum Associates Inc., NJ, 1989.

31 Rissland, E.L., and D. B, Skalak, *Combining case-based and rule-based reasoning: A heuristic approach*, In Proceedings of the Eleventh Joint Conference on Artificial Intelligence, Morgan Kaufmann Publishers, Inc., San Mateo, CA, August 1989.

32 Barletta, R., and W. Mark, *Explanation-based indexing of cases*, In Proceedings of the AAAI-88, Morgan Kaufmann Publishers, Inc., San Mateo, CA, 1988.

33 Ashley, K., and E. Rissland, *Dynamic assessment of relevancy in a case-based reasoner*, IEEE Expert, 1988.

34 Schwartz, E.I., and J.B. Treece, *Smart Programs go to Work*, Business Week, pp. 47-51, March 2, 1992.

35 Schwartz, E.I., and J.B. Treece, *Smart Programs go to Work*, Business Week, pp. 50, March 2, 1992.

# Part III

### Implementing strategic knowledge-processing applications

Having discussed the core technologies of knowledge processing in Chapters 2 and 3, it's now possible to explore their application in organizations. This part of the book focuses on the process of creating and implementing strategically advantageous knowledge-based system (KBS) applications. There are three major dimensions — technological, organizational, and strategic — to the implementation of KBSs. Chapters 4 and 5 explore each of these aspects in more detail.

Important technological issues in the process of designing and developing KBSs are the foci of Chapter 4. Relevant aspects of rules and frame hierarchies are described in detail, and different phases in the process of creating KBSs with these technologies are explained. The discussion is supported by examples, and challenges in the implementation process are highlighted. The chapter concludes with an analysis of different types of commercial tools available for developing KBSs, and status of and trends in the evolving commercial market for KBS products. More details on a wide range of commercial KBS tools are found in Appendix 2.

Complementing the above discussion, Chapter 5 focuses on organizational and strategic issues in the implementation of KBSs. These aspects are crucial because successful KBS applications have to satisfy strategic needs in the organizational context. There is an intimate relation between organizational knowledge and the knowledge-processing capabilities offered by KBSs. This issue is explored in detail in the chapter, and the organizational impacts of different types of KBSs are identified. The influence of KBS applications on corporate strategies and industry structure is also discussed. The chapter ends with an extended discussion of different strategies for developing competitively advantageous KBS applications. Important issues in the overall management of the process of developing KBSs within organizations are also identified.

# Chapter 4
## *Creating knowledge-based systems*

Rules and frame hierarchies (described in Chapter 3) are two important techniques for representing and reasoning with knowledge. This chapter focuses on the creation of knowledge-based systems (KBSs) using these two technologies. The process of — and tools used for — developing rule-based and hybrid KBSs are described below. While rule-based systems only support rules — either simple or complex, hybrid KBSs integrate frame hierarchies and rules.

Rules are useful for developing KBSs, when one or more of the following conditions are true:

(a) the domain is relatively simple, or

(b) heuristics form the dominant component of domain knowledge, or

(c) the end-user is a non-programmer and has to be able to develop/modify the KBS, or

(d) the KBS has to be developed relatively cheaply and quickly.

By integrating frame hierarchies and rules, hybrid systems can effectively and efficiently represent both domain models and heuristic knowledge. Objects and frame hierarchies[1] are useful for representing domain models, and for modelling the interactions between different domain entities. Rules are most effective for representing heuristic knowledge in the domain. Most current commercial KBSs are hybrid systems.

Hybrid systems are useful for building KBSs in complex domains. They maintain their modularity on scaling up, and offer the best approach for managing complexity in real-life domains. Though they are usually adequate for building most KBSs, they are not necessarily always the best choice. Rule-based approaches may be preferred if the domain is simple, and rapid development by end-users or computer-naive experts is desired.

Professional knowledge engineers are usually required for developing hybrid systems, due to the complexity of the underlying technology. Rule-based systems would also be preferable, if the users or experts are expected to modify and maintain the KBS independently.

In the following discussion, we assume for simplicity that the KBS is built by a knowledge engineer with the aid of a domain expert. In practice, users play an important role in and have a significant impact on the development process[2]. The utility of involving users in the development of KBSs and the mechanics of doing so are discussed in the following chapter.

## Creating rule-based systems

Generally, there are five important phases in the process of creating rule-based systems:

(1) problem description — this is the first phase, in which the overall problem has to be studied, and the suitability of a rule-based solution determined

(2) problem decomposition — except for small or simple domains, the problem should be suitably decomposed into sub-problems. The relationships between the various sub-problems should also be clearly identified

(3) initial prototype — next, an initial set of rules has to be obtained for a particular sub-problem. The choice of which sub-problem to begin with is domain-dependent. One can choose a sub-problem which is critical, or near the final goal(s), or close to the initial data, or perceived as being easy to solve

(4) incremental evolution — the small rule-based KBS of step (3) has to be incrementally expanded for the entire problem domain. Steps (1) through (4), have to be performed in close cooperation with the domain expert

(5) customization — when a reasonably complete rule set has been obtained for the problem, the entire KBS has to be customized to meet user requirements. Recall that users of KBSs are typically different from the expert(s) helping to build them.

The above design stages are explained now as the basis of a simple rule-based KBS for career counselling. A subsequent section describes some of the advanced features available with complex rules in structured rule-based systems.

## Problem description

The aim of the problem description phase is to get an overall perspective on the problem, and the domain. As not all domains are amenable to rule-based solutions, the applicability of rules to the problem has to determined during this stage.

A person seeking career advise usually goes to a professional career counsellor, or to an employment agency to get assistance and recommendations for a change in career. The career counsellor's job consists of three steps: client evaluation, employer evaluation, and matching clients and employers.

A number of conventional tools are available for evaluating clients: résumés, direct interviews, open questions, structured interviews, questionnaires, personality tests, and references. There is no one ideal tool for client evaluation, and the counsellor typically utilizes one or more of the above options. Problems faced by the counsellor at this stage include determination of which test(s) to use and maintaining consistency among the results of the various tests.

As a counsellor can only spend limited time with each client, it is difficult to ensure a systematic evaluation of each client's profile and goals. This problem is usually exacerbated by a client's inability to express personal strengths and weaknesses clearly, and objectively.

The counsellor needs access to a reasonably complete database of information about current openings in the job market. As this listing can potentially be very large, it is difficult for a counsellor to go through each item individually. Even if database queries are used, current commercial query languages lack the expressiveness to be able to intelligently retrieve the 'correct' set of job opening descriptions[3].

The final step in the counsellor's job consists of matching a client's background and strengths to an employer's requirements. Considerable expertise and experience is required for performing this match, as there is no objective measure for determining the 'goodness of match'. The payoffs to all three parties (the employer, client and the counsellor) can be substantial if this match is performed satisfactorily. As experience helps in developing expertise to perform this match, junior counsellors are often at a disadvantage in this step.

A KBS can improve effectiveness of a counsellor by performing a more consistent and systematic analysis of client strengths, weaknesses, and goals, helping the counsellor counsel more clients with a higher degree of quality and satisfaction, intelligently querying the job database to incorporate tradeoffs between job requirements and client qualifications as well as aiding the matching process by suggesting possible matches between clients and employers. A rule-based solution is appropriate for such a KBS because:

(1) the domain is relatively simple
(2) heuristics play an important role in the process — there is no accepted domain model in career counselling
(3) the end-user — the counsellor — is a non-programmer and has to be able to understand and modify the system
(4) low development costs are important.

## Problem decomposition

The strategy behind problem decomposition is: divide and conquer. By dividing up a problem into sub-problems, it is possible to focus attention on selected sub-parts of the original problem, and avoid getting bogged down in the complexity of the domain.

The counsellor's problem can be decomposed into the three stages mentioned earlier: client evaluation, employer evaluation, and client-employer matching. These three phases are also usually performed in order: first the client is evaluated, then the job openings are scanned, and finally a match is suggested.

## Initial prototype

The initial prototype provides the core around which the complete KBS can be incrementally developed. An enhanced understanding of the domain results from building the prototype. This facilitates the rapid development of the remainder of the KBS.

In our example we start with our focus on the sub-problem of client-evaluation. Assume the problem is to determine which of the following different career paths is most suitable for the client[4]: entrepreneur (with a focus on building up a new businesses), or expert (a specialized job such as a technical specialist), or manager (with a focus on general management), or consultant (in general management).

The knowledge engineer can adopt a top-down approach for determining how the expert counsellor decides upon a suitable career path. Initial questioning may reveal that the expert considers three major client characteristics, knowledge, job objectives, and personality traits, for making this decision. The counsellor decides how the client rates along each attribute, then uses expert knowledge to decide the career profile best suited for the client.

This knowledge consists primarily of a set of heuristics, as there is no 'correct' methodology for determining the right career path. It is the job of the knowledge engineer to extract this heuristic knowledge, and express it by a set of rules. This top-down knowledge extraction process can be carried one step further by asking the expert how the value of the characteristics, knowledge, job objectives, and personality traits are determined. At this stage the knowledge engineer may decide that enough knowledge has been acquired to build an initial prototype.

Dependency diagrams and decision tables are two useful tools for representing the logical structure of rule-based systems. Figure 4.1 describes a possible dependency diagram for the logical structure of the initial prototype in our example. Note that the attributes affecting the evaluation of each of the above three characteristics, Knowledge, Job objectives, and Personality traits, are also depicted in Figure 4.1. For example, the attributes, intelligence and skills, determine the value of the client characteristic, knowledge.

Each major decision point or characteristic is represented by a rectangular box. The different possible results at each decision point are represented along the arcs emanating from the box. Triangles in Figure 4.1 represent sets of rules. These rules specify how the various input conditions are combined to produce the different output results. A possible set of rules for 'rule set 2' is shown in Figure 4.2. Note that the rules of Figure 4.2 can also be equivalently represented by the (simple) decision table of Figure 4.3. Similarly, other rules have to be derived for rule sets 1,3 and 4. Note that even in this simple domain, 204 different rules can potentially be formulated for the dependency diagram of Figure 4.1.

The process of knowledge acquisition yields the various decision points, the possible results, and the applicable rules. The cumulative sum of the different attributes and rules represents the extracted expertise of the expert counsellor. Note that the expert is generally unable to correctly specify all relevant attributes and rules in one session. It usually takes a few iterations to arrive at a reasonably complete dependency diagram for the initial prototype. Building the prototype also helps the expert in better understanding the structure and functions of the KBS. The knowledge engineer can use the feedback from the expert on the prototype to validate the extracted knowledge[5].

# Initial prototype

## Figure 4.1

[Diagram: Top-level dependency diagram]

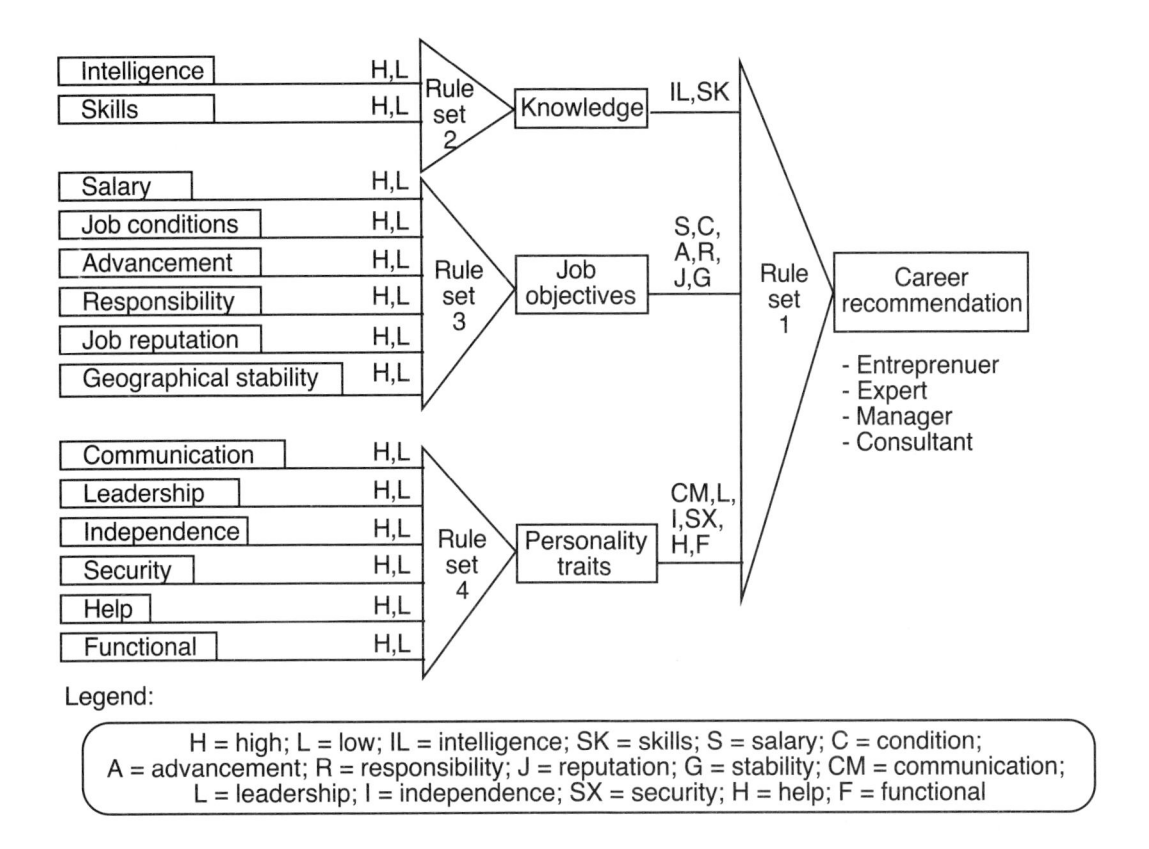

Inputs to Rule set 2 (Knowledge): Intelligence (H,L); Skills (H,L).

Inputs to Rule set 3 (Job objectives): Salary (H,L); Job conditions (H,L); Advancement (H,L); Responsibility (H,L); Job reputation (H,L); Geographical stability (H,L).

Inputs to Rule set 4 (Personality traits): Communication (H,L); Leadership (H,L); Independence (H,L); Security (H,L); Help (H,L); Functional (H,L).

Rule set 1 combines Knowledge (IL, SK), Job objectives (S, C, A, R, J, G), and Personality traits (CM, L, I, SX, H, F) → Career recommendation:
- Entreprenuer
- Expert
- Manager
- Consultant

Legend:
H = high; L = low; IL = intelligence; SK = skills; S = salary; C = condition; A = advancement; R = responsibility; J = reputation; G = stability; CM = communication; L = leadership; I = independence; SX = security; H = help; F = functional

**Figure 4.1** Top-level dependency diagram

## Incremental evolution

The construction of the complete KBS is based on the initial prototype, and is incremental and evolutionary in nature. The knowledge engineer takes a small part of the partially completed KBS, expands it, validates it with the domain expert, and repeats the process till the entire KBS is completed.

The initial prototype in our example captures the important high level characteristics considered by the expert while determining the profile of the client. However, the second level attributes shown to the left in Figure 4.1, are still too coarse to be directly answered by the clients/counsellors. Each of these attributes can be further decomposed into compositions of more easily measurable lower level attributes, or data. As before, these decompositions can be represented by a combination of dependency diagrams and decision tables. For example, Figure 4.4 represents the dependency diagram for the decomposition of the characteristic, knowledge. While the dependency diagram of Figure 4.1 only specified that the attributes intelligence and skills, were important for determining the characteristic, knowledge, Figure 4.4 probes further down to determine attributes

## 100 Creating knowledge-based systems

```
IF skill is high   AND intelligence is high   THEN knowledge is IL   AND SK
IF skill is high   AND intelligence is low    THEN knowledge is SK
IF skill is low    AND intelligence is high   THEN knowledge is IL
```

**Figure 4.2** Samples rule for the rule set of Figure 4.1

|        | Intelligence Low | Intelligence High |
|--------|------------------|-------------------|
| Skills Low  |              | IL                |
| Skills High | SK           | IL & SK           |

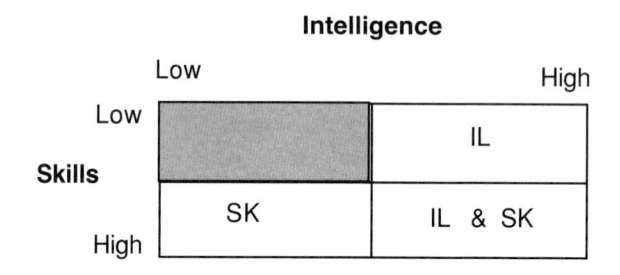

**Figure 4.3** A decision table for the rules of Figure 4.2

which can be combined to yield measures of the client's intelligence and skills. Note that all low level attributes shown (shaded) to the left of Figure 4.4 are easily measured. For simplicity, possible values of all attributes (in Figure 4.4) are limited to the two values: high (H) and low (L), which are to be interpreted appropriately for the attributes. The triangular boxes represent the various rule sets required to express knowledge about possible combinations of different attributes and their values. The potential number of rules required for the dependency diagram of Figure 4.4 is significantly higher than that required for the dependency diagram of Figure 4.1. The number of rules increase further if more attributes and values would be considered.

Analogous to Figure 4.4, detailed dependency diagrams need to be drawn for the client features, job objectives and personality traits. Cumulatively, these dependency diagrams define the structure of the rule-based system we are trying to design. It is important to emphasize that dependency diagrams, such as those shown in Figures 4.1 and 4.4 represent (simplified) end results of the knowledge-acquisition process. Usually, several cycles of the basic knowledge-acquisition cycle (elicitation, review, analysis, and elicitation...) are required to obtain such dependency diagrams. The expert counsellor has to be involved in making all incremental modifications to the evolving system. The development of the KBS in this example has adopted a top-down approach. It is also conceivable to use a bottom-up approach by first looking at what data about the client is available, then enquiring how the expert uses these data to arrive at relevant conclusions about the suggested career path. The decision about the appropriate development approach to choose is domain-dependent, and has to be selected to facilitate the knowledge-acquisition process. Usually, a judicious combination of top-down and bottom-up approaches is used.

While the dependency diagrams of Figures 4.1 and 4.4 depict the logical structure of the problem, they do not specify the type of inference strategy to use, or the order in which

# Incremental evolution 101

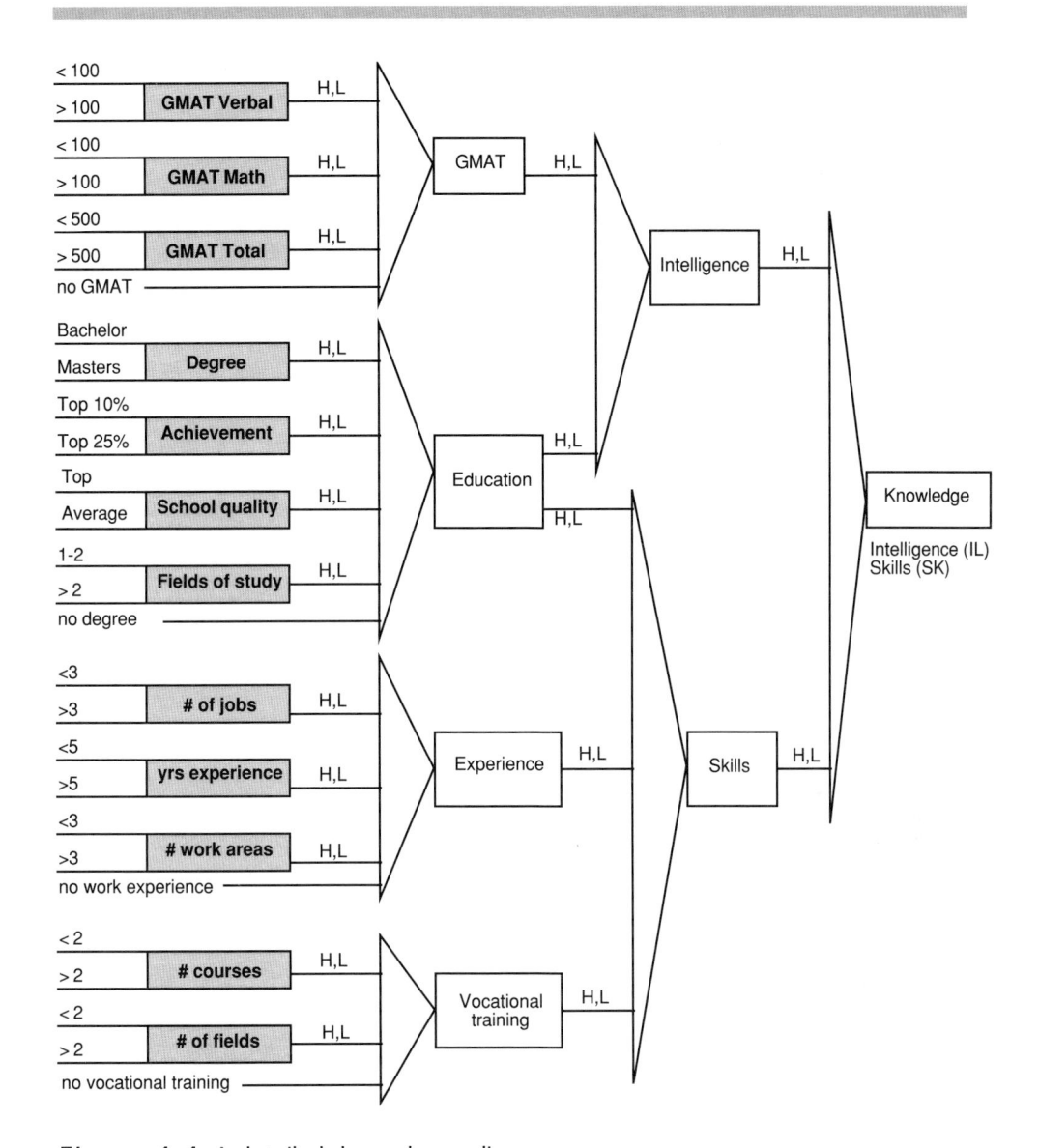

**Figure 4.4** A detailed dependency diagram

to solve the problem. The knowledge engineer has to choose the appropriate inference strategy (in consultation with the domain expert), such that the order of problem solution is natural for the domain. In this example, both backward and forward chaining inference strategies can be used. Backward chaining can be used to answer specific questions like, 'is the client profile that of a manager?'. Forward chaining can be use to solicit data from the client, then determine which profile is satisfied by the client ('here is the client data, give me the appropriate profile'). Dependent upon which question seems more natural or common, an appropriate inference strategy can be chosen.

## Customization

The goal of the customization phase is to ensure that the developed KBS is deployed successfully. Several important concerns have to be addressed at this stage:

- efficiency — is the system efficient and quick? Often, the rules and inference strategies have to be tuned to increase speed, and the efficiency of inferencing

- user demands — does the system meet the needs of the users? As the end-users of the KBS are usually different from the expert(s) who aided the development process, they tend to have different expectations from the system

- inference strategy — are the inference strategies correct, and appropriate for the end-user? Are questions asked in the right order? Will the user be able to provide the required answers?

- user-interface — is the interface friendly? Is it easy for the user to navigate through, and use the system? Attention needs to be paid to even small details, such as the exact wording of questions or recommendations (produced as output).

The customization phase can be time consuming. It is, however, very important because it is a strong determinant of the level of acceptance of the KBS by the user. The friendliness of the interface is perhaps the most important factor to be customized in our simple example. Given that the system is targeted at a group of computer-naive professionals, the system has to be friendly to use, and must provide the user with detailed explanations of particular conclusions.

All questions and answers have to carefully phrased, so as to avoid conveying the wrong meaning to either the clients, or the counsellors. More details on issues related to effective user-interface design are described later, in the section on the customization of hybrid KBSs.

## Structured rule-based systems

Note that even for relatively simple situations, numbers of rules can be fairly large. For example, potentially more than 200 different rules can be formulated for the simple dependency diagram of Figure 4.1. When the number of rules increases beyond a few hundred, simple rule-based systems can lead to inefficiency (as the inference engine has to sequentially search all rules to find matching rules), a loss of modularity (due to the difficulty in tracking inter-relationships between rules), and an accompanying decrease in the ease of comprehension and modifiability of the KBS.

Structured rule-based systems provide additional features to alleviate some of these problems. One simple approach is to allow the assignment of priorities to rules. Thus, the inference engine can search the rule base in a decreasing order of priority (or in some other specified manner). While this is useful for small systems, the assignment of priorities often becomes a difficult, and (sometimes) a meaningless task when the number of rules increase to a thousand, or more.

## Structured rule-based systems 103

Another more sophisticated solution is to provide mechanisms for bunching together rules into groups and hierarchies, with associated contexts. Though many different definitions of the term 'context' exist in commercial KBS tools[6], the term 'context' generally refers to a set of conditions associated with a group of rules. Contexts can specify different things, such as the conditions under which the rules in that rule set are to be searched (by the inference engine), and specific sequences of steps to be taken when control is passed (during the inference process) to that group of rules. Often, contexts are used to define the structural decomposition of a particular problem, and to enforce more control over the inference process.

For example, the rules of Figure 4.1 can be organized into a hierarchy of rule sets as shown in Figure 4.5. The three rules comprising rule set 1 (as shown in Figure 4.2) would be stored under the group 'rule set 1' in Figure 4.5 (and so on for the other rule sets). The context of each rule set specifies the conditions under which the rules in the rule set should be searched for matching rules. A simple context condition for rule set 1 can be something like: 'search this rule set if client career path is desired'. Thus in response to the question 'what is the client career path?', the inference engine can begin by first only searching rule group 1, then sequentially considering the other rule groups as control is passed to them by the rules of rule set 1 (to determine client skills and personality characteristics necessary for determining the appropriate career path). Note that the hierarchy of rule sets of Figure 4.5 does not have the properties of inheritance and specialization associated with object-oriented frame hierarchies (as described in Chapter 3).

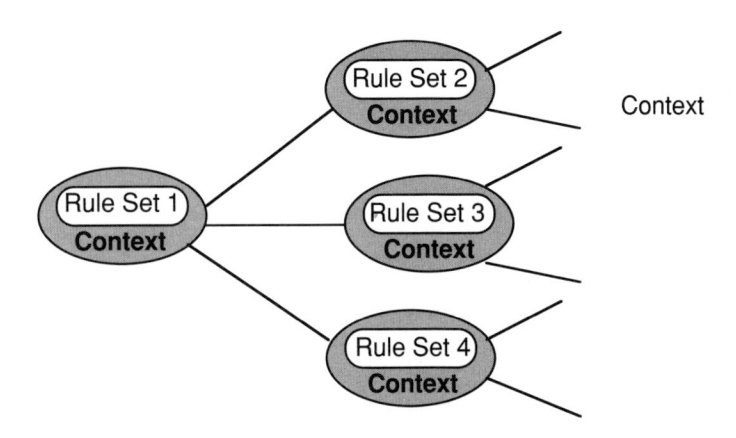

**Figure 4.5** A rule group hierarchy

The facilities of rule group hierarchies and contexts in structured rule-based KBSs allow for increased efficiency (as the inference engine can selectively search the most appropriate rule groups), improved modularity (because interactions between rules are isolated to interactions between rule groups), enhanced ease of maintenance (due to the improved modularity), and an increased level of comprehension of the domain knowledge (due the structure imposed on the rules). Thus, structured rule-based systems are preferable (as compared to simple rule-based systems) if rules are going to be used to structure knowledge in a moderately large and complex domain.

## Creating hybrid knowledge-based systems

The following five phases can be identified in the process of designing and creating hybrid KBSs:

(1) problem description — this phase is analogous to that for the development of rule-based systems, and is concerned with defining and understanding the overall problem to be solved

(2) frame hierarchy identification — relationships between different domain entities have to be recognized, and suitable parent-child relationships identified to define an initial frame hierarchy

(3) structure and behavior identification — the structure and behavior of each object have to be defined. This requires the identification of the primary attributes and relevant behaviors of the domain entities modelled by the objects. Structures are defined by the slots inside objects. Methods are used to specify the behaviors of objects

(4) prototyping and incremental evolution — it's usual to begin with a prototype built on the basis of the knowledge learnt in phases (2) and (3). The prototype evolves incrementally to yield the complete KBS for the domain. This incremental evolution involves expansion of the frame hierarchy and specification of the complete structure and behavior of each object in the frame hierarchy

(5) customization — this phase is similar to that during the creation of rule-based systems and focuses on customizing the user-interface and inference strategies to meet user requirements.

The above design stages are explained now for Brandframe[7], a hybrid KBS for assisting a brand manager.

## Problem description

The typical situation in a mature market for fast-moving consumer goods is as follows. A brand competes with other competitors in the market for market share. Brands compete with two sets of instruments. First, the marketing instruments that are directly aimed at consumers such as advertising, price, coupons and other sales promotion activities. The second set concerns the marketing instruments with which a brand manufacturer influences sales through a retailer: number of outlets where the brand is available, shelf space, point-of-purchase promotions and so on. A brand can be characterized by a number of aspects such as awareness, perception, consumer profile, market share, distribution, and price level.

Links between different brands are primarily antagonistic in that they compete for the same consumers. One brand's gain is usually some other brand's loss. In addition to these antagonistic links, there may also be synergistic links: two different brands may be from the same manufacturer. Links between brands and retailers are partly cooperative (common interest in large sales), and partly antagonistic (negotiation about price). There is a very direct brand-retailer link in the case of private labels (brands owned by the retailer).

# Problem description 105

The above constellation of brands (brand manufacturers), retailers, and their mutual links within the environment of a particular (consumer) market can be conceived of as an interactive system. An action of one of the actors will have direct consequences for some of the other actors in the system, and will also often invoke reactions from those actors. The brand manager is responsible for developing and carrying out the marketing strategy and tactics for a particular brand. Given the complex nature of the links and interactions between different players, determining the effects of the actions of a player on others is a non-trivial task requiring the use of both quantitative and heuristic reasoning. A few mathematical models do exist for supporting some of these decisions, but they have significant limitations, particularly in their handling of qualitative factors/relationships, and their treatment of incomplete, uncertain, and heuristic knowledge.

A KBS such as Brandframe can play a valuable role in this situation by providing an effective and realistic model of the domain, which can be used to support the decision processes of the brand manager. Objects and frame hierarchies can be used to encapsulate the structure and behavior of individual domain entities (such as brands and retailers), and exploit the relationships between different entities (such as the properties common to all brands). Rules can be used to express heuristic knowledge in the domain. A simple rule-based representation would fail to capture the complex interactions between different domain entities in an effective and modular fashion.

## Frame hierarchy identification

There is a need to determine the important classes and sub-classes of domain objects early on in the development process. A properly-defined frame hierarchy can significantly ease subsequent phases of development. Note that this stage does not require the frame hierarchy to be defined completely and accurately. It is common to begin with a simple frame hierarchy, and incrementally expand the hierarchy in later stages of development. An important objective at this stage is to ensure that all important classes of domain entities and parent-child relationships between the various classes have been identified.

For Brandframe, the problem description has identified several classes of interest in the domain such as brands, product classes, sub-product classes, retailers, and marketing instruments. An initial frame hierarchy for these entities can be constructed as shown (partially) in Figure 4.6. It is assumed in Figure 4.6 that the system is used by a brand manager responsible for a certain beer brand. There is no one unique method to build the frame hierarchy. It is quite likely that two knowledge engineers would arrive at two different hierarchies for the same problem. But there are certain natural parent-child relationships which cannot — and should not — be ignored. For example, the marketing instrument 'sales promotions' can be conducted in many different ways, such as by distributing coupons, or samples, or by holding contests. It is 'natural' to make the objects representing the specific sales promotions instruments ('coupons', 'sampling', and 'contests') sub-classes of the object representing the class of all sales promotion instruments ('sales_promotion') — as shown in Figure 4.6. It would be unnatural to place the object 'contest' as a child of an object representing another unrelated class, such as 'occupation'. Also, note that the list of specific sales promotions instruments shown in Figure 4.6 is incomplete. For example, it does not include objects for other sales promo-

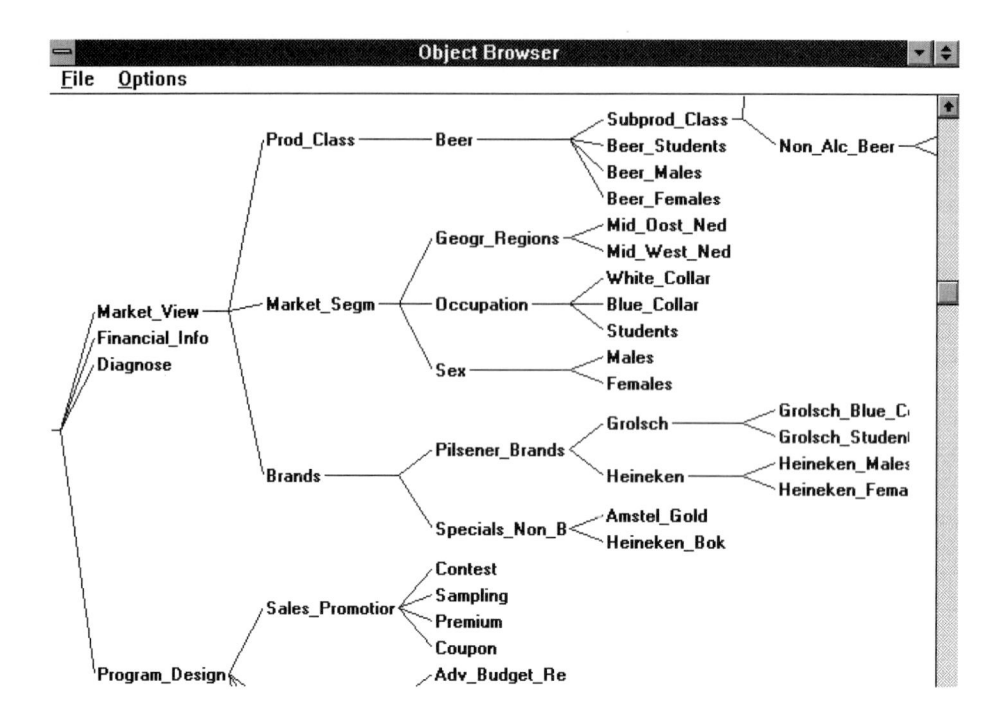

**Figure 4.6** An initial frame hierarchy for Brandframe

tion instruments such as cash refunds and price discounts. For simplicity, we may choose to ignore them now, and include them later as the system is incrementally expanded. Including them later is easy, because all children of the object 'sales_promotion' inherit common attributes and behaviors from it.

## Structure and behavior identification

After the specification of an initial frame hierarchy, attention has to be focused on the task of defining the structures and behaviors of the objects representing the different classes and instances. The process of structure definition requires the identification of the relevant attributes of domain entities, the creation of appropriate slots in objects modelling those entities, and the specification of whether the slots are passed down to its children or are local to that object. Behaviors of objects are specified by isolating distinct behaviors of domain entities and defining appropriate methods within the concerned objects. Methods, like slots, can either be passed down to children objects, or kept local to an object. Only selected aspects of the structures and behaviors of domain entities are specified initially. It is important to define structures and behaviors at the highest level of abstraction (for the most general class in the frame hierarchy). Analogous to the initial frame hierarchy (stage 2), the structures and behaviors of objects are also expanded, and incrementally refined during the later stages of development.

## Structure and behavior identification 107

Figures 4.7 and 4.8 depict the partial structures[8] of the objects 'sales_promotion' and 'sampling' respectively. The slots and methods of Figure 4.7, describe the attributes and behaviors characterizing the class of all sales promotion instruments. For example, all sales promotion instruments have an associated cost ('direct_costs'), and a measure of implementation complexity ('complexity'). These slots are passed onto the child objects as shown in Figure 4.8[9]. Figure 4.9 depicts the structure of a simple method called 'explain_devices', which is defined at the level of the object 'sales_promotion', and is passed down to the child object 'sampling' (Figure 4.8). When activated, this method has the effect of displaying a textual description of the various sales promotion instruments available to the brand manager.

Methods can be fairly complex in structure and function. They usually represent procedural knowledge, but can also contain calls to activate forward or backward chaining of rules. Just as there is no unique frame hierarchy, there is no one correct specification of slots and methods. Slot definitions should cumulatively give a reasonably complete set of attributes describing the class, or instance represented by that object. Methods should aim to isolate specific aspects of the behavior of the class or instance of domain entities modelled by that object. Emphasizing modularity, and minimizing interactions between different types of behaviors are desirable objectives while defining methods. For example, it is preferable to define separate methods (such as 'score_advertizing' and 'score_attention' in Figure 4.7) for evaluating a particular sales promotion instrument along separate

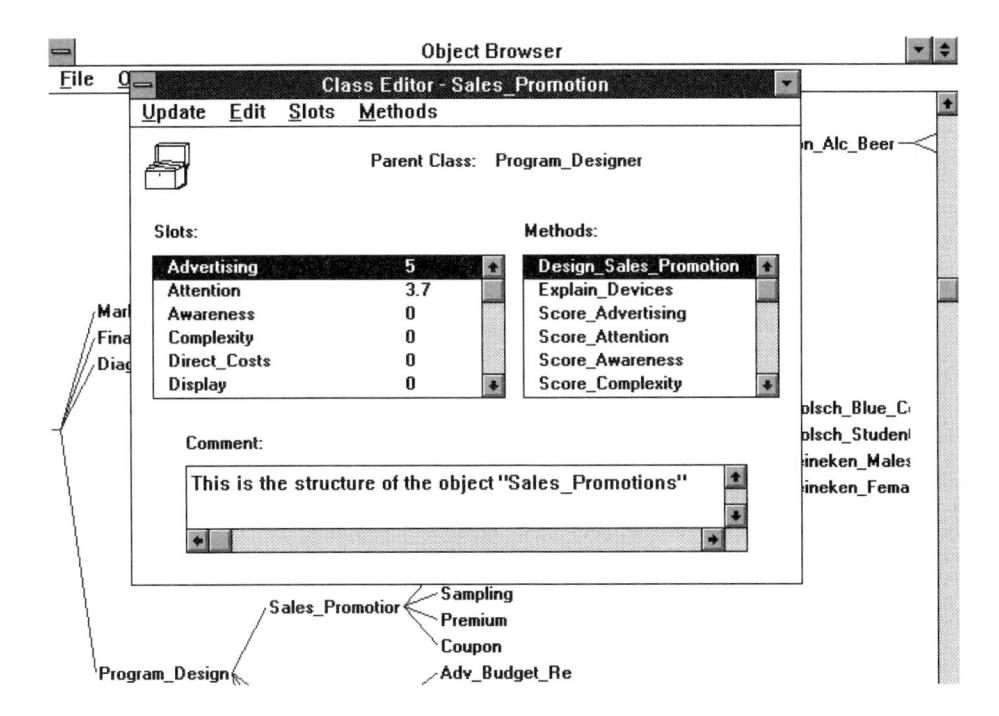

**Figure 4.7** An initial definition of slots and methods for the object Sales_Promotion

## 108 Creating knowledge-based systems

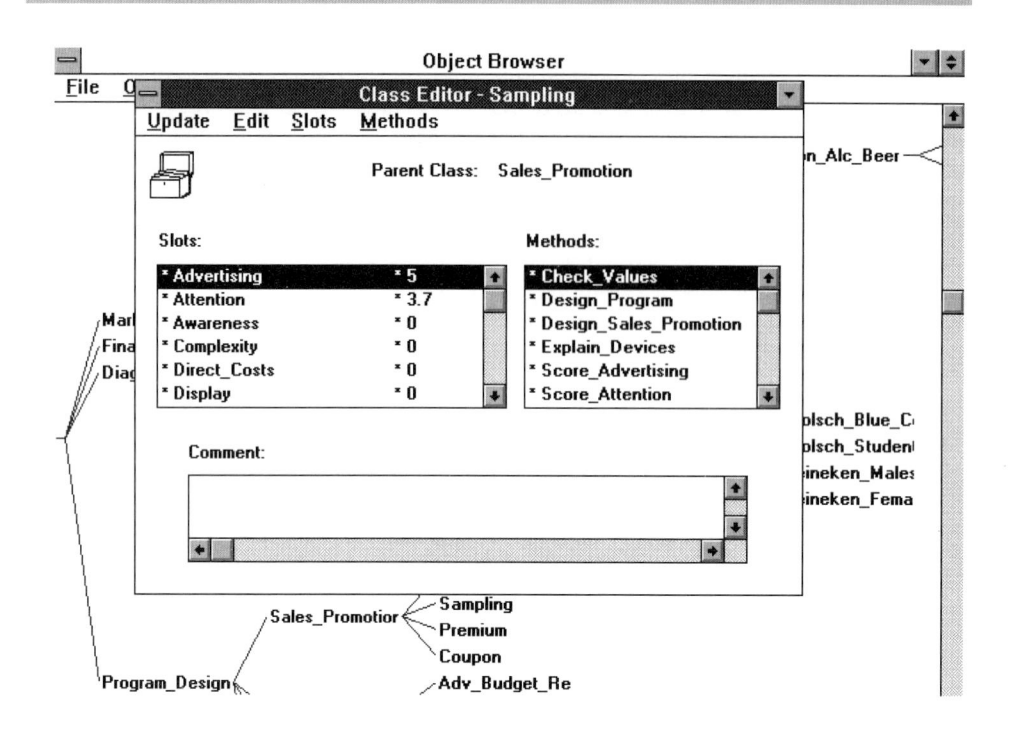

**Figure 4.8** An initial definition of slots and methods for the object Sampling

dimensions (advertising and attention, respectively), rather than consolidate them into one big method. Particular attention has to be paid to the pattern of inheritance of slots and methods in the frame hierarchy.

### Prototyping and incremental evolution

Except for relatively small and simple domains, it is not advisable to attempt to design the complete frame hierarchy, and specify all object structures and behaviors in a single iteration. Rather, it is preferable to first build a prototype (Figures 4.6 through 4.9) by utilizing the knowledge gained during the previous two stages. Building the prototype serves the important purpose of validating the domain model (frame hierarchy, and object structures and behaviors) learnt thus far. It also allows the knowledge engineer to present something concrete to the domain expert, and enlist his/her help in the incremental evolution of the system. It is difficult for the domain expert to validate the KBS design without a working prototype.

Analogous to rule-based systems, the initial prototype has to be incrementally expanded in consultation with the domain expert. Major steps in this process include expanding the frame hierarchy by adding new classes and instances of domain entities,

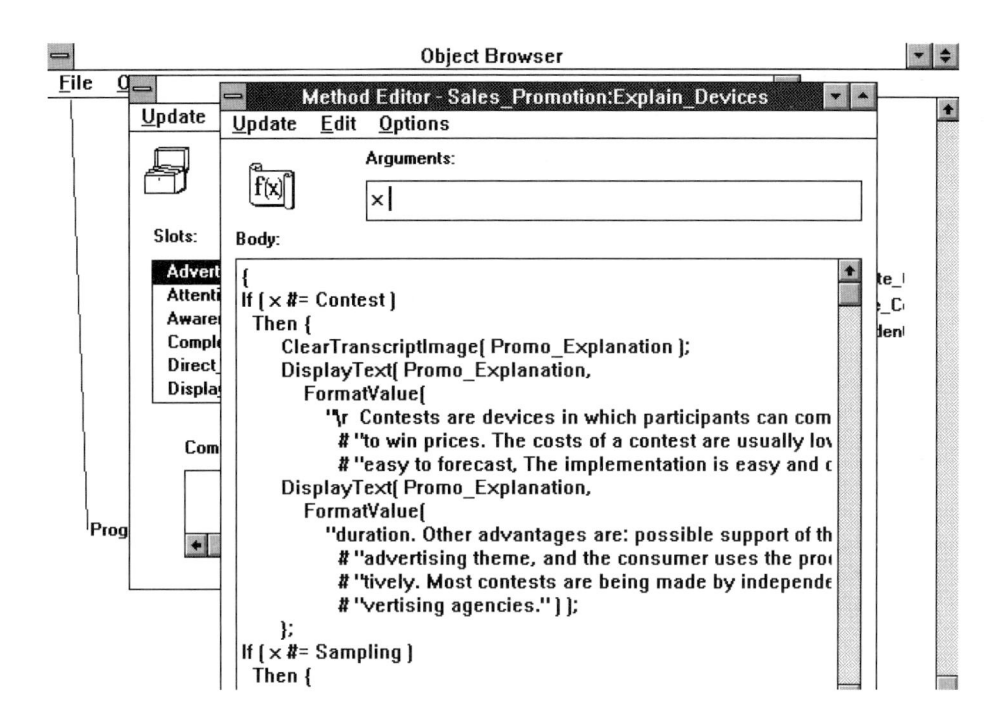

**Figure 4.9** Partial structure of the method Explain_Devices in the object Sales_Promotion

completing the structure and behavior definitions of objects in the frame hierarchy, and creating an initial user-interface. Figure 4.10 depicts an expanded version of a part of the frame hierarchy for the prototype of Figure 4.6. Note how the children of the object 'brands' have been expanded to include many additional sub-classes and instances. Though not shown in Figure 4.10, a similar expansion has occurred for other branches of the frame hierarchy of Figure 4.6 during the incremental evolution. A comparison of Figures 4.6 and 4.10 also yields insight into the reasons for emphasizing an initial global view of the frame hierarchy in stage 2 of the development process. Had the object for the class 'brands' not been defined at the appropriate level in the frame hierarchy, it would have been difficult to easily make the enhancements shown in Figure 4.10. The definitions of the slots and methods for the various objects in the frame hierarchy are also made more complete during the incremental evolution.

As Brandframe evolves towards a complete system, it is important to start building an interface to facilitate interaction of the knowledge engineer and the expert with the KBS. Defining interface components as objects eases the process of building user-friendly interfaces rapidly. For example, Figure 4.11 depicts the interface used to ask the user to rank (on a scale of -3 to 3) the perceptual attributes of a certain beer brand ('Grolsch'). There are many different objects on this screen: sliding scales specifying the user's ranking of the perceptual attributes, text buttons giving the qualitative value of the overall perceptual

## 110 Creating knowledge-based systems

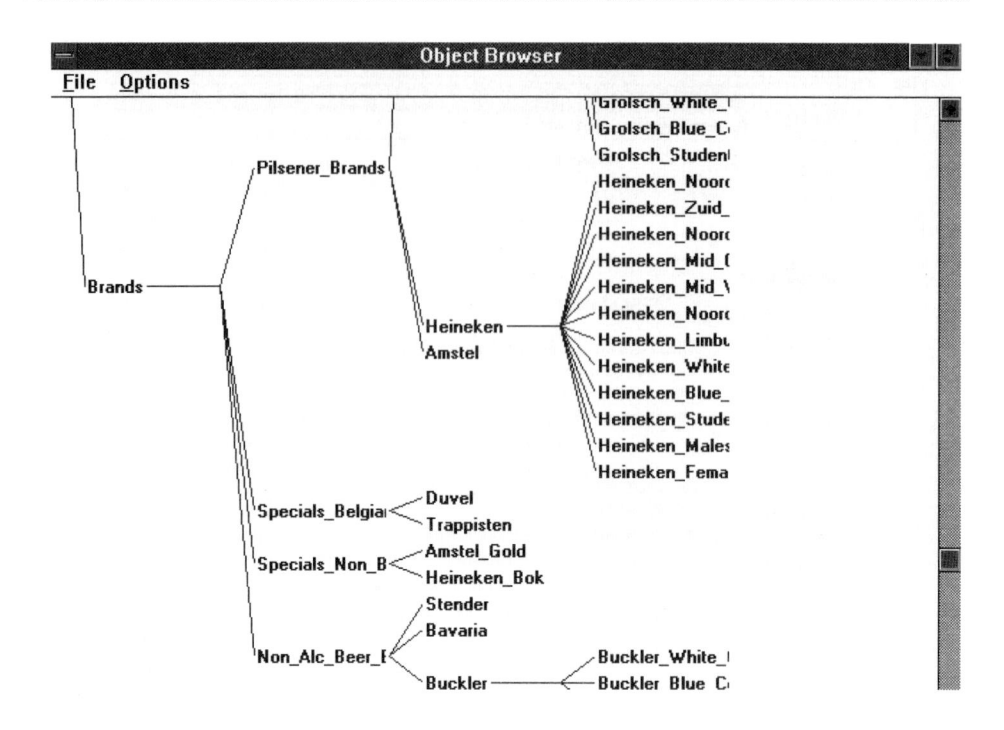

**Figure 4.10** Partial frame hierarchy of Brandframe after a few iterations of incremental evolution (compare with the frame hierarchy shown in Figure 4.6)

score, an analog meter giving the value of the overall perceptual score, and a 'finished' button at the bottom (to be clicked after finishing the assignment of ranks to the perceptual attributes). Like other objects in the system (such as 'brands' and 'sales_promotion'), each of these interface objects have special attributes (slots such as 'X_location', 'size', and so on), and behaviors (actions to be taken under specific conditions). For example, if the user moves the bar of any sliding scale (object) with a mouse, appropriate methods defined within that 'sliding_scale' object define what actions are to be taken. In this case, the actions include updating the numerical value below the bar to reflect the new value of the sliding scale, sending a message to the object representing the analog meter for computing the new value of the overall perceptual score (which is reflected immediately), and sending a message to the text buttons which are updated to reflect the new perceptual score.

Of course, other actions (such as posting a message to the user) could have been defined in the above sequence of actions, but the choice of what to include is dependent on the problem, and the desired interface characteristics. Most KBS shell tools (such as Kappa) with facilities for building frame hierarchies provide default definitions for generic interface objects such as sliding scales, text buttons, and analog meters. This makes it possible to build fairly complex interfaces, such as that shown in Figure 4.11, with a series of mouse clicks, and minimal programming.

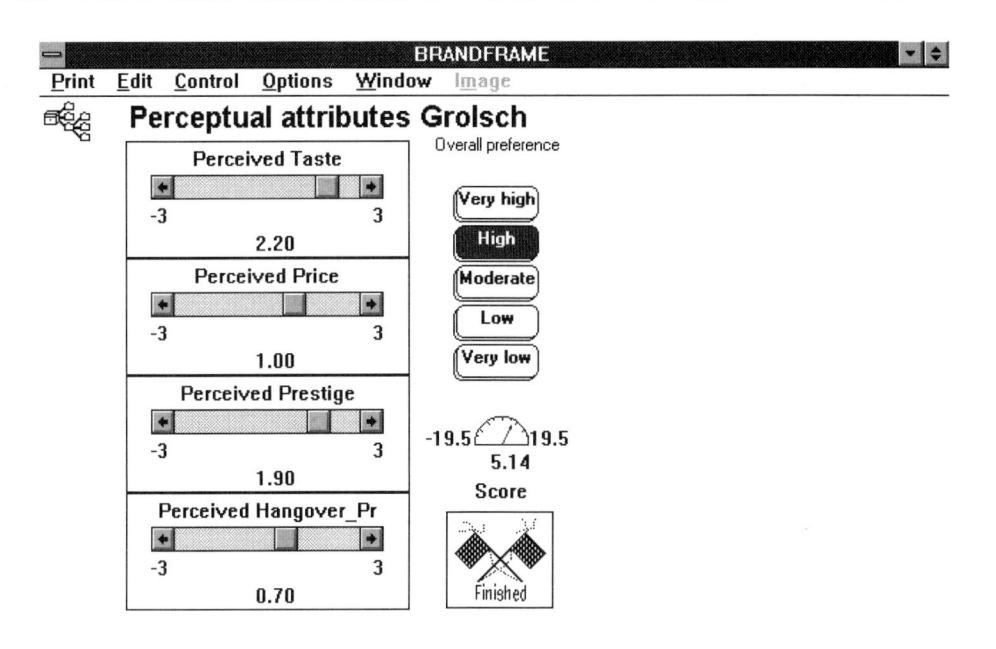

**Figure 4.11** A sample user interface for facilitating the input of data by the expert while incrementally expanding Brandframe

## Customization

The primary concerns of this phase are customizing the user-interface, ensuring that the frame hierarchy and object definitions are complete and accurate, and interfacing the KBS with external databases and other information systems. The following description focuses on the design of the user-interface, and the provision of links to external databases.

### Customizing the user-interface

Object-oriented programming enables the rapid development of complex (from a system perspective), but user-friendly interfaces. As the interface is a major determinant of acceptance of the KBS by the user, the knowledge engineer has to carefully consider the following issues:

● user expectations — what do users expect from the system in terms of functions performed, and information provided?

● user access — can the user easily access the available functions and information? Can the user switch between different access modes?

## 112 Creating knowledge-based systems

- system start, termination, and help procedures — can the user easily start, or terminate an interaction with the system? Is there an on-line help function? How easy is it to access the help function?
- interface dialogs — is the text (both questions and explanations) appropriately worded? Are there graphical icons to guide the user?

Figures 4.12, 4.13, and 4.14 depict selected user-interface screens from the completed version of Brandframe. Figure 4.12 depicts the opening screen of Brandframe which specifies clearly the different activity options available to the user. The user can select an activity by clicking the appropriate option. Note the graphical icons specified to the left of each activity name. They are used to guide the user in later stages of interaction.

By clicking on the icon titled 'analysis of a specific period' in Figure 4.12, the user can use Brandframe to analyze the market position of a brand during a specific period. Figure 4.13 depicts the results after such an analysis. Brandframe has ranked (after using its domain knowledge, and asking relevant questions to the user) the suitability of different marketing instruments to help improve the market position of the brand under consideration. The degree to which each instrument is desirable is depicted both graphically and numerically.

There is a 'home' button at the bottom of the screen. Clicking this button takes the user (brand manager) back to the opening screen (Figure 4.12). The graphic icon at the top-left corner of the screen reminds the user that the 'analysis' module of Brandframe is currently active. Of particular interest in Figure 4.13 is the bulletin window shown at the bottom-

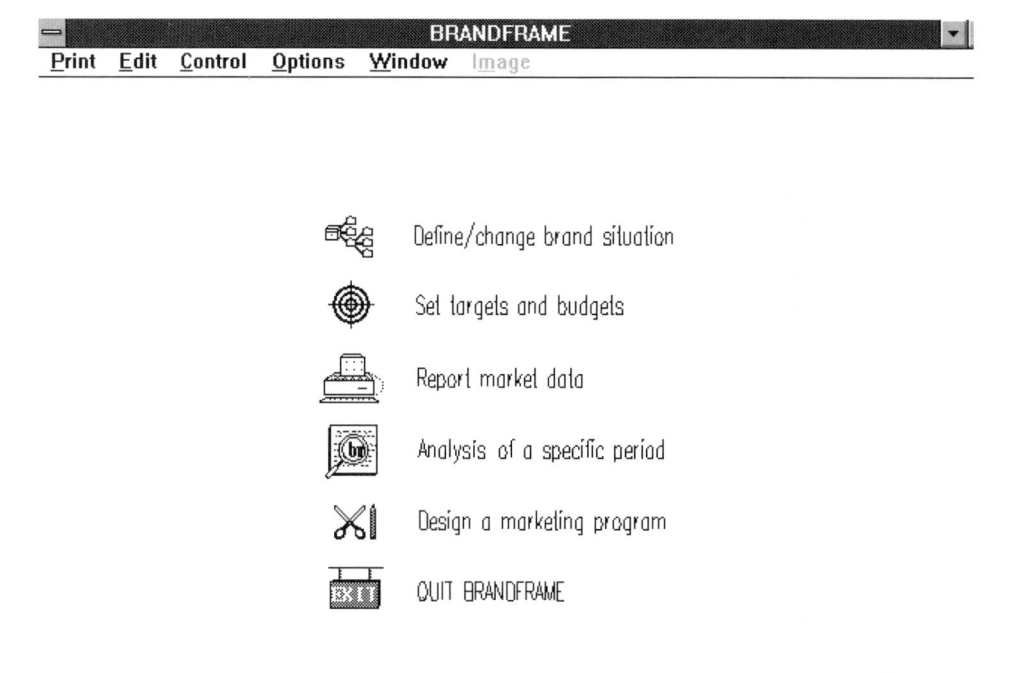

**Figure 4.12** Top-level interface screen for Brandframe

left. The bulletin provides a summary of the major issues arising in the current analysis session, and recommendations for action (augmented with justifications). Only a part of the bulletin is visible in Figure 4.13 (the rest can be read by scrolling upwards). Such a natural language record of the interaction/problem-solving process is valuable to the user who can take a print out of the bulletin, and either keep it for personal reference, or use it as evidence to justify decisions.

If the user asks for the design of a suitable advertising program (by clicking the button titled 'continue' in Figure 4.13), Brandframe starts the 'design a marketing program' activity, and designs an advertising program as shown partially in Figure 4.14. Note that this screen offers new possibilities to the user, such as the facility to ask for new estimations, or conduct 'what if' analyses, or view market data and models.

It should be clear from this description that effective user-interface design relies on a judicious use of graphics, text and icons, and a careful study of the process of interaction between the user with the system. As the end-user of a KBS is typically not an expert the interface should make aim to provide a comfortable and easy interaction environment, with emphases on the ease of experimentation (such as 'what if' analyses), and explanations of recommendations.

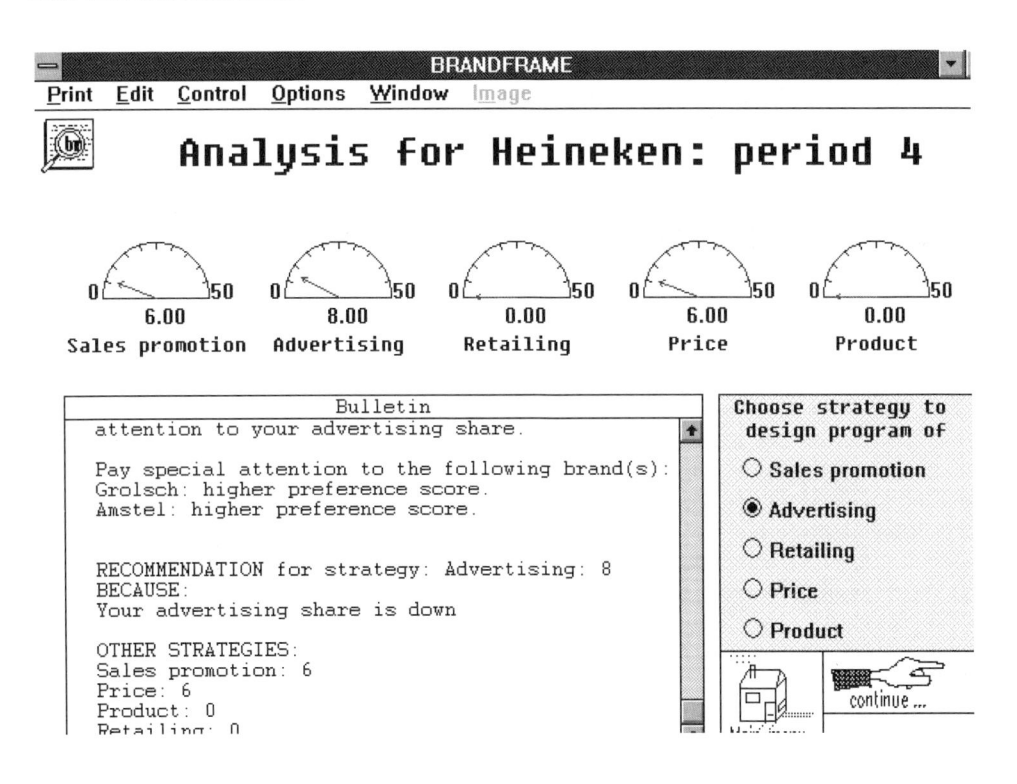

**Figure 4.13** An example of a customized user interface screen in Brandframe, for analyzing the market situation in a particular period. Note the use of graphics and text, and the natural language summary of the interaction appearing in the window titled Bulletin

## 114 Creating knowledge-based systems

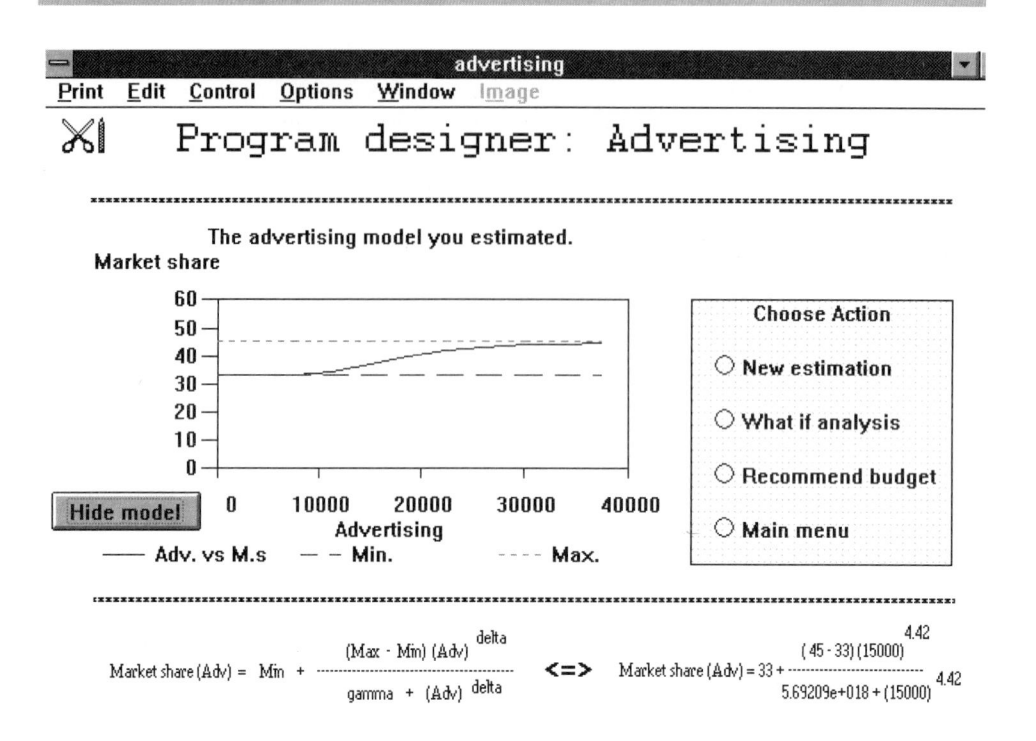

**Figure 4.14** An example of a customized user interface screen in Brandframe for designing a marketing program

### Interfaces to databases

There are two approaches to feeding data from external sources into the knowledge base of a KBS: direct, in which data is directly input into the KBS by the user or via an automated mechanism; and indirect, when the data is stored in a conventional database, and the knowledge base interfaces with the database to obtain the required data. Direct data input is preferred if one or more of the following conditions are satisfied: data amounts are small, data input frequency is low, data collection requires the user to answer questions, or the data needs manual interpretation before input.

Indirect data input mechanisms are essential for commercial KBSs for two important reasons. First, most organizations have large stores of data in conventional databases. These data are accessed by different computer applications. It is also useful to have a KBS share this data. This obviates the redundant act of entering data directly into the KBS, and reduces problems of data consistency and accuracy. Second, databases are optimized programs designed for storing and manipulating large volumes of data, and provide several useful data management features such as data security. Knowledge bases of KBSs allow greater flexibility in modelling and data representation, but are not designed for efficiently performing data management functions. When large amounts of data are

# Interfaces to databases 115

involved (such as market data in Brandframe), it is important to use conventional databases for efficiently storing and manipulating these data.

Most commercial KBS shell tools provide data bridges to link knowledge bases to external databases. While building the data bridge, the knowledge engineer has to define a mapping between the knowledge base object hierarchies and the database tables. Thus, if a slot in an object is linked to a particular database value, the data bridge automatically obtains the value from the database when it is required for inference in the KBS. If a new value is generated after inferencing, this new value is stored back in the appropriate database slot.

Figure 4.15 illustrates this process for a mapping between the slot 'total_sales' of the object 'Grolsch' and the table 'sales' in the marketing database. Similar data bridges are also available between most KBS shell tools and common spreadsheet packages. In general, both types of data input — direct and indirect, are required for building effective KBSs.

The nature of the link between databases and knowledge bases may change in the future, when object-oriented databases[10] become popular commercially. Object-oriented databases can potentially provide high level tools for data representation, similar to those currently available in knowledge bases.

This might cause the distinction between the terms 'knowledge base' and 'database' to blur. Commercial object-oriented databases are still in their infancy, and as yet do not focus on supporting reasoning strategies common in KBSs.

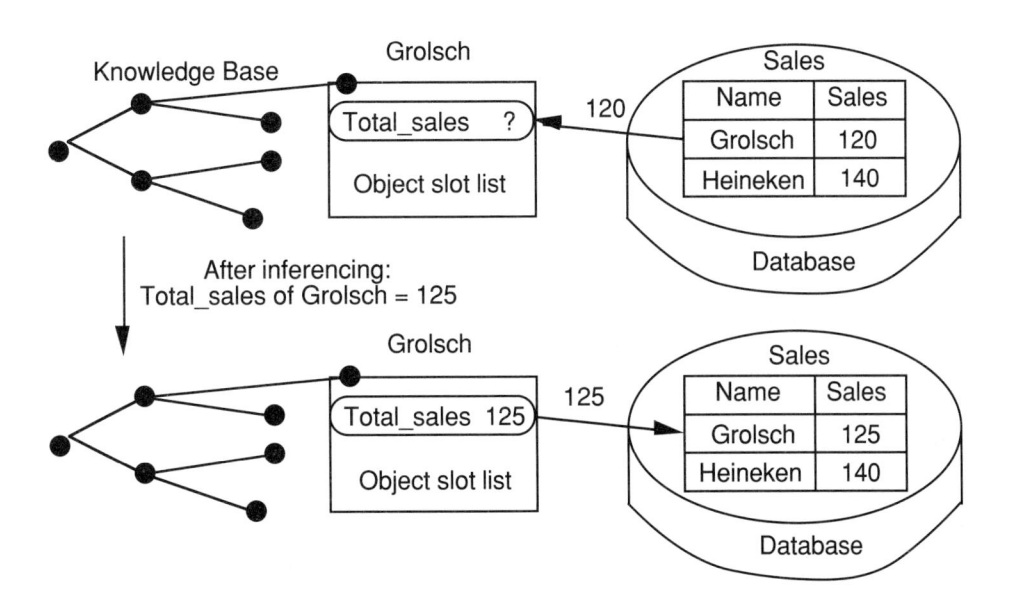

Figure 4.15 A databridge between a KBS and a database

## Tools for building knowledge-based systems

A variety of tools and products are available for building KBSs. Appendix 2 contains brief descriptions of selected commercial KBS products. These tools and products can be classified into the following five categories:

- enhanced conventional languages — many conventional programming languages such as C, Pascal, and Basic have been augmented with object-oriented concepts. This makes it possible to use an enhanced conventional language such as C++[11] to build KBSs

- conventional artificial intelligence languages — several programming languages have been designed for the specific purpose of developing artificial intelligence (AI) systems. The best examples of such languages are Prolog and Lisp[12]

- generic shell tools — a generic shell tool consists of an inference engine and an user-interface. Shell tools are commonly used for building KBSs (Figure 2.4). Many generic shell tools are available commercially. A good example of a commercial shell tool is Kappa

- application-specific shell tools — these tools are similar in structure to generic shell tools, but differ in being specially designed to facilitate the development of KBSs in a specific domain. Thus, they usually incorporate many domain-specific functions and models[13]. For example, Syncore, an application-specific shell tool for the financial domain (marketed by Syntelligence of Sunnyvale, California) contains many special built-in financial functions, such as easy methods to calculate cash flows, and net present values

- skeletal KBS products — these represent nearly-completed KBS applications, which only need to be customized for a particular problem before deployment. It is possible to take a skeletal KBS, and obtain a ready-to-run KBS by either changing a few parameters, or by making minimal modifications. Lysia Ltd. of London, UK, markets a series of skeletal KBSs for financial domains. Some examples of its skeletal KBSs are: the Client Portfolio Management System (CPS), and the Investment Risk Assessment Model (IRAM).

Each of the above approaches for building KBSs has its own advantages and disadvantages (as illustrated in Figure 4.16). Clearly, the application-specificity increases as one moves towards skeletal KBS products. Generic shell tools can be used to build KBSs in any domain. Application-specific shell tools are applicable for a specific domain, and skeletal KBSs can be used for specific problems only. Along with the increase in application-specificity, there is an increase in the speed and ease of development. As these tools provide more domain functionality, it becomes possible for the end-users, or the domain experts to take a more active role in the development and maintenance of the KBS. But there is a price to be paid for these benefits. This price is paid in terms of decreased flexibility, lower portability (across different hardware platforms), and inefficiency. Languages (both conventional and AI) provide the maximum flexibility, portability, and opportunities for optimizing specific aspects of the system's performance. But they also require professional programmers or knowledge engineers to shoulder the development efforts. Shell tools provide high-level structures for knowledge representation, inferencing and user-interface construction, but they sacrifice a certain degree of flexibility, efficiency, and portability in the process.

# Tools for building knowledge-based systems 117

```
               Application-specificity
              Ease and speed of development
          End-user/expert's involvement in development
          ──────────────────────────────────────────▶
```

| Enhanced conventional languages | AI programming languages | Generic shell tools | Application-specific shell tools | Skeletal KBS products |

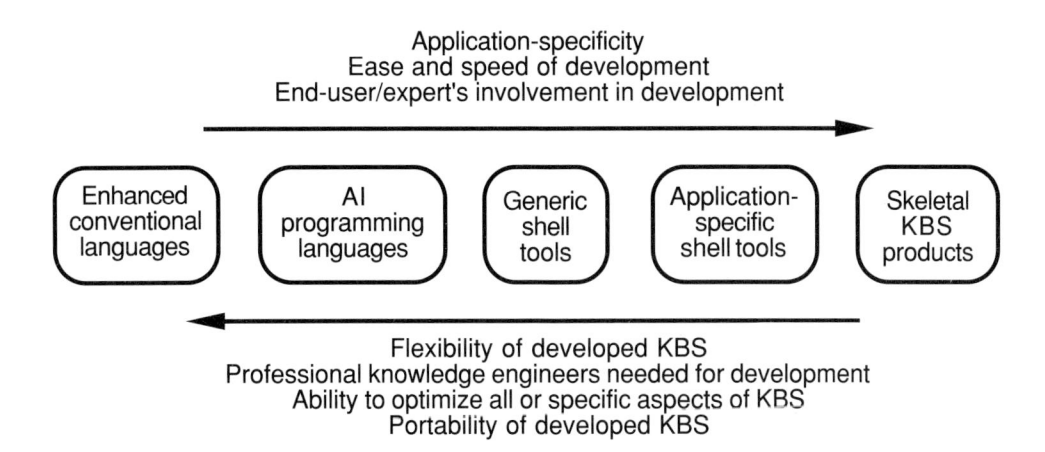

```
          ◀──────────────────────────────────────────
                 Flexibility of developed KBS
       Professional knowledge engineers needed for development
           Ability to optimize all or specific aspects of KBS
                    Portability of developed KBS
```

**Figure 4.16** Types of tools available for developing KBSs

Though generic shell tools provide the best compromise for building KBSs, there is an increasing emphasis on the development of application-specific shell tools or skeletal KBSs, which can be (relatively) easily used by the end-user or the domain expert to rapidly develop a KBS. Note that the lack of adequate flexibility is a frequent complaint with application-specific shell tools and skeletal KBSs. Thus, users should carefully evaluate the knowledge representation and reasoning structures contained in such tools, and the degree to which they can be modified, before committing to their use. For the development of KBSs which are large, or need to produce optimized results (such as in real-time systems), it is common to either develop the entire system using an programming language, or to use a generic shell tool in conjunction with a programming language. The most common choices for languages are object-oriented versions of C, Lisp, and Prolog. However, there is usually a large development cost associated with such systems.

## Types of shell tools

Generic (and application-specific) shell tools can be classified on the basis of the types of knowledge representation and inferencing techniques supported in the tool:

- simple rule-based shells — these shell tools support simple rules with backward or forward chaining. They usually provide data bridges to databases and spreadsheets, and sometimes even include rudimentary uncertainty schemes. An example of a simple rule-based shell is VPExpert (marketed by Paperback Software of Berkeley, California). These systems usually run on personal computers (PCs), and can be used to develop simple rule-based systems

- structured rule-based shells — these shell tools allow use of complex rules for the development of structured rule-based systems. Rules can be organized into groups and hierarchies, and contexts can be defined for rules and rule groups. Provisions exist for exercising control over the inference strategy, and for supporting reasoning under uncertainty. They also provide more sophisticated support facilities like graphic tracing and debugging facilities, and good interfaces with other databases and spreadsheets. An example of such a shell tool is the Guru system (marketed by MDBS Inc. of Lafayette, Indiana). These systems usually run on PCs, but can also run on workstations and mainframes

- hybrid shells — these shells integrate the power of object-oriented programming and structured rules. They offer the possibility to build frame hierarchies and rule groups, and allow the developer to exercise fine control over the inference strategy. They also provide sophisticated support facilities for graphics, and for interfacing with other information systems such as application programs and databases. Hybrid systems usually run on workstations and mainframes, but some also run on PCs. The KAPPA shell tool is a good example of a hybrid shell for the PC.

Figure 4.17 illustrates relative advantages and disadvantages of the different types of shells. For simple domains (where the number of rules is less than 500), simple rule-based shells are adequate. If the domain knowledge can be adequately represented by rules, but the number of rules is large, then structured rule-based systems are preferable. Due to the simplicity of rules as the basic knowledge representation structure, a higher degree of involvement of the end-user or the domain expert in the development process is possible with rule-based tools. Hybrid tools are best suited for complex domains. However, they require that professional programmers or knowledge engineers be used for the development process. Hybrid tools cost more than simple rule-based tools, and the entire development process is also usually more time consuming and expensive. Though rule-based tools are still used for many systems, the general trend is towards the use of hybrid shells. This has been accelerated by the introduction of hybrid shells for PCs, and the development of easy to use visual interfaces for programming these systems. The future will probably see a predominance of hybrid tools.

## Hardware platforms for shell tools

Till the early 1980s, most KBS shell tools ran on specialized AI workstations. AI workstations had special architectures, which were optimized to enable the rapid execution of AI languages (commonly Lisp). Two common problems with AI workstations were their high costs (each Lisp machine typically cost around $70,000 to $100,000 in the early 1980s), and their incompatibility with other computers. The scenario has changed rather dramatically today. The most common hardware platform today for shell tools and KBS applications is the PC. The rapidly increasing computing power of PCs has certainly had a major rôle in causing this transition. But this change has also occurred partly due to the crisis faced by the AI industry during the late 1980s, when customers revolted against the high costs and isolated architectures of AI workstations. After the PC, the next most common hardware platform for KBS shells and applications are generic engineering workstations (such as those manufactured by Sun and Hewlett Packard). Specialized AI workstations are today used only for research, or for very special applications. Though PCs and engineering workstations together form the overwhelming majority of hardware

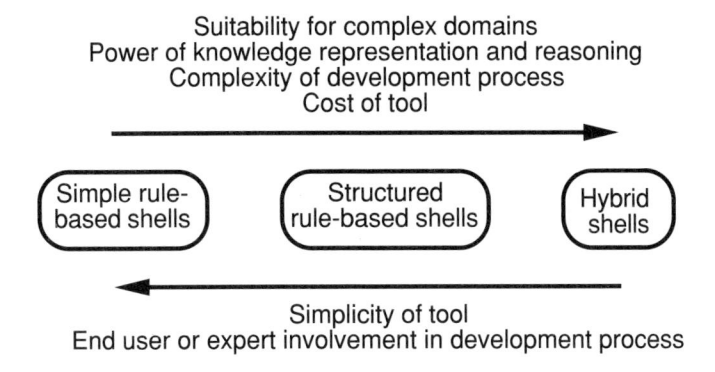

**Figure 4.17** Types of shell tools

platforms used for KBS shell tools, many shell tools are also appearing for mainframes. This is significant because the information technology architecture of most organizations today is still centralized, with conventional application programs running on large mainframe computers. For KBSs to be accepted by the information system departments of organizations, it is necessary to have them running in harmony with other computer programs on the mainframes.

## Guidelines for the selection of shell tools

Given the diversity of KBS shell tools available today in the commercial market, selecting the right tool can be a challenging task. Some guidelines for evaluating and selecting shell tools are described now.

● domain evaluation — the application domain has to be carefully studied to determine the nature of knowledge representation and inferencing techniques required for effective problem solution. Questions such as the following have to be answered: are rules adequate? If yes, is backward or forward chaining more natural for problem solution? If not, are object hierarchies necessary for adequately representing the domain knowledge? What kind of interfaces are required?

● tool evaluation — vendors of shell tools provide technical information about the capabilities of their respective products. The knowledge representation, inferencing, and interface development capabilities of tools have to be evaluated to see if they match the needs of the problem domain

● vendor characteristics — as the KBS market is evolving and relatively immature, particular attention has to be paid to the business stability of the vendor (many startups have gone bankrupt over the past few years). This factor is also important for evaluating the degree of support and maintenance of the shell tool in the long term

● other users — it is useful to learn about the experiences of other users with the KBS tool. If the tool is new, and there are few other users, then caution should be exercised.

## 120 Creating knowledge-based systems

One can have more confidence in a tool if it has been successfully and satisfactorily used by other users. Talking to other users also helps to sort though the marketing hype generated by vendors, and to arrive at a true assessment of the strengths and limitations of the tool

● development characteristics — most KBS development projects are constrained by the available money and time, and the skills of the development staff. This can also affect the choice of appropriate tools. For example, hybrid tools require more experienced programmers and longer development times, in contrast to application-specific shells

● deployment characteristics — the deployment characteristics of the domain can also impose restrictions on the choice of the tool. For example, enhanced conventional languages may be preferred if real-time performance in industrial settings is required. On the other hand, simple rule-based systems might be more appropriate if the end-user is to play a major rôle in the maintenance of the KBS.

### Commercial market for knowledge-based products

The market for commercial KBS products and tools is relatively new (a little more than a decade old). However, there are today many vendors selling a variety of KBS products. Appendix 2 contains a partial list of KBS vendors and a description of their major products. A recent survey[14] of nearly 100 KBS vendors and their products, determined the following characteristics for the commercial KBS product market:

● most KBS product vendors are small in size. The annual revenues of even the industry leaders range in the order of only a few tens of millions of dollars. Moreover, most vendors seemed to have KBS products as the core of their business

● there is a large number of start-up companies. This is a characteristic of the relative immaturity of the market. This is also a cause for some concern, as there are questions about the long-term survival of many start-ups. The industry is going through a phase of restructuring, and this can be expected to continue during the 1990s also

● the product bases of most KBS vendors are small. Nearly 45% of the companies surveyed marketed only one or two KBS products. Only about 10% of the surveyed companies are marketing 4 or more KBS products

● the most common KBS products being sold are generic shell tools (which constituted nearly 50% of the surveyed products). However the number of application-specific shells and skeletal KBSs are increasing (11% and 17% respectively, in the survey)

● most companies are technology focused, and emphasize the technical capabilities ('truly hybrid', 'really graphic', 'powerful user-friendly interfaces', and so on) of their products in their marketing campaigns. Few seem to have a true customer focus in their marketing and development efforts

● the most common hardware platform being offered is the PC (35% and 13% of the sample supported the IBM PC and the Macintosh platforms respectively), which is closely followed by generic engineering workstations (27% of the sample)

● KBS products exist within a wide price range, with costs ranging from $50 for the cheapest system (simple PC shells), to well over $100,000 for the most expensive products (usually skeletal products). There is also a marked increase in the sophistication and power of cheap PC-based KBS products

● though some industry leaders (such as Intellicorp of Palo Alto, California) are still product-oriented, many companies are moving towards emphasizing services. Services are often a major source of revenue and profits for these companies

● the market is characterized by fierce competition and weak product differentiation (many products offer similar technical capabilities).

Though there is significant diversity in the number and types of vendors, and their associated products, there is a distinct shift towards sophisticated, low-cost shells for PC platforms which are integrated with other information system programs (such as databases and spreadsheet packages).

While it's difficult to accurately estimate size of the worldwide KBS market (estimates range from $1 to 2 billions[15]), it is still a small percentage of the global software market (which is estimated to be more than $50 billions). Two kinds of growths can be identified for the KBS product market during the coming years, direct growth and diffusion growth. Direct growth refers to the gradual growth in the worldwide market for KBS products and services, which is estimated to reach a value of more than $10 billions by the mid 1990s[16]. Diffusion growth will result from the increasing use of KBS technology in other software products, such as in databases (see following section). Though the latter growth is difficult to measure and value, it will have a major impact on design and use of software at large.

Comparing across countries, the USA is widely seen as being the leader in both the production of leading-edge KBS products, and in their application. Estimates by consulting companies[17] rate the KBS market in the USA to be more than twice the size of the corresponding market in Europe. Japan seems to be lagging behind at present in this area, although it has recently invested (and is currently investing) significantly in KBS technology. The effects of these investments may be felt during the 1990s.

Comparing across industry sectors, the dominant users of KBS technology have been[18] manufacturing, financial services, and defense. All these three sectors are information-intensive, and it is not surprising that they have invested relatively heavily in KBS technology. There are some minor variations across different countries. The USA has invested most in defense and manufacturing, while other countries such as Germany and Japan have invested relatively more in manufacturing and financial services.

## The database and knowledge-based product markets

A development which can potentially have important consequences for the entire KBS product market, is the trend of major database suppliers attempting to incorporate many features of KBSs (such as support for rules, and inferencing strategies) into enhanced versions of conventional databases. The incorporation of selected features of the technology of KBSs can be seen as a natural expansion of the capabilities of products offered by database suppliers. However, this is a cause for concern for the KBS product market because the database industry is larger, and more mature. Major database suppliers are much bigger than the KBS industry leaders, and have more well-developed customer bases. Most organizations have established databases, and it may be easier for them to accept enhanced (more 'intelligent') versions of databases from database vendors, rather than accept isolated versions of KBS products from KBS vendors.

An example of such a trend is Software AG, the largest European software company, which markets the Adabas (relational) database package for large IBM mainframes. Since 1990, Software AG has been selling 'Natural Expert', a KBS addition to Adabas, which is completely integrated with Adabas, and other programs running on Adabas. Software AG is successfully targeting its large customer base of major banks, financial institutions, and industries to buy Natural Expert, and use its KBS features (such as inferencing strategies) for the development of KBSs which are wholly integrated with other Adabas application programs.

This encroachment of database vendors on the KBS product market will intensify in the future if object-oriented databases become commercially successful. This is because object-oriented databases can offer most of the features of shell tools relatively easily. Thus, there might be a consolidation and restructuring of the KBS and database markets in the coming decade.

## Summary

This chapter has focused on technological issues in the process of creating rule-based and hybrid KBSs. Important considerations discussed in the above sections are mentioned below:

● Simple rule-based KBSs use only rules (simple or complex). Hybrid KBSs integrate frame hierarchies and rules.

● Rules are useful if the domain is simple or heuristics are important for problem solution or end-user involvement (in the development process) is desirable or quick and cheap development (of the KBS) is necessary.

● There are five important phases in the process of creating rule-based systems: problem description, problem decomposition, initial prototyping, incremental evolution, and customization. The problem description phase attempts to study the problem to determine the suitability of a rule-based solution. Problem decomposition reduces complexity by decomposing the problem into sub-problems, and prototyping facilitates the incremental evolution of the system. The major goals of the customization phase are to increase user satisfaction and system efficiency.

● Structured rule-based systems offer additional features (such as rule contexts) which increase system efficiency and aid the comprehension and maintainability of rules in the knowledge base.

● Hybrid KBSs combine the benefits of rules and frame hierarchies. Thus, they are a popular choice for KBS applications. A large majority of commercial KBSs are hybrid in nature.

● The five phases in the development of hybrid KBSs are: problem description, frame hierarchy identification, structure and behavior identification, prototyping and incremental evolution, and customization. While similar in some respects to the development of rule-based systems, it is important to identify major classes of domain objects and their properties and interrelationships early in the development of hybrid systems. Both the frame hierarchy and the structures and behaviors of individual objects are expanded during the incremental evolution of the system.

● The design of an effective user-interface requires judicious use of graphics, text, and icons, and a careful study of the process of interaction between the user and the KBS. Proper interface design is very important for developing a successful KBS.

● Data can be input either directly or indirectly to the knowledge base of a KBS. Indirect data input mechanisms (data bridges) are necessary for linking KBSs to organizational databases.

● Different types of tools can be used for building KBSs — enhanced conventional languages, artificial intelligence languages, generic shell tools, application-specific shell tools, and skeletal KBS products. Though generic shell tools provide the best compromise of features for building general KBSs, there is a trend towards an increased use of application-specific shell tools and skeletal products.

● While specialized hardware platforms for KBS tools were common in the early 1980s, personal computers (both IBM and Macintosh) are adequate for most KBS tools today.

# 124 Creating knowledge-based systems

- Several factors such as characteristics of the domain, tool, vendor, and the deployment environment affect the evaluation and selection of shell tools.
- The market of commercial KBS product vendors is fragmented and immature, and is characterized by fierce competition and weak product differentiation. Significant consolidation in the industry can be expected during the coming decade. Of particular interest is the gradual merger of the database and KBS markets caused by major database vendors gradually incorporating different knowledge-based technologies within their database products.
- The KBS market in the USA is more than twice the size of the corresponding market in Europe. The dominant industry sectors using KBS products are manufacturing, financial services, and defense.

This chapter has covered only one — the technological — dimension to the process of creating KBSs. Other important perspectives — the strategic and organizational impacts of KBS applications — are detailed in the next chapter.

## Bibliography and suggested readings

A good general reference for details on the process of creating knowledge-based systems is the book by Harmon and Sawyer (Harmon & Sawyer 90). Details on creating rule-based systems are given in references (Hayes-Roth 85), (Holsapple & Whinston 86), (Mockler 89), and (Hicks & Lee 89). The book by Mockler is particularly noteworthy because it includes detailed dependency diagrams for rule-based systems in many different domains. More technical descriptions of the process of developing rule-based systems can be found in references (Hayes-Roth et al 83) and (Cooper & Wogrin 88). Details on object-oriented programming concepts, and hybrid approaches to KBS development are available in references (Kunz et al 84), (Fikes & Kehler 85), (Cox 86), and (Rich & Knight 91). The user and reference manuals of commercial hybrid shell tools (such as Kappa, marketed by Intellicorp, Palo Alto, CA) are also useful sources for practical details related to the implementation of hybrid KBSs. A good general reference devoted to KBS products is the book by Harmon, Maus and Morrissey (Harmon et al 88). Many of the other references mentioned above also contain descriptions of selected KBS products. Market information about KBS products can be found in the reports of consulting companies (such as Ovum Consultants, London, UK), and industry newsletters (such as Expert Systems Strategies (Harmon, Ed), and AI Trends (Newquist, Ed)).

Cooper, T.A., and N. Wogrin, *Rule-Based Programming with OPS5*, Morgan Kaufmann, Palo Alto, CA, 1988.

Cox, B.J., *Object-oriented Programming*, Addison-Wesley, 1986.

Fikes, R., and T. Kehler, *The Role of Frame-Based Representation in Reasoning*, Communications of the ACM, Vol. 28, No. 9, pp. 904–920, Sep. 1985.

Harmon, P., (Ed.), *Expert Systems Strategies*, (Newsletter), Cutter Information Publications, Arlington, MA.

Harmon, P., and B. Sawyer, *Creating Expert Systems*, John Wiley, 1990.

Harmon, P., R. Maus, and W. Morrissey, *Expert Systems: Tools and Applications*, John Wiley, 1988.

Hayes-Roth, F., D.A. Waterman, and D.B. Lenat, (Eds.), *Building Expert Systems*, Addison-Wesley, Reading, MA, 1983.

Hayes-Roth, F., *Rule-Based Systems*, Communications of the ACM, Vol. 28, No. 9, pp. 921–932, Sep. 1985.

Hicks, R., and R. Lee, *VP-Expert for Business Applications*, Holden-Day Inc., Oakland, CA, 1989.

Holsapple, C.W., and A.B. Whinston, *Manager's Guide to Expert Systems using GURU*, Dow Jones-Irwin, Homewood, IL, 1986.

Kunz, J.C., T.P. Kehler, and M.D. Williams, *Applications Development Using a Hybrid AI Development System*, AI Magazine, 5(3), 1984.

Mockler, R.J., *Knowledge-Based Systems for Management Decisions*, Prentice-Hall, 1989.

Newquist, H.P., (Ed.), *AI Trends*, (Newsletter), D.M. Data, Scottsdale, AZ.

Rich, E., and K. Knight, *Artificial Intelligence*, Mc-Graw Hill, 1991.

## Notes

1 Each frame in a frame hierarchy represents a class, or a sub-class, or an instance in the domain, and is modelled as an object. As in Chapter 3, we use the term 'object' and 'frame' (in the context of a frame hierarchy) synonymously.

2 Leonard-Barton, D., *The Case for Integrative Innovation: An Expert System at Digital*, Sloan Management Review, pp. 7–19, Fall 1987.

3 This problem is similar to that faced by users while querying library databases. Chapter 6 describes how multiple queries are necessary (with conventional 'dumb' database query languages) to retrieve the correct set of books related to a certain concept or topic.

4 For the sake of this example, we will assume that MBA students represent the major clients for using this system.

5 Recall the possibility of using 'trial runs' for knowledge acquisition (Figure 2.7).

6 A good description of issues in the development of structured rule-based systems with contexts can be found in: Harmon, P. & B. Sawyer, *Creating Expert Systems*, Chapter 10, John Wiley, 1990.

7 The Brandframe system has been jointly developed by the author with Prof. B. Wierenga and A. Dalebout of Erasmus University, Rotterdam. The Brandframe KBS is implemented using the hybrid shell tool, Kappa (marketed by Intellicorp, Palo Alto, CA). A detailed description of Brandframe is available in: Dutta, S., Wierenga, B., and Dalebout, A., *An Integrated Perspective on Designing Management Support Systems*, INSEAD working paper number 93/15/TM, 1993.

8 Only some of the slots and methods are visible in Figures 4.7 and 4.8 (the rest can be accessed by scrolling down the appropriate windows).

9 Recall from Chapter 3 that inherited slots and methods are marked by an asterisk (*) to the left within Kappa.

10 Verity, J., and E.I. Schwartz, *Software Made Simple*, Businessweek, pp. 58–63, Sep 30, 1991.

11 Stroustrup, B., *The C++ Programming Language*, Addison-Wesley, Reading, MA, 1986.

12 Prolog was described in Chapter 3. There are several good references on Lisp, such as: Steele, G.L., Jr., *Common LISP: The Language*, Digital Press, Billerica, MA, 1984.

13 Some researchers describe these application-specific shell tools as integrating concepts from knowledge-based systems and decision support systems. Thus these tools can be used to build 'intelligent decision support systems'. A good reference on these topics is: Klein, M. and L.B. Methlie, *Expert Systems: A Decision Support Approach*, Addison Wesley, 1990.

14 Grunspan, M., *Expert Systems - A Market Survey*, Project report, INSEAD, October 1991.

15 Schwartz, E.I., and J.B. Treece, *Smart Programs go to Work*, pp. 50, Businessweek, March 2, 1992. This article states that, according to International Data Corp., $200 million of artificial intelligence software was sold in North America in 1991. However this figure

does not include the value of related services and consulting fees, which is estimated to be more than $500 million.

16 Based on data in a management report on expert systems prepared by Ovum Consultants, London.

17 Based on data in a management report on expert systems prepared by Ovum Consultants, London.

18 Based on data in a management report on expert systems prepared by Ovum Consultants, London.

# Chapter 5
# *Strategic and organizational issues in knowledge processing*

Chapter 2 explores the definition of the term 'knowledge' from a predominantly individual or task perspective. To effectively understand and evaluate the rôle of knowledge-based systems (KBSs) in organizations, it is important to understand the meaning of the term 'knowledge' and the implications of 'managing knowledge' in the more general organizational context.

Knowledge exists in many different forms in organizations. Some of them are tangible, while others are more subtle and intangible in nature. Examples of tangible knowledge assets are patents, company databases (of customers, clients, and so on), written procedures ('how to' knowledge about certain tasks), books, manuals, software programs, and research and development outputs such as published papers, and new products. Intangible knowledge assets of a company include company 'culture', the experience and expertise of employees, informal associations, and synergies from group interactions.

Managing knowledge is an challenging task because it is hard to identify, and even more difficult to value and deploy to give the organization a competitive edge in the market place. While many tangible knowledge assets such as software programs can be identified easily, it is often difficult to value them, and thus they rarely make it into the company's balance sheets. It is a more difficult task to identify the intangible knowledge assets of an organization, and most executives do not understand how to value them (if at all they are identifiable). Even the identification and valuation of the most fundamental unit of knowledge assets, the individual knowledge worker, is poorly understood and rarely accounted for. For instance, few companies know how to compute the value of their research laboratories. Moreover, knowledge after identification has to be shared so that the organization is able to translate it into a competitive advantage. Isolated islands of knowledge are not very useful to an organization. A company derives true benefits from its knowledge assets only when they are leveraged via a knowledge network, and diffused throughout the organization (and its partners, if appropriate). Complicating the scenario further is the fact that knowledge is never static; it is continuously changing and evolving. Tracking and managing a dynamic asset is always harder.

Partly due to the above reasons, traditional management methods have largely ignored knowledge assets. Standard accounting practices are poor at capturing intellectual assets, and except for a few exceptions (such as book publishers), the market does not ascribe a value to knowledge assets. However, companies are today realizing the importance of the competitive differentials achievable by effectively managing knowledge assets. In a recent cover story on this subject, Fortune magazine[1] stated this concisely as:

> Intellectual capital is becoming corporate America's most valuable asset and can be its sharpest competitive weapon. The challenge is to find what you have - and use it.

## Levels of organizational knowledge

An organization's knowledge assets can be analyzed in different ways. A useful classification is along the following four categories:

● individual — the individual knowledge worker is the fundamental unit for knowledge creation, storage, and use within an organization

● group — networks, both formal and informal, are usually an intangible, but important knowledge asset within a company. Groups of individuals often develop a cumulative expertise that is more than the sum of their individual skills, and can produce results of true competitive significance

● organizational — in a sense, the entire organization with its own peculiar structures, division of functions, and processes can be viewed as embodying the result of a certain cumulative body of knowledge. The organization is designed to facilitate and direct knowledge flows, and evolves with changing knowledge needs

● knowledge links — every company develops specific links with other firms (such as suppliers and customers) to exchange knowledge. Analogous to groups, knowledge links between groups of organizations can lead to the development of expertise and knowledge not possible with isolated organizations.

## Managing knowledge in organizations

Figure 5.1 reflects essential components of the process of strategically managing knowledge. A company has to identify its knowledge assets, leverage them by forming a knowledge network, and learn from experience (to adapt to the dynamic nature of knowledge). All of this has to be done, of course, within the context of the strategic objectives of the organization.

# Managing knowledge in organizations 131

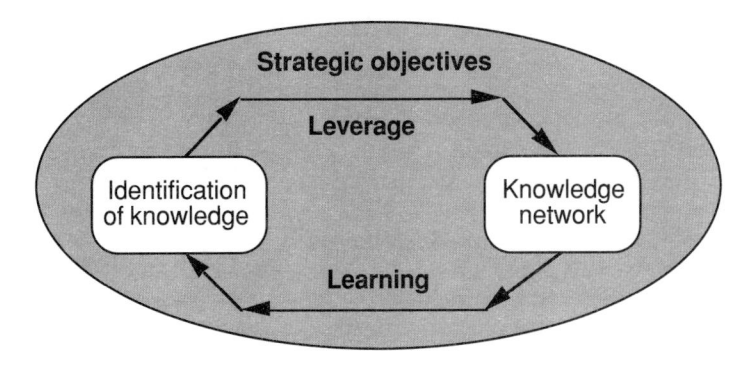

**Figure 5.1** Strategic management of knowledge

Identification of specific assets at each of the levels of knowledge mentioned earlier is a challenging task for any organization. Individual expertise is not restricted to a company's professionals, or its top management. Often the best experts are found low down in the ranks of an organization[2]. It is also sometimes difficult to distinguish between a true expert (a knowledge asset), and someone who just has better access to certain information based on the power of his/her position.

Locating group knowledge assets is difficult because formal groups seldom mirror real intellectual assets. Rather, informal networks of individuals often tend to form the most effective knowledge assets. Similar identification problems are also experienced at the organizational and inter-organizational levels. Many organizations are unable to clearly identify their core competencies, and relate their special skills to their structures, functions, and knowledge needs. Only certain links across organizations are true knowledge links, and they can go unidentified if the company has not studied its own knowledge assets at the individual, group, and organizational levels.

Isolated knowledge is of little strategic benefit to an organization. The larger the extent to which knowledge is shared and disseminated within an organization, the higher the return on it. For example, most organizations are today making determined efforts to from groups of inter-disciplinary and cross-functional individuals in order to facilitate transfer and dissemination of knowledge (both within the company, and across cooperating partner organizations). This is helping them to design better products, reduce time to market, achieve a higher degree of customer satisfaction, and be more competitive on the whole.

Knowledge is inherently dynamic. To ensure long-term competitiveness in the market place, every organization has to be able to learn. The emphasis is on how closely an organization can track and adapt to the changing knowledge needs of its internal and external environment. The CEO of a leading company has correctly emphasized the importance of learning as[3]:

> ...the rate at which individuals and organizations learn may become the only sustainable competitive advantage.

## 132 Strategic and organizational issues

### Knowledge-based systems and the management of knowledge

KBSs have a direct impact on the management of knowledge within organizations. By its very definition and development process, a KBS aims to extract a piece of the organization's intellectual capital, and capture it in an automated or semi-automated system. Thus, development of a KBS results in creation of a tangible knowledge asset which can be distributed within the company.

The processes of knowledge acquisition and knowledge engineering (Chapter 2) aim to capture intangible organizational knowledge, and represent it in a KBS. The intangible knowledge targeted by a KBS can be about tasks, processes, or about tangible knowledge assets such as manuals and documents. While a conventional computer program can capture the information in a document or a manual, the additional advantage of a KBS lies in its ability to also store how the document or manual is interpreted by experts (i.e., capture the intangible knowledge associated with the use of the tangible knowledge asset). The degree of automation with KBSs can be either complete or partial, as shown in Figure 5.2. In the former case, the KBS captures the specific intangible knowledge asset in its entirety, and can be deployed as a complete or partial replacement for the intangible knowledge asset. However, such situations are rare. The latter situation in which the KBS only partially captures the intangible knowledge asset, is more common. Here the KBS is used to augment the intangible knowledge asset as an 'intelligent' assistant, or as an 'intelligent' interface.

Most commercially successful KBSs have captured (usually partially) the intangible knowledge associated with individuals (more often) and groups (less often). It is also possible for KBSs to capture knowledge at the organizational and knowledge link levels. A good example of this is Digital Equipment Corporation. Chapter 2 described Digital's XCON computer configuration KBS in some detail. The XCON system is a piece of a

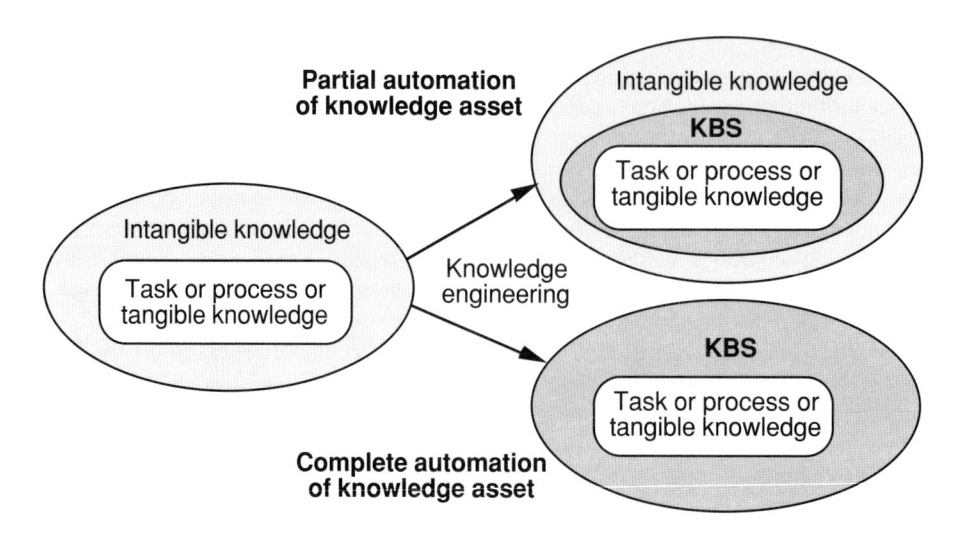

**Figure 5.2** Creation of a tangible knowledge asset using a KBS

# Knowledge-based systems and management 133

larger VAX-based knowledge network (Figure 5.3), which integrates and facilitates knowledge flow related to the sale of computers across several different functions (including sales, engineering, manufacturing, and customer service) within Digital. Major KBS components in Digital's VAX-based knowledge network are: XSEL (used to support field sales people in translating a customer's computing needs into computer orders which can then be configured by Digital), XCON (used to validate the technical correctness of customer orders and guide the assembly of these orders), CAN BUILD (used for inventory scheduling), MOS (used for manufacturing planning[4]), NDR (used to control the scheduling of trucks), XFL (used for diagramming a computer room floor layout for the proposed configuration), XNET (used for designing local area networks), and SIZER (used for sizing computing resources according to customer needs). These KBSs together capture important aspects of the organizational knowledge of Digital in the domains of sales, manufacturing, and service of its computer products. By facilitating the sharing of knowledge common to different functions, these KBSs form an effective knowledge network at the organizational and knowledge link levels within Digital.

KBSs are tangible knowledge assets, and can be distributed widely within an organization. Even inexperienced users can improve their performances significantly with the help of a KBS. This is depicted in Figure 5.4. The larger the difference between the performance levels of experts and inexperienced employees, the more noticeable are the improvements in performances with the use of KBSs. Such applications of KBSs are particularly suited to geographically distributed tasks, such as remote diagnoses and repairs of equipment, and credit analyses at different locations. KBSs offer a practical and easy solution for companies to apply their critical knowledge at many different sites simultaneously.

KBSs also have an important impact on the rate of learning within an organization. With the help of a KBS, an inexperienced employee can reach a higher level of perfor-

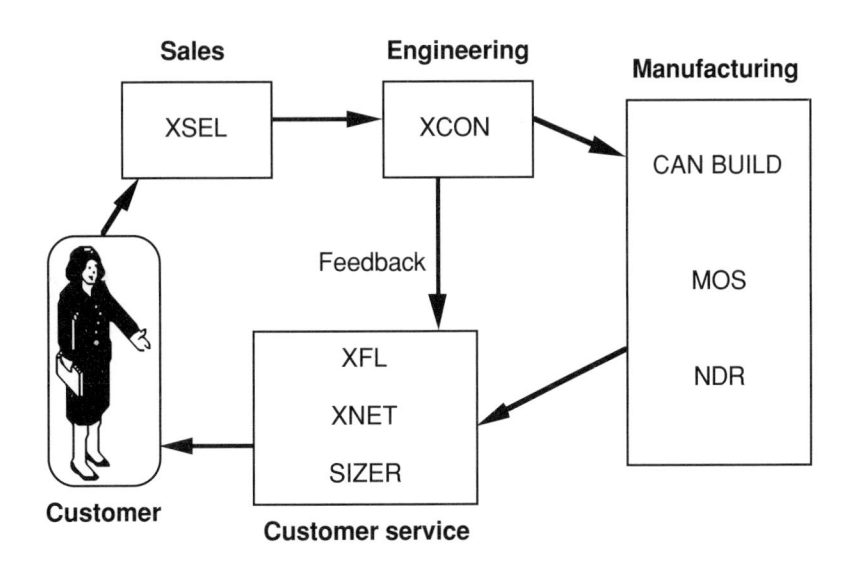

Figure 5.3 Digital's VAX-based knowledge network

## 134 Strategic and organizational issues

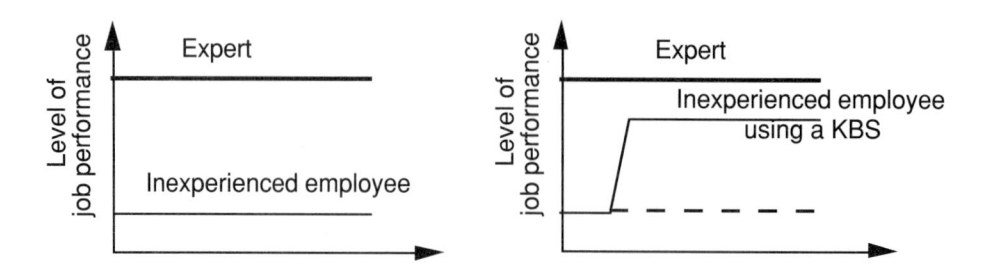

**Figure 5.4** Improvement in performance with a KBS

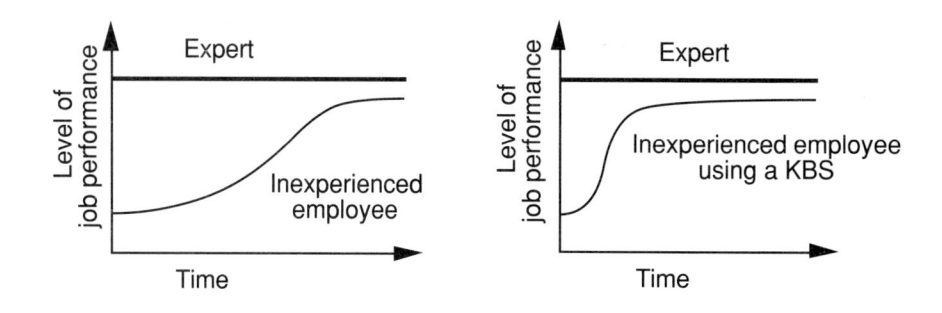

**Figure 5.5** Improvement in rate of learning with a KBS

mance faster. The slower the normal rate of learning, the larger the impact of the KBS in speeding up the learning process. This is shown in Figure 5.5. KBSs can also help in enhancing the learning rate of the entire organization. As an example, consider the ExperTax KBS of Coopers and Lybrand. ExperTax assists junior accountants in the tax auditing and planning tasks. A central office in Coopers and Lybrand is responsible for maintaining all changes in the knowledge base of ExperTax. Whenever tax laws change (and they do so frequently), the central office in Coopers and Lybrand makes the appropriate changes in ExperTax's knowledge base, and the revised version is shipped out to the hundreds of Coopers and Lybrand field staff all over the USA. As all field staff use the same ExperTax KBS, the changes in tax laws are immediately reflected in their task performances. Thus Coopers and Lybrand is able to propagate the effects of changes in the knowledge contents of critical tasks rapidly. When the US tax laws were changed radically in 1986, Coopers and Lybrand was able to incorporate and implement these changes nationwide within 6 weeks[5], and with minimal additional training. A short turnaround time in implementing such changes in a knowledge-intensive company can lead to major competitive advantages in the marketplace.

## Applications of knowledge-based systems in organizations

The applications of KBSs in industry and business can be analyzed from the four different perspectives of task, user, system, and activity. The task perspective classifies the different types of tasks to which KBSs have been applied. The user dimension describes the relation between deployed KBSs and the end-users. The degree of integration of KBSs with the information systems architecture of organizations is the focus of the system perspective. Finally, the activity dimension analyzes the application of KBSs in the context of the firm's activities and business processes.

### The task perspective

From the task perspective, KBSs have been used for the following types of applications (Figure 5.6):

● monitoring — these are problems which require a constant or periodic monitoring of a certain set of parameters, and the emission of a warning signal when certain aberrations occur. In complex systems such as chemical refineries, nuclear plants, and intensive-care medical units, there are hundreds of different interacting parameters, and monitoring for aberrations (which, if undetected, can cause very expensive, or life-threatening problems) is a knowledge-intensive, but often a boring and repetitive task. KBSs can be used to perform such tasks effectively and reliably

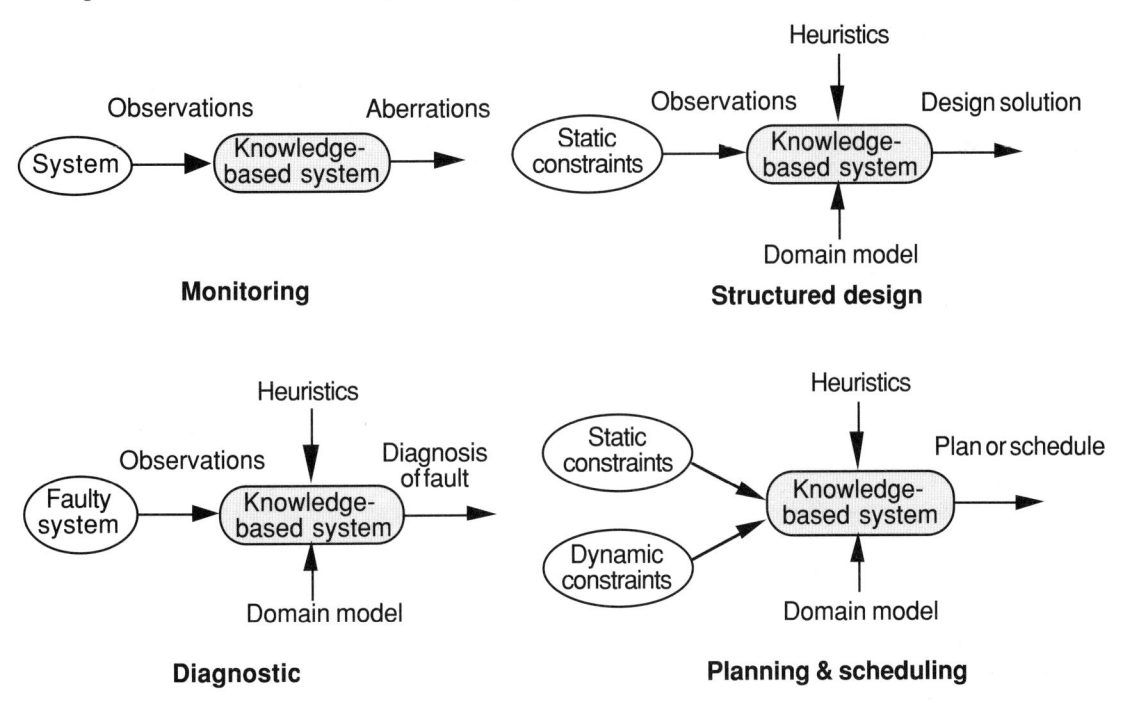

Figure 5.6 Different KBS applications along the task dimension

## 136 Strategic and organizational issues

- diagnostic — the diagnostic task consists of choosing one (or more) of a limited set of options or recommendations, given data about some problem or aberrations. Common examples are diagnoses of doctors about patients, auto mechanics about defective cars, and financial analysts about merger strategies. Effective diagnosis relies on a combination of domain models (knowledge about the human body, the structure and functions of auto parts, and so on), and heuristic knowledge (relating symptoms to certain diseases, auto breakdown conditions to faulty parts, and so on). KBSs can solve many diagnostic problems effectively

- structured design — KBSs are useful for structured design problems, in which certain actions have to be designed in the context of a set of well-specified (though possibly complex) static constraints. The task of configuring computers (as performed by XCON) is a good example of a structured design problem. KBSs are not very useful if the design constraints are not well-structured, as in creative art design. Both domain models (which provide the structure), and heuristics (which help in shortening the design process) are required for solving structured design problems. An important difference between diagnostic and structured design problems is that the list of possible outcomes (designs) are less constrained in the latter task. Also, knowledge about domain models is more dominant in KBSs used for structured design tasks, as compared to those used for diagnostic problems

- planning and scheduling — planning and scheduling problems are similar to structured design problems, except that they also include the additional complexities of a temporal dimension (all plans and schedules are executed over a period of time); multiple, temporally separated, and possibly interacting goals (each temporally separated action can be seen as achieving a goal); dynamic constraints (resource constraints typically change over time); and real-time changes (often caused by unanticipated situations). Thus, both static and dynamic constraints are present in planning and scheduling problems. Well-defined domain models and extensive heuristic knowledge are required for solving such problems. Thus, they are often the most complex KBS applications. There are several applications of KBSs in industry for planning and scheduling tasks. For example, many KBSs have been designed for planning factory flows and schedules, because they are good at including heuristics to accommodate unanticipated changes in real-time.

### User support types
From the perspective of user support, KBSs have been used for several types of applications (Figure 5.7). Note that the end-users of KBSs are typically different from the expert(s) helping to build them. Application types are:

- replacement — KBSs can be used to directly and completely replace a human worker. Though such applications are not very common, they are sometimes desirable e.g., for operations in hazardous situations, such as in radioactive environments, and in outer space. In most such applications, a KBS acts as the 'brain' for a robot, or some other mechanical device

- partial replacement — this is a special case of the previous situation in which a KBS partially replaces the end-user. Some proportion of the problems are passed through the KBS, and the rest are solved by the end-users. Care should be exercised in such applications because the performance of most KBSs, while better than the average end-user, is typically inferior to that of the expert

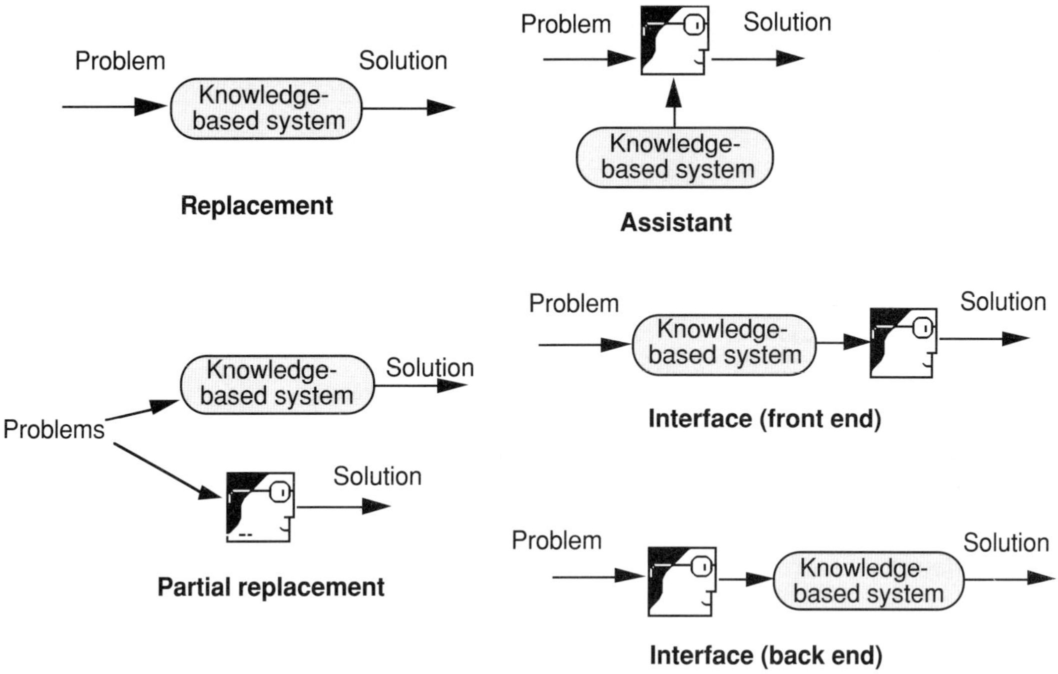

## Applications in organizations

**Figure 5.7** Different KBS applications along the user dimension

- assistant — here a KBS plays the rôle of an 'intelligent assistant' to the end-user. The end-user is in command all the time, but at times (at his/her discretion) asks for help/advice from the KBS. The KBS can also be seen as playing the rôle of a decision-support system in this scenario. The recommendation of the KBS is not binding in any way. The user can either reject, or modify, or ignore the recommendation of the KBS. This is the most common form of KBS applications from a end-user perspective

- interface — in such applications, a KBS is used to pre-process input data, or post-process the output produced by an user. In the former case, input data or problem descriptions are first analyzed by a KBS, and the output of the KBS is given to the user for problem-solution. This is useful in situations where large amounts of data need to be screened for important features. In the latter case, the recommendation or problem-solution given by an expert is transformed and processed before final presentation. This is useful when the presentation format of the output is important, but is a time-consuming chore.

### The systems perspective

From a systems perspective, KBS applications can be classified into the following categories (as depicted in Figure 5.8):

- standalone — there are two types of standalone KBSs — isolated, and linked. Isolated standalone KBSs have no links to other computer programs. While many early KBSs were of this type, isolated KBSs are rare today. Linked standalone KBSs operate independently

**138** Strategic and organizational issues

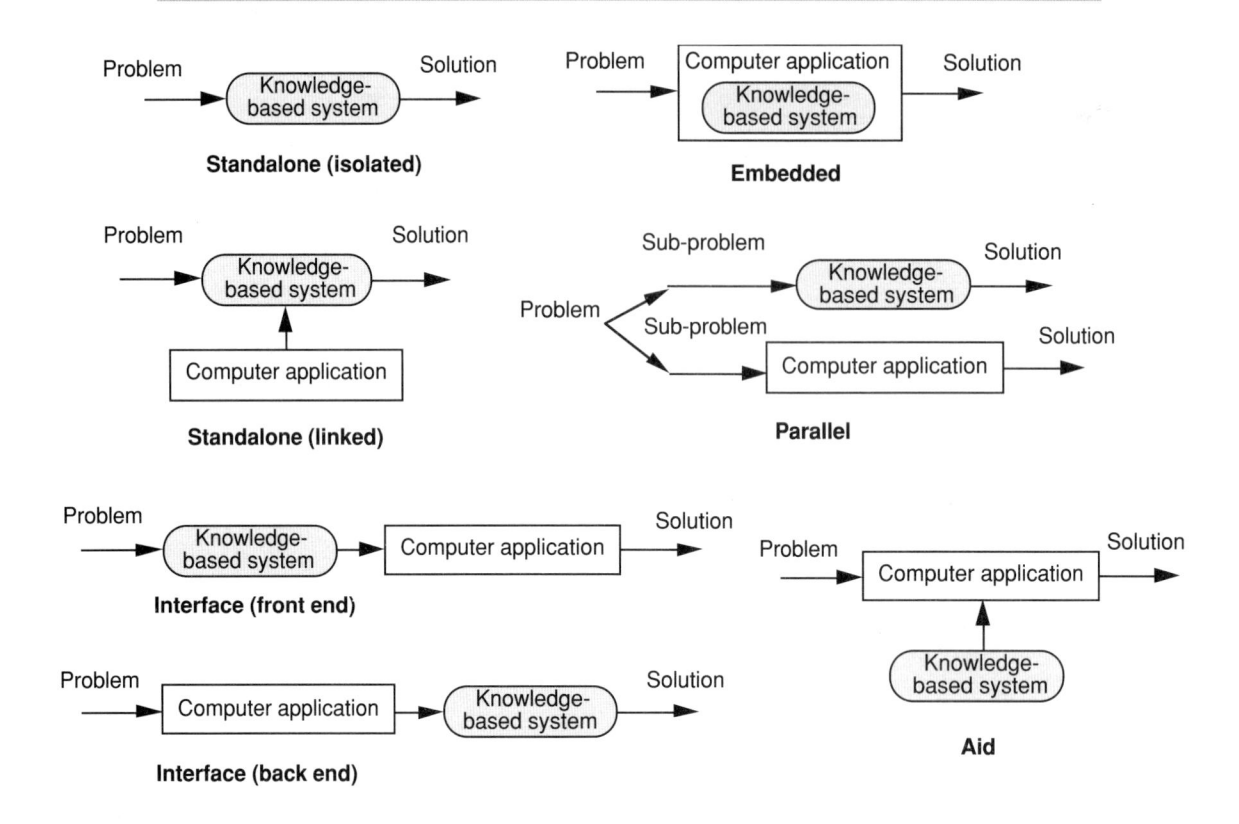

**Figure 5.8** Different KBS applications along the system dimension

for the most part, but maintain links to some other computer programs (usually databases and spreadsheets) for performing selected functions (such as obtaining or writing data). Many current KBS applications are of this type

● interface — a KBS can act as a front-end or a back-end for a conventional computer program. Acting as a front-end, a KBS can screen large amounts of input data, or reformulate problem descriptions such that it can be solved by the conventional program. For example, a front-end KBS can take user queries in natural language, understand it, transform it into an equivalent query in a database language (such as SQL), then feed it to a conventional database program. A back-end KBS can take the output of a conventional computer application and post-process it using specific domain knowledge. For example, a back-end KBS to a database can take the output of the database to a certain query, and present answer(s) to the user in natural language, with hints about how to progress next (the specification of which requires domain knowledge)

● embedded — a KBS can be embedded in a larger computer application program. The overall application program can, when required, activate the KBS and use the results of the KBS in its internal processing. An example is a financial transaction processing program running on a mainframe database which incorporates an embedded expert system

# Applications in organizations 139

to detect fraud in fund-transfer transactions. The emphasis on embedded KBSs is increasing in commercial applications

● parallel — a KBS can be used in parallel with a conventional computer program to solve a particular problem. It differs from embedded KBSs in that the KBS is the master of its own part of the problem-solution (the larger computer program is always in command in embedded systems). This is useful if the task can be broken down into distinct components, and KBS technology is required for solving some of the decomposed problem components. The choice between embedded and parallel KBSs is problem-dependent

● aid — a KBS can also be used as an external aid to a conventional program. It can be thought of as a one-way link existing between conventional application programs and a KBS. Under certain conditions, the conventional computer program calls the KBS to provide some assistance on a certain topic. The KBS is however not embedded in the conventional program.

### Activity types

We use the value chain[6] model of a firm to understand applications of KBSs from the perspective of a company's activities. The value chain concept divides a company's activities into the set of technologically and economically distinct activities that it performs to do business. Each of these activities is termed as a 'value activity'. The value a company creates is measured by the amount that buyers are willing to pay for a product or service. Each value activity makes a contribution to the total value created by the company. A business is profitable if the value it creates exceeds the cost of performing the value activities. A company can gain competitive advantage over its rivals by either performing these activities at a lower cost, or in such a way that it leads to differentiation of product, and a premium price (more value). A company's value chain is part of a larger system called a 'value system', which additionally comprises the value chains of the suppliers, distribution channels, and final buyers.

Using the value chain framework, a firm can be modelled by a set of interdependent value activities. This is shown in Figure 5.9, where each node represents a particular value activity and links represent dependencies between activities. Linkages exist when the manner in which one activity is performed affects the cost or effectiveness of other activities. An activity can create value directly (through the processes taking place within that activity), or by influencing the links emanating from it. Careful management of these linkages is often a powerful source of competitive advantage because of the difficulty rivals have in perceiving them. A company can also create competitive advantage by coordinating, or optimizing links to the outside i.e., to suppliers and customers.

Using the value chain framework, the following categories of KBS applications can be identified from the perspective of a firm's activities (as shown in Figure 5.10):

● knowledge processing at value activities — Porter and Millar[7] have postulated that every value activity has a physical component and an information component. The physical component includes all physical tasks necessary to perform the activity, and the information component includes 'the steps required to capture, manipulate, and channel the data necessary to perform the activity'. KBSs can be used to capture the knowledge related to the information processing component of value activities. In such a rôle, KBSs can significantly enhance the value generated by that activity, specially if that activity has

## 140 Strategic and organizational issues

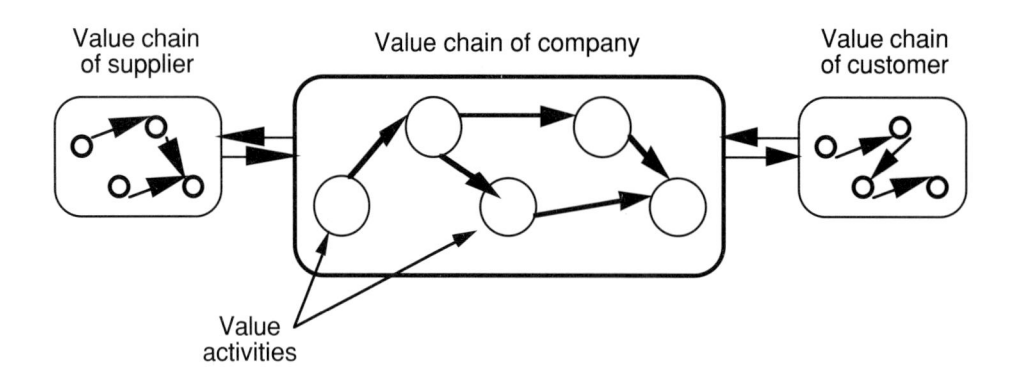

**Figure 5.9** Value system for a company

to be performed in geographically distributed locations simultaneously. For example, the XCON KBS (Chapter 2) enhances knowledge processing in the configuration activity within Digital

- knowledge transfers across links — links between activities represent dependencies caused by transfers of products, and information/knowledge between activities. KBSs can capture and enhance the information/knowledge transfers across these links. The enhancements in the information and knowledge transfers can be experienced in the form of

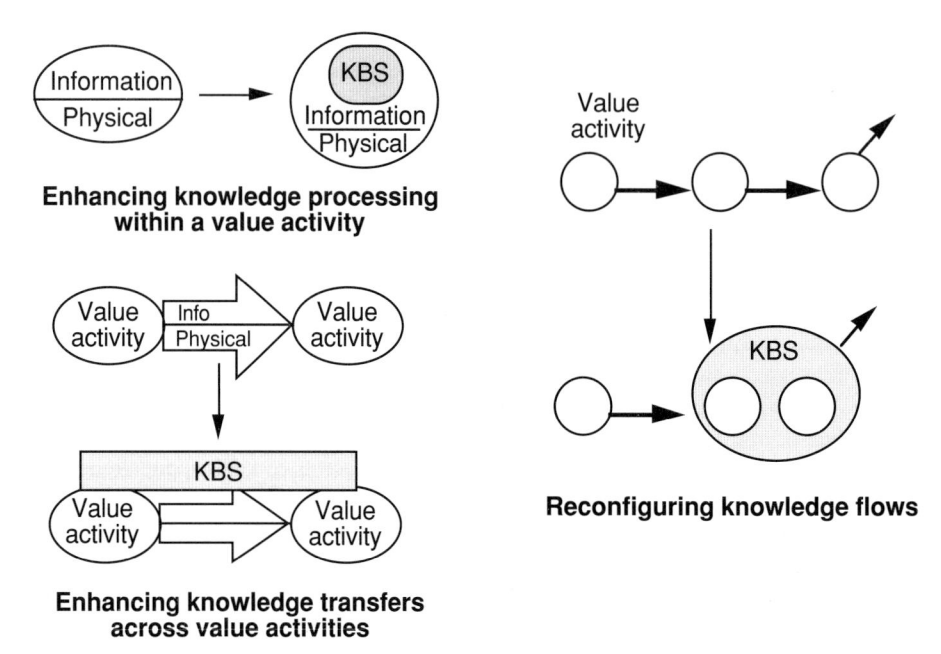

**Figure 5.10** Different KBS applications from the perspective of a firm's activities

# Applications in organizations 141

increased sharing, faster transfers, better reliability, and increased consistency. For example the XSEL and XCON KBS applications (Figure 5.3) provide for an enhanced knowledge transfer between the sales and engineering activities within Digital. Salespeople have a better idea of what can be configured (due to the knowledge about configuration shared between XSEL and XCON), and this also helps the engineering activity (which has to consequently deal with fewer configuration problems). KBSs can aid knowledge transfers across links both internal to a company, and between the firm and its external partner organizations

● reconfiguration of knowledge flows — KBS applications can also change the structure of the value chain of the company. In doing so, they help in reconfiguring the knowledge flows within the organization such that the organization realizes a competitive advantage. For example, the tax activity within Coopers and Lybrand consists of three major value activities[8]: compliance (filing forms), accrual (reflecting liability for books and taxes), and planning (designing business practices to minimize taxation). Prior to 1987, the usual approach to performing the accrual activity was to send junior accountants to client field offices to collect data, and have relatively senior accountants analyze the collected data at Cooper's & Lybrand's offices for planning issues. In 1986, Coopers and Lybrand started building ExperTax, a KBS to help increase the effectiveness of junior accountants while performing the accrual activity. Initially, ExperTax was conceived of as a long questionnaire which served as a checklist to help standardize data collection during accrual. However, it was soon realized that ExperTax provided the valuable opportunity to Coopers and Lybrand to include knowledge (of senior tax experts) about tax planning in the accrual process. This resulted in a merger of (parts of) the two value activities of accrual and planning. Coopers and Lybrand was able to obtain a competitive advantage from this knowledge flow reconfiguration by enhancing the speed and quality of its tax service.

## Organizational benefits

Some of the benefits of KBS applications in organizations are mentioned below. More details on selected KBS applications, and their specific benefits are given in Appendix 1. Benefits include:

● management of task complexity — the complexity of many tasks in industry and business is increasing. This is partly the result of the increasing information intensity of tasks, shrinking business cycles, and rapid environmental changes (which accentuates information uncertainty). KBSs can play an important rôle in managing the information intensity of complex tasks. For example, the XCON KBS (Chapter 2) is vital to Digital for managing the complexity of the computer configuration task. The performance of XCON is today rated to be better than a good human expert

● performance of hazardous tasks — certain tasks (such as cleaning up nuclear meltdowns, and repairing spacecrafts in distant outer space) are too hazardous, or difficult, to be performed by humans. KBSs can act as the 'brains' for suitable mechanical devices (robots and robotic manipulators), and help in accomplishing such tasks

## 142 Strategic and organizational issues

- knowledge preservation — experienced employees are valuable knowledge assets for an organization. However, employees are never permanent, and usually either leave the organization (for other opportunities), or simply grow old and retire. In either case, they walk away with a valuable part of the intellectual asset base of the company when they leave. This was the problem faced by Campbell Soup when Aldo, an experienced employee was about to retire (Chapter 2). KBSs can provide a possible solution to this problem by capturing and preserving expertise of experienced employees.

- distribution of knowledge — KBSs increase the portability of knowledge. Expertise can, in principle, be captured in a KBS and distributed widely. This has important implications for business and industry. Consider the routine task of repairing machines (such as photocopiers, laser printers, and computers) which are distributed over a large area. Any service company has only a limited set of qualified, skilled technicians. It is difficult for a handful of experts to service all locations. If every (ordinary) company technician were equipped with a KBS that captured the essential knowledge of the best technician, then the quality of customer service can be improved. Many major service companies are using KBSs for such purposes

- guided information access — increasing levels of information strains parts of the organization which act as interfaces, or conduits for the information. For example, with rapid increases in the product ranges of many companies, and the accompanying (sometimes complex) interactions between products, customer sales representatives are typically unprepared to deal effectively with all this information. A KBS can help to structure and store product-related information, and also help in increasing performance-effectiveness by using heuristics about opportunities for cross-selling the company's products. A variety of application-specific KBSs are available commercially for structuring and providing a guided access to information at a help desk[9]

- business process redesign — the ability to re-engineer business processes to radically transform organizations is seen as an important business capability today. Business process redesign is intimately related to redistribution of knowledge stores and reconfiguration of knowledge flows within an organization[10]. As evident from the preceding discussions, KBSs can play an important rôle in supporting such process innovation initiatives. For example, Digital's VAX-based knowledge network (Figure 5.3) is a good example of how a company can redesign its business processes (of computer manufacture and sale in this case) to obtain significant competitive benefits

- consistency of decisions — there are many situations where it is important to keep decision-making processes consistent throughout the organization. For example, it is important for American Express to take consistent decisions about similar credit requests from similar customer profiles. Achieving this consistency is difficult in practice, because the staff taking such decisions differ in their levels of experience and knowledge and are, in addition, subject to a variety of local constraints. KBSs can help to keep decision processes consistent within a narrow range. As a KBS captures knowledge about a particular process of decision making, it gives the same (or similar) result for similar input problems. Companies such as American Express (Chapter 2) use KBSs to partially achieve the goal of enhanced consistency in decision making

- faster response — decision processes are often hampered by increased amounts of information. These delays can be unacceptable for success in many business sectors. For example, American Express requires its credit agents to arrive at a yes/no decision about a particular credit request within an average time of 90 seconds, during which the agent might be required to access and go through several screens full of data (Chapter 2). A KBS can automate parts of the decision-making process, and allow human staff to take faster and more informed decisions

● learning — KBSs are usually used by relatively less-experienced users. It has been seen that repeated observations and analyses of the reasoning of a KBS can have an important learning effect on end-users (Figure 5.5). The impact of KBSs on learning can also be observed at the organizational level of knowledge. By helping each knowledge worker learn faster, the entire organization can learn and adapt faster to changes in the environment

● financial savings — data about real financial savings is often hard to obtain because sometimes companies do not want to release them publicly, and at other times it is difficult to accurately measure the financial benefits accruing from the automation of the intangible knowledge associated with KBSs. However, there are several indications in related literature that most KBS applications have lead to real financial savings. Some companies[11] which have quantified their financial savings from KBSs applications are DuPont (annually more than $100 million), and Digital (about $200 million annually).

## Organizational hazards

Like any other technology, KBSs have their downsides. Without adequate care and precaution, KBSs can have dysfunctional impacts on the organization. This can stall the deployment and use of the application within the organization. Some important organizational hazards of KBSs are the following:

● knowledge stagnation — KBSs typically capture a particular state of knowledge about a task. As techniques for learning and autonomous evolution are lacking in most current KBSs (based on rules and frame hierarchies), there is the danger of the knowledge in the KBS being outdated, irrelevant, and erroneous. The consequences of such knowledge stagnation can be significant if employees are using the KBS regularly and depend upon system responses for effective task performance. As an example, consider the potential damage to Coopers and Lybrand if the tax knowledge in its ExperTax system (which is being used by hundreds of field staff) is wrong and outdated. The solution to this problem is to ensure that a knowledgeable group of experts takes responsibility for keeping the knowledge in the KBS updated and correct after its deployment

● innovation freeze — KBSs usually simplify the task of end-users by providing answers to specific problems with appropriate explanations. If end-users become totally dependent upon the system, there is the possibility that they stop thinking about new innovations in their task and passively accept the recommendations of the KBS. This might have strong negative impacts on the organization in the long run, and in extreme cases can even lead to a de-skilling of the employees. It is important that adequate managerial measures are taken to prevent this from happening. Possible managerial actions in this context includes making changes to increase the level of challenge in end-user tasks, and providing specific incentives for innovation

- asymmetry with management processes — KBSs have a profound impact on the tasks performed by end-users. It is important that management recognizes this change and takes appropriate measures to ensure that no dysfunctional situation arises. A common example is the division of responsibility between the system and the users. Without management directives, it is often not clear to end-users about the degree to which they are responsible for wrong actions resulting from the acceptance of the recommendations of the KBS. Such confusion and ambiguity has to be resolved effectively by the management of the company.

## Impact on industry structures

According to Porter[12], there are five primary forces of competition shaping the structure of any industry: barriers to entry, the threat of substitute products, buyer power, supplier power, and industry rivalry. Certain combinations of the above forces can lead to sustainable, above average, long-term profits i.e., a good industry structure. These forces are not static, and changes in the different forces can have major impacts on the industry structure.

Sviokla[13] has noted that KBSs can affect each of the earlier five competitive forces, and can consequently have a strong impact on the industry structure. For example, the configuration system of Digital (Figure 5.3) has lowered the bargaining power of buyers (Digital's customers) by providing them with an enhanced level of service and support which Digital can provide. Digital's investment in KBS technology has helped to increase the entry barriers for new entrants in the niche of minicomputers. This is because the VAX-based knowledge network enables Digital to provide a more integrated and higher quality service to its customers. Cooper & Lybrand's ExperTax KBS has allowed Coopers and Lybrand to differentiate the tax service provided to its customers, and thus reduced the threat of substitute services. The ExperTax system has also reduced the bargaining power of many third-party tax preparation companies whose services used to be utilized by Coopers and Lybrand. This is because ExperTax performs many of the functions provided earlier by these suppliers. Since the late 1980s, many large financial planning firms have started using KBSs to cut costs and time in financial planning. However, KBSs have caused an increase in rivalry in the market for financial planning by lowering the entry barriers (smaller players are also able to use KBS technology to produce complex plans at low costs).

KBSs can have both a positive or negative (or neutral) impact on the competitive forces shaping industry structure. It is important to understand the nature of these effects, and use KBS technology to support a company's particular competitive strategy. According to Porter[14], companies can adopt one of three generic strategies: (1) be a low-cost leader, (2) differentiate own products and services, (3) focus on particular market segments. KBSs can be used to aid the company in following any of these strategies. For example, Digital has the strategy of differentiating its products and services by allowing customers to order computers 'a la carte' i.e., giving them complete flexibility and freedom in their choice. Such flexibility complicates the processes of configuring and manufacturing computers. The configuration KBSs and the VAX-based knowledge network (Figure 5.3) of Digital have been instrumental in supporting this strategy of differentiation.

## Managing the development process in organizations

The successful development of KBSs in organizations requires a balance between the dimensions of technology, strategy, and organization (Figure 5.11). The technological perspective in developing KBSs was described in Chapters 3 and 4. This section focuses on the link between successful KBS applications and the firm's strategic objectives, and the impact of KBSs on different aspects of the organization.

Five important phases can be identified in the process of managing the development of KBSs within organizations (Figure 5.12):

● corporate knowledge processing strategy selection — the development of KBSs within an organization has to follow an overall strategy determined by the knowledge and resource profiles of the organization

● application identification — though many different KBS applications may be possible within an organization, resource constraints and competitive needs of the organization dictate selection of an appropriate set of possible KBS applications

● application feasibility — this phase aims to determine feasibility of building competitively desirable KBS applications

● application creation — once an application has been selected and deemed to be feasible, it has to be created i.e., designed and knowledge-engineered

● deployment and maintenance — after creation, a KBS application has to be deployed in the field, and suitable arrangements have to be made for its maintenance.

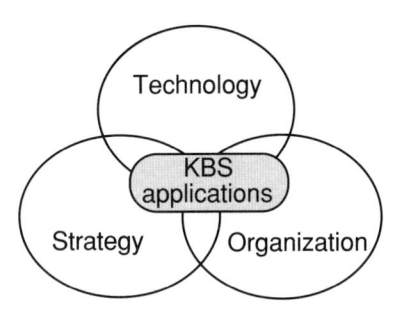

**Figure 5.11** Important dimensions in development of a KBS

## Choosing a corporate strategy for knowledge processing

Two dimensions affect the choice of an appropriate corporate strategy for KBS development:

● development strategy — this dimension relates to the nature of the groups responsible for the development of KBSs. At one extreme, a centralized group can be made responsible for all aspects of the development of KBSs within the organization. At the other extreme it is possible to have a completely decentralized approach to KBS development in which end-users, or groups of end-users, are responsible for most aspects of KBS development

## 146 Strategic and organizational issues

```
Choose corporate
strategy for KBS
development
    ↓
  Identify potential
  KBS application
        ↓
      Determine
      feasability of
      KBS application
            ↓
          Create KBS
          application
                ↓
              Deploy &
              maintain KBS
              application
```

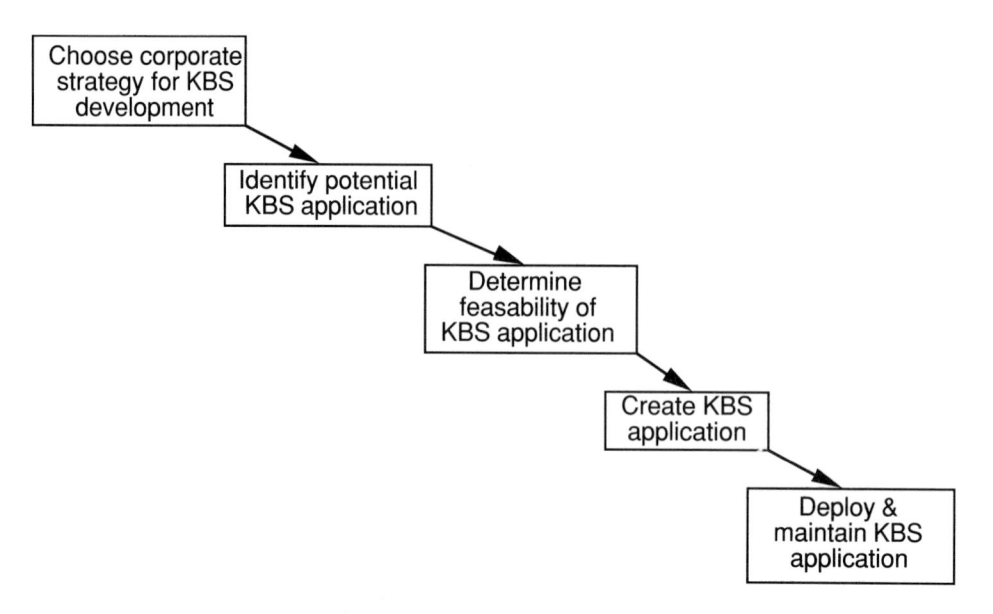

**Figure 5.12** Steps in management of KBS development

- level of knowledge — the organization has to decide about the level(s) of knowledge (individual, group, organizational and knowledge link) targeted by KBSs. We consider only two levels of knowledge in a following analysis — individual and organizational. KBSs focused at the individual level of knowledge tend to capture and encode expertise of an expert (or a group of experts) for a specific task. KBSs targeted at the organizational level tend to impact knowledge flows across different tasks or functions within the organization.

Based on the different possible values along these two dimensions, four different broad strategies can be identified for KBS development within organizations (Figure 5.13):

- guided — this reflects a centralized approach to developing KBSs targeted at the individual level of knowledge. Corporations adopting this strategy typically form a centralized task force/development group for exploring the utility of KBSs for enhancing the effectiveness of individual performances. The emphasis is on capturing and distributing the knowledge of specific experts within the organization, whose expertise would be of use to other less-experienced employees performing the same (or similar) task. The centralized KBS development group provides all resources - such as tools and knowledge engineers - for building the KBSs. It also usually controls all aspects of the development process. This is the cautious approach adopted by many companies experimenting for the first time with KBS technology. The developed systems are generally small in size as they attempt to capture the expertise of one (or a few) expert(s). Risks are low, and successful KBSs can be developed if the central group is capable, well-qualified for the task, and has the support of management

- specialists[15] — this strategy also requires a centralized KBS development group, but it differs from the guided strategy in being focused on the development of KBSs which span

|  | Centralized | Decentralized |
|---|---|---|
| Organizational | Specialists | Dispersed clusters |
| Individual | Guided | Dispersed points |

Level of knowledge (vertical axis) / Development strategy (horizontal axis)

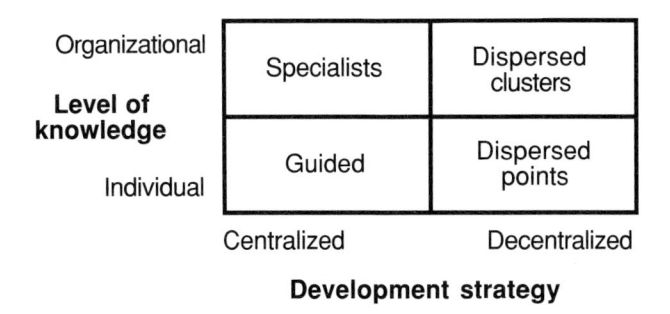

**Figure 5.13** Different corporate strategies for KBS development

task/functional boundaries, and influence knowledge flows across the organization. Due to the large potential impact of the developed KBSs, the adoption of such a development strategy requires the total commitment of the top management of the company to the KBS development efforts. The central KBS development group is larger than in the guided strategy, and the developed KBSs are also more complex. The complexity arises from not only an increase in size and scale of the problem being tackled (organizational as opposed to individual), but also from a need to integrate the KBSs across different functional or task boundaries with the aim of improving knowledge flows within the organization. The risks are high in this approach, and it calls for the best caliber professional knowledge engineers, good funding, and total and sustained top management support.

A good example of a company adopting such a strategy is Digital[16]. Digital has established a major centralized KBS technology group called the Artificial Intelligence Technology Center (AITC) at Marlborough, Massachusetts. The AITC has a large staff (about 300) of specialized programmers and knowledge engineers, devoted to implementing and maintaining a number (about 50) of the large KBSs which constitute Digital's VAX-based knowledge network. The VAX-based knowledge network integrates different functions, and facilitates flow of knowledge across different parts of the organization. For example, the XSEL, XCON, XFL, XNET, and SIZER KBSs (Figure 5.3) integrate and facilitate flow of knowledge regarding computer configuration across the functions of sales, engineering, and customer service within Digital. Building the VAX-based knowledge network requires experience in building KBSs, and sustained top management support. Digital has been a leader in the commercialization of KBSs since the early 1980s. Though the AITC does not control all aspects of KBS development within Digital, it serves as an important locus for activities related to KBSs, and for ensuring that the developed KBSs meet certain communication and data standards so that they can be easily integrated into the organization

● dispersed points[17] — this strategy is almost diametrically opposite to the specialist strategy in that it puts all (or most) of the burden of developing and managing KBSs on end-users. In this approach a KBS shell tool is promoted as a tool for enhancing personal productivity, in much the same way as spreadsheet and database packages. End-users are trained on a particular shell tool, then given the freedom to develop KBSs to aid their own tasks or decision processes. The end-users are the experts, the knowledge engineers, and the users of the developed KBSs. Most of the developed KBSs are targeted at the individual knowledge level, and are typically small (in size) and simple (in complexity). Consequently, they are also developed rapidly, and maintained easily (by the users themselves). Risks and costs are fairly low in this approach, but it requires a reasonably large base of computer literate end-users who are willing to invest time and energy in learning about KBS tools, and developing working KBSs. As this strategy assumes little centralized control, there can be problems of coordination, duplication, and standardization amongst the developed KBSs. Strong user groups (both formal and informal) are desirable for minimizing such problems.

A company such as DuPont is perhaps the best example for illustrating such a strategy. Since 1985, DuPont has been training its end-users to develop their own KBSs. By 1990, approximately 600 different small PC-based KBSs were installed in different business units. This strategy is possible to a large degree because DuPont had in 1990, about 30,000 Lotus-literate managers, and this number is expected to grow to 60,000 by the end of the 1990s. As a direct result of this strategy, it's estimated that in 1990 about 1,800 DuPont managers were able to use KBS shell tools as readily as spreadsheets, electronic mail, and other office automation packages. As most KBSs are developed on personal computers with shell tools, the development cost of most KBSs is small (about $40,000 each). Though DuPont follows the dispersed points strategy, a centralized initiative was necessary to start the process. This was provided by limited seed money ($3 million given by top management), and a small centralized task force (of about a dozen people) which started and coordinated the process of training end-users on KBS shell tools

● dispersed clusters — this strategy can be considered as a hybrid between the pure specialist and dispersed point strategies. There is no one strong locus of centralized control, but rather a few loci of activities related to KBS development. These clusters can exist in different business divisions, subsidiaries, or groups. Each cluster is responsible for development of KBSs within its own span of control. This strategy is conceptually similar to the dispersed point strategy, except for the difference that the 'points' are not direct end-users, but rather small specialist groups. Problems of coordination can arise if there are many clusters. Thus, such a strategy is useful if the organization is in a few distinctly different businesses.

Xerox is following a KBS development strategy that is a mix of the specialist and dispersed clusters approaches. Since 1989, Xerox's centralized KBS Competency Center (KBSCC) has initiated an innovative KBS Circles Program[19] to leverage Xerox's 'leadership through quality' program.

Each KBS circle consists of a group of individuals who operate as a 'quality improvement team'. KBSCC provides hardware and software support to each KBS circle, and helps them to interface with departmental information management departments. Each KBS circle attempts to use KBS technology to address a high corporate priority, knowledge intensive problem. Ten circles were started in April 1989, and the benefits from their efforts exceeded $20 million by the end of 1992.

## Factors affecting the knowledge processing strategy

No one KBS development strategy is inherently superior. The choice of the correct strategy to adopt is dependent on the following factors:

- familiarity — if a company is new to the domain of KBSs, it is best to pursue a guided strategy because it minimizes risk and costs, and provides a good environment for experimenting with the technology. Though the dispersed points strategy is of low cost, it should be avoided if KBS technology is new to the company because end-users can be easily misguided during the experimental stages, and their initial results (or failures) can be misinterpreted by management. All other strategies require a larger degree of commitment, and should be chosen only after the company has acquired a certain degree of familiarity with, and confidence in KBS technology

- knowledge flows — a centralized approach, such as the specialist strategy, is desirable if there is a high degree of integration in knowledge flows across different functions in an organization. This integration can be easily seen in Digital which is in the sole business of selling (a large variety of) computers, and requires a tight integration of knowledge flows across sales, engineering, manufacturing, and customer service. Decentralized strategies are more preferable if the organization has many different sub-units, each of which is relatively independent in its knowledge requirements. DuPont is a good example of such an organization. DuPont has some 1,700 different product lines, with relatively independent knowledge profiles. To stay at the leading edge in so many different products, DuPont encourages a strong sense of independence and technical excellence amongst its employees. Thus a dispersed point strategy seems appropriate for the knowledge flows within DuPont

- resources — resources such as people, capital, and information systems architectures also impact the choice of a KBS development strategy. If a company has a large base of computer-literate end-users (as in DuPont), decentralized strategies may be appropriate; but if there is a limited number of computer literate end-users, centralized strategies may be better. Large capital investments are required for the specialist and dispersed cluster strategies. The guided and dispersed points strategies are relatively less expensive to implement. Centralized strategies are facilitated by the presence of an uniformly consistent information systems architecture. For example, Digital has fairly uniform data and communication standards throughout the company. Digital's centralized AI Technology Center ensures that developed KBSs fit into this information technology architecture. However for a company such as DuPont, there is no common information systems architecture with IBM mainframes, Digital and HP minicomputers, and IBM and Apple personal computers being used in a relatively uncoordinated manner. It is not possible to enforce use of only one (or a small number of) KBS development tools, or system integration strategies. A decentralized development strategy is thus more suited to the information systems architecture of DuPont.

An organization is not limited to any one strategy for nurturing development of KBSs. It may change strategies with time and can even pursue more than one strategy simultaneously. For example, an organization may initially use the guided strategy to gain familiarity with KBS technology and, with time and increased confidence, adopt a combination of the specialist and dispersed points strategies. Regardless of the chosen strategy, it is important there is some thought and consensus about it. The selection of an appropriate KBS development strategy helps to avoid a haphazard allocation of resources to KBS development. This was a frequent pitfall for companies in the mid 1980s, when they often experimented in AI with little coordination and sense of strategy. This usually resulted in a expenditure of resources on KBSs with meagre benefits.

## Identification of potential knowledge-based applications

KBS applications, even if successful and technically advanced, may fail to impress and win management support if they do not yield a competitive advantage to the firm in the long run. A KBS application, if identified as of strategic benefit to the firm, will (with proper communication) be better placed to win sustained management support and resources even if it is technically complex. To identify potentially strategic applications of KBSs, it is necessary to first determine the company's competitive strategy. This can only be obtained from the top management of the company. Next, islands of knowledge which are the true sources of competitive advantage have to be identified. This can be done by analyzing the following types of activities and links within the value chain[20] of the company.

● high value activities — activities which create high value to the company (in the context of its overall competitive strategy) are obvious first places to look for potential KBS projects. The knowledge processing occurring within high value activities should be analyzed carefully to determine whether it may be possible to leverage that knowledge with a KBS. For example, computer configuration is a high value activity for Digital, and Digital's first big KBS project (the XCON system) was designed for that activity

● activities interfacing with high value activities — activities which either influence or are influenced by high value activities are sources for potential KBS projects. Such activities are important, but frequently overlooked sources of value to a company. For example, within Digital the activities of selling and manufacturing computers respectively influence, and are influenced by the high value engineering activity of configuration. Digital has therefore appropriately built KBSs for these activities also (Figure 5.3)

● junctions — activities which serve as a junction for many different linkages (both incoming and outgoing) can also lead to strategic KBS projects. Though such activities may not obviously appear as high value activities, they are often areas for intense knowledge processing corresponding to the incoming and outgoing links

● bottleneck activities — bottleneck activities are undesirable because they slow down the generation of value in the value chain. KBSs can potentially be used in such activities to alleviate bottlenecks. Though many high value activities are bottlenecks, the two need not always be the same. For example, invoice processing can be a bottleneck (but not a high value) activity within a particular firm

● boundary linkages — linkages across boundaries, both external (such as those between a firm and its suppliers or customers) and internal (such as those between different subdivisions of the same firm) are usually associated with intense knowledge flows. KBSs can potentially be used to facilitate flow of knowledge across these boundary linkages. For

# Identification of potential knowledge-based applications 151

example, a KBS can be used by a supplier to get 'intelligent' assistance while ordering products from the company. Such a KBS can facilitate the flow of knowledge about a company's products across to its customers.

Potentially strategic applications of KBSs can best be identified by users and management who are knowledgeable about both the business and the basics of KBS technology. This can be done by either having a centralized center to educate end-users and managers about KBS technology (as in Digital[21]), or forming teams of business users and technology specialists to focus on KBS applications (as in Xerox[22]).

## Cost-benefit analyses of potential applications

All potential KBS projects should be subjected to a preliminary cost-benefit analysis. Performing such a cost-benefit analysis is not always easy for KBSs due to the intangible nature of knowledge captured by systems. The list of KBS application benefits mentioned earlier can be used as a guide to determine the potential benefits from a KBS project. For example, if a KBS leads to a task being performed faster, this can (with some care) be translated into a quantifiable benefit. However, there are other benefits of KBSs such as 'improved quality and consistency of decisions', which are much harder to quantify. All attempts should be made to carefully analyze (and perhaps quantify) possible benefits accruing from a potential KBS project. While estimating costs of developing KBSs, attention should be paid to the following cost drivers:

● knowledge acquisition — acquiring knowledge is expensive because it consumes many hours of an expert's time (most experts are typically highly-paid employees), and the entire process of knowledge acquisition can require many weeks or months

● development team — a well-qualified team of knowledge engineers and programmers is usually required to actually develop a KBS (except in the dispersed points strategy). Such professionals are expensive and add to the costs of the KBS project

● training and education — a significant amount of effort and time has to be expended in training end-users (about how to use the system), and educating managers (about how the KBS impacts rôles, functions and knowledge flows within the organization). Costs arise from both the efforts needed to develop comprehensive training programs, and the time commitment needed from end-users and managers to attend these training sessions

● maintenance — due to the continuously evolving nature of knowledge, knowledge bases of KBSs have to be regularly updated. This is critical for ensuring the usefulness of the KBSs in the long-term. However, this means the process of knowledge acquisition and system building never really stops. The cost of maintaining the knowledge of a KBS in the long run can be a significant proportion of the cost of building the first version of the KBS.

At this stage, it should be possible to obtain a set of potential high-value KBS projects with justifiable returns. As resources of any company are limited, these KBS projects have to be prioritized to determine a limited subset of projects which can be attempted.

## Determining feasibility of applications

Before major resources are actually expended on KBS projects, it's important to determine the feasibility of developing those KBS applications. While the previous stage of application identification is driven primarily by business considerations, this phase of feasibility determination is driven by technological, domain, and task considerations. This phase can not only help in eliminating unfeasible KBS projects (and thus prevent the wasteful expenditure of resources), but can also provide insights into possible problems arising during the construction and implementation of the proposed KBSs (for which suitable precautions can be adopted).

The feasibility of developing KBS applications can be analyzed along the dimensions of task, development process, and deployment environment. Along the task dimension, the following characteristics are important determinants of the KBS project feasibility:

● domain constraints — the task should be relatively well-structured and constrained. Current KBS technology is not very suitable for loosely constrained tasks (such as creative art design)

● task type — it should be possible to classify the task as one of the four task types mentioned earlier: monitoring, diagnostic, structured design, and planning (Figure 5.6). Particular care should be taken to analyze the task if there is some doubt about the true nature of the task

● knowledge requirements — the knowledge required for problem solution should be amenable to representation in KBSs. Effective task performance should not require the extensive use of physical or perceptual skills (as in driving a car), because it is difficult to encode such skills with current KBS technology. Care should also be taken to ensure that the available domain knowledge is fairly complete and certain

● changes — domains with frequent changes are not very suitable for KBS development, as the knowledge of the KBS can be rendered ineffective fairly easily and quickly. Also, uncertainty in the domain should not be large, because then the conclusions obtained with the KBS can be suspect.

The following feasibility issues can be identified along the dimension of development process:

● expert — an expert should be available, articulate, and cooperative. If any one of these conditions is not satisfied, then successful development of the KBS can be jeopardized. If there is more than one expert, then the experts should agree on the correct solution to the problem

● management support — adequate management support at all stages of the development process is essential. Management commitment to and sponsorship of the project is facilitated by the selection of KBS applications with a high strategic impact on the organization

● project champion — like any other project, a successful KBS needs a project champion. Someone within the organization has to be ready to take the responsibility for championing the cause of the KBS project

● project management — an effective project management team is required to ensure the KBS is developed on time, within budget and according to specifications. A team of qualified professionals either from within the company, or hired from external sources should be available to take responsibility for the project.

The following issues are important for determining feasibility of KBS applications with respect to the deployment environment:

● integration — depending on the nature of the developed KBS along the system dimension (Figure 5.8), it should be possible to interface the KBS effectively with all other relevant application programs. Poor integration in the deployment environment can render a well-developed KBS useless

● user acceptance — care has to be taken to ensure the user community will accept the KBS. If the user community perceives the KBS as a threat and is hostile to its installation, then it may not be possible to implement a KBS successfully. User acceptance can be enhanced by involving them in the development process

● maintenance responsibility — knowledge in a KBS has to be updated on a continuing basis. Certain groups within the organization (either the experts, or the users, or the information systems professionals) have to take responsibility for maintaining the KBS.

By analyzing each potentially strategic KBS application along the above dimensions, it is possible to determine which KBS projects are feasible. At the end of this phase, it is possible to choose one (or a small number) of KBS projects which can be put through the next stages of actual implementation and deployment.

## Creation of knowledge-based applications

This phase is concerned with the actual construction of the KBS project(s) identified at the end of the previous stage. Technological issues in the process of creating both rule-based and hybrid KBSs are explained in Chapter 4, and are thus not repeated here. Important managerial issues related to the creation of KBSs include the following.

● project management — an effective project champion and good project management are crucial for successful completion of KBS projects. Note that KBS development projects suffer from the twin evils - cost and time overruns - plaguing conventional software projects, and more. There is significant uncertainty associated with the knowledge acquisition phase, and it is possible that even with the best efforts of knowledge engineers, acquired knowledge is not good enough for a deployable KBS. It is difficult to initially guarantee quality of knowledge acquired during the knowledge acquisition phase. This is because problems can occur even with cooperative experts and good knowledge engineers (Chapter 2). Good planning is necessary to ensure that budgeted costs and estimated times are not exceeded. Particular care should be taken to manage the time dimension because the knowledge acquisition phase is time consuming, and is dependent on the schedule of the expert(s). If the expert is occupied with another task, and does not have time for the knowledge engineers, the entire KBS development effort can stall. Proper communication with top management can help in ensuring availability of the expert during development of the KBS

● management support — management support is essential for not only getting a KBS project started, but also to keep it going till successful completion. The most important guideline for obtaining sustained management support is open and regular communication. The KBS development team has to communicate expected benefits and current progress of the system in clear and non-technical terms to management. There should be no mysterious shroud surrounding the development of the KBS. Regular reports to, and meetings with management are useful in this regard. Prototyping is also critical for both improving communication with management, and providing regular proofs of continuous progress. Demonstrations of prototypes can explain to management how the KBS will achieve the expected benefits. Note that most managers have never seen a working KBS, and thus may have a hard time in visualizing the relation between the proposed KBS and its benefits. Obtaining positive feedback on various stages of the prototype from potential users of the system is also useful for demonstrating value of the KBS to management. Good communication can help top management better appreciate pitfalls of KBS development processes, and control damage should the project yield poor results, or have to be abandoned midway (for example, due to poor acquired knowledge)

● managed expectations — the KBS development team has to manage expectations from two communities — management and users. It is important that both groups have realistic expectations from the KBS, because undesirable situations can result from mismanaged expectations. For example, management can stop funding for the KBS project, and users can refuse to accept a working KBS. If there is a good communication channel with management (see above), then it is likely they will not have misplaced expectations from the KBS project. Similarly, communication with users is the key to managing their expectations. This can be achieved by regular meetings with user groups, and by involving selected users (or user groups) in the development process[23]. The latter can be done by demonstrating prototype versions to users, obtaining their feedback, incorporating requested changes in the system, and iterating through this process. Care should be taken to ensure that users (or user groups) involved in the development process are representative of the user community (to avoid biases) and have a reasonable grasp of the potential of KBS technology (to be able to suggest useful and possible changes). The KBS development team should not make undeliverable promises to either community (management and users). Creating over-expectations is often the worst evil in the development of KBSs

● integration — most commercial KBSs are required to interface with other application software packages in the deployment environment. It is important to plan the necessary interface adaptations in the KBS during actual construction of the KBS. Deploying an isolated standalone KBS, then trying to make the integration links in the field usually leaves a bad impression (of the system not being very useful and friendly) on most users (besides taking their time and causing them a variety of inconveniences). Integration of the KBS to other information systems such as databases also requires interactions with the managers of these systems. As managers are typically possessive about their own data and software packages, such interactions should be handled with care. Top management support can facilitate these demands of the integration process

● validation — due to the heuristic nature of processing within most KBSs, it is often difficult to guarantee the 'correctness' of the answers generated by systems. The problem is compounded by the fact that knowledge in a commercial KBS is typically updated on a regular basis. With each update, the complexity in the interactions between the different rules and/or objects magnifies. These factors make it very difficult to completely validate many KBSs. Though some formal validation procedures have been devised, they are usually applicable to small and simple KBSs. The most common technique for 'validating' a KBS is to repeatedly try out different scenarios, and present the solutions (along with the generated explanations/justifications) to the expert for comments. If the expert finds a flaw in the reasoning process of the KBS, then the cause for this flaw is isolated, and appropriate changes are made in the knowledge base of the system. This process is repeated with many different scenarios, till a reasonable confidence is achieved in the answers generated by the KBS. It is possible to facilitate validation of the system by incorporating certain validation checks into the design of the KBS during its creation.

## Deployment of applications

Proper management of this final phase in the development of KBSs is crucial for successful commercial applications. A KBS cannot succeed unless it is accepted by users in the field. Note that the typical end-user of a KBS is a junior inexperienced employee who has had little participation in the process of designing the KBS. Factors affecting the acceptance of KBS applications by end-users are described now:

● phased deployment — most KBSs are deployed in multiple locations. This must be done in a phased manner. There are several benefits from a phased deployment. First, it gives the opportunity to engage in 'organizational prototyping'[24]. The ultimate impact and boundaries of a KBS application cannot be specified with full confidence initially. The incremental deployment of a KBS allows for a better understanding of the relation between the KBS and the organizational context, and leads to a more successful KBS application. Second, because it is difficult to guarantee the knowledge of a KBS as 'correct', greater confidence in the system can be obtained with gradual use in real-life settings. Third, any problems or errors in the KBS can be located early, and rectified with minimal impact on the deployment environment. Finally, this gives the opportunity to learn incrementally about the 'desired' user interface, and to design suitable protocols for interaction

● task integration — the developed KBS has to be integrated into the tasks performed by end-users. User acceptance of the system is hampered if the KBS requires the user to unnaturally change the normal sequence of task performance. An important issue related to task integration is the question of accountability. The degree of accountability of users with respect to the recommendations made using the KBS should be made explicit. This is particularly important if the KBS is being used to aid the users in making critical decisions

● system integration — also important is the degree to which the KBS is integrated in the information systems environment of the end-user. For example, if the KBS needs data from a database used by the user, then this link should be integrated in the deployed system. Users do not like the inconveniences of poorly integrated KBSs

● task enrichment — the deployed KBS should enrich the tasks performed by the end-users. Most KBSs are usually deployed as assistants (Figure 5.7) to end-users. Users should be made aware of the beneficial effects of KBSs, such as helping them to enhance their rate of on-the-job learning (Figure 5.5). Some thought in the design of KBSs can enhance the degree of task enrichment possible with their use

● customization — particular care should be taken to customize the KBS for the users. Attention should be focused on system and task integration (see above), and on the design of the user interface. Even minor details like the wording of questions, or allowed options at a particular stage can have an important impact on ease of use (and hence the acceptance) of the system. The deployed KBS should also be efficient. Users should not have to wait for long periods to obtain responses

● user support — a comprehensive program has to be organized for providing adequate support to end-users. This support program should consist of organizing training sessions for users and creating a network of internal advocates for the KBS. Training sessions should explain both how the users can use the KBS, and how it can be used to enrich their jobs and enhance their effectiveness. Proper training can remove much of the fear and hostility that user groups may possibly experience with the KBS. Training sessions should be synchronized with the deployment schedule of the KBS. A network of internal advocates is essential for motivating users into using the KBS and for ensuring the success of the KBS. The project champion has to create the network of advocates for the KBS by marketing the project effectively to key players within the organization

● management processes — most KBSs have an impact on the nature of the tasks performed by end-users. It is important to identify these effects, and change the incentive structure and management processes to keep the users motivated and productive. For example, if users are paid on the basis of number of hours worked, then there is no incentive for them to use a KBS to be more productive.

## Maintenance of applications

The maintenance of KBS applications is different from that of conventional information systems. The maintenance of conventional software programs typically focuses on system issues like upgrading the program to a newer version of a programming language, or porting the system to a new generation of hardware, or making minor changes in selected program modules. The maintenance of KBS applications includes the above issues, and the efforts of trying to keep the knowledge in the knowledge base of the KBS updated and current. This is critical for keeping the KBS useful in the long term. For example, the XCON KBS would get quickly outdated if all new Digital product descriptions were not immediately incorporated into the knowledge base of the system. The magnitude of such changes in the knowledge base can be fairly large. For example, it is estimated[25] that about 40% of the rules (which currently number more than 12,000) in the knowledge bases of the configuration KBSs at Digital change each year. Performing these changes poses a formidable maintenance task, but is critical for the renewal of the knowledge contained with the configuration KBSs. Thus, the knowledge acquisition task has to be continued, albeit at a reduced level, even after a KBS is deployed. The following steps should be taken to ensure adequate maintenance of a KBS

● system maintenance — information system professionals should be given responsibility for system maintenance of the KBS, such as ensuring integration of the KBS with changing generations of hardware and software

● knowledge maintenance — either the expert(s) helping to build the system, or another knowledgeable person (or group of persons) should be assigned responsibility for ensuring the knowledge base of the KBS is updated when required. Careful thought has to be given to the selection of persons authorized to make changes in the knowledge base. If these persons have different views about the problem solution than that contained within the knowledge base, the KBS can get distorted fairly rapidly. Also, if several different persons are given authority to change the knowledge base with little coordination, then it is possible to end up with as many different, incompatible (from a knowledge perspective) versions of the original KBS after some time. Management support is required to ensure that an expert is available for spending time on the maintenance of the knowledge in the KBS

● cost budgeting — maintaining a KBS is expensive because in addition to the usual system maintenance costs, there is the additional cost for knowledge maintenance. This extra cost has to be budgeted into the total costs of the KBS. A failure to budget for this cost may result in a dispute over funding for maintenance at a later stage, and could possibly result in the KBS being rendered useless.

## Summary

Knowledge assets are an important source of competitive advantage for organizations. KBSs store and process knowledge, and influence the management of knowledge assets within corporations. To obtain the maximum benefits from KBSs it is necessary to identify strategically important KBS applications and to effectively manage their development and deployment. Strategic and organizational aspects of KBS applications have been described in this chapter. Important issues mentioned in the above sections include the following:

● Organizational knowledge exists in both tangible and intangible forms. Managing knowledge is challenging because knowledge assets are difficult to identify, value, and deploy effectively. Knowledge is most useful when it is shared.

● An organization's knowledge assets can be classified into four categories — individual, group, organizational, and knowledge links.

● KBSs capture and automate (partially or completely) intangible knowledge about tasks, processes, and tangible knowledge assets. While most KBSs have been used for capturing knowledge at the individual level, greater benefits are obtained by using KBSs to manage knowledge at the organizational and knowledge links levels.

● From a task perspective, four types of KBS applications can be identified — monitoring, diagnostic, structured design, and planning and scheduling. Planning and scheduling tasks integrate static and dynamic constraints and are the most challenging for KBSs.

● KBSs can support users in four different ways — replacement, partial replacement, assistant, and interface. Most KBSs are used as assistants.

● From a system perspective, KBS applications can be classified into the following categories — standalone (linked or isolated), interface, embedded, parallel, and aid. Standalone (linked) KBSs are most common today.

● KBSs can impact business activities by enhancing knowledge processing at value activities, enhancing knowledge transfers across links, and by reconfiguring knowledge flows.

● Major organizational benefits of KBS applications include — managing task complexity, performing hazardous tasks, preserving knowledge, distributing knowledge, providing guided information access, enhancing consistency of decisions, enabling business process redesign, increasing learning, allowing for faster responses, and yielding financial savings.

● KBS applications can also have an important impact on industry structures and the competitive strategies of corporations.

● Five important phases to be managed in the development of KBSs in organizations are — selection of a KBS development strategy, identification of a KBS application, determination of the application feasibility, creation of the KBS, and deployment and maintenance of the application.

● Four different strategies can be selected for developing KBSs — guided, specialists, dispersed points, and dispersed clusters. Factors affecting the choice of the appropriate strategy include — familiarity with KBS technology, knowledge flows within the organization, and available resources.

● It is crucial to identify KBS applications which can potentially have a significant strategic impact. Such KBS applications are typically found in one of the following regions of a firm's value chain — high-value activities, activities interfacing with high-value activities, junctions, bottlenecks, and boundary linkages.

● Important cost drivers in the development of KBSs are — knowledge acquisition, developmental staff, training and education, and maintenance of the KBS.

● Before actually committing to building a KBS, it is important to determine the feasibility of its successful implementation. This feasibility has to be analyzed along three different dimensions — task (is a KBS appropriate for the task?), development process (are resources necessary for development available?), and deployment environment (can the KBS be deployed effectively?).

● Important management concerns during the process of creating KBSs are — effective project management, strong management support, managed expectations, validation of the KBS, and integrated application deployment.

● It is important to deploy KBSs in a phased manner, and to ensure task and system integration. The emphasis should be on enriching the jobs of end-users and on making appropriate changes in the management processes (to reflect organizational changes caused by the deployment of the KBS).

● Maintenance costs of KBSs include those for traditional system maintenance and for updating knowledge in the knowledge base. This latter cost is significant and is frequently overlooked.

Several advanced AI technologies (such as fuzzy logic and neural networks) are discussed in succeeding chapters. It is important to note that strategic and organizational concerns raised in this chapter for KBSs also apply to applications using these other technologies.

# 160 Strategic and organizational issues

## Bibliography and suggested readings

Some excellent references on the management of the development of KBSs are books by Harmon et al (Harmon et al 88), Mumford and Macdonald (Mumford and Macdonald 89), and Prerau (Prerau 90). While Harmon et al's book explains the process of managing development of KBSs in general, the latter two books describe the experiences of Digital and GTE with development of the XSEL and COMPASS KBSs respectively. Other useful references are (Feigenbaum et al 88), (Mockler 89), (Harmon & Sawyer 90), and (Turban & Liebowitz 92). Articles by Barker and O'Connor (Barker & O'Connor 89), and Sviokla (Sviokla 90) describe organizational impact of the XCON KBS (and other related KBSs) on the configuration task within Digital. Other articles of general interest on issues related to the application of KBSs within organizations are (Sviokla 86), (Braden 89), (Maletz 90), and (Sharma 91). Appendix 1 contains descriptions of selected commercial KBSs and their benefits. The reader is referred to the bibliography of Appendix 1 for additional references on commercial applications of KBSs.

Barker, V.E., and D.E. O'Connor, *Expert Systems for Configuration at Digital*, XCON and Beyond, Communications of the ACM, Vo. 32, No. 3, pp. 298–318, March 1989.

Braden, B., J. Kanter, and D. Kopcso, *Developing an Expert Systems Strategy*, MIS Quarterly, pp. 459–466, Dec. 1989.

E. Turban, and J. Liebowitz, (Eds.), *Managing Expert Systems*, Idea Publishing Group, Harrisburg, Pennsylvania, 1992.

Feigenbaum, E., P. McCorduck, and H. Penny Nii, *The Rise of the Expert Company*, Times Books, 1988.

Harmon, P., and B. Sawyer, *Creating Expert Systems*, John Wiley, 1990.

Harmon, P., R. Maus, and W. Morrissey, *Expert Systems: Tools and Applications*, John Wiley, 1988.

Maletz, M. C., *KBS Circles: A Technology Transfer Initiative that Leverages Xerox's 'Leadership Through Quality Program'*, MIS Quarterly, pp. 323–329, Sep. 1990.

Mockler, R. J., *Knowledge-Based Systems for Management Decisions*, Prentice-Hall, 1989.

Mumford, E., and W. Bruce Macdonald, *XSEL's Progress: The Continuing Journey of an Expert System*, John Wiley, 1989.

Prerau, D. S., *Developing and Managing Expert Systems*, Addison-Wesley, 1990.

Sharma, R. S., D. W. Conrath, and D. M. Dilts, *A Socio-Technical Model for Deploying Expert Systems — Part I: The General Theory*, IEEE Transactions on Engineering Management, Vol. 38, No. 1, pp. 14–23, Feb. 91.

Sviokla, J. J., *An Examination of the Impact of Expert Systems on the Firm: The Case of XCON*, MIS Quarterly, pp. 127–140, June 1990.

Sviokla, J. J., *Business Implications of Knowledge-based Systems*, Data Base, Vol. 17, No. 4, pp. 5–19, part I; Vol 18, No. 1, pp. 5–16, part II, summer and fall 1986.

## Notes

1 Steward, T. A., *Brainpower,* Fortune, pp. 42–60, June 3, 1991.

2 Prietula, M. J. and H. A. Simon, *The Experts in your Midst*, Harvard Business Review, pp. 120-124, Jan–Feb. 1989.

3 Steward, T. A., *Brainpower,* Fortune, pp. 42–60, June 3, 1991.

4 The MOS KBS also helps managers within Digital in determining the impact of major changes (in pricing, resources, demands, and other variables) on the workload and capacity of manufacturing plants on a world-wide basis.

5 ExperTax, Harvard Business School Case Study, No. 9-187-007, 1988.

6 Porter, M. E., *Competitive Advantage: Creating and Sustaining Superior Performance*, Free Press, NY, 1985.

7 Porter, M. E. and Millar, V. E., *How Information Technology Gives You Competitive Advantage*, Harvard Business Review, July–Aug 1985.

8 ExperTax, Harvard Business School Case Study, No. 9-187-007, 1988.

9 Barr, A., *Automating Knowledge Flow at the Help Desk, Intelligent Software Strategies*, P. Harmon (Ed.), Vol VI, No. 11, pp. 1–9, Cutter Information Corp., Arlington, MA, Nov., 1990.

10 For more details on the links between information technology and business process redesign, see (a) Davenport, T. H., *Process Innovations*, Harvard Business School Press, 1993; and (b) Davenport, T. H., & J. E. Short, *The New Industrial Engineering: Information Technology and Business Process Redesign*, Sloan Management Review, pp. 11–27, Summer 1990.

11 Meador, C. L. and E. G. Mahler, *Choosing an Expert Systems Game Plan*, Datamation, August 1, 1990

12 Porter, M. E., *Competitive Advantage: Creating and Sustaining Superior Performance*, Free Press, 1985.

13 Sviokla, J., *Business Implications of Knowledge-Based Systems*, Part 1, Database, pp. 5–19, Summer 1986.

14 Porter, M. E., *Competitive Advantage: Creating and Sustaining Superior Performance*, Free Press, 1985.

15 The term *specialist* has been used by Meador and Mahler to describe the KBS strategy of Digital in the article: Meador, C. L. and E. G. Mahler, *Choosing an Expert Systems Game Plan*, Datamation, August 1, 1990.

16 Meador, C. L. and E. G. Mahler, *Choosing an Expert Systems Game Plan*, Datamation, August 1, 1990.

17 The term *dispersed* has been used by Meador and Mahler to describe the KBS strategy of DuPont in the article: Meador, C. L. and E. G. Mahler, *Choosing an Expert Systems Game Plan*, Datamation, August 1, 1990.

18 Meador, C. L. and E. G. Mahler, *Choosing an Expert Systems Game Plan*, Datamation, August 1, 1990.

## 162 Strategic and organizational issues

19 Maletz, M. C., KBS *Circles: A Technology Transfer Initiative that Leverages Xerox's 'Leadership Through Quality Program'*, MIS Quarterly, pp. 323–329, Sep. 1990.

20 Porter, M. E., *Competitive Advantage: Creating and Sustaining Superior Performance*, Free Press, NY, 1985

21 Meador, C. L. and E. G. Mahler, *Choosing an Expert Systems Game Plan*, Datamation, August 1, 1990.

22 Maletz, M. C., *KBS Circles: A Technology Transfer Initiative that Leverages Xerox's 'Leadership Through Quality Program'*, MIS Quarterly, pp. 323–329, Sep. 1990.

23 A good discussion of important issues in using users as co-developers can be found in the following reference: Leonard-Barton, D., *The Case for Integrative Innovation: An Expert System at Digital*, Sloan Management Review, pp. 7–19, Fall 1987.

24 Organizational prototyping is discussed in the following reference: Leonard-Barton, D., *The Case for Integrative Innovation: An Expert System at Digital*, Sloan Management Review, pp. 7–19, Fall 1987.

25 Barker, V. E., and D. E. O'Connor, *Expert Systems for Configuration at Digital: XCON and Beyond*, CACM, Vol. 32, No. 3, pp. 298–318, March 1989.

# Part IV

## Intelligent interfaces

The design of man-machine interfaces is of critical importance for the success of computer applications in organizations. Computing applications, regardless of their technical sophistication, may fail if they cannot interface effectively with relevant components (such as users) of their organizational contexts. Design of effective interfaces with a judicious combination of text messages, graphics, and icons is discussed in Chapter 4. However, the potential for building more sophisticated interfaces extends well beyond the use of graphics and text to the incorporation of natural language, and image and speech processing capabilities. It is possible to build interfaces which are intelligent, and which possess many of the same perceptual skills as us. These aspects are covered in detail in the two chapters (6 and 7) forming this part of the book.

The term 'natural language' refers to languages in common and everyday use such as English, French, and Spanish. This is in contrast to computer languages such as Fortran, Pascal, and Basic. Chapter 6 describes how intelligent systems can be augmented with capabilities for processing natural language, and for translating between different natural languages. Selected commercial tools with natural language capabilities are described and guidelines are provided for evaluating natural language interfaces. The chapter illustrates the commercial impact of natural language processing with selected commercial applications.

The description of knowledge-based technology in previous chapters has focused on the automation of logical problem-solving behavior. The logical mode of problem-solving is characterized by a dominant emphasis on a sequential mode of thinking and actions (such as in backward or forward chaining). Chapter 7 focuses on another important aspect of human intelligence — the ability to recognize patterns from visual and auditory sensory data. The first part of this chapter covers the processing of visual information, while the second part focuses on the processing of speech. Again the commercial impacts of these technologies are illustrated with actual applications

The advanced artificial intelligence technologies described in Chapters 6 and 7 utilize the core concepts of representing and reasoning with knowledge described in Chapters 2, 3 and 4. Thus it is important that the reader is familiar with the contents of these earlier chapters before starting on this part of the book.

# Chapter 6
## Natural language processing

Natural languages are interesting because they constitute the most important medium for human communication[1]. Language has also been accorded a central position in the philosophical school of thought of logical positivism. Ludwig Wittgenstein, an important logical positivist, wrote[2] that all philosophy was a critique of language because the limits of language defined the limits of the world. He also believed that humans cannot think what they cannot say. From these perspectives, the understanding of natural language is of central importance to artificial intelligence. Two introductory examples are described below to illustrate the commercial significance of natural language processing (NLP) in industry. They also highlight the two central concerns within NLP: natural language understanding, and machine translation.

### The Securities and Exchange Commission

The Securities and Exchange Commission (SEC) is a regulatory agency of the US government which was established in 1934 (in response to the stock market crash of 1929) with the aim of providing full and fair disclosure about traded securities. Companies are required to file periodic financial statements and other documents with the SEC. In 1985 about seven million pages of information were received by the SEC from over 10,000 companies[3]. Since 1986, companies are able to file the necessary documentation with the SEC directly in an electronic format. While it is easier and quicker to receive documents electronically, the incoming information still has to be indexed[4] so as to enable the SEC analysts to answer questions about their contents.

# 166 Natural language processing

Merely indexing by words or phrases complicates formulation of the correct queries to get the desired answers. Figure 6.1[5] illustrates a possible query to answer the question 'how many amendments are there to the company's by-laws relating to the authorization of securities?', when a key-word based indexing scheme is used. Note that formulation of the search string is dependent on the terms and phrases used to index the various documents. Complicating matters is the fact that there is (usually) no unique and complete set of terms and phrases to use for indexing. For example, the query of Figure 6.1 assumes that all amendments are captured by the terms 'increase/increasing', 'raise/raising', and 'change the number/changing the number'? Relevant documents indexed by other expressions are not retrieved by this query. Thus, often several trials (with different query formulations) by an experienced analyst are required to get the correct answer to the original question.

A more natural way to frame the query of Figure 6.1 would be something like that shown in Figure 6.2. While writing the query of Figure 6.2 is much simpler and more natural, it is also more difficult to process. Special knowledge and processing techniques are required to recognize presence or absence of the concept 'amendment of authorization of securities' in the concerned documents. NLP offers capabilities to accept such queries, and retrieve the correct set of relevant documents. Arthur Andersen has built the ELOISE (English Language-Oriented Indexing System for EDGAR) NLP system for the SEC. ELOISE detects the presence of concepts of interest to the SEC, and performs the required knowledge-based indexing to facilitate 'natural' queries of the form shown in Figure 6.2. It has increased the accuracy, reliability, and efficiency of processing electronic filings at the SEC[6].

## Siemens-Nixdorf

Siemens-Nixdorf estimates[7] that an ordinary personal computer (PC) requires about 10,000 pages of documentation for its constituent hardware and software. If Siemens-Nixdorf wants to sell its PC in different countries, it has to provide the documentation in as many different languages. A skilled technical translator can only translate about 1000 pages per year. This implies that about 10 special technical translators are required to work for one year to produce each foreign language version of the PC's documentation. The amount of documentation is much larger for more complex products.

```
FIND Companies
     WHERE SEARCH_STRING =
              (Amendment OR (Be Amended) OR Revision OR (Be Revised))
     AND     (By-laws OR Charter OR (Articles of Incorporation) OR (Restated
              Articles of Incorporation) OR (Restated Certificate of Incorporation))
     AND     (Increase OR Increasing OR Raise OR Raising OR (Change the
              Number) OR (Changing the Number))
     AND     (Common Stock))
```

**Figure 6.1** A possible query in a keyword-based system

```
FIND Companies
       WHERE SEARCH_STRING =
            (Amendment to authorization of securities)
```

**Figure 6.2** Query of Figure 6.1 rephrased in natural language

Certain industry trends are aggravating the need for documentation. The complexity of products is on the rise, life cycles of electronic products are decreasing, and an increasing number of functions inside products are being realized with software. In addition, there are competitive pressures on large multinational companies (such as Siemens-Nixdorf) to simultaneously cater to an international market and maintain a strong local focus. Providing all documentation in the local language is a small, but important step in satisfying local sensibilities. Alonso and Schneider[8] mention that in 1986 more than 100 million pages were translated in Western European countries alone. In 1987, they conservatively estimated the worldwide bill for translation services to be about $25 billion with a 15% annual growth rate.

Human translators are in short supply and they can only translate a limited number of pages each year. Rapid changes in technology and the resulting explosion in technical terminology is further straining the output of human translators. Machine translation technology can help to alleviate the problem by automatically converting text from one language to another.

Technical literature, though voluminous, is generally simple in structure and content, and is more amenable to automatic translation systems. The commercial market for machine translation services is huge, even if it represents only a fraction of the $25 billion worldwide market for translation services.

Siemens-Nixdorf realized the importance and need of machine translation technology back in the 1970s, when it started building the Metal machine translation system. Metal is today a successful commercial product, and can be used for translating text between 6 different languages. The output translation is not perfect, and usually needs further editing (by a human translator), but nevertheless, it increases the productivity of human translators significantly.

## Components of natural language processing

Natural language processing (NLP) is a sub-field of artificial intelligence (AI) that deals with the processing of natural language. The emphasis in NLP has been on devising procedures which are computationally effective i.e., ultimately result in the techniques being encoded in a suitable computer program. This emphasis distinguishes NLP from the study of natural languages within other disciplines such as linguistics and cognitive psychology. The emphasis in linguistics has been on formulation of formal models which allow capture of regularities in language. Within cognitive psychology the goal has been to model the use of language in a psychologically plausible manner (backed by experimental data).

The field of NLP can be divided into two broad streams. One stream termed here as cognitive NLP (also alternatively known as general NLP) can be viewed as taking the perspective of cognitive psychologists, and giving it a grounding in computation. Thus the goal within cognitive NLP is to generate models of the use of language (between humans) which are both psychologically plausible and computationally effective. The other stream of NLP is termed as applied NLP, and as the term implies, is more concerned with the communication interfaces between humans and computers (machines). The emphasis is not on a cognitive simulation of the communication processes between humans, but rather on the pragmatics of communicating with computers/machines using natural language. This chapter focuses only on applied NLP, the commercially important part of NLP.

There are two major categories of applied NLP systems: natural language understanding systems, and machine translation (MT) systems. Natural language understanding systems are concerned with the 'understanding' of instructions specified in natural language such that the computer can respond appropriately to the specified instructions. The ELOISE system of the SEC is an example of a natural language understanding system. MT systems take written text in one natural language (the source language) and produce as output text translated in another natural language (the target language). Competent MT systems not only have to 'understand' incoming natural language statements, but also have to generate the appropriate text in another language. Thus MT systems utilize many ideas and processing techniques from natural language understanding systems. The Metal system of Siemens-Nixdorf is an example of a MT system.

## The nature of understanding

The concept of 'understanding something' is closely related to and as difficult to define as the general notion of 'intelligence'. In Turing's test (Chapter 1), the ability of a computer to engage in a meaningful conversation[9] is dependent on its ability to understand the topic of conversation and the various dialogs. Roger Schank[10] has argued for the following three stages of understanding:

● making sense — at this level of understanding, a system is able to 'make sense' of some input text. Examples of tasks at this level would be making summaries of news stories, or translating a piece of text into another language

● cognitive understanding — this level of understanding uses domain and common-sense knowledge to analyze and answer questions about the content of a certain piece of text. An example is a system which is able to take as input the description of events in a certain domain, and answer questions which require it to reason deeply (such as explain why certain actions were taken in preference over others)

● complete empathy — this is the highest level of understanding, and refers to the often unspoken, implicit understanding which exists between individuals (such as couples, twins, and close friends) who have shared many common experiences.

Figure 6.3 maps the proficiency of applied NLP systems on the above spectrum of understanding. Current systems are good for the first level (making sense) of understanding, and are only recently starting to push into the second level of cognitive understanding. The box on the top of the Figure 6.3 depicts different technological approaches (described in more detail in the following sections) to understanding natural language. The available technology is fairly well suited for 'making sense' of natural language text. Genuine cognitive understanding requires large amounts of domain knowledge. Some applied NLP systems are providing cognitive understanding by restricting themselves to a narrow restricted domain, and handling only a limited set of queries. As of now, there are not many clues about how to, if at all possible, reach the complete empathy level of understanding.

## Ambiguity in natural language understanding

Understanding natural language is not easy. The most important problem in understanding natural language is ambiguity. Some examples of ambiguity in natural languages are:

● syntactic ambiguity — consider the statement: 'Bob saw the Eiffel tower flying into Paris'. Syntactically, the above sentence is ambiguous: 'is the Eiffel tower actually flying into Paris', or 'did Bob see the tower while flying into Paris'?

● multiple word meanings — many words have more than one meaning, and this can be a source of ambiguity. For example in the sentence, 'John washed his glasses', the word 'glasses' can refer to either John's spectacles, or his drinking glasses

● pragmatics — consider the sentence: 'Can you open the door?'. Though a 'yes or no' answer would be appropriate under some circumstances, the 'normal' meaning of this sentence is something like 'please open the door'. This meaning is very different from that conveyed by a direct interpretation of the words in the sentence

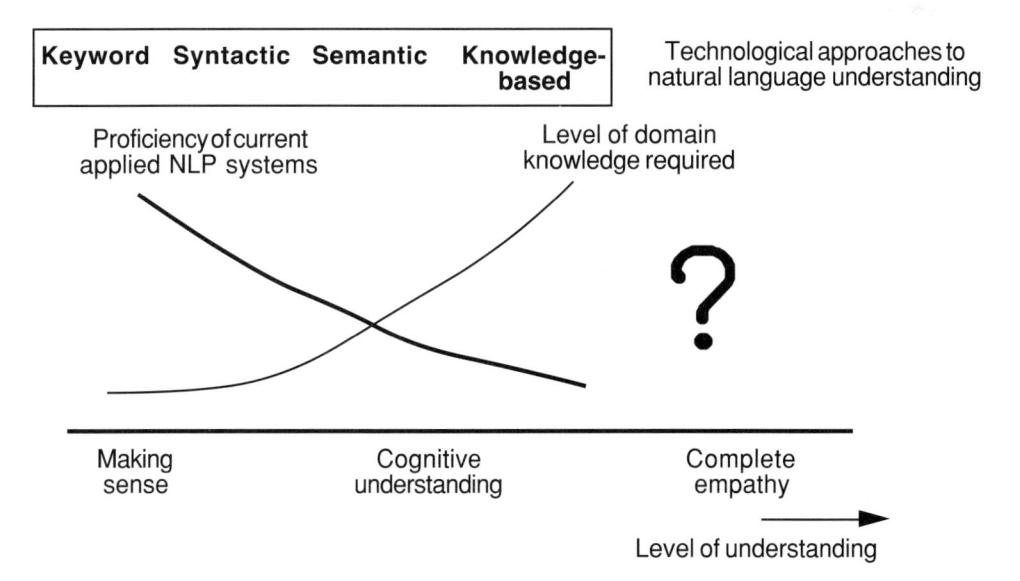

Figure 6.3 Levels of understanding

- referential — consider the example 'Bob took the cake and the plate and ate it'. Here the pronoun 'it' can potentially refer to either the cake or the plate.

The level of ambiguity increases significantly while considering multiple sentences. We usually resolve such ambiguity by using extensive domain and commonsense knowledge. In the sentence, 'Bob saw the Eiffel tower flying into Paris', we easily infer that Bob was flying into Paris because we know that the Eiffel tower is a fixed physical landmark in Paris, and is not capable of flying. In the example, 'John washed his glasses', we realize that the word 'glasses' refers to drinking glasses because we know that (usually) only drinking glasses are washed. When presented with a question of the form, 'Can you open the door?', we know from experience that it is really a request to open the door. In the sentence, 'Bob took the cake and the plate and ate it', we understand that the pronoun 'it' refers to the cake and not the plate, because we know that while cakes can be eaten plates are not edible.

The importance of using background domain knowledge to resolve ambiguity is evident. It is difficult to incorporate a large and sufficiently complete store of background knowledge to build a NLP system that is applicable to all (or a large number of) domains. To overcome this problem, most applied NLP systems store knowledge about a limited domain. For example, if the query, 'How many terminals are operating?', is given to a NLP system operating in the computer domain, the system will restrict the meaning of the word 'terminal' to a 'computer terminal' (and not consider other meanings, such as an 'airport terminal').

## Approaches to natural language understanding

Computational procedures to natural language understanding have been researched since the 1960s, and can be classified into three broad categories: keyword matching, syntax and semantics, and knowledge-based.

### Keyword matching

Keyword matching is the simplest and oldest approach to understanding natural language. The essence of keyword matching is the recognition of specific keywords in the input text. Keywords can vary from individual words to phrases and complete sentences. No attempt is made in this approach to arrive at a meaning of the input text by an analysis of how the various words and phrases in the sentence interact to give a specific meaning to the sentence. The best way to understand such an approach is to consider a simple example.

Figure 6.4 depicts a simple Prolog program (named Fast-Talk) which is capable of engaging in an 'apparently intelligent' conversation. An example of a dialog with Fast-Talk is shown in Figure 6.5. Note that the responses seem 'fairly intelligent' for a program that occupies less than a page! Without going into details, consider the two most important clauses, 'modify' and 'change', in the program Fast-Talk. All other clauses in Figure 6.4 are used for controlling input and output of the program. Note some of the transformation patterns specified in the various 'change' clauses. The clause change(my, your) changes all occurrences of 'my' in the input sentence to 'your' in the output sentence. The transfor-

# Approaches to natural language understanding 171

```
talk IF write("hello") AND nl AND nl AND interact.

interact IF readln(Line) AND modify(Line, Out) AND
            fronttoken(Out,First,Rest) AND type_out(Out, First).

type_out(Out, First) IF First = "bye" AND nl AND write(Out) AND nl AND nl.
type_out(Out, First) IF nl AND write(Out) AND nl AND nl AND interact.

modify(In_st, Out_st) IF
      fronttoken(In_st, First, Rest) AND
      change(First, Ch_first) AND
      modify(Rest, Ch_rest) AND
      concat(Ch_first, " ", Sp_first) AND
      concat(Sp_first, Ch_rest, Out_st).

modify("","").

change(what, "").
change(my, your).
change(your, my).
change(you, i).
change(do,"").
change(i, you).
change(any, "").
change(about, "").
change(because, "").
change(is,"").
change(name, "name is Fast-talk").
change(are,"").
change(interests, "interests are reading and art").
change(actress, "actress. She is Meryl Streep").
change(why, "can you be more clear").
change(streep, "streep because she acts well").
change(oh, "do you agree").
change(sure, good).
change(X,X).
```

**Figure 6.4** The Fast_Talk 'conversation' program

mations of all other change(.,.) clauses is analogous. A special transformation is specified by change(X, X). This is the 'catch-all' transformation pattern which causes all words[11] not identified as special keywords (by the other occurrences of the change(.,.) clause) to be repeated verbatim in the output sentence. Now it is easy to see how Fast-Talk responds to the input sentences shown in Figure 6.5. Consider the input sentence 'do you like going to the cinema'. Figure 6.6 shows how the various change(.,.) clauses specify the transformation patterns which determine the output sentence.

## 172 Natural language processing

| | |
|---|---|
| Fast_Talk: | hello |
| User Input: | what is your name |
| FT: | my name is Fast-talk |
| UI: | what are your interests |
| FT: | my interests are reading and art |
| UI: | do you like going to the cinema |
| FT: | i like going to the cinema |
| UI: | do you have a favorite actress |
| FT: | i have a favorite actress. She is Meryl Streep. |
| UI: | what do you like about meryl streep |
| FT: | i like meryl streep because she acts well |
| UI: | oh |
| FT: | do you agree |
| UI: | sure |
| FT: | good |
| UI: | bye |
| FT: | bye |

**Figure 6.5** A sample 'intelligent' conversation with Fast_Talk

Fast-Talk is a very simple program. It is possible to conceive of a more sophisticated version of Fast-Talk, which is able to match and transform a few thousand templates and keywords. Some early 'conversation programs' such as ELIZA[12] (which simulated a Rogerian psychologist), and PARRY[13] (which simulated a paranoid patient) were built using similar keyword matching techniques. ELIZA and PARRY were able to engage in fairly convincing conversations, and PARRY even managed to fool certain human psychiatrists. However, the level of 'understanding' within ELIZA and PARRY was fairly poor (only slightly better in quality than Fast-Talk), and this became apparent to any user who engaged in long conversations with the programs. The level of understanding obtainable

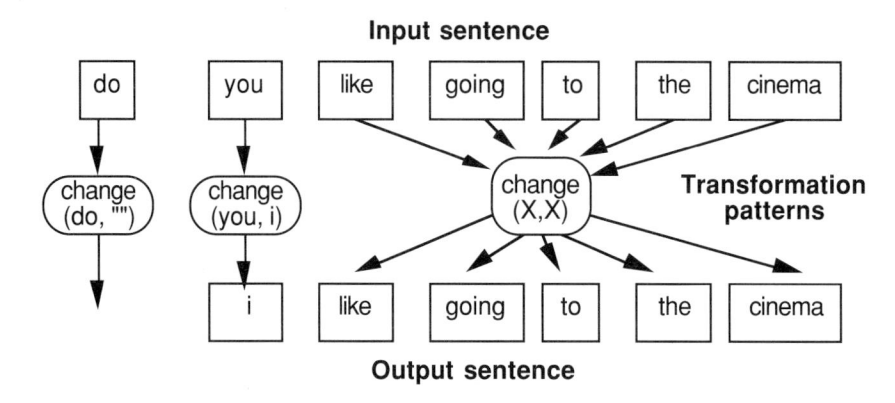

**Figure 6.6** Generation of output sentences in Fast_Talk

## Syntax and semantics 173

with such simple keyword matching techniques borders at the lower end of the 'making-sense' level of Schank's spectrum of understanding (Figure 6.3).

Keyword matching approaches to understanding natural language are simple to implement and are quite common. For example, most libraries contain books indexed by words and phrases (i.e., specific keywords), and library database queries use keyword matching techniques to retrieve the set of relevant books. The inability to incorporate an 'appropriate level of understanding' in keyword matching techniques limits their applicability to many tasks. Many 'natural language interfaces' to commercial programs also utilize keyword (or phrase) matching techniques for understanding natural language. It's important to realize the limited 'understanding' possible with such interfaces.

## Syntax and semantics

Most successful commercial applied NLP systems use some combination of syntax and semantics in understanding natural language. The syntactic analysis of an input sentence determines the relations between the different words in the sentence according to a grammar of the language. The semantic analysis process attempts to determine the meaning of the sentence by assigning domain-specific interpretations to the individual components (words) of the sentence.

### Syntactic analyses

Syntactic analyses are done by application of a grammar that determines legal sentence structures. Consider a simple grammar[14] for a subset of the English language as shown in Figure 6.7. This grammar determines how (some) sentences in English are constructed. For example, the first line of the grammar specifies that a sentence in English is composed of a noun phrase and a verb phrase. The next few lines define what qualifies as noun and verb phrases. Such a grammar can be applied to an input sentence such as, 'John hit the red ball', to check whether the sentence satisfies the structure specified by the rules of the grammar. The output of the application of a grammar to a sentence is known as a parse tree. The parse tree produced by applying the grammar of Figure 6.7 to the sentence 'John hit the red ball' is given in Figure 6.8. Note that the possible structure of the parse tree is limited by the rules of the grammar used for parsing.

| | |
|---|---|
| Sentence = | Noun_Phrase + Verb_Phrase |
| Noun_Phrase = | Noun OR (Determiner + Noun) OR (Determiner + Adjective + Noun) |
| Verb_Phrase = | Verb OR (Verb + Noun_Phrase) |
| Adjective = | red |
| Noun = | John OR ball OR moon OR glasses |
| Verb = | hit OR filled |
| Determiner = | the |

Figure 6.7 A simple grammar for the English language

## 174 Natural language processing

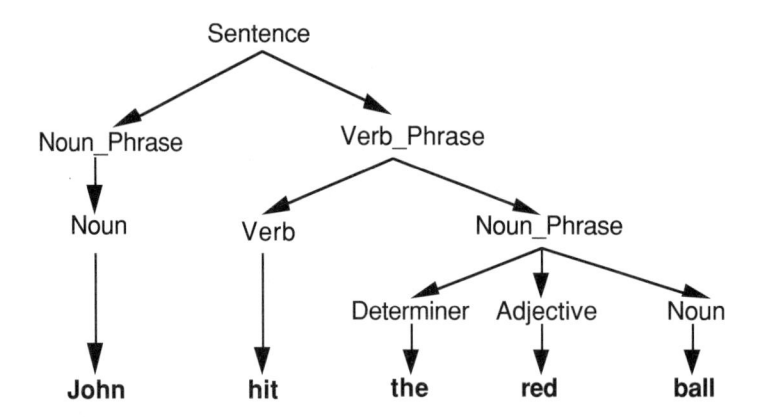

**Figure 6.8** A simple parse tree

Parse trees and grammars have been extensively studied within computer science. This is because parsing is an important component of the process of compiling a computer program. Every computer programming language (such as Fortran, Basic, and Pascal) has a well specified grammar (similar in form to that shown in Figure 6.7). This grammar is used for parsing sentences of an input program to verify that there are no syntactic mistakes in the program. Parsing techniques of computer languages cannot be used equally profitably for natural languages because it's difficult to devise a grammar which covers all possible sentences within a natural language. Unlike computer languages (which are artificially designed to satisfy strict rules), natural languages have evolved over centuries and have many exceptions and special structures. Despite the impossibility of devising a grammar for the entire English language, syntactic analyses are useful and used often. A reasonably complex form of the grammar shown in Figure 6.7 can parse a large enough subset of English sentences to satisfy the communication requirements of a restricted domain.

As noted earlier, many sentences have syntactic ambiguity i.e., they can have many possible parse trees. A classic example is: 'Bob saw the boy in the park with a telescope'. This sentence has three distinct syntactic parse trees corresponding to (a) Bob using the telescope to see the boy, (b) the boy in the park carrying a telescope, and (c) the telescope being a distinguishing feature of the park. Syntactic analyses alone cannot determine which parse tree represents the correct meaning. Domain-specific information is required to resolve such ambiguities.

Syntactic analyses have another important limitation. The process of parsing only checks structures of the sentences with no regard for their meanings. Thus a grammar can accept sentences which, though syntactically correct, do not have any meaning. A famous example[15] of a syntactically correct, but meaningless sentence is: 'colorless green ideas sleep furiously'. The dual limitations of (a) being unable to effectively resolve syntactic ambiguity, and (b) accepting sentences with no meaning, highlight the need for semantic analysis to assign correct meaning to a sentence.

## Semantic analyses

There are different approaches to performing semantic analyses. A common approach is to use semantic markers. Every NLP system has an associated dictionary (alternatively known as a lexicon) which stores meanings and parts of speech information about words. Using semantic markers would imply the storage of additional domain-specific 'semantic information' along with the meanings in the dictionary.

For example consider the simple dictionary[16] shown in Figure 6.9 for the grammar of Figure 6.7. The sentence, 'John filled the glasses', would be accepted as syntactically correct by the grammar, but there would be ambiguity about its meaning because the word 'glasses' can have two possible interpretations. A semantic analysis of the sentence would notice that the verb 'filled' requires that the object has an enclosure. Of the two possible meanings of 'glasses', the associated semantic markers indicate that only one meaning (as glasses for drinking) has an associated enclosure. This match between the semantic markers of the verb 'filled' and the noun 'glasses' helps to disambiguate the sentence, and assign it the correct meaning. Note that the semantic markers provide the background knowledge required for resolving the ambiguity in the input sentence. Real-life NLP systems have more complex lexicons, and the semantic disambiguation procedure is more sophisticated.

## Combining syntax and semantics

Some approaches to NLP attempt to combine both syntactic and semantic analyses. Semantic grammars represent one such popular technique. Semantic grammars were first used in 1976 to build a computer-aided instruction system named SOPHIE[17]. Semantic grammars quickly gained popularity, and were later used to provide natural language access to a large distributed database for the US Navy[18]. Semantic grammars are similar in structure and function to the syntactic grammars used for parsing (Figure 6.7) except for one major difference: the structure of the grammar rules is defined using both syntax and semantics. For example, consider the simplified semantic grammar shown in Figure 6.10. Note that the categories used in the grammar rules are not simply parts of speech (such as nouns and verbs), but rather semantic phrases (such as attribute and ship). This simple

| Word | Category | Semantic Markers |
|---|---|---|
| John | noun | human; animate |
| ball | noun | inanimate; round |
| moon | noun | inanimate; heavenly body; round |
| glasses | noun | inanimate; fragile<br>1st meaning: for drinking, hollow<br>2nd meaning: for reading |
| hit | verb | needs actor to hit subject |
| filled | verb | object needs enclosure |
| the | determiner | |

Figure 6.9 A simple lexicon with semantic markers

```
Sentence =     Question + the + Attribute + of + Ship
Question =     what is OR give me
Attribute =    length OR location OR class OR speed
Ship =         (the + Ship_Name) OR (Ship_Type + class + ship)
Ship_Name =    kennedy OR enterprise
Ship_Type =    carrier OR submarine
```

**Figure 6.10** A simple semantic grammar

semantic grammar can recognize input sentences such as: 'What is the length of the kennedy?', 'What is the location of the enterprise?', and 'Give me the speed of carrier class ships'.

Note that the parsing procedure with semantic grammars combines both syntactic and semantic analyses. Thus, it avoids many of the limitations of pure syntactic parses. For example, the utilization of semantic information in the grammar helps to resolve syntactic ambiguities, and focuses attention on correctly parsing and understanding only the relevant set of sentences. This narrow focus is also a limitation for semantic grammars. They are only able to handle inputs from a relatively small and preset group of sentences. They cannot understand and process arbitrary sentences.

Semantic grammars are popular, and sophisticated variations (of the basic structure illustrated in Figure 6.10) are used in many commercial NLP systems. Many interfaces to databases require the formulation of queries from a small subset of sentences. Semantic grammars can provide the requisite natural language processing capabilities easily and efficiently.

## Knowledge-based

Knowledge-based approaches to natural language understanding emphasize the use of domain and commonsense knowledge to aid the understanding process. Two common examples of knowledge-based natural language understanding are conceptual dependency diagrams and scripts, both proposed by Roger Schank of Yale University.

### Conceptual dependency diagrams

Conceptual dependency diagrams[19] aim to reduce natural language statements into a certain canonical semantic representation. Consider two examples mentioned by Schank: 'John gave Mary a ball', and 'Mary took a ball from John'. Though these two statements are different in their structures, their underlying meanings are similar. The different conceptual dependency diagrams[20] of both sentences are given in Figure 6.11. 'Atrans' is a particular primitive that represents the action of transfer of an abstract relationship (possession of the ball in the above sentences).

Schank claimed that 11 basic primitives (shown in Figure 6.12) were sufficient for representing all actions which could possibly be contained in the meaning of natural language statements. While this claim has been controversial, it has the attractive implica-

| | | |
|---|---|---|
| PRIMITIVE: | Atrans | Atrans |
| ACTOR: | John | Mary |
| OBJECT: | Ball | Ball |
| SOURCE: | John | John |
| RECIPIENT: | Mary | Mary |
| | *John gave Mary a ball* | *Mary took a ball from John* |

Figure 6.11 Conceptual dependency diagrams for two sentences

tion that any NLP system using conceptual dependency diagrams would only have to deal with a small subset of primitives (and not many dozens of keywords or grammar rules). A system using conceptual dependency diagrams also needs to have a set of inference rules to determine the conditions under which a particular primitive is applicable. For example, the primitive 'Atrans' is also applicable for other verbs such as donate, sell, and buy. The ability of conceptual dependency diagrams to capture and represent meaning canonically has made them popular in NLP systems utilizing a knowledge-based approach. Note that the conceptual dependency diagram shown in Figure 6.11 can be easily represented by a frame (see Chapter 3).

### Scripts

Scripts[21] are special knowledge structures used to represent certain stereotypical situations and sequences of events. Their structure is similar to an extended version of frames. A simple ride-a-train script is shown in Figure 6.13. The script has several slots (name, rôles, props, and so on) which are filled by certain values. There are certain rôles (e.g., traveller) and physical structures (e.g., train station and ticket machine) associated with the script. There are also associated entry and exit conditions which represent activation and termina-

| Primitive | Action Described by Primitive |
|---|---|
| PTRANS | transfer of location of a physical object |
| ATRANS | transfer of an abstract relationship (e.g., ownership) |
| PROPEL | application of physical force to an object |
| MOVE | movement of a body part |
| GRASP | grasping of an object by an actor |
| INGEST | an animal taking in (e.g., eating) some object |
| EXPEL | an animal expelling (e.g., sweating, spitting) an object |
| MTRANS | mental transfer of ideas between animals |
| MBUILD | using old information to build new information |
| SPEAK | action of producing sounds |
| ATTEND | focusing a sense organ to a stimulus |

Figure 6.12 Primitives of conceptual dependency diagrams

tion states of the script respectively. The various scenes describe different distinct action sequences associated with the subject of the script. Note that conceptual dependency diagrams can be used to represent the various actions in a script. Thus a script can be seen as being composed of a hierarchy of related conceptual dependency diagrams. The script of Figure 6.13 can be used for understanding text describing a situation in which someone is riding a train.

Scripts are useful for understanding text describing standard, stereotypical situations. A NLP system using scripts would typically contain many different scripts. A challenging task in using scripts for understanding natural language is determining the appropriate script to use. Different parts of the script (such as entry conditions, rôles, props, and various scenes) are used to determine applicability of scripts. For example, if a certain part of a natural language text contains references to a train station, then this reference can trigger the ride-a-train script. Once the applicability of a certain script has been identified, the process of understanding the text can be driven by the components of the script. Continuing with our example, if a NLP system is able to identify that the 'ride-a-train' script is applicable to a piece of text, it knows the kind of rôles and action sequences to expect based on its knowledge of the contents of the script. This feature of generating 'expectations' based on the script is very useful for understanding and explaining stories and texts about complex tasks.

While scripts are useful for understanding text dealing with stereotypical situations, they are limited in their capability to handle atypical problems and explain non-standard situations. For example, the 'ride-a-train' script of Figure 6.13 would have problems in dealing with text describing situations in which a ticket has to be bought from a manual ticket counter. Of course, this additional possibility can be added onto the script of Figure 6.13, but one can always think of new exception conditions. Scripts are commonly used in applied NLP systems which are used for specific restrictive tasks or domains.

| Script Name: | Ride-a-train |
|---|---|
| Roles: | Traveller |
| Props: | Station, Ticket-machine, Train, Seats |
| Entry condition: | Traveller wants to PTRANS (move) himself to another location |
| Exit condition: | Traveller is PRTANSed to new location |
| Scene 1: | Traveller enters station |
| | Traveller buys ticket from ticket-machine |
| | Traveller waits for train |
| Scene 2: | Train arrives at station |
| | Traveller enters train |
| | Traveller takes a seat in the train |
| Scene 3: | Train stops at destination |
| | Traveller leaves train |
| | Traveller exits destination train station |

**Figure 6.13** A simple 'ride-a-train' script

## Understanding multiple sentences and dialogs

Except for scripts, all other approaches to understanding natural language described above are best suited for understanding single sentences. Understanding multiple sentences is more complex than understanding a single sentence as an additional level of ambiguity has to be dealt with — relationships across sentences. Some examples of problems in understanding multiple sentences are:

- common objects across sentences — consider the text;

    *John bought a newspaper. He wanted to read the headlines*

Here 'headlines' refers to the content of the newspaper

- common actions across sentences — consider the examples;

    *Bill was riding a cycle. He fell down*

Here the action of 'falling' is related to riding a cycle

- causal chains across sentences — consider the text;

    *Bill wanted to go to the city. He went to the train station*

Here Bill went to the train station because he wanted to take the train to the city.

Domain knowledge is again required for resolving ambiguity across sentences. For example, domain knowledge is needed to known that 'headlines' refers to something found in newspapers. Similarly, knowledge about the action of riding a cycle would indicate that Bill fell down from the cycle (and not from somewhere else). The 'ride-a-train' script of Figure 6.13 can be used to understand the last example. The first sentence of the example, 'Bill wanted to go to the city', indicates that Bill wanted to 'Ptrans' (Figure 6.12) himself to another location. This matches the entry condition of the script 'ride-a-train'.

This match should trigger the script. Note that because the ride-a-train script has been activated, the NLP system can already generate a hypothesis about what to expect next. The second sentence, 'He went to the train station', matches with the first sentence of scene 1 of the script, and fulfils the expectations of the NLP system. Note that now all the additional information in the script can be used by the NLP system to answer questions 'intelligently' about the provided text. For example, in response to the question, 'Why did Bill enter the station?', the NLP system can respond something like, 'To buy a ticket to take the train and go to the city'.

Understanding interactive dialogs is in general a harder problem than understanding multiple sentences because:

- dialogs contain a large number of references to situations and objects mentioned earlier in the conversation

- people often use incomplete sentences which require to be interpreted in the context of the dialog (e.g., 'The 7 am flight?')

- occurrence of ungrammatical constructions is also higher in dialogs. Most parsing techniques are not robust enough to handle many grammatical exceptions

- dialogs are often strongly determined by the implicit beliefs of the participants. These beliefs complicate the language understanding procedures.

## Machine translation

The term 'machine translation' (MT) was coined around 1955[22], and the field received a major boost in 1957 when the Russians surprised the West by successfully launching the Sputnik satellite. Western scientists realized that due to a language barrier, they had been unable to follow Russian scientific journals and accurately judge the pace of Russian technical developments. Partly in response to this unexpected development, about 20 different MT projects were started in the USA alone, most of them with a focus on translating text between Russian and English. Similar MT projects were simultaneously started in the UK, France, Canada, and the USSR.

In 1966, the Automatic Language Processing Advisory Committee (ALPAC) reviewed the MT projects started with government funding about a decade ago. Their report[23] came to the disappointing conclusion that 'there is no immediate or predictable prospect of useful machine translation'. There were two major reasons for their conclusion. First, the idiosyncrasies of natural language and the complexities of translating languages had been grossly underestimated by researchers. As a result, even the best systems of that period produced text, whose quality was way below that produced by human translators. Second[24], the cost of manually keying in text to computers (there were no optical scanners then) drove up the costs of MT. Translated text also needed to be revised before it could be used.

As a reaction to the ALPAC report, most governmental funding of MT in the USA (and the UK) was cut off. Work on MT continued on a much lower scale over the next decade. The field enjoyed a rejuvenation again in the late 1970s. This was due to rapid improvements in computing technology, together with advances in AI and NLP. Optical scanners and other developments (such as word processors) simplified transfer of text to computers. The rôle of heuristics and knowledge came to be recognized as vital for MT, and expertise in heuristic programming from knowledge-based systems was transferred over to MT projects. The goal of MT was also made more realizable: the emphasis shifted from producing output text of equivalent quality as a human translator, to producing text which required minor editing by a human translator.

## Approaches to machine translation

Analogous to natural language understanding, three different approaches to MT can be identified: pattern-based translation, a combination of syntax and semantics, and knowledge-based.

### Pattern-based translation
This is the simplest and the oldest approach to MT. The basic set up is as shown in Figure 6.14. The fundamental component of the MT system is a large dictionary that takes patterns in the source language text, and translates them into an equivalent pattern in the target language. Patterns in this context are usually words or phrases, and in some instances (e.g., idioms) complete sentences. Such MT systems do not (and cannot) understand the text to be translated in any meaningful manner. As a result, these systems are often seriously limited in the range and type of text they can translate.

## Approaches to machine translation 181

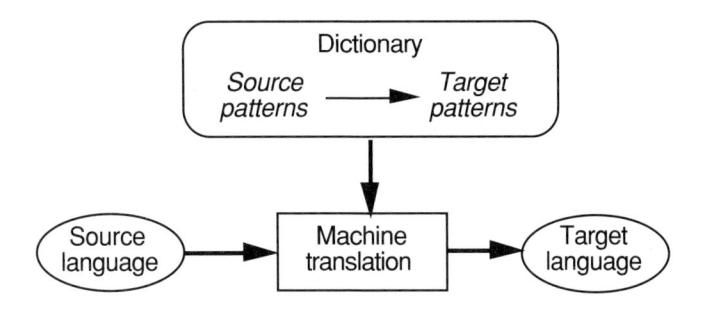

**Figure 6.14** Machine translation based on pattern matching

A notable example of a MT system using a pattern-based approach was the SYSTRAN[25] MT system, which was built at Georgetown University for conversion of Russian into English. SYSTRAN contained about 700,000 Russian words and phrases, and made up to 16 different passes over the same sentence. Its performance was surprisingly good for a limited class of Russian documents, and it had the useful feature of allowing the user to add new words and phrases automatically to the system dictionary. It also enjoyed a fair amount of commercial success for a period of time[26].

### Using syntax and semantics for translation

These approaches to MT translate text with the aid of syntactic and semantic analyses of sentences in the source language. They utilize many of the ideas described in the section on syntactic and semantic approaches to NLP. An example of a MT employing such an approach is the Metal[27] system (developed by Siemens-Nixdorf). A simplified representation of its basic structure and mode of operation is given in Figure 6.15.

Metal contains two lexicons, one each for the source and the target languages. The lexicons contain grammatical, syntactic, and semantic information about the concerned languages, and are arranged in a hierarchical organization of 'modules'. The highest module contains function words (such as conjunctions and prepositions). The next lower module contains general vocabulary words. For Indo-European languages, it is observed that about 5000 words are sufficient to cover most (about 90%) of general text. Below the general vocabulary module, there is a common technical vocabulary module. Next in the

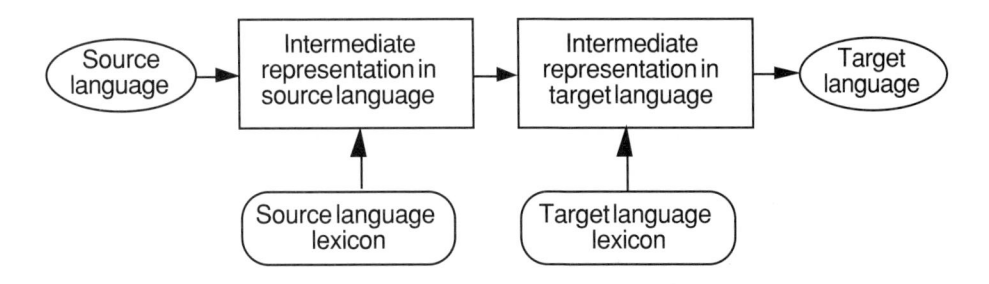

**Figure 6.15** Machine translation using syntax and semantics

hierarchy are one or more modules containing specialized technical vocabulary (such as those relating to hardware or software). Before a translation run is invoked, the user can instruct the system to give priority to one particular module (and thus bias the translation process). For example, if the hardware technical module is emphasized, the German word 'Fehler' is translated as 'fault'. If the software technical module is given priority, then the same word is translated as 'error'.

Metal accepts a sentence in the source language, and uses the source language lexicon to generate an intermediate representation of the structure and meaning of the sentence. The grammar rules in the lexicon are weighted using probabilities (based on semantics and the context — such as the prespecified subject area of the text) to determine which rules are most applicable. The intermediate representation in the source language resembles a parse tree (Figure 6.8) with the important difference that additional information (derived from the source language lexicon) about the applied rules and determined meanings is stored with each 'fork' or 'node' in the parse tree. This additional information is used to transform the source language intermediate representation into an equivalent intermediate representation in the target language. The entire process is computationally expensive as usually there are many different translation possibilities.

Note the difference between Figures 6.14 and 6.15. While the translation in Figure 6.14 is 'direct', the translation of Figure 6.15 proceeds by generating an 'intermediate' representation. This helps to increase accuracy of translation and the range of text handled by the system. The proficiency of MT systems is difficult to measure as there is no one objective measure of the 'goodness' of translation. Tests with the Metal system for translations between English and German have indicated that more than 60% of all sentences are 'accurate', while the rest are good enough to serve as a basis for post-editing.

**Knowledge-based translation**

High quality MT requires extensive domain-specific and commonsense knowledge to resolve ambiguities in the text. The generic structure of knowledge-based approaches to MT is shown in Figure 6.16. An important step in this approach is the extraction of 'meaning' from the source language text, and its storage in a suitable knowledge representation scheme (such as conceptual dependency diagrams — Figure 6.11). The stored meanings of the source language sentences can be used by a language generation module to generate text in the target language. In principle, the target language can be changed by varying the language generation component. Few commercial MT systems exist which use knowledge-based approaches exclusively. However, this is the direction in which future MT systems will evolve. Many existing commercial MT systems (such as Metal) are incorporating limited domain knowledge during their analyses. This domain knowledge is usually represented by small rule-based (knowledge-based) systems which guide the disambiguation and parsing processes.

The MT procedures described in Figure 6.15 and 6.16 differ in two important aspects. First, there is only one intermediate representation in Figure 6.16, and this intermediate representation attempts to capture the 'meaning' of the sentence (as opposed to its structure). Second, there is no store of domain-specific and commonsense knowledge in Figure 6.15.

Though not discussed in this chapter, it must be mentioned that language generation is a deceptively hard problem. Most researchers believe it to be an equally (if not more) difficult problem as language understanding. The difficulties arise in generating text

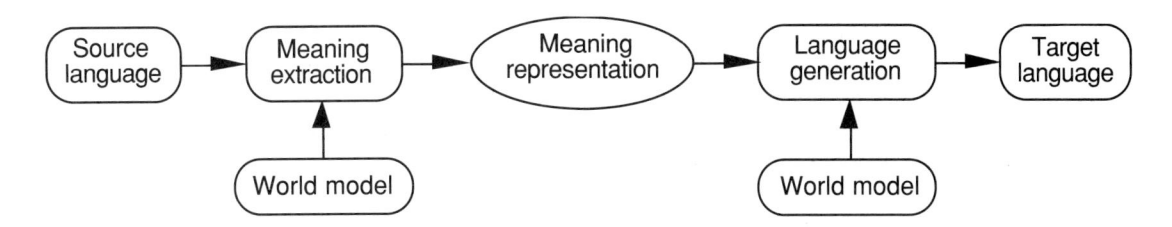

**Figure 6.16** Knowledge-based machine translation

which is both 'readable' (and not full of repetitious constructs, as is typical of automated procedures) and coherent. Surprisingly, little research has been done on the issue of language generation, and most of the effort within NLP has been spent on language understanding.

## Machine translation in industry

During the 1960s and the early 1970s, industrial translators typed documents manually, and scrutinized original technical literature in the source and target languages (due to a lack of technical dictionaries) for product specific terminology. The translation process was cumbersome, error prone, and quite disorganized. Translation demands of industry were low and were generally satisfied by the translators. From the mid-1970s onwards, computers started entering industrial translation departments in the form of word processors, multi-lingual databases, and technical dictionaries. Though all translation was still done manually, these tools enhanced the efficiency of the translation process. Nevertheless, the translation departments were overwhelmed by increased translation demands caused by rapidly increasing product ranges. Schneider[28] notes that when Siemens-Nixdorf launched its EWS public switching system in the late 1970s, complex software requiring extensive documentation accounted for about 80% of the new product's development cost. Companies such as Siemens-Nixdorf found it was virtually impossible to meet the growing need for translation services with human translators alone. This caused them to explore the use of MT technology for meeting the translation challenge.

Since the mid-1980s, many major industrial corporations of the world have been utilizing MT technology. These MT systems are not fully automated, and typically their outputs have to be post-edited by human translators. They have however helped to increase efficiency of human translators significantly. For example, the Metal system can produce a raw translation of a 10,000 page manual in 50 normal working (8 hour) days as opposed to 200 days for a full-scale translation by 10 translators working at the rate of five pages a day. MT technology is best suited within industry for translating technical materials. They are not well suited for translating legal documents or advertising materials. They help the language departments of industries in accepting large translation assignments, and producing quick and rough translations of documents when required.

Some professional associations of translators have protested against the use of MT systems in industry by arguing that they take away jobs. However, the truth is just the opposite. MT systems enrich the jobs of human translators by removing much of the drudgery in their work, and enable them to take on larger and more challenging assignments. Also, experience (at Siemens-Nixdorf) has shown that the use of MT systems increases the demand for translation services (from the rest of the organization), and thus creates new jobs for human translators.

## Evaluating natural language interfaces

Natural language interfaces to computer systems are useful when one or more of the following conditions are satisfied:
- most users are computer non-specialists
- users are not interested in formulating complex queries
- the system interface is complex
- users cannot undergo special training to use the system
- range and domain of queries are moderately restricted.

Though having natural language interfaces seems appealing, they are not always desirable. Some conditions under which natural language interfaces are not desirable are:
- the content and type of interactions are limited (so that menu type interfaces can perform the functions easily and efficiently)
- physical controls are essential for performing the task (such as in driving a car)
- complex queries are needed (special computer languages are best suited for formulating special, complex queries)
- wording of queries is not restricted to a manageable subset of the natural language (it is difficult to build interfaces to successfully understand general natural language sentences).

Natural language interfaces are available commercially for interfacing to various application programs (such as databases and statistical programs) on a variety of machines ranging from desktop PCs to large mainframes. Many developers of fourth generation languages and special application development packages have started incorporating 'English interfaces' in their systems. Claims of vendors selling systems possessing natural language interfaces should be taken with caution. Some interfaces are entirely based on keyword matching techniques. These interfaces cannot truly understand text. Other script-based interfaces may provide deep knowledge-based understanding, but they are usually limited in their domain of applicability. Careful analyses need to be done to evaluate the true capabilities of the NLP tool, and to match them to the communication needs of the concerned interface. Some criteria on which to evaluate a natural language interface, and relevant questions to be asked are mentioned below:
- lexical coverage — how large is the size of the relevant vocabulary? How easy is it for the user to add new words to the dictionary? Many domain-specific terms are needed in the lexicon for a natural language interface to be effective. The ability for the user to add such words at a later point of time is important (every lexicon grows with time)

# Evaluating natural language interfaces 185

- syntactic coverage — what is the range of syntactic structures (such as relative clauses, passives, and comparatives) which the system is capable of handling? Are these syntactic structures sufficient for formulatingthe required queries?
- semantic coverage — does the natural language interface understand the underlying domain of application? Or does it simply translate the incoming natural language query into a database retrieval language query without using any domain knowledge? An interface of the latter type would only allow queries such as, 'Is there a teacher record for John', and not as, 'Was a student named John ever taught by Professor Zadeh'?
- built-in inference — does the interface have the capability to make knowledge-based inferences about the information requested in the query? For example, a query such as, 'Do Bill and John know each other', might prompt a natural language interface with inference capabilities to check whether Bill and John ever worked together or lived nearby, and then deduce whether they know each other
- robustness — how robust is the system to errors (such as ungrammatical sentences and abbreviated words) in the input statements? How well can the system handle different kinds of ambiguities?
- special-purpose or general-purpose — special-purpose natural language interfaces tightly integrate syntax, semantics, and domain knowledge and are usually only applicable to a restricted domain. Other interfaces are general-purpose to the extent that domain-dependent knowledge is separated from general syntactic and semantic knowledge within the system. General-purpose systems need longer development and adaptation periods, but can be used in different domains.

## Commercial tools for natural language processing

Intellect[29] is one of the oldest and most successful general-purpose NLP tools. It interfaces to many different databases, graphical systems, and statistical packages on a variety of hardware platforms including PCs and IBM mainframes. Intellect relies primarily on a combination of syntax and semantics in understanding natural language. It however also allows a limited amount of domain-specific information to be utilized during the understanding process. Intellect has two different lexicons: one for general English (supplied with the product), and one which is domain-specific (created specifically by the user for a particular application). Each lexicon contains information about both syntax and semantics. When interfacing to databases, Intellect also utilizes knowledge of the database structure (such as the records and fields in the database). This allows the system to exhibit reasonable inference capabilities, and frees the user from the responsibility of having to know about the underlying database structure. When confused, the system returns to the user for help and clarification. Recently, the Intellect system has been linked to a knowledge-based system tool called KBMS (Knowledge-Based Management System), and today both packages are sold together as a knowledge-based application shell tool with a natural language interface.

A company called Cognitive Systems sells natural language interfaces based on conceptual dependency diagrams and scripts. These interfaces contain many different scripts for a particular application, and use domain-specific knowledge extensively. Thus they are entirely special-purpose natural language interfaces, and each new application needs the development of a new set of scripts.

A natural language interface called Language Craft[30] takes an approach similar to conceptual dependency diagrams, but combines it with syntactic and semantic analyses. Language Craft has a set of frames for different actions (similar to, but not the same as the primitives given by Schank — Figure 6.12). Each action frame has an associated set of rôles and structure (like the conceptual dependency diagram of Figure 6.11). The syntactic and semantic analyses attempt to identify which action frame is appropriate for 'understanding' the input sentence. Language Craft is linked to a knowledge-based system development tool called Knowledge Craft. It also provides links for Language Craft to access (if needed) the knowledge within the knowledge base of Knowledge Craft.

Another natural language system called Natural Link takes a more simple and restricted approach as compared to the above systems. Rather than allowing users to frame arbitrary queries, it restricts the type of queries by letting users choose between different words/phrases. Such an approach is also alternatively known as a menu-based natural language interface. Figure 6.17 depicts a simple menu-based natural language interface. Note the similarities between Figures 6.17 and 6.10. A menu-based natural language interface has the advantages of simplicity, efficiency, and of never allowing the user to make a mistake in the input query. However, it has the important limitations of restricted applicability, and not being able to perform any 'understanding'.

## Applications of natural language processing

Due to the wide use of natural language, NLP systems are being applied in a variety of domains ranging from financial institutions to manufacturing industries and hospitals. A few examples of NLP applications in different domains and using different technological approaches are described below.

### The Securities and Exchange Commission[31]

Arthur Andersen & Co. has built two major NLP systems — FSA and ELOISE — for the Securities and Exchange Commission (SEC) in the USA (see introductory section).

The SEC receives electronic filings (such as 10Q and 10K filings) directly from various companies through the EDGAR system. Though available in the computer (in text

| Choose one item from each group to form query: |||
| --- | --- | --- |
| What is the<br><br>Give me the | length of<br>location of<br>class of<br>speed of | the Kennedy<br>the Enterprise<br>carrier class ship<br>submarine class ship |

Figure 6.17 A simple menu-based natural language interface

## Applications of natural language processing 187

format), this information by itself cannot be used for automatic processing. SEC analysts have to scan the statements manually to retrieve financial information that can be used for performing various analyses, such as calculation of ratios. Complicating matters is the fact that filed documents are not of a uniform format (the SEC, as a matter of policy, does not enforce a uniform format), and differ widely in their wording and level of detail. Thus simple pattern matching is not sufficient for retrieving the required information. The FSA (Financial System Analysis) system 'reads' the documents in the EDGAR database, and retrieves the financial information required by the SEC analysts. To do this successfully, FSA must 'understand' the document because the same information can be located in distinct parts in different documents and be worded variously. To assist in NLP, FSA relies on an extensive knowledge base (built on frames) about the underlying domain model. Some of the capabilities of FSA are:

● captions — FSA understands a variety of captions i.e., interprets them specially in the context of the financial domain (e.g., the caption 'Other' is interpreted as 'Other current assets')

● textual notes — FSA looks at the parenthetical notes listed besides a caption (e.g., it highlights temporary cash investments mentioned in parenthesis, but included in the value of cash)

● footnotes — FSA analyzes information available in footnotes

● inference — beyond retrieving financial numbers, FSA can (with the help of knowledge-based techniques) highlight trends and abnormal situations (e.g., companies which are significantly lower or higher than the average).

Initial tests with the FSA system have indicated it handles about 94% of cases supplied by the SEC correctly.

The ELOISE (English Language Oriented Indexing System for EDGAR) system is used for identifying concepts of interest in the documents stored in the EDGAR database. This identification is useful for indexing the stored documents. The NLP technology in ELOISE is also knowledge-based. ELOISE contains many different frames (similar to the conceptual dependency diagrams shown in Figure 6.11) for the different concepts of interest to the SEC. During its initial scan of the text, ELOISE attempts to find a building word or phrase which can signal presence of one or more of the concepts of interest. After the frame for a particular concept of interest is triggered, ELOISE tries to 'fill' in the various slots in the triggered frame (using an expectation-driven process — similar to the use of scripts) till all (or most) slots are filled with information in the document, and the presence of that concept is confirmed. Initial results of the ELOISE system indicate it is capable of correctly identifying target concepts in 85% of the cases supplied by the SEC.

### The Intelligent Banking System at Citibank[32]

Electronic transfer of messages is very important for international banks such as Citibank. Though major banks have adopted several industry-wide structured message formats for the most common banking transactions, a significant minority of these messages are still transmitted using English. These messages are usually very terse, highly abbreviated, and often typed (at their source) by operators who are operating under severe time pressures, and for whom English is not the first language. These messages usually require costly and error-prone manual processing by operators who also need to be knowledgeable about international banking operations. Also, specific conditions in the environment require that each of these messages be processed within 60 seconds.

The IBS (Intelligent Banking System) is a special-purpose NLP system developed for Citibank to scan and understand banking messages written in English. It contains modules for handling messages belonging to three different categories: fund transfer, letter of credit issuance, and letter of credit reimbursement. It also has facilities to answer queries regarding fund transfer problems and classify messages based on certain parameters. The underlying NLP technology includes semantic grammars and a small knowledge-based component. The semantic grammar exploits the available structure in the message units, and the knowledge-based component attempts to put the various message units together into one coherent package. This application has been deemed as successful by Citibank because it helps to identify over 80% of messages automatically (the remaining 20% is done manually), and has reduced message processing time to 30 seconds per message. Quantifiable cost savings have reportedly been achieved by reducing head count, increasing customer satisfaction and lowering data-entry errors.

### The Direct Labor Management System at Ford[33]

At Ford, process sheets form a critical means for transmittal of assembly information from initial process planning to assembly at the plant. Process sheets are used to generate work allocation sheets (containing detailed assembly instructions assigned to each assembly worker), and to provide consistent and accurate estimates of direct (actions that directly contribute to the assembly process) and non-direct (actions that are necessary to effect the direct actions) labor times during the assembly process. An additional factor is the international nature of many of Ford's assembly operations. Process sheets have to be translated into foreign languages for use in foreign assembly locations.

Due to these reasons, Ford has built the Direct Labor Management System (DLMS), a NLP system which is a major sub-system in a multi-phase Manufacturing Process Planning System (MPPS). For 'understanding' process sheets, the DLMS system relies on a large lexicon of automotive assembly terms related to parts, process equipment, standard operations, and geometric workstation models.

Analogous to the ELOISE system of the SEC, the DLMS system attempts to identify concepts of interest in the process sheet specifications with the help of a frame-based representation scheme (each frame with its various slots represents a particular concept). Based on its understanding of the process sheet instructions, the DLMS system generates data for the work allocation sheets, and estimates the direct and indirect labor components. The DLMS system was introduced experimentally in December 1988, and about 300 engineers were using it in 1989. Ford views this project a success, and as a critical component in its plans to assist production and planning personnel in all aspects of the manufacturing process through the next decade.

### Content-based indexing of news stories at Reuters[34]

The Historical Information Products Division at Reuters sells a variety of textual and numerical products (such as Reuters Country Reports and Reuters Company Newsyear). To aid their customers locate relevant stories, Reuters supplies an indexing scheme specifying a set of index terms for each document. Producing this indexing scheme with human editors is a labor intensive, expensive, slow, error-prone, and repetitive task.

To overcome these problems Reuters has been using (since April 1988) the Construe natural language understanding system to understand a broad range of news stories, and categorize each story into one or more of 674 distinct categories. Each story is processed in less than five seconds and overall accuracy of the system is higher than 89%. The Construe system was custom designed for Reuters by the Carnegie Group (involving a total effort of nearly 6.5 person years), and is today sold as a general text categorization shell. The technical approach used in Construe is a combination of semantics and shallow domain knowledge (about how human editors categorize stories). Reuters estimates that the use of natural language understanding techniques for the indexing of news stories has reduced costs by $700,000 in 1990, and by more than $1 million in 1991. Indexing staff members displaced by the automated system have been moved to other projects where their skills are used more effectively. Reuters' customers are also benefiting from a faster and more consistent indexing of stories.

### Patient medical records system at Hartford Hospital[35]

Hartford hospital is a well-respected hospital in Connecticut with a 900-bed facility. Since the early 1980s, Hartford Hospital has been utilizing the Intellect NLP tool to provide natural language access for its employees to its databases containing medical records. The primary benefit of the NLP system at Hartford has been to provide faster and easier access to medical records. Doctors and nurses are usually computer-naive, and tend to have little patience with sophisticated computer languages. Intellect has helped them to directly access (in English) required information. The inference capabilities of Intellect has enabled these medical professionals to ask complex queries (such as, 'give me the total charge for all heart surgery patients over the last five years') which combine data from different departments. Other mentioned benefits of the Intellect system have been in reducing training time for MIS staff, reducing the number of PCs (as all users directly access data from the central mainframe), and minimizing duplication of data (as all data is stored and accessed centrally).

### Natural language applications at Steelcase[36]

Steelcase is a $1.5 billion company which is well-known in the office furniture industry. It has successfully used the Intellect NLP system for human resources and manufacturing applications. Today all Steelcase employees from company chairman to factory foremen have been trained to use the Intellect system to query the human resources database. Telephone operators and mailroom clerks regularly use the system to make about 1600 queries a week on employee names, departments, and phone extensions. In addition, the Intellect system is used within manufacturing for inventory control, factory capacity planning, and shop floor design. For example, more than 800 users have the capability to directly access the 80,000 item manufacturing database to locate inventory data, and make better decisions about scheduling materials and labor by combining that data with customer order information. Directly as a result of the improved information access capabilities offered by the NLP system, Steelcase has been able to cut its production lead time for many items by two days, and greatly reduce materials and parts inventories. Intellect has automated information retrieval on the factory floor to the extent that it is today possible for a shop-floor foreman to retrieve, using a single English query, the bills of material and drawings for all parts involved in manufacture of a product.

## The business impact of natural language processing

The most important benefit of NLP applications is that they aid the process of *informating*[37] the organization. NLP applications allow the easy access of information by all employees within an organization. This can be observed in the NLP application examples described above. At Hartford hospital, NLP is giving doctors and nurses fast and easy access to medical records. At Steelcase, all employees (ranging from factory foremen to the chairman) can access company databases with equal ease. The result of this ease of access to information is that employees are more informed about their work and business contexts. This in turn leads to more efficiency and innovation as employees, empowered by the available information, are able to evaluate current business practices and suggest useful changes. Based on the improved information available via NLP, doctors at Hartford hospital can provide more effective medical treatment, and Steelcase has been able to cut its production lead times and greatly reduce inventories.

Huge amounts of information need to be processed by organizations daily. This is evident in the examples of the SEC and Citibank. The SEC has to annually process more than seven million electronic filings of all listed companies and provide rapid access to this information. Banks like Citibank are critically dependent upon quick and accurate processing of electronic text messages. It is very expensive and inefficient to process all this information manually. NLP can help organizations in processing incoming information and flagging important conditions which need further attention from experts. Besides the benefit of being able to digest enormous amounts of information, NLP can yield quantifiable savings, lower errors, and increase satisfaction (as illustrated in the example of NLP at Citibank).

The world economy is getting more and more integrated, and most companies today can no longer operate isolated within the security of one particular business environment. An ability to conduct business in different languages is important to be competitive in the global market. NLP and MT technologies can play important rôles in aiding corporations to adapt to different business environments. As explained earlier, benefits of NLP such as an ability to provide documentation for products in local languages is important for multinational corporations. Using human translators is both difficult and expensive. The Metal MT system of Siemens-Nixdorf is a good example of how MT technology can supplement human translators and enhance the competitive positions of organizations.

Finally, NLP can provide new business opportunities for organizations. By using the capabilities of NLP to process and access information, organizations can potentially make the selling of information into a profitable business.

## Summary

Natural language is the most important medium for human communication. Thus it is very useful to have man-machine interfaces which are capable of communicating in natural language. This chapter has described important technological challenges in natural language processing and has provided examples to illustrate commercial impacts of the technology. The highlights of the chapter can be summarized in the following manner:

- Natural language processing (NLP) is the sub-field of AI that deals with understanding and generating natural language. The sub-field of NLP consists of two streams — cognitive NLP and applied NLP. The emphasis in this chapter is on applied NLP.

- There are two major categories of applied NLP systems — natural language understanding systems and machine translation (MT) systems. The former is concerned with 'understanding' natural language instructions, and the latter focuses on understanding and translating natural language text from one language into another.

- The concept of 'understanding something' is hard to define and is closely related to the notion of 'intelligence'. Three levels of understanding have been identified by researchers — making sense, cognitive understanding, and complete empathy. The understanding capabilities of current NLP systems are slowly reaching into the second level of cognitive understanding.

- Understanding natural language is difficult, primarily due to different types of ambiguities in natural language text — syntactic, multiple meanings, pragmatics, and referential. Extensive domain knowledge is needed for effectively resolving such ambiguities.

- Three broad approaches to understanding natural language are possible — keyword matching, syntax and semantics, and knowledge-based. Keyword approaches are simple to implement and are commonly used. However they have several limitations. A combination of syntax and semantics is more powerful and attempts to find the meaning of sentences by assigning meanings to its individual components. Knowledge-based approaches use extensive domain-specific knowledge to aid the understanding process.

- Understanding multiple sentences and dialogs is harder than understanding single sentences due to an increase in the level of ambiguity (such as common actions and objects across sentences).

- There is a large commercial market for MT as the worldwide bill for translation services is estimated to be more than $30 billion with an annual growth rate of around 15%. MT technology is vital for organizations selling products and services in different countries.

- MT is harder than simple natural language understanding as it has to both understand and generate text. Language generation is a deceptively hard problem.

- Analogous to natural language understanding, there are three broad approaches to MT — pattern-based, combining syntax and semantics, and knowledge-based. State-of-the-art commercial MT systems combine syntactic and semantic analyses, and use scattered amounts of domain knowledge in the translation process.

- Natural language interfaces to computer systems can be evaluated on the following criteria — degrees of lexical, syntactic, and semantic coverage, the ability to perform inferences, robustness, and domain-specificity.

- Several commercial tools offer different degrees of natural language processing capabilities.
- Natural language applications can significantly impact processing, distribution and availability of information within an organization. They can help in reconfiguring work flows and informating the organization.

Natural language processing systems need to use domain-specific knowledge to aid the understanding process. Thus they utilize techniques for representing and reasoning with knowledge elaborated upon in Chapters 2, 3, and 4. Organizational considerations for knowledge-based system applications as outlined in Chapter 5 also apply for implementing natural language applications in organizations.

## Bibliography and suggested readings

Books by Schank and Abelson (Schank & Abelson 77) and Wilensky (Wilensky 83) provide excellent descriptions of important issues in natural language processing in the context of understanding stories. A cognitive perspective on language is described in reference (Winograd 82). Relatively technical overviews of natural language processing can be found in references (Barr et al 89), (Carbonell & Hayes 92), (Bates 90), (McDonald 92), and (Rich & Knight 91), Selected chapters of the book by Rauch-Hindin (Rauch-Hindin 88) provide a good description of commercial tools for natural language processing. Other useful books on NLP are references (Winograd 73), (Wallace 84), and (Harris 85). Articles by Nagao (Nagao 92), and Alonso and Schneider (Alonso & Schneider 87) provide a technical overview of and an industry perspective on machine translation respectively.

Alonso, J. A. and T. Schneider, *Machine Translation Technology: On the Way to Market Introduction*, Siemens Review, Vol. 54, No. 6, Nov/Dec 87.

Barr, A., P.R. Cohen, and E.A. Feigenbaum, *The Handbook of Artificial Intelligence*, Vol 4, Chapter 19, Addison-Wesley, 1989.

Bates, M., *Natural Language Interfaces, in Encyclopedia of Artificial Intelligence*, Vol. 1, S.C. Shapiro (Ed.), pp. 655–660, John Wiley, 1990.

Carbonell, J.G. and P.J. Hayes, *Natural Language Understanding*, in *Encyclopedia of Artificial Intelligence*, Vol. 2, S.C. Shapiro (Ed.), pp.997–1015, John Wiley, 1992.

Harris, M.D., *Introduction to Natural Language Processing*, Reston Pub. Co., Reston, VA, 1985.

McDonald, D. D., *Natural Language Generation,* in *Encyclopedia of Artificial Intelligence*, Vol. 2, S.C. Shapiro (Ed.), pp.983–997, John Wiley, 1992.

Nagao, M., *Machine Translation*, in *Encyclopedia of Artificial Intelligence*, S. C. Shapiro (Ed.), Vol. 2, pp. 898–902, John Wiley, 1992.

Rauch-Hindin, W., *A Guide to Commercial Artificial Intelligence*, Chapters 11–14, Prentice-Hall, 1988.

Rich, E., and K. Knight, *Artificial Intelligence*, Chapter 15, Mc-Graw Hill, 1991.

Schank, R.C., and R. Abelson, *Scripts, Plans, Goals and Understanding*, Lawrence Erlbaum, 1977.

Wallace, M., *Communicating with Databases in Natural Language*, Ellis Horwood, Chichester, UK, 1984.

Wilensky, R., *Planning and Understanding*, Addison-Wesley, Reading, MA, 1983.

Winograd, T., *Language as a Cognitive Process*, Vol. 1, Syntax, Addison-Wesley, Reading, MA, 1982.

Winograd, T., *Understanding Natural Language*, Academic Press, NY, 1973.

## Notes

1 There is some debate over the fact whether chimpanzees and other primates can also communicate using natural language. Some experiments have reportedly shown that chimpanzees can communicate using sign language. While a fascinating field of research in biology, this aspect has been ignored in this chapter, as it has little commercial potential today.

2 Wittgenstein, L., *Tractatus Logico-Philosophicus*, New York, Routledge and Kegan Paul, 1961. Original German version published in 1921.

3 *The Securities and Exchange Commission*, Case Study, Harvard Business School, No 9-186-279, 1986.

4 Indexing is necessary as it is not possible to physically search all documents in their entirety during retrieval.

5 Adapted from: *The Securities and Exchange Commission*, Case Study, Harvard Business School, No. 9-186-279, pp. 12, 1986.

6 The problem faced by the SEC is similar to that faced by users of library databases. Books in most libraries are indexed by words, and/or phrases (subject, title, author, and so on). The retrieval of books on a desired topic requires the formulation of queries of the form shown in Figure 6.1. Experiments with different forms of queries are often required to obtain the correct set of books. A natural language processing system can accept the description of the desired topic in natural language, and retrieve only the relevant books, based on its knowledge of the specified topic, and of the contents of the various books in the library. Similar benefits can be obtained by using natural language processing techniques in the interfaces to other databases also.

7 Alonso, J. A. and T. Schneider, *Machine Translation Technology: On the Way to Market Introduction*, Siemens Review, Vol. 54, No. 6, Nov/Dec 87.

8 Alonso, J. A. and T. Schneider, *Machine Translation Technology: On the Way to Market Introduction*, Siemens Review, Vol. 54, No. 6, Nov/Dec 87.

9 Some programs (such as PARRY — see following sections) which claimed to fool human observers were by themselves not very intelligent, and did not really understand the topic of the conversation.

10 Schank, R. C., *Explanation Patterns*, pp. 6–13, Lawrence Erlbaum Associates, Hillsdale, New Jersey, 1986.

11 Note that X represents a variable in Prolog and thus can represent any input word.

12 Weizenbaum, J., *ELIZA — A computer program for the study of natural language communication between man and machine*, Communications of the ACM, 9(1), Jan, pp 36–45, 1966.

13 Parkinson, R. C., K. M. Colby and W. S. Fraught, *Conversational language comprehension using integrated pattern-matching and parsing*, Artificial Intelligence, 9, pp. 111–134, 1977.

14 The notation used here for representing the grammar is non-standard. This is for increasing the ease of comprehension by the non-technical reader.

15 Chomsky, N., Syntactic Structures, Mouton, The Hague, 1969.

16 A non-standard representation is adopted for the lexicon to ease comprehension by the non-technical reader.

17 Burton, R. R., *Semantic Grammar: An Engineering Technique for Constructing Natural Language Understanding Systems*, BBN Report 3453, Bolt, Beranek and Newman, Cambridge, MA, Dec. 1976.

18 Hendrix, G. G., *Human Engineering for Applied Natural Language Processing*, Proceedings of the 5th International Joint Conference on Artificial Intelligence, Cambridge, MA, pp. 183–191, 1977.

19 Schank, R. C., *Conceptual Information Processing*, North-Holland, Amsterdam, 1975.

20 A non-standard representation is used here for depicting conceptual dependency diagrams to ease comprehension by the non-technical reader.

21 Schank, R. C. and R. P. Abelson, *Scripts, Goals, Plans and Understanding*, Lawrence Erlbaum, Hillsdale, NJ 1977.

22 Weaver, W.; *Translation*, reprinted in F. Lockheed and T. Booth (Eds.), Machine translation of languages, pp. 15–23, Wiley, 1955.

23 *ALPAC, Languages and Machines: Computers in Translation and Linguistics*, National Academy of Sciences, National Research Council Publication 1416, Washington, DC, 1966.

24 Taie, M., *Machine translation*, in the *Encyclopedia of Artificial Intelligence*, Vol 1, pp. 564–571, S.C. Shapiro, (Ed.), John Wiley, 1990.

25 Bruderer, H., *Handbook of machine translation and machine aided translation: Automatic translation of natural languages and multilingual terminology data banks*, North-Holland, Amsterdam, 1977.

26 Nagao, M., *Machine translation*, in the *Encyclopedia of Artificial Intelligence*, Vol 2, pp. 898–902, S.C. Shapiro, (Ed.), John Wiley, 1992.

27 Bennett, W. S., *A general overview of the METAL machine translation system*, Siemens-Nixdorf, 1991.

28 Schneider, T., *Breaking the language barrier*, Siemens Magazine, COM 1/88, 1988.

29 The Intellect system is marketed by AICorp of Waltham, Massachusetts.

30 Language Craft is marketed by the Carnegie Group, Inc., Pittsburgh

31 Further information on these systems can be found in the following documents: [a] *The Securities and Exchange Commission*, Harvard Business School Case Study, No. 9-186-279, 1986. [b] Arthur Andersen & Co., *Final Report on the Financial Statement Analyzer to the Securities and Exchange Commission*, Technical Report, Dec. 1985 [c] Mui, C. and W. E. McCarthy, *FSA: Applying AI techniques to the Familiarization Phase of Financial Decision Making*, pp. 38–48, IEEE Expert, Feb. 1989.

32 K. Sahin and K. Sawyer, *The Intelligent banking system: Natural language processing for financial communications*, in *Innovative Applications of Artificial Intelligence* (H. Schorr & A. Rappaport, Eds.), AAAI Press/MIT Press, Menlo Park, 1989.

33 J. O'Brien, H. Brice, S. Hatfield, W.P. Johnson and R. Woodhead, *The Ford motor company Direct Labor Management System*, in *Innovative Applications of Artificial Intelligence* (H. Schorr and A. Rappaport, Eds.), AAAI Press/MIT Press, Menlo Park, 1989.

34 Hayes, P. J., and S. P. Weinstein, *Construe-TIS: A System for Content-Based Indexing of a Database of News Stories*, in *Innovative Applications of Artificial Intelligence 2*, A. Rappaport and R. Smith (Eds.), pp. 48-64, AAAI/MIT Press, 1991.

35 Description based on publicity materials from AICorp, Waltham, Massachusetts

36 Description based on publicity materials from AICorp, Waltham, Massachusetts.

37 Zuboff, S., *Automate/Informate: The Two Faces of Intelligent Technology*, pp. 5–18, Organizational Dynamics, Autumn 1985.

# Chapter 7
## Image and speech processing

While logical problem-solving behavior is usually learnt, pattern recognition appears to be an inherent intelligent characteristic of humans (and other lower forms of intelligence). For example, babies are able to recognize their parents, and most of us are able to read handwritten characters or follow spoken speech (in spite of large variations across different individuals). Attempts to directly apply conventional knowledge-based systems (KBSs) technology to pattern recognition tasks have generally met with poor results. This is due to the inherently different nature of pattern recognition tasks, as compared to logical problem solving processes.

Besides producing results of interest from the cognitive perspective, artificial intelligence (AI) research in pattern recognition has lead to the growth of several practical technologies with significant commercial payoffs. Document image processing (DIP), optical character recognition (OCR) systems, medical imaging systems, and industrial sensing systems are examples of such technologies. To appreciate their commercial significance, consider DIP technology as an example. The information explosion in business and industry has nearly quadrupled the amount of paperwork over the last 25 years. Studies[1] show that the average business has five filing cabinets for each employee, with 33% of all files never being retrieved. It costs nearly $20 to file and retrieve a single document, and the cost of a misfiling can be up to $120. DIP technology is helping to manage the increased paperwork by automating the storage, retrieval, analysis, and transfer of documents. These benefits are causing a rapid adoption of DIP technology by business, and creating a multi-billion dollar market (estimated to be around $12.2 billions in 1994[2]) for DIP systems.

Pattern recognition is a separate discipline in its own right, and is influenced by several fields such as statistics, decision theory, mathematics, and computing. It is beyond the scope of this book to cover all important approaches to pattern recognition. This chapter focuses on pattern recognition as applied to visual and auditory data processing from the perspective of applied AI.

## Computer vision

The Handbook of Artificial Intelligence[3] has defined computer vision as 'the science and technology of obtaining models, meanings, and control information from visual data'. Within the field of computer vision, two broad approaches can be identified. One approach, known as computational vision, attempts to develop a coherent theory of visual perception, with an emphasis on the formulation of computational models of biological vision processes. The second approach, known as machine vision, focuses on the design and construction of practical, economical applications of artificial vision systems in industry and business, with little emphasis on development of new theories or models of visual perception. Our interest in this chapter is primarily on machine vision.

## Biological roots

The ability to see and recognize objects in the environment is a fundamental and important human ability. The ease and rapidity of our perceptual skills (we can open our eyes, and instantaneously recognize objects in the surrounding domain) provides little clues about the complexity of even mundane perceptual tasks like recognizing a chair, or a table. Perceptual skills in humans (and lower forms of life, such as flies and insects) are performed by complex, highly specialized biological organs which have evolved over many tens of thousands of years into their current forms. Automated vision systems are very primitive compared to such biological vision systems. For example, the human eye has a resolution about 1000 times better than modern television cameras.

It is instructive to begin by looking at how humans process images (Figure 7.1). The human eye forms the basic camera in the human vision system. The transparent lens in our eyes focuses and projects rays of light from illuminated objects in the environment on a light-sensitive screen called the retina. The retina in each eye has more than 110 million light sensors (rod and cone cells). When excited by light rays, these rod and cone cells send impulses to the visual cortex of the brain via the optic nerve. The visual cortex contains hundreds of layers of cells where the received electrical impulses are progressively refined to ultimately yield recognizable object identifications.

Note that light rays from the three-dimensional external environment (also referred to as the scene) are converted into a two-dimensional image on the retina inside the eye. The image is captured by the cumulative excitation signals of the more than 100 million rods

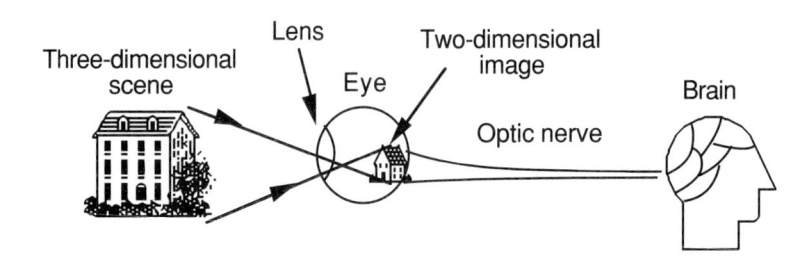

Figure 7.1 Human vision system

# Biological roots 199

and cone cells in the retina. The electrical encoding of each image is transmitted to the brain from the retina by about a million nerve fibres (which together constitute the optic nerve). From an information processing perspective, vision is much more than the mere transmission of these electrical image intensities. The intensity of excitation of any one nerve fibre is of little use in making sense of the entire image. Understanding an image is intimately related to how different parts of the image (different nerve fibre excitations) relate to each other at different levels of abstractions. Critical steps in this process of visual information processing are: detecting edges in the image (given by the relationships between different neuronal excitations); identifying objects in the scene (specified by the relationship of different edges to each other), and; associating a semantic meaning to the various objects (with the help of knowledge about the scene being 'seen'). Though the transformation of electrical signals into semantically recognizable objects is a complex and relatively poorly understood phenomenon, there is biological evidence to suggest that layers of cells in the visual cortex do perform the above tasks, such as that of edge detection[4]. There are additional sophistications in human vision systems. Each human eye produces a slightly different image of the same scene (known as stereo vision) as shown in Figure 7.2. The visual cortex has the ability to fuse these two different images to give us a sense of depth in the scene (this process of fusion is known as stereopsis). The human perceptual system is also capable of making fine discriminations between different textures, shapes, and lighting patterns.

## Computational requirements

The computational requirements of visual information processing in humans are significant. The human eye has a resolution of about 100 million pixels, and calculations indicate that up to a billion personal computers are needed to match the computational complexity of certain tasks performed by our eyes[5]. Though human nerve fibres are relatively simple structures, with individual processing speeds much smaller than current desktop computers, the human brain is able to perform all the complex computations necessary for 'instantaneous vision' with the help of large-scale parallel computing. Millions of individual nerve elements process information simultaneously to produce results of an exceptionally high quality in real-time.

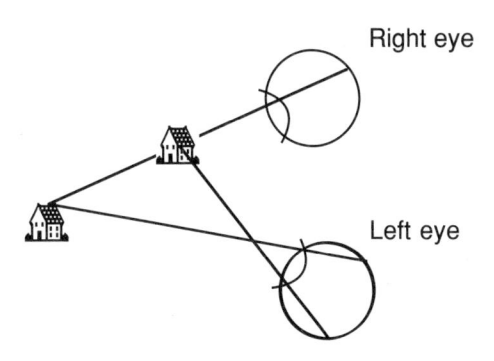

Figure 7.2 Stereo vision in humans

## 200 Image and speech processing

Modern machine vision systems have a much lower resolution than the human eye, but still present quite formidable computational requirements, specially for real-time processing (necessary for 'instantaneous vision'). The computational requirements for real-time vision can only be satisfied with parallel computers.

However, parallel computing is still in its infancy today. Most commercial parallel computers use only a few dozens of processors in parallel. Compared with the million or more nerve fibres processing information simultaneously, parallel computing still has a long way to progress.

Computational barriers have prevented the use of sophisticated artificial vision systems for applications in industry and business. However, progress is surely and continuously being made, and machine vision systems are used today in a number of domains (Table 7.1). Even relatively advanced features, such as stereo vision, are available today in many commercial vision systems.

### Problems and ambiguities

Building practical and economical machine vision systems is not easy. Besides the significant computational requirements imposed on machine vision systems, there are several additional complications in the process of understanding images:

| Domain | Example applications |
| --- | --- |
| Manufacturing | Parts inspection |
|  | Automatic sorting and packaging |
|  | Robotic manipulators |
| Business | Document imaging |
|  | Design aids for engineers/architects |
| Defense | Remote sensing |
|  | Target identification and tracking |
|  | Weapons guidance |
|  | Photo reconnaisance |
| Medical | Analysis of medical images such as X-Rays, Ultrasound and tomographies |
| Science | Analysis of images from outer space |
|  | Explorations in atomic structures |

Table 7.1 Some sample applications of machine vision systems

## Problems and ambiguities 201

- relative views — depending upon the particular angle and distance of viewing, the same object can appear quite different. Figure 7.3 illustrates how the same house can look different when viewed from the front and from the side. Figure 7.4 depicts how the distance of viewing can give different appearances to the same object. This means is that it is difficult to use simple pattern recognition techniques for image recognition

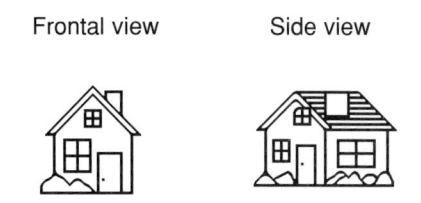

Frontal view     Side view

**Figure 7.3** Viewing the same object from different angles

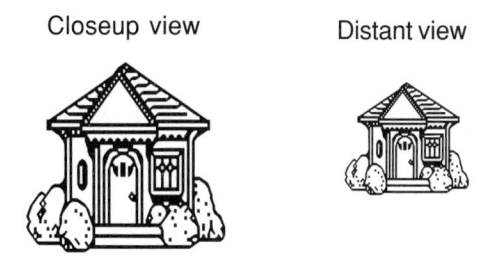

Closeup view     Distant view

**Figure 7.4** Viewing the same object from different distances

- ambiguity — there can be local ambiguity in the image of a particular scene. For example, it is not clear in Figure 7.5 whether A1 and A2 are parts of the same object or whether they are two separate objects

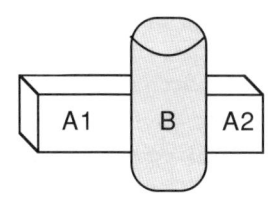

**Figure 7.5** Local ambiguity in an image

- incomplete information — the interpretation of a general scene may be complicated by the fact the image presents partial information about the scene. For example in Figure 7.6, there appears to be only one house, while in reality there are two houses (stereo vision can rectify this problem — see Figure 7.2)
- lighting conditions — the same object can look quite different depending upon the particular orientation of light sources (as shown in Figure 7.7).

## 202 Image and speech processing

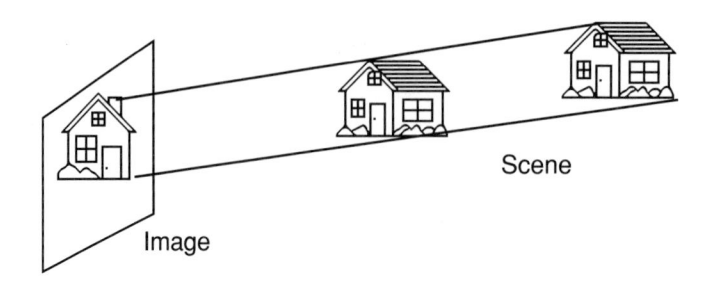

**Figure 7.6** Incomplete information in an image

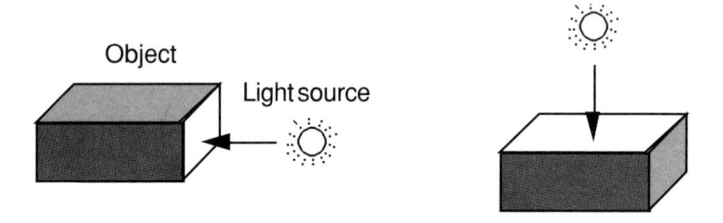

**Figure 7.7** Effect of variations in lighting conditions

These interpretation problems can become acute in images of general cluttered scenes. For example in Figure 7.8, it is not clear whether objects B and D are cylinders, or rectangular blocks, or rectangular surfaces. Domain knowledge is useful and important for overcoming such ambiguity and incomplete information in images. For example, given the domain knowledge that only cylindrical objects are present in the scene, the image of Figure 7.8 can be disambiguated to recognize that objects B and D are cylinders. Because external conditions (such as the placement of light sources) can also have an impact on the nature of the image, most industrial vision systems adopt relatively rigid pre-determined environmental conditions to facilitate the identification and disambiguation of domain objects in images.

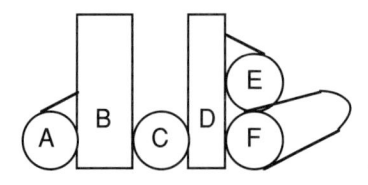

**Figure 7.8** An image of a cluttered scene

## Information processing in machine vision

The input to a generic machine vision system is an image of a certain scene produced on a light-sensitive screen with a camera. Note that the image is a two-dimensional representation of an external three-dimensional scene. Much of the effort within machine vision systems is spent on inverting the image i.e., on recreating the three-dimensional scene from its two-dimensional image. Three stages of information processing (Figure 7.9) can be identified in this inversion process:

- signal processing — the collected image is subjected to a variety of low-level processing operations with the aims of reducing noise, converting the analog image into digital signals, and performing certain operations to enhance the detection of edges in the image
- image processing — this phase takes the processed image signals from the previous stage, and determines connecting edges and surfaces to arrive at an initial partition of the image into distinct regions.
- image understanding — this is the last stage of visual data processing in which the surfaces identified during the previous phase are aggregated into distinct objects, and each object is associated with a semantic meaning establishing its relationship to the external environment.

The computational requirements are the highest for the low-level task of visual signal processing, and the knowledge demands are maximum for the high-level task of image understanding. This is because procedures to reduce noise or detect edges require the processing of intensities of all pixels in the image in relation to other neighboring pixels. As the number of pixels in an image can be very large (about 1 million), the computational requirements for such tasks are significant. In contrast, the number of objects for image understanding is limited to the number of distinct objects in the image (usually a small number), and procedures at this level attempt to utilize domain-specific knowledge to identify and associate semantic labels with individual objects. The ultimate aim of many

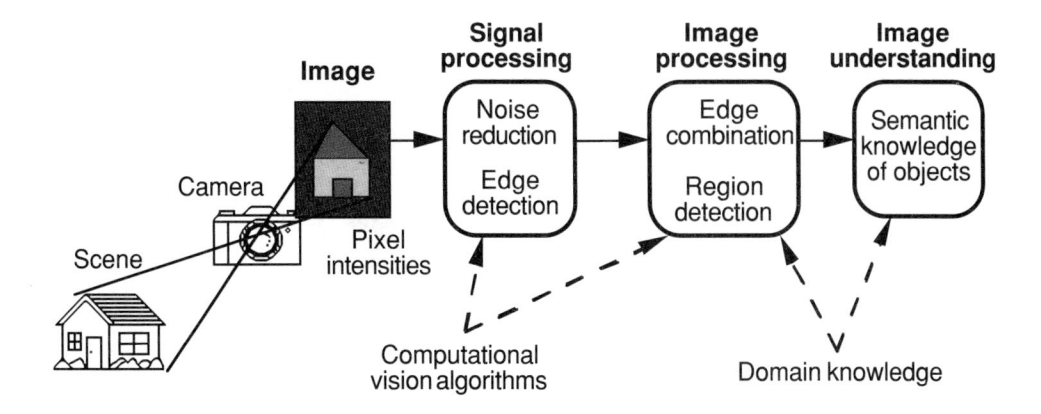

**Figure 7.9** Stages of visual information processing

## 204 Image and speech processing

machine vision systems is to produce an interpretation of a scene which can be used in a meaningful manner by a reasoning component, such as a KBS. The following sections describe (qualitatively) the stages of visual information processing in more detail[6].

## Signal processing

### Digitizing and sampling

The first task in this stage is to convert the image produced on the light-sensitive screen within the camera into a digitized pixel image. This is typically done (within the video cameras used in machine vision systems) by using an electron beam to scan the light-sensitive screen sequentially from left to right and from top to bottom, then sampling the produced continuous electrical signal at regular intervals (Figure 7.10). Note that between sequential left-to-right scans, the electron beam flies back 'instantaneously' to its starting position on the left (of the light-sensitive screen), and immediately below the starting position of the previous scan.

So the analog signal produced corresponds to left-to-right sequential scans only. Each individual small square in the digitized image (to the right in Figure 7.10) is known as a pixel. The number inside each pixel gives the average signal (image) intensity corresponding to that particular area on the original image (according to the sampled intensity values). The number of pixels in the image is related to the rate at which the analog electrical signal is sampled.

Note that the larger the number of pixels in an image, the greater is the resolution of the image. The resolution of good machine vision systems is of the order of 1000 by 1000 pixels. The resolution of the human eye is of the order of 10,000 by 10,000 pixels. The numerical image intensity of each pixel can be mapped onto a gray-scale (from white to black) to produce an image.

Figure 7.11[7] depicts such a digitized image of a cat. While we can see and 'understand' such an image, a machine vision system needs to further process such a raw digitized image, before it can be understood in any useful manner.

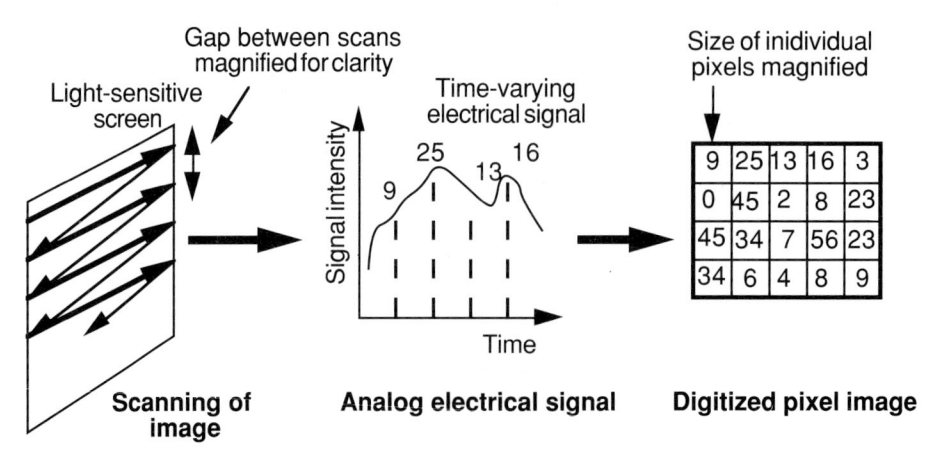

**Figure 7.10** Initial stages in low-level signal processing

Information processing in machine vision 205

**Figure 7.11** A sample digitized pixel image

### Thresholding

A common operation during signal processing is thresholding, which entails choosing a certain image intensity level T as the threshold. All pixels having intensities below T are mapped onto a particular gray level (say white), and all pixels with intensities above T are mapped onto another gray level (say black). Figure 7.12 depicts the result of such a thresholding operation on the image of Figure 7.11. As evident, thresholding helps to sharpen

**Figure 7.12** Image resulting after thresholding operation

## 206 Image and speech processing

object boundaries, and reduce noise and distortions in the image. Thresholding can also ease subsequent processing steps by simplifying the digitized pixel representation of the image.

The choice of the particular threshold level T used is important, and is dependent upon the image. By analyzing a histogram of the different pixel intensities (Figure 7.13), it is possible to identify the level T which separates concentrations of different pixel intensity levels. The choice of a wrong threshold level can actually reduce the quality of the image by obscuring essential details. Depending upon the nature of the image, it may be necessary to consider thresholding with more than one threshold level.

Thresholding is a common operation in machine vision systems used for routine industrial tasks such as parts inspection, where it is used to enhance discrimination between the part to be examined and the surrounding environment (such as the conveyor belt carrying the part).

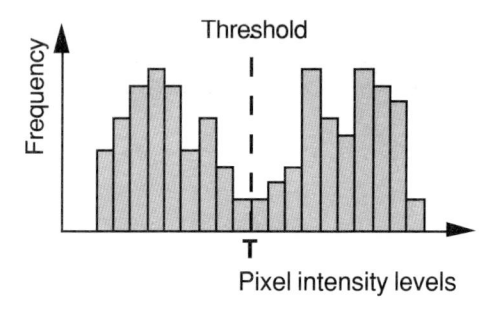

**Figure 7.13** Histogram of pixel intensities

### Smoothing

Another operation typically performed during this stage of visual information processing is smoothing of the image by the use of digital filters. A common technique to perform smoothing is to replace the intensity of each pixel in the image by a weighted average of the intensities of the neighboring pixels. A digital filter to perform such a task can look like the following:

| -1/17 | -1/17 | -1/17 |
|---|---|---|
| -1/17 | **9/17** | -1/17 |
| -1/17 | -1/17 | -1/17 |

where the central boxed number in bold identifies the pixel being smoothed. Such a weighted smoothing is also known as convolution. Note that because the above filter has to be applied to each individual pixel, convolution is a computationally expensive operation. Figure 7.14 depicts the image of Figure 7.11 after convolution with the above digital filter.

# Information processing in machine vision

**Figure 7.14** Image of Figure 7.11 after convolution

## Edge detection

The last operation of interest in signal processing is edge detection. Edges are thin lines or arcs in the image which act as boundaries of distinct objects or regions in the image. For edge detection, the rate of change of the pixel intensities is more useful than the actual intensities themselves. This is because the rate of change in the pixel intensities is highest across boundaries (Figure 7.15). Figure 7.16 depicts the image of Figure 7.14 after edge detection.

Edge detection forms the basis for the much of the higher levels of visual information processing. Many false edges are often generated in the image during edge detection. They are caused by noisy signals, variations due to local lighting conditions, and the varying texture and surface features of objects. Appropriate thresholding and smoothing operations prior to edge detection can help in reducing the number of false edges.

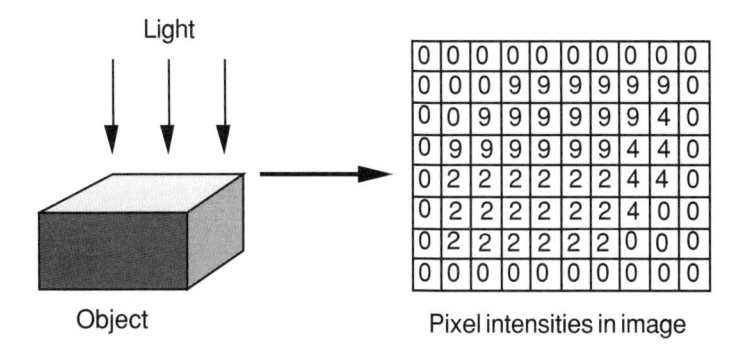

**Figure 7.15** Rate of change of intensities across edges

## 208 Image and speech processing

**Figure 7.16** Image of Figure 7.14 after edge detection

Other operations aimed at determining texture, color, and surface features of objects, and resolution of stereo images (in case two cameras are used) are also performed during signal processing. However, a description of these operations is beyond the scope of this chapter.

## Image processing

The input to this stage of visual information processing is (usually) the image after edge detection. Two major operations are performed in this phase: segmentation, and labelling. The general process of determining the boundaries of objects and regions in the image is known as segmentation. To segment a image correctly, it is necessary to be able to discriminate between noise (random edges), false edges (lines which appear as edges in the image, but do not correspond to edges in the scene), and true edges. Labelling is the process by which different regions in the image are assigned labels describing their primary features. The output of this stage of image processing is a labelled assignment of regions, which can be used to identify and associate semantic meanings to distinct objects in the scene during the next stage of image understanding.

Though Figure 7.16 represents the actual transformation of the image of Figure 7.11 after convolution and edge detection, it is much too complex to aid us in easily understanding the processes of segmentation and labelling. As an alternative, consider Figure 7.17 which is a hypothetical image after edge detection for the simple image of Figure 7.5. There are 6 different regions or surfaces (labelled by bold capital letters) to be recognized in this simple image. The edges constituting the boundaries of these regions are not clearly demarcated in Figure 7.17. For example, the line segments a and b form part of the

# Image processing 209

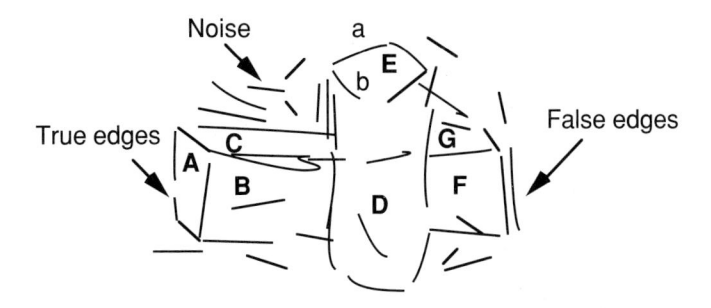

**Figure 7.17** Edges in an image (also see Figure 7.5)

boundary of the same surface E, but are not joined together. A machine vision system has to be able to infer edges forming boundaries of particular regions. Note also that there is considerable distortion and noise in the image. This complicates the task of distinguishing true and false edges in the image considerably.

## Segmentation
Some general approaches to segmentation include the following:

● graphical techniques — graphical algorithms for segmentation start with a particular edge and, based on a heuristic function of certain image variables (such as distance and pixel intensity), attempt to find connecting edges and build the contour of the region containing the starting edge. For example in Figure 7.17, a graphical procedure might start with edge a, find the closest neighbor edge, b and connect it to a to produce part of the boundary for region E. Graphical techniques work well for clean (not noisy) images of simple scenes

● mathematical programming — the problem of edge finding can also be formulated (under certain conditions) as a dynamic programming problem by assigning costs to edges (based again on image variables such as pixel intensity and arc length), and defining the edge contour as the path having the minimum cost

● model-based — in certain cases, domain knowledge (in the form of models) is available about the properties of objects in the scene. This knowledge can be used to quickly and efficiently detect edges in the image. For example, given the domain knowledge that the image of Figure 7.17 is about a scene containing only rectangular boxes and cylinders, the task of segmentation can be made more efficient

● region segmentation — rather than take the output image after edge detection as the starting point, this approach begins with the pixel intensities of the image (usually after operations such as smoothing and convolution), and attempts to build regions by locating groups of adjacent pixels sharing common properties, such as similar intensities, color, or texture. This segmentation can be performed in either a bottom-up or a top-down manner. The former approach begins with a single pixel, then attempts to build a region by finding other adjacent similar pixels. The latter approach starts with the entire image, and iteratively breaks it down into smaller homogeneous regions (for example, by using multiple thresholds in a recursive manner).

# 210 Image and speech processing

## Labelling

After segmentation, the different regions and surfaces have to be labelled. These labels typically include parameters specifying the size, orientation, area, average intensity, number of vertices, and shape of the region. The task of assigning labels becomes more complex for three-dimensional objects as additional dimensions of interpretation (such as depth and orientation) are introduced. For three-dimensional objects, local ambiguities in the image can give rise to different possible labellings. For example, given the knowledge that the image of Figure 7.18 is of a three-dimensional object, there is ambiguity about the relative orientation of surfaces A and B. The literature of computer vision[8] contains several constraint satisfaction algorithms which attempt to find the correct labelling for surfaces, given certain constraints about the properties of different surfaces.

Pre-stored domain knowledge can also be used for labelling objects. If a particular surface in the image is identified with a certain surface in the domain model, the relevant properties from the domain model can be easily transferred to the label of the appropriate surface in the image. For example, given the domain knowledge that the image of Figure 7.17 only contains cylinders and rectangular boxes, appropriate descriptive information can be transferred to the description of the surfaces in Figure 7.17.

Another interesting technique for labelling is to use a syntactic grammar for recognizing and describing surfaces or objects in the scene. A syntactic grammar is similar to the grammars described in Chapter 6, except for the fact that the basic components of the grammar here are line segments and arcs and not parts of speech (as was the case for natural language grammars). Figure 7.19 illustrates a simple syntactic grammar and its application for labelling surfaces in an image. Note that significant domain knowledge is required for devising an appropriate syntactic grammar. Syntactic grammars are domain-specific, and the same grammar cannot (usually) be used to label images from different domains. Syntactic grammars have also been used for problems such as handwriting recognition. For example, by using the syntactic grammar of Figure 7.19, the letter N can be labelled as: N = bfb. Obviously, the above information alone is not sufficient for recognizing N in all cases. The labels produced by a syntactic grammar have to be augmented with other descriptive information to provide a more complete and useful description of the surface or region under consideration.

## Image understanding

This is the highest, but the least structured level of information processing with visual data. This phase takes as input the set of labelled regions or surfaces in the image, and performs two major tasks: identification of objects and interpretation of the image. The

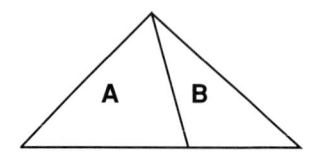

Figure 7.18 Ambiguity in the relative orientation of surfaces

# Image understanding

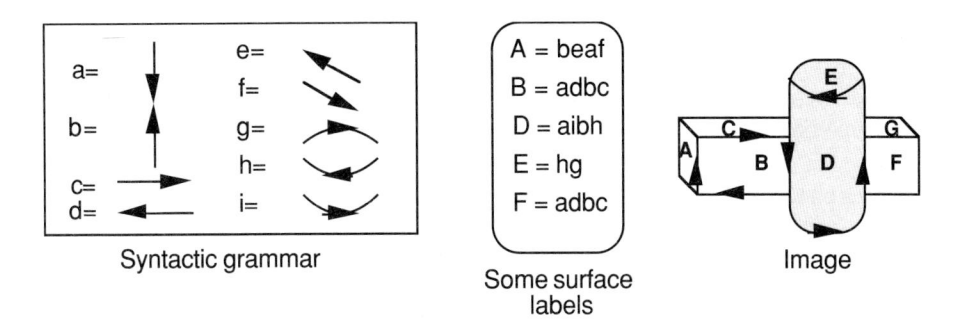

**Figure 7.19** Use of a syntactic grammar for labelling surfaces

former task is concerned with aggregating different regions in the image into distinct objects, and assigning a unique identity to each object. The latter task of interpretation is closely related to our general notion of understanding an image, and is consequently more open and less structured. It is concerned with interpreting the identified objects with regard to their function, purpose, and inter-relationships. The degree of interpretation required is dependent upon the final use of the image by the machine vision system. For many industrial uses, such as for parts inspection, a simple identification of objects may suffice. If the machine vision system is being used to provide visual input to an autonomous agent (such as a robot), then a more sophisticated interpretation of the image in the context of the general knowledge base of the agent is necessary.

### Identification

Domain knowledge and models are useful for identification of objects. For example, in the image of Figure 7.17, the knowledge that cylinders have curved parallelopiped surfaces, capped at both ends by flat circular surfaces, is useful for recognizing that surfaces E and D together form a cylinder, surface D is a curved surface, and surface E is a flat circular region. Even for the simple image of Figure 7.17, there is ambiguity about whether the object identified by surfaces A, B, and C, and the object identified by the surfaces F and G, are the same. It is difficult to determine the answer by using the information from the image only. Domain knowledge may help in resolving such ambiguities. For example, given the knowledge that all rectangular boxes in the domain are of a certain length, one can use this domain-specific knowledge for resolving the above ambiguity.

Often, additional information is required for disambiguating images. For example in military reconnaissance by spy planes, it is difficult to separate dummy tanks (or other dummy military equipment) from actual tanks. One solution is to gather additional information in the form of infrared pictures of the same area. Because dummy tanks are usually made of cardboard or non-metallic structures, they show up in infrared pictures in very different ways from normal metallic tanks. Thus by combining the information available from a photographic image with that obtainable from an infrared picture, it is possible to have a better understanding of the objects in the scene.

General world knowledge is also useful for identifying objects in images. For example consider Figure 7.20, which contains an image of a particular scene. A military commander would be interested in knowing whether object A represents a road or a river.

# 212 Image and speech processing

Assuming it can be determined that object B is a bridge, it can be reasonably inferred that object A in Figure 7.20 is a river. Note that here we are using our general world knowledge that bridges are usually across rivers (and not roads) while making this disambiguation.

### Interpretation

For vision systems with limited output objectives, such as in industrial part recognition systems, the output of the image understanding phase can be a simple identification of parts (or defects). However, for systems which are linked to the reasoning and planning processes of a KBS (as in autonomous robots), it is necessary to interpret the result of the image understanding phase and represent it in an appropriate knowledge representation scheme.

Figure 7.21 partially depicts the interpreted output of the simple image of Figure 7.17 after image understanding. The amount of detail (about properties of objects and their inter-relationships) necessary to be provided in such an interpretation is dependent upon the application task for which the machine vision system is utilized. It is quite common to use frame hierarchies (Chapters 3 and 4) to represent domain knowledge, and to express the interpreted output of images.


## Commercial applications of machine vision

Brief descriptions of selected examples of commercial applications of image processing technologies from different domains are now given.

### Industrial vision applications

Machine vision systems are used for many sensing applications in industry. The most common use of machine vision in an industrial setting is for the purpose of automated inspection of parts and products. The basic structure of an industrial parts inspection system is shown in Figure 7.22. The machine vision system matches the image recorded by the camera of the object on the moving conveyor belt against the (known) image of a correct part. If a defect is found, an appropriate signal is sent to a mechanical device (such as a robot arm) to physically remove the defective part. To simplify the task of image processing, the lighting conditions and the position of objects on the conveyor belt are fixed within certain limits.

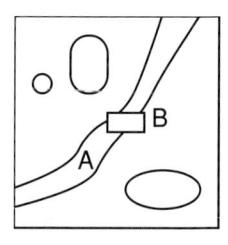

**Figure 7.20** Ambiguity in object identification

# Commercial applications of machine vision 213

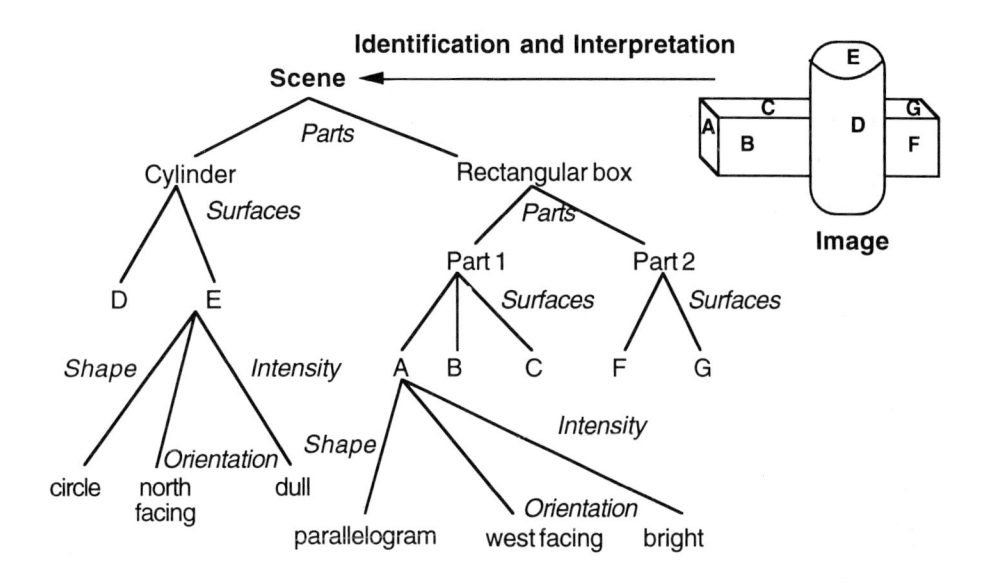

**Figure 7.21** Interpretation of a simple image

Commercial systems for such recognition tasks are numerous, and differ in the degree of their sophistication. The simplest of these systems use thresholding of the digitized pixel image (Figure 7.12), and match the resulting (black and white) image with a known template image to determine defects in two-dimensional surfaces (such as washers and steel plates). These systems are typically not able to determine surface features such as texture and color. More sophisticated vision systems can detect edges in products. Figure

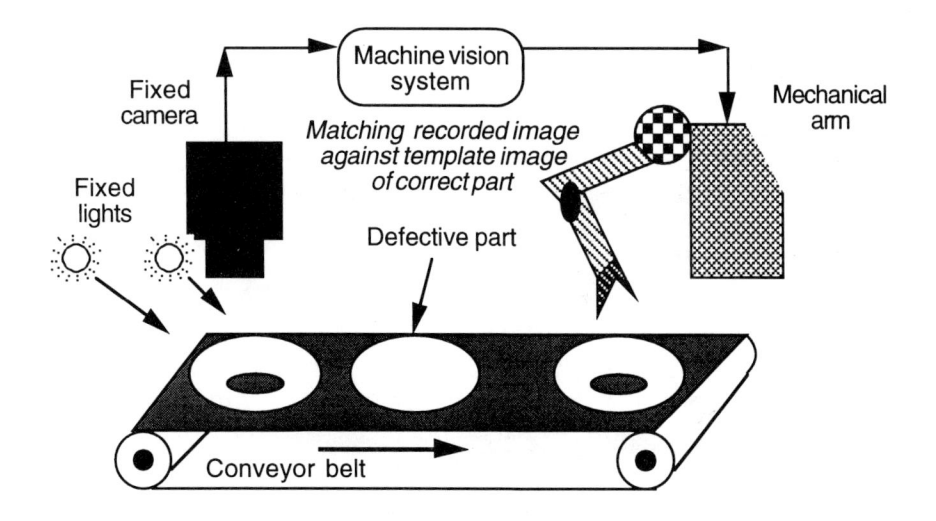

**Figure 7.22** Typical industrial parts inspection system

## 214 Image and speech processing

7.23 shows an example of an object for which edge detection capabilities are necessary for proper inspection (thresholding is not sufficient as it cannot find defects along the side edges).

Recent technological enhancements to machine vision systems have significantly enhanced the sophistication of industrial machine vision applications. The addition of true color sensing has opened a whole new dimension in industrial packaging and assembly operations. Color vision systems merge three images (red, green, and blue scans) to obtain information about the color of objects in the scene. Color vision systems can perform intricate tasks such as sort similarly colored pecan and walnut shells, sort blanched and unbalanced peanuts, measure the degree of browning of baked products, and reject slightly off-color products. Other enhancements to vision systems include the use of laser beams (for finer discrimination in the image), and X-rays and infrared photography (to yield additional information about the image). For example, Clayton Durand Penetect (of Raleigh, NC, USA) has developed an infrared vision system to detect pits in singulated cherries, olives, and dates. Also, Test Equipment Distributors (of Troy, Michigan, USA) and Videx (of Canandaigua, NY, USA) have jointly developed a system using X-rays that can detect a 1mm glass bead inside a baby-food jar.

Several commercial vendors offer integrated machine vision packages for industry. Table 7.2[9] lists selected industrial vision system vendors, and limited details of the applications and technological choices offered by them. Modern vision systems are sophisticated enough to inspect over 600 cans per minute, locate as many as 16,000 objects every 1/30 of a second (possible with the RAM Vision system of R. A. McDonald), detect bones in 'boneless' chicken, and smart enough to alert operators of impending packaging problems long before significant rejects begin to occur (a feature available in systems offered by Pattern Processing Technologies and Videk). Many vendors are moving towards offering integrated hardware and software solutions which blend into the production environments of the targeted industries.

Machine vision systems offer important benefits to industry by automating and enhancing quality and speed of inspection, assembly, and packaging. A good vision system can have an important impact on competitiveness of a company's manufacturing operations, and on quality of its products. However, vision systems are rarely cheap, and

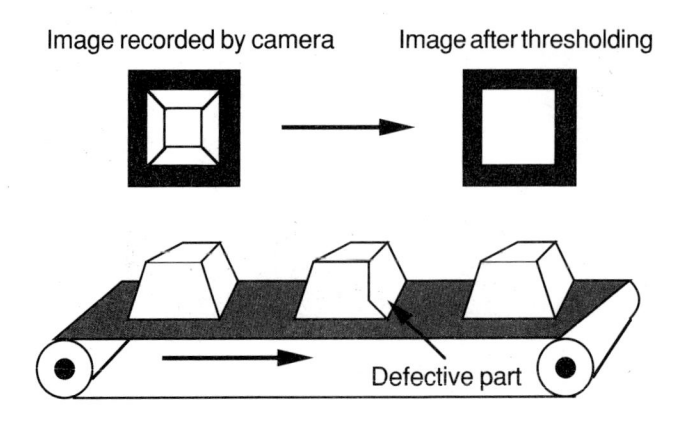

Figure 7.23 Defects for which edge identification is necessary

# Commercial applications of machine vision 215

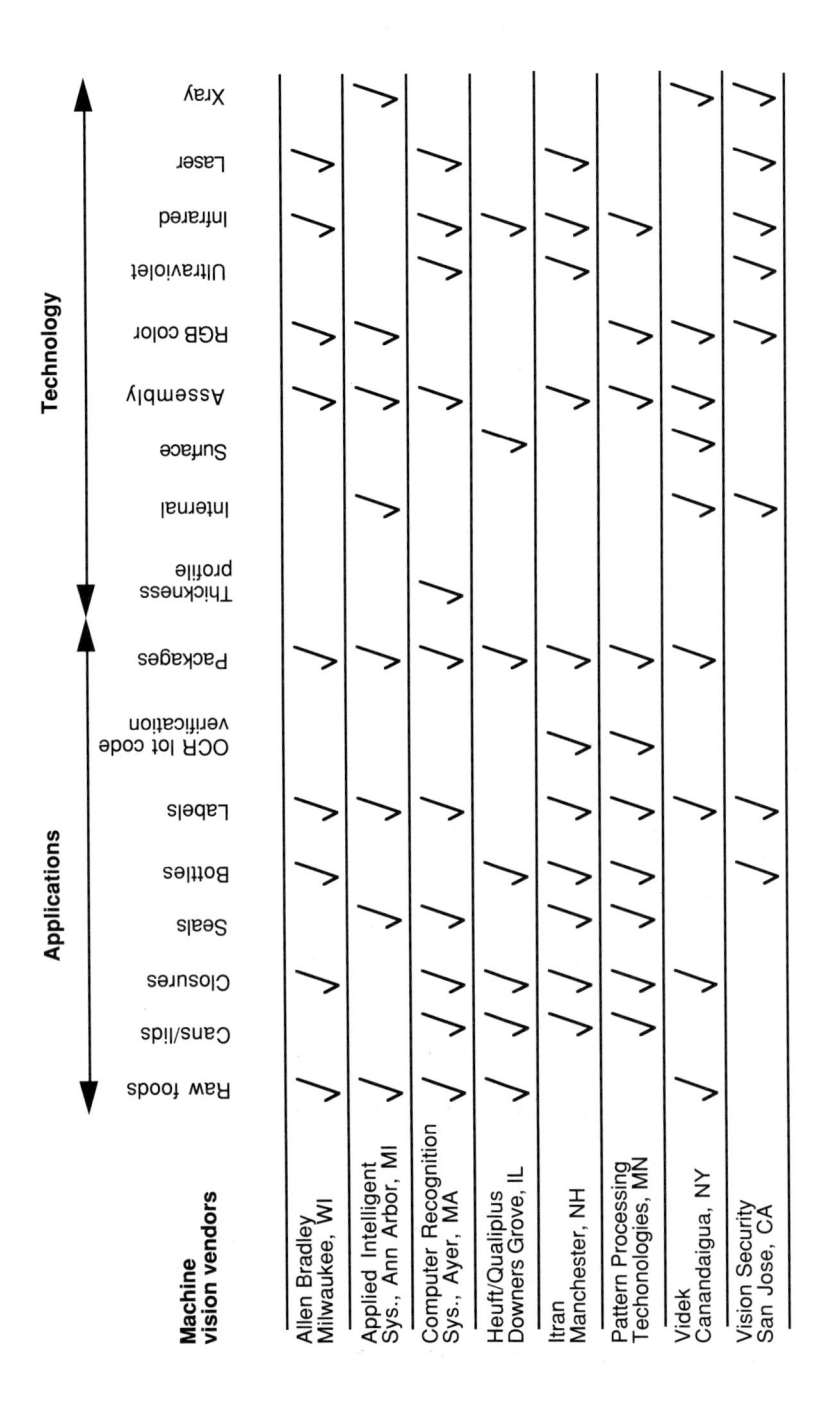

| Machine vision vendors | Raw foods | Cans/lids | Closures | Seals | Bottles | Labels | OCR lot code verification | Packages | Thickness profile | Internal | Surface | Assembly | RGB color | Ultraviolet | Infrared | Laser | Xray |
|---|---|---|---|---|---|---|---|---|---|---|---|---|---|---|---|---|---|
| Allen Bradley Milwaukee, WI | ✓ | ✓ | ✓ |  | ✓ | ✓ |  | ✓ |  |  |  | ✓ | ✓ |  | ✓ | ✓ |  |
| Applied Intelligent Sys., Ann Arbor, MI | ✓ |  | ✓ | ✓ | ✓ | ✓ |  | ✓ |  | ✓ |  | ✓ | ✓ | ✓ | ✓ |  | ✓ |
| Computer Recognition Sys., Ayer, MA | ✓ | ✓ | ✓ | ✓ | ✓ | ✓ |  | ✓ |  |  |  |  | ✓ | ✓ | ✓ | ✓ |  |
| Heuft/Qualiplus Downers Grove, IL |  | ✓ | ✓ | ✓ | ✓ | ✓ |  | ✓ |  |  | ✓ |  |  |  |  |  |  |
| Itran Manchester, NH |  | ✓ | ✓ | ✓ | ✓ | ✓ |  | ✓ |  |  |  | ✓ |  |  | ✓ | ✓ |  |
| Pattern Processing Techonologies, MN |  |  | ✓ | ✓ | ✓ | ✓ |  | ✓ | ✓ | ✓ |  | ✓ |  |  |  |  |  |
| Videk Canandaigua, NY | ✓ |  |  |  |  | ✓ |  |  |  | ✓ |  | ✓ | ✓ | ✓ | ✓ | ✓ | ✓ |
| Vision Security San Jose, CA |  |  |  |  | ✓ | ✓ |  |  |  | ✓ |  | ✓ | ✓ | ✓ | ✓ | ✓ | ✓ |

**Table 7.2** Selected commercial machine vision vendors

## 216 Image and speech processing

typically require investments of a million dollars or more. As the cost and risk of failure is high, careful coordination and cooperation between management, engineering, and manufacturing is necessary to ensure that the right financial, technical, and process decisions are taken. With continuous progress in computer vision, and the steady decline in the price/performance ratio of computing, machine vision systems will play an increasingly important rôle in industry in the future.

### Document image processing

Most businesses generate more paper documents than which they can cope with. While asking for approval for a new drug, say, manufacturers may have to submit up to 100,000 pages of supporting documents (on issues such as proof of safety and effectiveness) to the governmental regulatory agency (FDA) in the USA. Other government offices, such as those which keep track of property rights, births and deaths, and motor vehicle records, are similarly flooded by large amounts of paperwork. Storage and selective retrieval of information under such circumstances is a formidable, but important task for organizations. For example, consider the state of Delaware in which 280 of the Fortune 500 companies, 40% of the big-board stock companies, and a total of 190,000 companies are incorporated. The franchise taxes and corporate filing fees — an amount of $200 million — amounts to nearly 20% of the total state tax revenues for Delaware. Companies file enormous amounts of paper documents with the State of Delaware, such as notifications of company by-law changes, stock offerings, and merger data. To prevent these companies from moving to one of the other 49 states (and thus protect a major source of its revenue), the State of Delaware has to efficiently process the information in all filed papers, and be able to satisfy the queries and information needs of companies quickly and correctly. The State of Delaware is using document image processing (DIP) technology to help it manage such vast amounts of information. Besides automating Delaware's existing record keeping operations, the DIP has also enabled it to offer new services (such as fast prioritized access to corporate information) to the filing companies, and create a new $2.5 million revenue generation business. The DIP system has also helped Delaware speed up the processing time of annual reports (190,000 companies file their annual reports in March each year) from 10 months to 6 weeks.

Document imaging technology can be viewed as an integration of image processing techniques (as described in this chapter) and natural language understanding technology (Chapter 6). The basic structure of an DIP system is shown in Figure 7.24. Documents are scanned, and processed by an machine vision system to yield an electronic image of the document. This electronic image is then processed to yield information about the contents of the document, and stored on optical discs. The kind of processing done varies from simple barcode recognition and optical character recognition (OCR), to the more complex task of natural language processing (NLP). For simple indexing and retrieval, OCR or barcode recognition is adequate. To be able to 'understand' the contents of the various documents, it is necessary to utilize NLP techniques. Most commercial DIP systems offer OCR (of printed characters) and barcode recognition abilities, with simple NLP facilities. However, advanced NLP facilities and OCR of handwritten characters are gradually

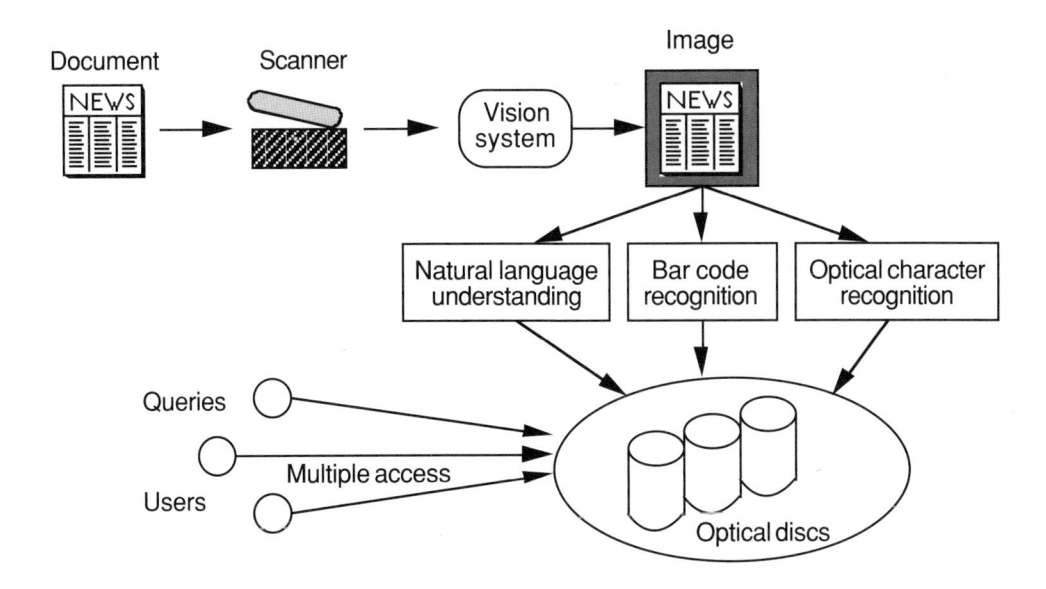

**Figure 7.24** Document image processing system

becoming available in commercial DIP systems. As the amount of paper documents processed by a DIP system can be very large (typically a few millions), optical disks are necessary to be able to store and retrieve document images.

Like industrial vision systems, DIP systems are also very expensive, and usually cost $1 million or more (for example, the DIP system of the State of Delaware cost $2 million) inclusive of all hardware and software. Costs for expanding the system are also usually significant. The huge amounts of data being processed can pose some technological challenges. For example, the size of a normal document image is approximately 75 kilobytes, and networks typically move data in bundles of 4 kilobytes. Thus if multiple users are accessing electronic documents over a network, the response times can be slow. To get the full benefits of DIP systems, it is important to integrate them into the existing office information systems architecture, and to redesign work flows within the office to leverage the capabilities of imaging technology. Table 7.3[10] lists some commercial document imaging systems.

Despite the high costs, document image processing is being widely adopted by businesses, and is expected to grow into a $12 billion industry by 1994. Table 7.4[11] lists selected applications of document imaging processing in business today. Two examples of the use of DIP technology are explained in more detail now.

### Retirement fund processing[12]
Home Savings of America is a large savings and loans organization in Southern California servicing more than 350,000 retirement accounts. Till 1984, most accounts were managed manually by paper files. The paperwork and errors with this system were significant, and this caused Home Savings to move to a system of microfilming existing and incoming documents. This process made the document unavailable for the initial few days it took to

| Vendor | Document image processing product |
|---|---|
| Bull HN Information Systems<br>Billerica, MA. | IMAGEWorks |
| Digital Equipment<br>Maynard, MA. | DECimage EXpress |
| Hewlett-Packard<br>Palo, Alto, CA | HP Advanced Image Management System |
| IBM<br>White Plains, N.Y. | IBM SAA ImagePlus/400<br>IBM SAA ImagePlus MVS/ESA |
| Laser Data<br>Tyngsboro, MA. | LaserView |
| NCR<br>Dayton, OH. | NCR Document Management System |
| TRW Financial System<br>Berkeley, CA. | Image Transaction Processing |
| Unisys<br>Blue Bell, PA. | InfoImage Folder |
| Wang Laboratories<br>Lowell, MA. | Wang Integrated Image Systems<br>OPEN/image |

**Table 7.3** Selected vendors of commercial document image processing products

batch, microfilm, review, and key the document indices. This was an important drawback because account information was frequently changed during the first week after it was opened, and any delays during this period resulted in poor customer service. In late 1985, Home Savings contracted with FileNet Corporation to use document image processing for automating its account management system.

The conversion from microfilms to images was converted by 1987 at an overall cost of 11 cents per image. Home Savings claims that its document imaging system has helped to increase productivity by nearly 25%, and has allowed it to provide a higher level of customer service to its clients.

Documents are accessible by multiple users simultaneously, and files can be updated on-line with greater consistency and accuracy. Staff requirements have also been reduced, and training times shortened.

## Document image processing 219

| |
|---|
| Employee retirement benefits management |
| Nuclear records management |
| Frequent flier program correspondence |
| Signature verification |
| Customer service |
| Insurance policy application and approval processing |
| Mortgage loan processing |
| Uniform commercial code document management |
| Patent and trademark management |
| Personnel tracking |
| Claims processing |
| Court document management |
| Chapter 11 bankruptcy filings |
| Press clippings management |
| Police department records management |
| Yellow pages classifieds management |
| New drug filings |
| Patient record management |

**Table 7.4** Sample applications of document image processing

### Yellow Pages advertising management[13]

US West Direct (USWD) publishes the white and yellow pages for three Baby Bell companies (Mountain Bell, Northwestern bell, and Pacific Northwest Bell) in 14 US states, and generates about $700 millions in advertising revenues. As a result of AT&T's divestiture, USWD was forced to develop its own system with the objectives of providing a single system to serve all three Bell companies, creating customers' advertising proofs faster and with more accuracy, and bringing in-house the outside contract work of preparing yellow-page graphics (which cost about $5 million annually for the largest of three Bell companies). Together with Plexus Computers, USWD set up a sophisticated document imaging system which included scanners to capture graphics for display advertisements, electronic routing of work, and a retrieval index to identify the status of each advertisement. Graphic images were stored in a relational database on magnetic disks for new advertisements, and optical disks for old advertisements (since a significant proportion of advertisements — around 70% — are renewed annually). The system helped USWD to achieve all its initial objectives and provide a higher level of customer responsiveness. It is now possible for USWD's salespeople to answer customer's queries quickly and efficiently.

### Diagnostic heart imagery[14]

The Thallium diagnostic workstation (TDW) is an AI system integrating machine vision, conventional KBS technology, and inductive learning for the task of screening US Air Force pilots for significant coronary artery disease. This diagnosis task is more difficult and complex for pilots (as compared to normal patients) due to the strict rules for aeromedical fitness (such as disqualification for even a 30% loss of diameter of the coronary artery — a condition which is hard to detect, and causes no major symptoms). A Thallium scan is often used to assist doctors in their diagnoses. Physicians show considerable variations in their skills in reading such thallium scans. A physician learns from on-the-job experience, and typically leaves for another assignment in three years' time. Studies have shown that physicians routinely miss about 30% of all abnormalities in medical images.

The TDW integrates machine vision and conventional KBS technology. Machine vision is required to extract high-level features (about size and intensities of hot and cold regions) from thallium scans. Thallium images are received by the TDW over a communication network (such as the Ethernet). These images of raw pixel intensities contain a lot of noise, and have to be preprocessed (to reduce noise) before useful features can be extracted. The extracted features are next stored in TDW's knowledge base, which also contains diagnostic rules. These rules are used to generate possible diagnoses for presentation to doctors. To facilitate knowledge acquisition, TDW has an inductive component which learns these diagnostic rules from previously diagnosed images. Doctors have access to this library of stored prior images, and can manipulate it as necessary. They can also modify the rules learnt inductively by TDW. The accuracy of the diagnoses of the TDW system averages around 82%. This is comparable to the level of consistency among doctors. Though difficult to measure accurately, TDW has lead to a higher degree of consistency and accuracy in the diagnosis of thallium images. It is also helping doctors, specially those who are less experienced, in its rôle as an intelligent assistant.

## Microfossil identification[15]

The identification of microfossil[16] samples is an important activity for companies drilling for oil. The knowledge required to correctly identify fossils is limited to a few experts, and any delays in fossil identification (sometimes experts have to be flown into the central research facilities from the field) can result in significant financial losses (amounting to a few millions of dollars) to the oil company. Vides is a KBS for fossil identification developed by British Petroleum. Vides integrates KBS technology with image processing to enable an easy visual approach to microfossil identification.

The knowledge base of Vides is object-oriented, and consists of two parts: a text component, and an image component. The object hierarchies for both the text and image components reflect the domain models used by the expert to classify microfossils. The knowledge about a certain phylum (several thousand species) can contain 3,500 images and more than 10,000 lines of textual information. The text object hierarchy runs from the top level of the general genus name down to more specific species names, and to specific attribute descriptions. The actual process of identification of microfossils by the user is driven by the images stored in Vides. The user first selects an appropriate level (usually the highest level at which assistance is sought) in the text object hierarchy. Next, Vides performs image processing to suggest the appropriate image (from its image knowledge base). This processing is based on the selected level in the hierarchy, comparisons with similar images, and certain features input by the user. Iteratively, the user uses Vides to arrive at a correct identification for the microfossil at every lower level in the text object hierarchy.

The Vides system has been used successfully within BP for assisting in oil exploration. It has helped to preserve knowledge about fossil identification, distribute scarce knowledge to remote locations, and accelerate the process of training young geologists.

## Speech processing

Written text has been the primary medium for communication in human-computer interfaces. With progress in applied AI, attempts are being made to use speech directly to communicate with computers. Speech processing can make computers more user friendly, and facilitate automation of tasks where verbal commands are given more easily (such as in the cockpit of a plane). Speech processing can also help disabled and less educated persons to use computers.

There are two major components of speech processing: speech recognition, and speech understanding. The former is concerned with the relatively limited task of associating an utterance to a set of unique words in a dictionary. The latter is more broad in scope, and is concerned with the general goal of understanding spoken speech. Speech understanding includes recognition of words and sentences, and natural language understanding. Most early research in speech processing (till the early 1970s) focused on speech recognition. Since the mid-1970s, the research focus has shifted to speech understanding. The following sections provide qualitative descriptions of some important concepts in speech recognition and speech understanding.

### Interpretation problems
Many of the problems in speech processing are quite similar to those faced during image processing:

● ambiguous termination points — in spoken speech, the mere detection of the point where a word begins and ends can be quite difficult. Figure 7.25 depicts the sound waveform for the two words Can I. As evident, it is difficult to tell where the waveform for Can ends, and where the waveform for I begins. This problem can get more acute with continuous flowing speech

● relative patterns — spoken speech can be affected by numerous factors such as size of the human vocal tract, rate of speech, variations in pronouncing patterns (even by the same speaker), and the normal variability associated with vocal articulators such as the

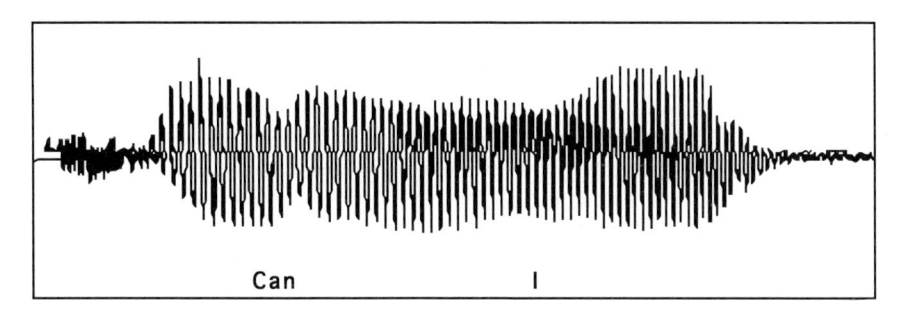

Figure 7.25 Ambiguous termination points of words

## 222 Image and speech processing

tongue, lips, and the jaw. As a result, the same word is almost never pronounced in exactly the same manner by different persons, and rarely so by even the same person. Figure 7.26 represents how different waveforms are produced when the phrase Can I is pronounced two times by the same person. Consequently, it is difficult to rely on absolute pattern matching techniques for accurate speech recognition

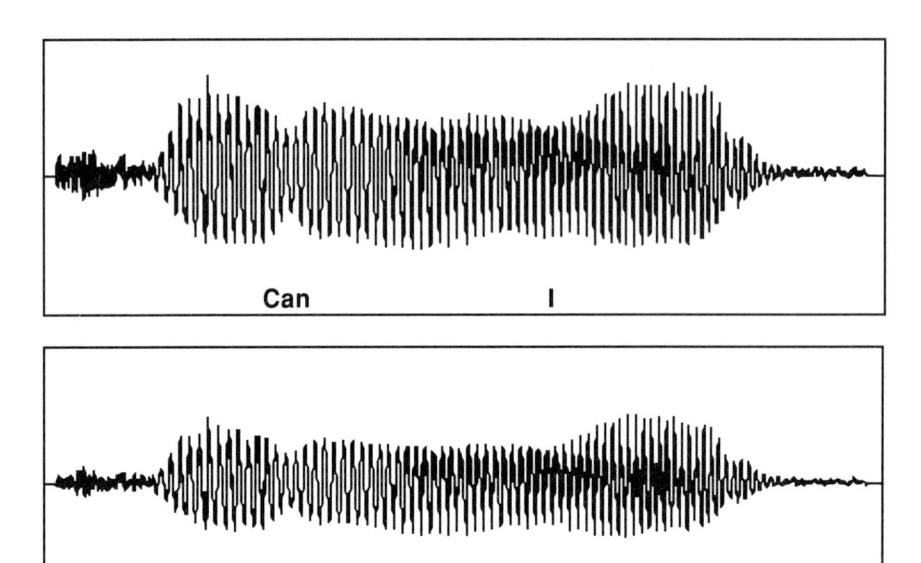

**Figure 7.26** Lack of absolute patterns in spoken speech

● multiple waveforms — speech waveforms are rarely generated in an isolated environment. More commonly, there is a variety of overlapping sound signals. Figure 7.27 depicts the cumulative waveform of numerous musical instruments playing in a symphony. Isolating the individual waveform of each instrument is a difficult task. Similar problems arise while trying to analyze and understand spoken speech when there is background noise (such as that caused by a crowd).

Many mathematical and heuristic techniques have been devised to overcome some of these problems in speech processing. Mathematical approaches include modelling of the source of speech (to predict the shape of the generated sound waveforms), dynamic time warping (selectively contracting and expanding the time axis to decrease variability), and a variety of filtering techniques (for example, to reduce noise). While mathematical approaches are more useful for lower levels of speech signal processing, heuristic approaches exploiting domain-specific knowledge are more applicable at higher levels of speech understanding. For example, assume that the following sounds have been isolated by the processing of speech signals[17]:

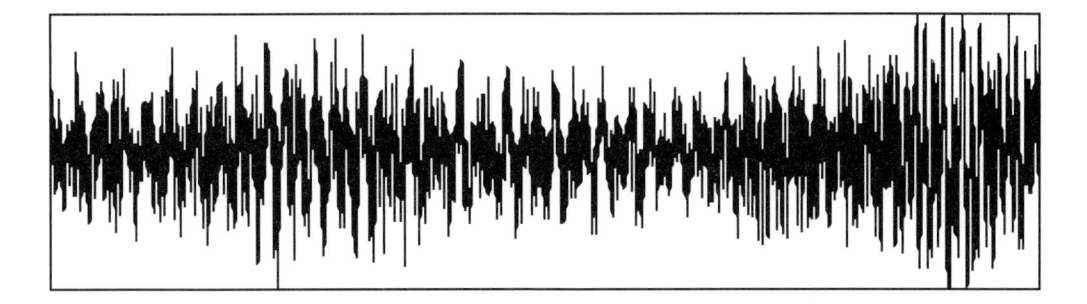

**Figure 7.27** Multiple sound waveforms generated by a symphony

*k a t s k a r s*

Now there are at least two possible interpretations to this combination of sounds: 'cat scares' and 'cats cares'

The correct interpretation is decided by the other words in the phrase or sentence, because either of the above interpretations is possible — as in:

*A cat scares away the birds.*

or;

*A cat's cares are few.*

## Speech recognition

Speech recognition has the limited goal of associating an input speech signal with a certain word or phrase in a dictionary. The structure of a simple speech recognition system is shown in Figure 7.28. The input speech signal is first subjected to a variety of low-level signal analyses such as filtering (to reduce noise levels), parameter extraction (aimed at extracting an information-rich set of parameters about the signal waveform), and determination of the end points of words/phrases (which is a non-trivial task). Next, if the system is being run in a training mode, selective parameters are stored as a template along with the known correct word/phrase in the template dictionary. If the system is run in recognition mode, one or more mathematical techniques such as time warping (to reduce variability), and speech-source modelling (to increase the predictability of spoken speech patterns) are used to help associate a particular dictionary entry with the input speech signal. Typically, absolute matches are not possible (Figure 7.26), thus the system usually lists a set of dictionary templates against which a partial match is found, and suggests the most similar dictionary sound as the 'correct' spoken word.

As the basic approach in speech recognition is pattern matching, the effectiveness of the system is largely determined by the accuracy of dictionary templates and the extent of variations allowed in the input speech signals. Most commercial speech recognition

## 224 Image and speech processing

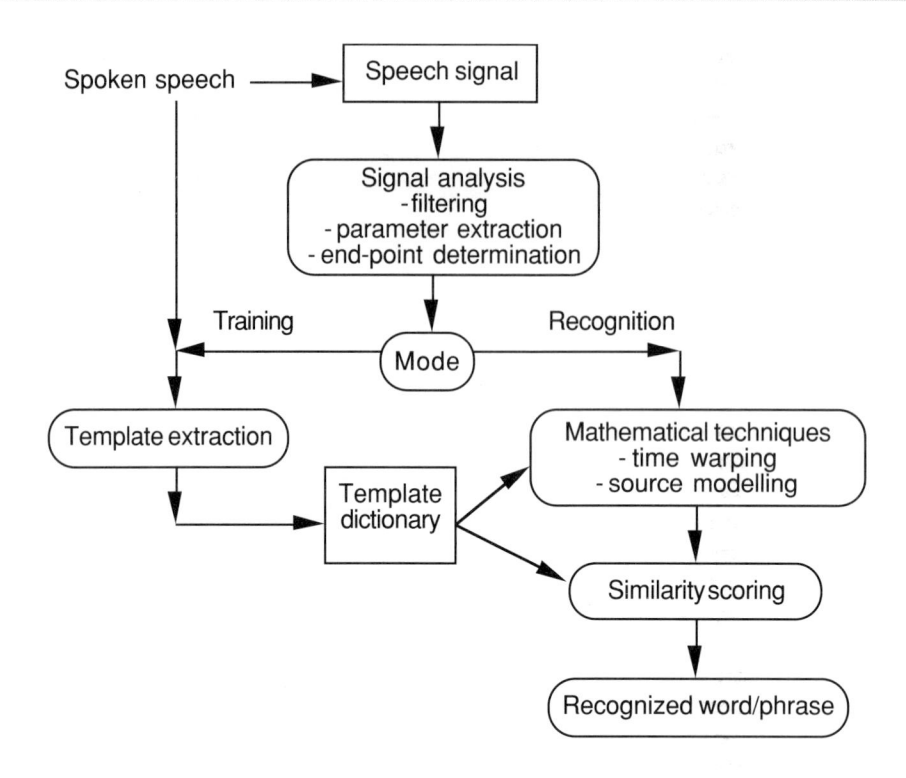

**Figure 7.28** Structure of a simple speech recognition system

systems are based on the architecture shown in Figure 7.28. Due to the required accuracy of the dictionary entries, these speech systems are usually applicable for a limited vocabulary of words/phrases spoken by a single speaker, and have to be trained to store the particular patterns of the allowed vocabulary in the template dictionary. Some sophisticated speech recognition systems include a knowledge-based module which contains knowledge about specific relationships between words/phrases, and the domain of application to aid the process of template matching. However, all speech recognition systems work best for individual words or small phrases, and do not extend very well to recognizing connected speech.

### Speech understanding

Speech understanding is broadly defined as the transformation of an acoustic signal into a representation of its meaning. The importance of speech understanding increased in the mid-1970s when it was realized that the ability of an automated system to respond intelligently to speech was more important than merely recognizing words and phrases. Speech recognition technology has been very successful for building speaker-dependent, limited-vocabulary, isolated-word recognition systems. However, to understand connected speech effectively, it is necessary to start with the identification of basic linguistic units (phonemes) of speech (speech recognition systems deal with entire word patterns), and preserve information about the timing and duration of the utterance (such information is typically discarded in speech recognition due to the use of variability reducing algorithms). As a simple example, consider the following two sentences[18]:

*Mice lick ice.*

and;

*My slick ice.*

The sound waveforms for both of the above sentences would (for most native speakers) look exactly alike. There would be no way for a speech recognition system to distinguish effectively between the two waveforms. However, most people have little difficulty in discerning between a reading of the above two sentences. This indicates that even though there is no physical information in sound waveforms about the beginning and end points of words, part of our knowledge about words is composed of abstract building blocks (called phonemes in linguistics). There has been considerable research within linguistics on the subject of phonemes and their definitions.

Speech understanding systems attempt to understand connected speech by identifying phonemes, then working upwards towards identifying words, sentences and their meanings. The various stages of information processing in a speech understanding system are shown in Figure 7.29. These stages can be classified broadly as belonging to either the recognition phase, or the understanding phase. The understanding phase is the same as that described in the previous chapter on natural language processing, and is omitted here. However, it is important to realize that due to the ambiguity and uncertainty inherent in speech understanding, processing has often to be passed back to an earlier phase (hence the broken backward arrows in Figure 7.29) in an attempt to find a different meaning for the acoustic signal. Described now are some details of the various stages in the recognition phase.

### Signal processing
The input acoustic signal is subjected to noise filtering techniques and digitized by sampling (analogous to that shown in Figure 7.10). Results from information theory indicate that a sampling rate of at least twice the highest frequency in the input waveform is necessary to capture all the information in the speech waveform. This translates into sampling requirements of about 20K to 30K bytes per second, a large enough figure to make the understanding of speech in real-time a difficult problem with current technology.

### Phonetic analysis
This stage is concerned with identification of the various phonemes in the input waveform. This is a crucial stage of processing, as mistakes at this stage can cause large errors and ambiguities in later stages of processing. Phonetic analysis has proven to be a difficult task because cues associated with phonemes are influenced to a large extent by neighboring segments. For example, the spectral cues to the presence of the phoneme /d/

## 226 Image and speech processing

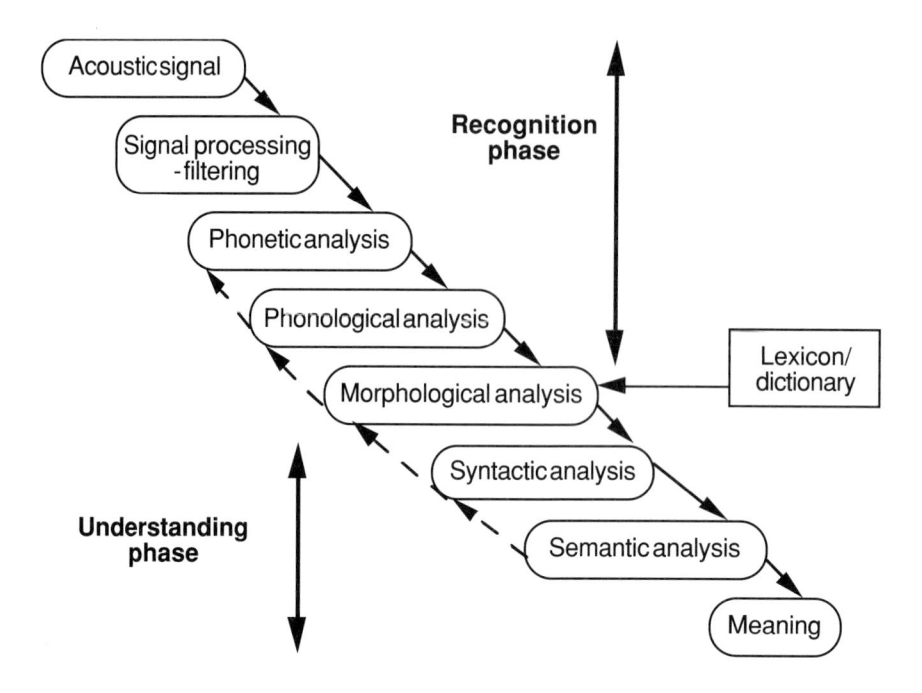

**Figure 7.29** Stages in speech understanding

in /di/ and /du/ are very different, as they are influenced by the following vowel. Moreover, it is not always possible to distinguish accurately between the /d/ and the following vowel. Modern systems still are able to achieve only about 70% accuracy in the identification of phonemes in speech signals.

### Phonological analysis
This stage is concerned with aggregation of phonemes into linguistically significant meaningful patterns of sound (i.e., recognizable words). A significant amount of linguistic knowledge is required (about particular preferred combinations of phonemes) for this stage of processing.

### Morphological analysis
Morphological analysis is necessary to relate inflected variants of words to their base forms. It is not possible to store in the speech understanding system dictionary all inflected variants of words identified during the previous phase of phonological analysis. Examples of inflected variations are plurals — formed by appending an 's' at the end of the word, and word combinations — such as great-grandfather, great-grandmother, and so on. The speech understanding system has to be able to access a dictionary to retrieve selected syntactic and semantic information about the identified word, before processing can be passed onto the following stages of syntactic and semantic analyses.

## The business impact of image and speech processing

Image and speech processing technologies are closely related to NLP and thus their business impacts are similar in many respects to those of NLP applications (Chapter 6). Image and speech processing can aid in informating[19] the organization by providing a means to process large amounts of information, and provide easy and rapid access to this information for all employees. This was observed in the DIP application examples described earlier. Image and speech processing applications can yield quantifiable cost savings and lower errors, as evidenced by the benefits of industrial vision systems. These technologies can also enable organizations, such as the State of Delaware, to create new business opportunities in repackaging and selling information.

An important business impact of image and speech processing technologies which deserves more careful attention is the induced change in business practices and organizational work flows[20]. Business processes in organizations can be viewed as being concerned with storage of information and configuration of information flows for achieving a particular task. Existing process designs in organizations are usually the result of several constraints (historical, organizational, and technological) and are rarely the best possible. Image and speech processing technologies offer the potential to transform storage and flow of information within the organization radically. This transformation provides ample opportunities to organizations for rethinking and redesigning their business processes. These opportunities are important because business process reengineering is an important technique for maintaining organizational competitivity. This ability of image and speech processing technologies to support the redesign of work flows and business processes was illustrated earlier in the examples of DIP at Home Savings of America and US West.

# 228 Image and speech processing

## Summary

Complementing the discussion of NLP in Chapter 6, this chapter has focused on two other important perceptual skills — the abilities to process visual and auditory data. These skills are different from logical problem-solving behaviors as they are dependent to a large extent on the ability to recognize patterns. NLP together with image and speech processing hold the potential for enabling the construction of truly intelligent man-machine interfaces. The main points of this chapter include the following:

- Computer vision can be defined as the field of obtaining relevant information from visual data. There are two broad approaches within computer vision — computational vision (the formulation of computational models of vision) and machine vision (the design of practical image processing systems). This chapter focuses on the latter.
- Biological vision is a highly complex and computationally-intensive process. The performance of modern machine vision systems is significantly poorer than that of the human eye.
- A major barrier in modern machine vision systems is the formidable computational requirements for real-time vision (as in the human eye). Other complications are caused by factors such as relative views, ambiguity, incomplete information, and varying lighting conditions.
- There are three major stages of information processing in machine vision systems (1) signal processing (2) image processing (3) image understanding. Signal processing subjects raw image data to a number of operations (such as digitizing, sampling, thresholding, smoothing, and edge detection) to yield distinct edges in the image data. Image processing performs segmentation and labelling to locate distinct regions and objects in the image. The last phase of image understanding assigns meaning to and interprets the different regions and objects in the image.
- Speech processing consists of two major components — speech recognition and speech understanding. While the former task focuses on simply associating utterances with words in a dictionary, the latter is more broad in scope and aims on understanding spoken speech.
- Analogous to image processing, problems in interpreting speech data can be caused by ambiguous termination points, relative patterns, and multiple waveforms. Domain knowledge is needed for solving such problems.
- Speech recognition systems are limited in many ways, but are common in commercial applications.
- Speech understanding encompasses NLP and needs several stages of processing (signal processing, phonetic, phonological, and morphological analyses) in addition to those needed for NLP. Speech understanding is complex and is yet to be properly exploited commercially.
- The business impacts of image and speech processing include informating the organization, yielding cost savings, lowering errors, and enabling business process redesign.

Like NLP systems, domain knowledge is needed for effective image and speech processing. Concepts from Chapters 2, 3, 4, and 5 are therefore also relevant for applications incorporating these applied AI technologies.

## Bibliography and suggested readings

Technical descriptions of computer vision algorithms are given in many books such as (Horn 86), (Fischler & Firschein 87), (Boyle & Thomas 88), and (Vernon 91). Technology-oriented overviews of machine vision can be found in references (Cohen & Feigenbaum 82), (Barr et al 89), (Patterson 90), and (Shapiro 92). Speech processing algorithms are described in references (Carter 83), (Carter 84), (Church 87), and (Shapiro 90). Ray Kurzweil's excellent book (Kurzweil 90) provides the best non-technical description of important issues related to vision and speech processing algorithms and applications. Kurzweil's book also describes his own personal experiences in building vision and speech applications.

Barr, A., P. R. Cohen, and E. A. Feigenbaum, *The Handbook of Artificial Intelligence*, Vol. 4, Addison Wesley, 1989.

Boyle, R. D., and R. C. Thomas, *Computer Vision — A First Course*, Blackwell Scientific Publications, Oxford, 1988.

Carter, J. P., *Electronically Speaking: Computer Speech Generation*, Howard W. Sam & Co., Indianapolis, 1983.

Carter, J. P., *Electronically Hearing: Computer Speech Recognition*, Howard W. Sam & Co., Indianapolis, 1984.

Church, K. W., *Phonological Parsing in Speech Recognition*, Kluwer Academic, Norwell, MA, 1987.

Cohen, P. R., and E. A. Feigenbaum, (Eds.), *The Handbook of Artificial Intelligence*, Vol. 3, William Kaufmann, Los Altos, CA, 1982.

Fischler, M. A., and O. Firschein, *Readings in Computer Vision: Issues, Problems, Principles, and Paradigms*, Morgan Kaufmann, Los Altos, CA, 1987.

Horn, B. K. P., *Robot Vision*, MIT Press, Cambridge, MA, 1986.

Kurzweil, R., *The Age of Intelligent Machines*, MIT Press, 1990.

Patterson, D. W., *Introduction to Artificial Intelligence and Expert Systems*, Prentice-Hall, 1990.

Shapiro, S. C. (Ed.), *Encyclopedia of Artificial Intelligence*, Vols. 1 and 2, John Wiley, 1992.

Vernon, D., *Machine Vision*, Prentice-Hall, 1991.

## Notes

1  Kinnucan, P., *Imaging Speeds Forms Processing*, Datamation, pp. 79–80, May 1, 1991.

2  Tapellini, D., *How Imaging can Change your Business*, Datamation, pp. 71–74, April 1, 1991.

3  Barr, A., P. R. Cohen, and E. A. Feigenbaum, *The Handbook of Artificial Intelligence*, Vol. 4, pp. 521, Addison-Wesley, 1989.

4  Poggio, T., *Vision by Man and Machine*, Scientific American, April 1984.

5  Kurzweil, R., *The Age of Intelligent Machines*, pp. 227, MIT Press, 1990.

6  A mathematical description of computational vision algorithms used at the different levels of visual information processing is beyond the scope of this chapter. The reader is referred to the bibliography of this chapter for pointers to references with more technical descriptions of image processing.

7  This image was produced using a sample image provided with Digital Darkroom software (marketed by Silicon Beach Software of California, USA) on the Macintosh personal computer.

8  See the bibliography at the end of the chapter.

9  White, K. W., *Machine Vision: At the Cutting Edge in Food Processing and Package Inspection*, Spectrum Food Industry Notes, Arthur D. Little, July 1989.

10  Davis, D. B., *Imaging Systems that Pay Off*, Datamation, May 15, pp. 80, 1991.

11  Arthur D. Little, *Survey of Document Image Processing*, 1991.

12  Sherry, M. E., *Critical Management Issues in the Introduction of Image Processing Technology*, Spectrum Information Systems Industry Applications, pp. 4–5, Arthur D. Little, Burlington, MA, Jan 1989.

13  Sherry, M. E., *Critical Management Issues in the Introduction of Image Processing Technology*, Spectrum Information Systems Industry Applications, pp. 7–8, Arthur D. Little, Burlington, MA, Jan 1989.

14  Saunders, R., *The Thallium Diagnostic Workstation: Learning to Diagnose Heart Imagery from Examples*, in *Innovative Applications of Artificial Intelligence*, Vol. 3, R. Smith and C. Scott (Eds.), pp. 105–118, AAAI/MIT Press, 1991.

15  Swaby, P. A., *Integrating Artificial Intelligence and Graphics in a Tool for Microfossil Identification for Use in the Petroleum Industry*, in *Innovative Applications of Artificial Intelligence*, Vol. 2, A. Rappaport and R. Smith (Eds.), pp. 202–218, AAAI/MIT Press, 1991.

16  Micro-fossils are remains of small organisms which lived many hundreds of millions of years ago and are typically found in rock layers during drilling for oil exploration. Their identification gives a geographical history of the drilling region and leads to the formation of an estimate about the probability that oil will be found in that region.

17  Example adapted from: Rich, E., *Artificial Intelligence*, pp. 346, Mc-Graw Hill, 1983.

18 Example adapted from: Keyser, S. J., *Phonemes*, in the *Encyclopedia of Artificial Intelligence*, Vol. 2, S. C. Shapiro (Ed.), pp. 744, John Wiley & Sons, 1990.

19 Zuboff, S., *Automate/Informate: The Two Faces of Intelligent Technology*, Organizational Dynamics, Autumn, 1985.

20 Tapellini, D., *How Imaging can Change your Business*, Datamation, pp. 71–74, April 1, 1991.

# Part V

## Alternative approaches to knowledge processing

Rules and frame hierarchies have been the fundamental techniques used for representing and reasoning with knowledge in earlier chapters. This concluding section of the book presents two alternative approaches for modelling intelligence — fuzzy logic (FL) and connectionism. Both of these techniques are important, and each offers advantages over conventional knowledge-based technologies. While FL allows for the modelling of approximate reasoning, connectionist approaches have powerful pattern-recognition capabilities and are able to learn and evolve autonomously. FL is a mature technology and is being widely exploited commercially today. Connectionist models are gradually evolving into a commercially viable technology.

The importance and popularity of FL has increased rapidly over the past few years. A fundamental impact of FL has been to alter the granularity of intelligence. With the help of FL processing on a chip, it is possible to embed intelligence inside individual products. This has unleashed a wide variety of 'intelligent' consumer products which are available in the commercial market today. Coupled with rule-based systems, FL has enabled modelling of the approximate and imprecise reasoning processes common in human problem-solving. Within industry, FL is being used to simplify modelling of complex systems and revolutionize product design. FL technology and its commercial applications are described in Chapter 8.

Connectionism has been gaining in importance and popularity since the mid-1980s because it has some powerful and attractive properties in the domains of pattern-recognition and learning. Connectionist systems hold the promise to potentially rectify important limitations of conventional knowledge-based systems: an inability to learn and poor pattern-recognition capabilities. Chapter 9 introduces connectionism and describes selected connectionist architectures. Guidelines for designing connectionist applications are presented, and selected connectionist applications are described. Appendix 3 provides additional details on commercial applications of connectionist architectures.

# Chapter 8
# *Approximate reasoning using fuzzy logic*

Fuzzy logic (FL) was invented about 25 years ago. The past decade has seen an extraordinary spurt in the commercialization of the technology. Not only has FL significantly enhanced knowledge-based technology, it has fundamentally altered the granularity of intelligence. Today, with the help of FL, manufacturers of home appliances are 'embedding intelligence' inside individual products. The application of FL has also transformed industrial process control, and enabled new product development strategies. Some introductory examples of the commercial applications of FL are described below.

### Hitachi: the Sendai subway control system[1]

Sendai is a major city in the northern part of Japan's main island of Honshu with one of the highest ratios of car ownership in Japan. Road capacity reached its peak in 1965 with the average speed of a municipal bus during rush hour dropping to a snail's pace of 8 km/hr within 10 km of the city's center. Against this background, Sendai's city planners started designing a municipal subway system that would alleviate the city's subway snarls, and also provide its citizens with the highest levels of comfort, safety, and efficiency.

While designing the subway system at Sendai, Hitachi engineers spent many years trying to automate train operations based on traditional industrial control methods. In the conventional approach, accurate operation is achieved by having a predetermined speed pattern and issuing (frequent) commands for acceleration or braking in order to adapt to changing conditions, such as gradient of track and braking force of rolling stock. The results obtained with the conventional methods were unsatisfactory. Next, engineers looked at how a human driver controlled the train. While operating a train, a skilled driver made control decisions based upon his knowledge of conditions of the track and his understanding of the performance characteristics of the train. His decisions and actions are approximations of what is reasonable and necessary at a particular instant of time, rather than the result of a series of detailed quantitative decisions. The engineers noted that a driver's internal reasoning might be something like:

*have to watch the speed along that stretch*

or;

*easy on the brakes coming in.*

These seemingly vague and imprecise decisions are actually the result of highly complex thought processes based on knowledge and experience, and allow constant readjustment of indices such as safety, speed, quality of ride, time table, and so on[2]. It is difficult to process the 'fuzzy' and 'imprecise' information used by a skilled motorman with conventional logic, or by traditional rule-based technology. The engineers next looked at FL for help with designing a radically different subway control system. FL allowed the Hitachi engineers to incorporate the knowledge of the experienced motorman and his ability to process fuzzy and imprecise information into the control procedures. The resulting system is not only simpler, but has resulted in significant improvements in the degree of comfort and safety, and has yielded cost savings. Since July 15, 1987, a nearly fully automated 'intelligent' subway system (designed by Hitachi) whisks passengers between stations with reputedly the highest degree of comfort and safety in the world — 'straphangers don't need to grip hard because station stops are gentle as a kitten'[3].

## Yamaichi Securities: intelligent trading programs[4]

Conventional trading programs for index-linked portfolios are common in Japanese financial companies. It is, however, widely recognized that the Tokyo stock market is more faddish than fundamental, and that standard computerized-program strategies based on traditional portfolio theory won't work perfectly there.

Experienced Japanese fund managers are adept at recognizing 'fads' and trends. Much like the skilled motorman running the Sendai subway, fund managers at Yamaichi Securities are experts at understanding and reasoning with imprecise and ambiguous data. For example, a reasoning rule in the mind of such a manager might be:

> If market sentiment is strong now and the previous session's market sentiment was normal, then sell futures in large volume.

The concepts strong, normal, and large in the above reasoning rule are fundamentally imprecise and vague. As explained later, they are not easily quantified or expressed as symbols in rule premises. FL enables the representation of and reasoning with such vague concepts. Since August 1989, Yamaichi Securities has been managing several billions of

Yen with a computerized trading system based on FL, and which attempts to capture the reasoning processes of an experienced fund manager. The computerized trading model looks at basic financial data such as stock prices and trading volumes, and integrates it with about 600 trading rules-of-thumb which represent the approximate reasoning processes of fund managers. The trading heuristics are represented by fuzzy rules (and not conventional IF..THEN.. rules). Fuzzy rules have special advantages as compared with conventional rules and are described in more detail later. According to company sources, a two year trial period in futures arbitrage was excellent — 'only one in 100 pros could have done better'[5].

## Matshushita: intelligent washing machines[6]

The latest washing machine sold by Matshushita in Japan makes the chore of washing clothes very simple for users. All the user has to do is insert laundry in the washing machine and press the start button. The machine takes care of the rest. It automatically selects wash, rinse, and spin cycles from among 600 possible combinations by analyzing dirt in the wash, size of the load, and other relevant factors. The result is a cleaner and more efficient wash. The first washing machines sold out the company's initial production run within weeks. It is not surprising that these latest models already (in early 1991) account for over half of Matshushita's washing machine sales in Japan.

Since 1989, FL processing has been available on a chip. This has dramatically changed the scope of applicability of FL technology. It has now become feasible to insert 'expertise on a chip' within individual products. The Matshushita washing machine is one example of an 'intelligent' product resulting from the integration of 'intelligence' into the product. Expert rules about the best combination of wash, rinse, and spin cycles are stored in a FL chip inside the washing machine. Various sensors in the washing machine provide data about the wash load to the chip which selects the best combination. A lot of the information used in this decision is also imprecise and vague, such as 'the degree of dirt'. FL chips are being used to incorporate expert knowledge into many other products. For example, Toshiba's cooking range incorporates the expertise of four professional chefs. Virtually every Japanese home appliance maker has integrated FL intelligence (on chips) into current models of cameras, video camcorders, vacuum cleaners, air conditioners, rice cookers, microwave ovens, toasters, and refrigerators.

## Rockwell: modelling stress on wings[7]

Engineers at Rockwell were facing the formidable task of modelling the stress on a wing while designing controls for the Air Force/NASA advanced technology wing. Stress on the wing is caused by many different variables — air speed, shape of the wing in flight, drag, and aerodynamics — all of which constantly change during flight. The domain is enormously complex to model precisely. After spending months using conventional modelling techniques, the engineers decided to use a novel method based on FL. The result: simpler rules, less math, and a more accurate representation of a complicated process. According to sources within Rockwell, the adoption of FL allowed them to get better results, faster.

Precision is expensive and often not required as demonstrated by the above example. Using FL, it is possible to exploit the tolerance for imprecision in many engineering situations. The results need not necessarily be less useful or less realistic. On the contrary, the models are usually simpler and the results often more accurate. Many real-world situations are too complex to model precisely.

Conventional approaches usually simplify the domain and develop precise models of the simplified situation. Results obtained using such models are precise, but typically apply to the simplified domain modelled. FL in contrast, allows an 'approximate model' of the actual domain to be developed with comparatively less effort. Experience shows that the results obtained with such an 'approximate model' are also usually very useful and usable.

## Development of fuzzy logic

FL was invented in the USA during the mid-1960s by Lotfi Zadeh[8], a professor at the University of California at Berkeley. Zadeh's initial motivation to develop FL came from his observation that traditional mathematics with its emphasis on precision was ill-suited for modelling 'soft, non-quantifiable' systems (such as those studied in the social sciences). The commercial successes of FL applications have however been in entirely different areas — industrial process control and knowledge-based systems (KBSs). FL began to find wide-ranging commercial applications when it was coupled with KBS technology because coupling the two technologies allows a better modelling of the imprecise reasoning processes of skilled human experts.

The first practical application of FL to the control of industrial processes was pioneered by Mamdani and Assilian in 1974 in connection with the regulation of a steam engine[9]. In 1980, F. L. Smith of Copenhagen[10] started marketing the first commercial fuzzy KBS to control the fuel-intake rate and gas flow of a rotating kiln used to make cement. Around the same time, Japanese companies realized the practical potential of FL and started investing in it seriously. The shot in the arm for the commercialization of FL came with the invention of the FL chip by researchers in Bell laboratories in 1985[11] (which became commercially available in late 1988). A FL chip enabled coding and execution of a set of fuzzy rules in hardware inside a chip. With the availability of the chip, it became possible to mimic human-like intelligence in a small package, and to do it cheaply — and quickly. FL chips can perform over 580,000 fuzzy inferences per second, and can be purchased for approximately $77 a piece. This invention lead to a proliferation of a wide range of 'fuzzy products' (primarily developed and marketed by Japanese companies) i.e., everyday appliances such as cameras, camcorders, rice cookers and air conditioners with an embedded fuzzy chip.

Recently announced in Japan is the development of the first fuzzy computer (designed by Professor Yamakawa and built by OMRON). The logic inside a fuzzy computer, in contrast to conventional computers (utilizing a binary logic of 1 and 0), is based on FL (utilizing a range of degrees of truth ranging between 0 to 1). Such a computer is not only able to perform fuzzy inferences at a very high speed (10,000,000 inferences per second), but more important, is looked upon as an important step towards the development of sixth-generation computers with a capability of processing uncertain and imprecise knowledge[12].

# Development of fuzzy logic

The importance that Japan attaches to these developments can be seen clearly from the fact that in 1989, Japan's Ministry of International Trade and Industry (MITI) setup a consortium of 48 top Japanese companies to develop fuzzy systems. The consortium, Laboratory for International Fuzzy Engineering, has a $70 million starting budget. Similar, but less ambitious, efforts are underway in Europe also.

The Ministry of Research in France is coordinating research and investment in FL and taking steps to increase cooperation between universities and industry, such as aiding in the formation (in 1991) of the club Logique Floue within the Association ECRIN (Echange et Coordination Recherche Industrie). Also in 1991, the European foundation, ELITE (European Laboratory for Intelligent Techniques Engineering), has been started in Aachen, Germany with the aim of enhancing research in FL and stimulating FL applications in European industry. Table 8.1 lists some important milestones in the commercial development of FL.

## Fundamentals of fuzzy logic technology

FL is today a vast field. However only a small part of FL technology — the integration of FL and rule-based reasoning — is being used at present in most commercial applications. This section provides a qualitative description of the fundamentals of fuzzy rule-based reasoning[13].

### Representational concepts

FL aims to model the imprecise modes of reasoning that play an important rôle in the remarkable human ability to make rational decisions in an environment of uncertainty and imprecision. Zadeh[14] has suggested that rather than regard human reasoning processes as

| Year | Development |
|---|---|
| 1965 | First paper on FL by Zadeh |
| 1972 | Theory of application of FL to industrial control is developed by Zadeh |
| 1974 | First implementation of fuzzy industrial control by Mamdani and Assilian |
| 1975 | Theory of merger of FL and KBS technology is developed by Zadeh |
| 1980 | First commercial fuzzy KBS is marketed by FL Smidth of Copenhagen |
| 1985 | First implementation of a fuzzy KBS on a chip by Togai and Watanabe at Bell Laboratories |
| 1987 | Sendai's advanced subway system based on fuzzy control is operational |
| 1988 | Fuzzy chips are available commercially from Omron |
| 1989 | ● Fuzzy home appliances start being sold in Japan |
|  | ● LIFE, a consortium of 48 top Japanese companies started in Japan by MITI |
| 1990 | The first fuzzy computer designed by Yamakawa and built by Omron |

Table 8.1 Milestones in development of fuzzy logic

themselves 'approximating' to some more refined and exact logical processes that could be carried out with mathematical precision, the essence and power of human reasoning lies in its capability to grasp and use inexact concepts directly. For example, we are usually quite comfortable dealing with problems of the sort:

- most wealthy actors live in Beverly Hills. Mary is a rich actress. What can be said about the location of Mary's residence?

- most players on the basketball team are quite tall. George is on the basketball team. How tall is George?

### Representation of vague concepts using fuzzy sets

Classical logical systems are usually based on Boolean two-valued logic i.e., in it, any proposition can be either true or false. This imposes an inherent restriction in its ability to represent vague and imprecise concepts such as wealthy and tall. To understand this better, consider the concept tall. Most people would agree that a person whose height is more than 7 feet is definitely tall, while someone whose height is below 5 feet is surely short i.e., not tall. How to then quantify the distinction between tall and short persons? A common approach is to use a threshold (above which everyone is tall and below which everyone is short). Let us choose the threshold height to be 6 feet. This threshold correctly classifies the height of 7 feet as tall, and of 5 feet as short. Next consider two persons A and B, with heights of 5 feet 11 inches and 6 feet 1 inch respectively. Assuming the earlier threshold of 6 feet, we see that A is classified as short and B as tall. Intuitively, this does not seem right. While A is indeed shorter than B, their heights are very similar. Note that this problem persists even if we move the threshold upwards or downwards (we can always find similar heights, each one on either side of the threshold). This problem exists because we are using a two-valued logical system in which middle-values such as 5 feet 11 inches and 6 feet 1 inch are forced into one of the two sets tall or not tall by the choice of the threshold height.

FL in contrast, would assign a 'degree of membership' to each height in the set of tall persons. Thus, a person with a height of 6 feet 1 inch would be tall to a certain degree, while a person with a height of 5 feet 8 inches would be tall to another degree. This allows the explicit representation of the fact that different heights can be tall to different degrees. Figure 8.1 illustrates how different heights can be assigned different degrees of membership in the representation of the imprecise concept tall using FL. The horizontal axis gives the height and the vertical axis specifies the corresponding degree of membership of the height in the set of tall persons. Persons with heights below 5 feet are tall to the degree 0 (i.e., they are not tall), while persons taller than 7 feet are tall to the degree 1 (i.e., definitely tall). All intermediate heights are tall to varying degrees (e.g., a person with a height of 6 feet 5 inches is tall to the degree 0.7). Figure 8.1 can be said to represent the fuzzy set tall. Note that fuzzy sets are a generalization of conventional Boolean sets. The degree of membership for domain elements in a Boolean set can be only either 0 (not a member of the set) or 1 (a member of the set). In contrast, the degree of membership in a fuzzy set can be any value between (and including) 0 and 1. It thus follows that models developed using FL are also applicable for 'crisp' (non-fuzzy) data.

Analogous to tall, the concepts short and average height can also be represented using FL. Figure 8.2 depicts one possible representation of these concepts. Note that a particular height can belong to different fuzzy concepts (i.e., fuzzy sets) and can have different

# Development of fuzzy logic

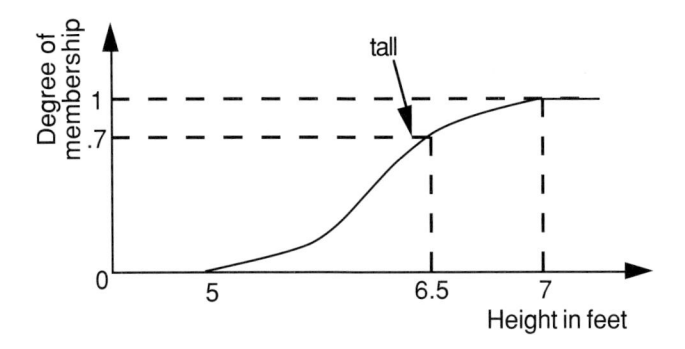

**Figure 8.1** Representation of the concept *tall* using fuzzy sets

degrees of membership in each of them. For example, the height, 6 feet 5 inches has a degree of membership 0.7 in the fuzzy concept tall and a degree of membership 0.49 in the fuzzy concept very tall. Also as would be intuitively expected, the degree of membership of the height 6 feet 5 inches in the concept tall is more than that in the concept very tall.

### Linguistic variables

In 1975, Zadeh[15] introduced the concept of a linguistic variable and it has played an important rôle in the commercial applications of FL. Zadeh's basic idea was to extend the possible values of a particular variable to include not only numerical values, but also linguistic values. For example, a variable such as height would typically have a particular number as its value. By treating it as a linguistic variable, it is possible to (also) assign as its value linguistic labels such as short, tall, very tall, very short and average. These linguistic labels are given a numerical interpretation by fuzzy sets similar to those shown in Figure 8.2. The use of linguistic variables makes it much easier for humans to express statements or conditions linguistically. (Recall the use of linguistic labels in the reasoning processes of the Sendai subway driver and the Yamaichi fund manager in the introductory

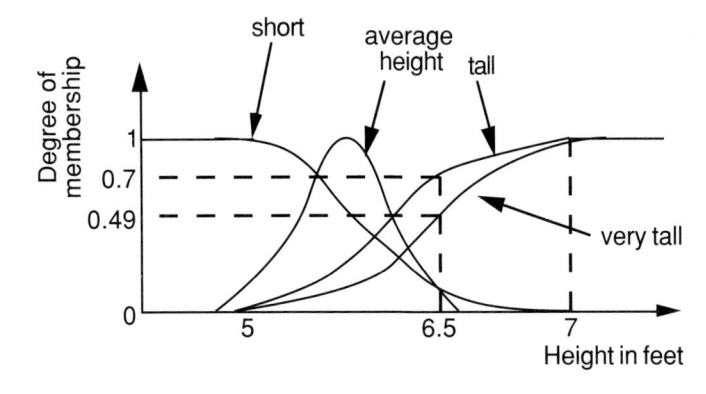

**Figure 8.2** Fuzzy sets *tall*, *short* and *average height*

examples) The use of linguistic variables in fuzzy reasoning procedures is explained in the following sections. Note that a linguistic variable can be viewed as a generalization of a conventional variable.

### Practical implications of fuzzy set representations

To see the practical implications of such a representation, consider the example of an air conditioner. A conventional air conditioner only recognizes two states: too hot or too cold. Under normal thermostat control, the cooling system either operates at full blast or shuts off completely. A fuzzy air conditioner can, by contrast, recognize that some room temperatures are closer to the human comfort zone than others. Its cooling system would begin to slow down gradually as the room temperature approached the desired setting. The result of this is a more comfortable room and a smaller electric bill. These principles have been used in fuzzy air conditioners marketed by Mitsubishi.

As another example, consider the formulation of a database queries. A typical query such as 'get all companies with revenues above $400 million' would not retrieve companies with revenues just below the threshold (such as $399 million). This problem can be solved by the use of FL. Assume that the concept high revenue is defined using an appropriate fuzzy set (analogous to that shown in Figure 8.1). Now a query such as 'get all companies with high revenues' will retrieve all companies whose revenues qualify as high to a certain degree. This facilitates intelligent information retrieval from databases[16].

### Reasoning procedures

The combination of FL and rule-based reasoning has found wide applications in control of industrial processes, modelling of complex systems, and development of fuzzy KBSs. Fuzzy rules are like ordinary IF..THEN.. rules, except for two important differences:

- the premises and conclusions of fuzzy rules contain linguistic variables
- the inference procedure with fuzzy rules is different from that with conventional IF..THEN... rules.

Consider a simple fuzzy reasoning problem. Assume that the following two fuzzy rules are given in a knowledge base:

>   IF voltage is small THEN current is medium     ...(rule a)
>
>   IF voltage is large THEN current is small      ...(rule b)

Here, voltage and current are two linguistic variables representing particular values of voltage and current in some unspecified electrical system. Small, medium and large are fuzzy sets defining the different linguistic values that can be assigned to the linguistic variables, voltage and current. Rules a and b relate the output value of current to the input value of voltage. A typical fuzzy reasoning problem in this context would be 'determine the value of current given that voltage is medium'.

# Reasoning procedures 243

Note that this problem is non-trivial as the input value of voltage (= medium) does not match exactly with the premises of either rule a or rule b above. Thus neither rule can be directly applied to obtain the output value of the current. However, rules a and b specify the value of the current when the values of the voltage are small and large. The inference mechanism of fuzzy rules allows us to compute the partial match of the input data with the premises of the above two rules, and obtain an interpolated current value as an answer to the posed problem. To understand how these partial matches are computed and how the fuzzy inference procedure operates, it is necessary to know about some basic mathematical operations on fuzzy sets. These are described qualitatively now.

## Mathematical operations on fuzzy sets

Fuzzy sets are extensions of classical sets. Thus it is possible to define the classical set theoretical operations of union, intersection, and complementation for fuzzy sets:

- union — the union, A∪B, of two fuzzy sets A and B is given by taking the maximum of the the degrees of membership of the elements in A and B. This is graphically depicted in Figure 8.3 for two arbitrary fuzzy sets A and B

- intersection — the intersection, A∩B, of two fuzzy sets A and B is given by taking the minimum of the the degrees of membership of the elements in A and B. This is graphically depicted in Figure 8.4 for two arbitrary fuzzy sets A and B. Note that only elements common to both sets are retained in their intersection

- complement — the complement of a fuzzy set A is obtained by subtracting from 1 the degree of membership (in the fuzzy set A) of the various elements in the domain. Figure 8.5 depicts a graphical interpretation of the process of obtaining the complement of a fuzzy set. Also note the fuzzy sets short and tall in Figure 8.2. The concept of short is the complement of the concept tall (and vice versa). Therefore the possibility distribution for short can be obtained by taking the complement of that for tall and vice versa.

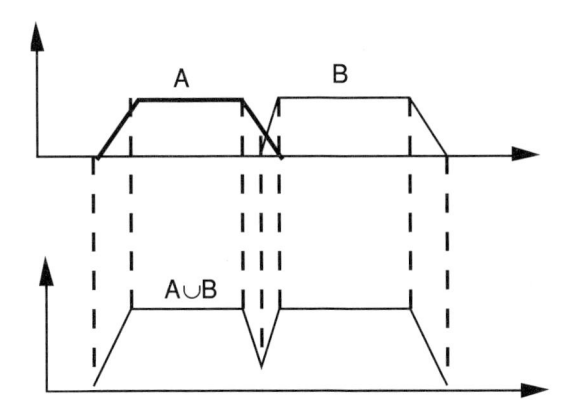

**Figure 8.3** Union of fuzzy sets

## 244 Approximate reasoning using fuzzy logic

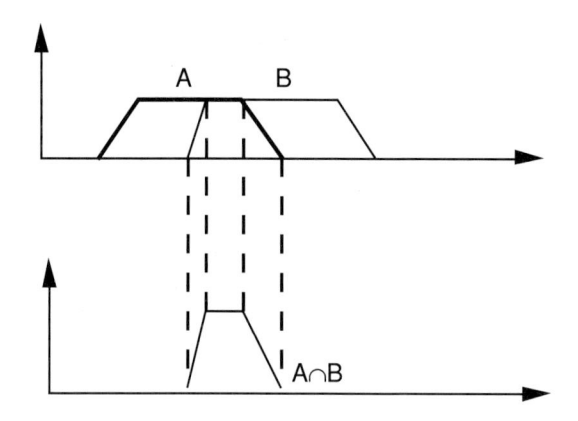

**Figure 8.4** Intersection of fuzzy sets

### Inference with fuzzy rules

For simplicity, let the fuzzy sets small, medium, and large in rules a and b have similar representations for both voltage and current as shown in Figure 8.6 (X-axis scales would be different for voltage and current). The appropriate value of current is to be determined by fuzzy reasoning.

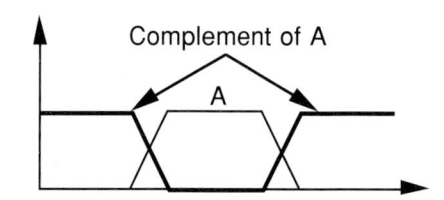

**Figure 8.5** Complement of a fuzzy set

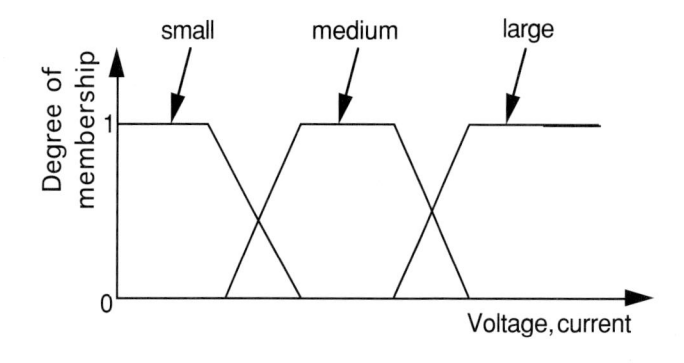

**Figure 8.6** Fuzzy sets *small, medium* and *large*

# Reasoning procedures 245

Figure 8.7 depicts the two fuzzy rules and the fuzzy input. For ease of visualization, the distribution of the input fact is superimposed (as a lightly shaded region) on the premises of the two fuzzy rules in Figure 8.7. Though there is no direct match between the premises of the two fuzzy rules and the input fact, note that a partial match with each rule does exist. Thus intuitively one can expect each of the two rules to contribute partially to the output answer. The desired value of current is computed as follows. First, the intersection of the input data with each of the fuzzy premises is computed (using the same operation as shown in Figure 8.4). The intersections are shown by the striped regions in the input premises in Figure 8.7. Second, the contribution of each rule to the output answer is determined by taking the portion of the output fuzzy distributions (shown shaded in the rule conclusions in Figure 8.7) which are contained within the intersections computed in the above step. Third, a union (as shown in Figure 8.3) is taken of the contributions of the conclusions of each rule to give the final output value of current (shown by the shaded region in the bottom right hand corner of Figure 8.7).

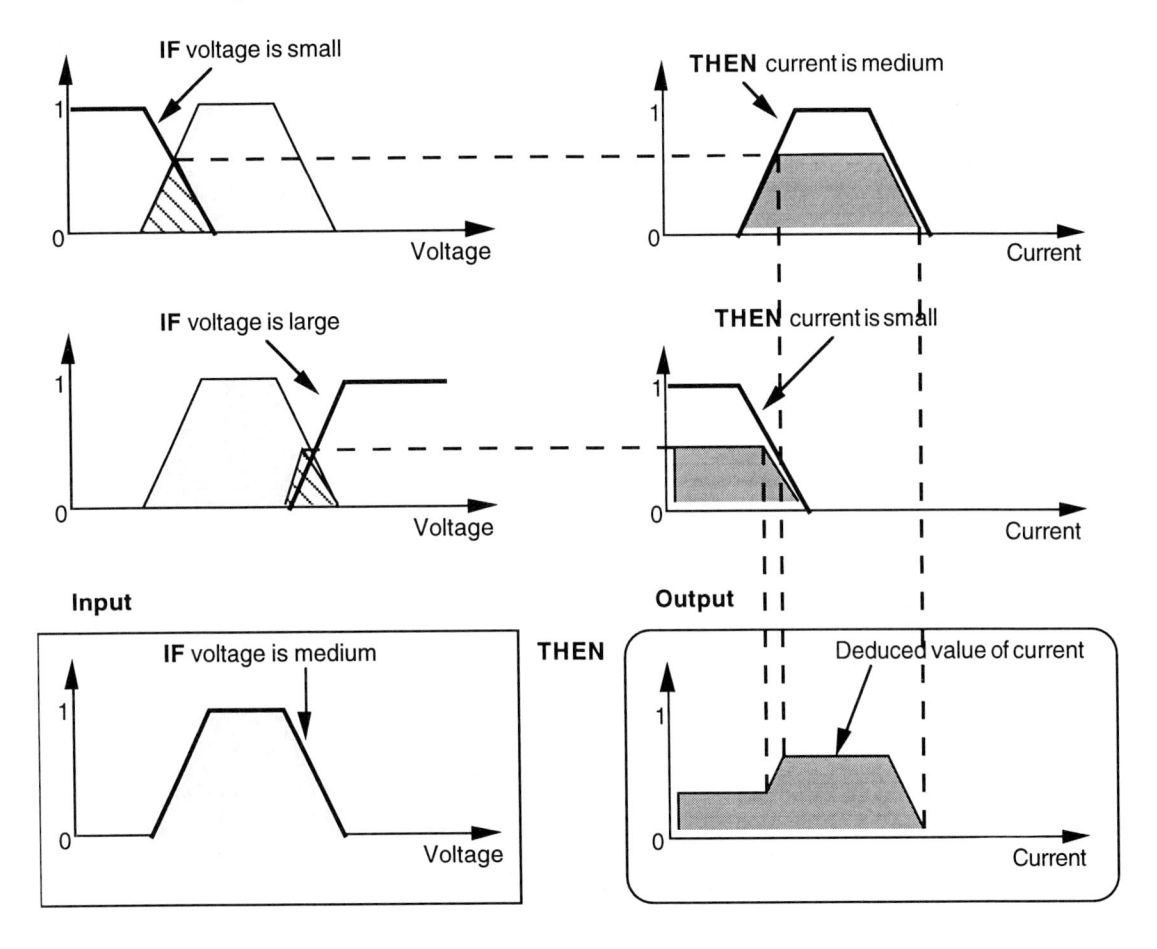

**Figure 8.7** Approximate inference using fuzzy rules (and fuzzy input)

Sometimes, a linguistic answer may be desired, specially if the output answer is to be given to a human. In such situations, a process known as 'linguistic approximation' is used. The output distribution of Figure 8.7 does not directly correspond to any distribution shown in Figure 8.6. Thus the fuzzy sets small, medium or large cannot be directly assigned to the output answer. Rather some combination of the fuzzy sets has to be determined whose distribution approximates the distribution of the output answer. The previously defined operations of union, intersection, complementation (and other operations not defined in this chapter) are used to obtain the linguistic label combination (such as 'not small and not large current') whose possibility distribution closely approximates the output distribution. This linguistic label combination is then output as the answer of the fuzzy inference procedure.

Note that the output value of current is in general a fuzzy set. Often the output fuzzy set has to be 'defuzzified' to give a crisp number. Crisp numbers are important for controlling physical systems because fuzzy sets may not make much sense by themselves. For example if the value of current has to be set, a crisp number is required (the value of current cannot be set to a distribution). Different methods for defuzzification have been proposed[17]. A popular defuzzification procedure (which has been used successfully in many applications) is to take the center of mass of the output distribution. Figure 8.8 illustrates the defuzzification of the output of Figure 8.7. Point A is the center of mass of the output fuzzy set. The coordinate, y, of A along the current (X) axis represents the defuzzified output value of current. A more concrete example of the defuzzification procedure is given in a later section describing the use of fuzzy rules for controlling an inverted pendulum.

## Comparing fuzzy and conventional rules

In contrast to the usual IF..THEN.. rules which are based on Boolean logic, fuzzy rules can accommodate partial matches. Assume for a moment that the labels small, medium, and large are treated as symbols (not as fuzzy sets) as in coventional rule-based systems. Then, because there is no rule (in the rule-base) for the value of current when the value of voltage is medium, the system is unable to produce an answer for current (as no rule will be triggered). However, the fuzzy inference procedure just described computes partial matches, and can produce a meaningful answer even when there is no direct match between rule premises and input facts. This feature causes fuzzy rules to be more robust to variability in the input descriptions.

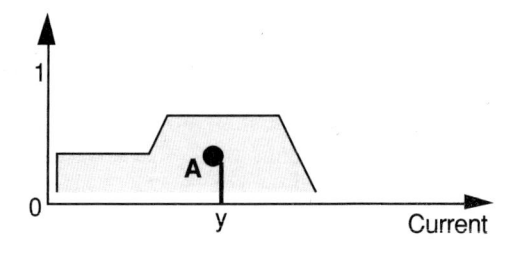

**Figure 8.8** Defuzzification of a fuzzy set

The number of fuzzy rules required for a particular inference is significantly less than that if conventional rules are used. This is primarily due to the ability of fuzzy rules to accommodate partial matches with inputs. The premises and conclusions of each fuzzy rule are fuzzy sets covering a certain range of domain values. A few rules are usually adequate for covering regions of interests in the domain. All possible values in each domain do not need separate rules (as would be required if conventional rules were being used). Even if a particular input does not match exactly with the rule premises, its partial match with a set of rules provides an answer. Thus systems using fuzzy rules are often simpler to build and maintain.

The conventional inference procedures of backward and forward chaining are essentially sequential procedures, with each step in the process being represented by a single rule firing. A rule fires, and that rule in turn triggers another rule. The fuzzy inference procedure described above is in contrast, a parallel procedure. The match of each rule premise with the input fact is computed in parallel. This makes the fuzzy inference procedure easily amenable to implementations on parallel computers (an attractive feature given the predicted future importance of parallel computers).

The parallel nature of the rule firing makes the inference process robust to breakdowns, and gives it the desirable property of graceful degradation. As each rule contributes (in proportion to its match with the input) to the final output, the removal of any one rule (due to mechanical breakdowns or other reasons) does not stall the system. The system still operates (due to the contribution of other rules), albeit not as effectively as before. In contrast, if a critical rule in a conventional rule-based system does not fire (due to a software bug or other reasons), then the entire system can crash suddenly. Graceful degradation provides advance warnings errors, and allows more time for repairs or corrective actions.

The exact shapes of the distributions in the premises and conclusions of fuzzy rules are not critical. As various rules contribute in parallel when presented with a particular input, there is some in-built tolerance for errors in the shapes of the distributions. This is in contrast to conventional rules, where the premise and output labels (values) have to be chosen carefully (to match the input data exactly). This property of fuzzy rules facilitates the engineering of fuzzy systems.

## Case studies of fuzzy logic applications

Two case studies of FL applications are described below. Both examples aim to provide the reader with a better idea of how fuzzy rules are actually used in applications.

### The inverted pendulum
The inverted pendulum is one of the classical systems used for studying control procedures. The problem consists of applying a suitable force to balance an inverted pendulum. In principle, it is very similar to balancing a stick on one's hand by moving the hand forward or backward as necessary. Figure 8.9 depicts a simple inverted pendulum in which a motor applies the required force for balancing the pendulum. In this simple system, there are two inputs and one output. The inputs are the angular displacement of the bob, $\theta$, and the angular velocity of the bob i.e., rate of change of $\theta$ with time ($d\theta/dt$).

## 248 Approximate reasoning using fuzzy logic

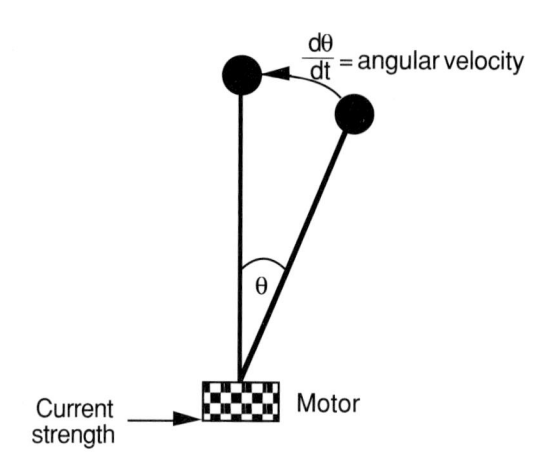

**Figure 8.9** An inverted pendulum

Despite its simplicity, the inverted pendulum is a non-linear system (i.e., the required current strength varies as a non-linear function of the angular displacement and the angular velocity). The system can be modelled accurately, but requires the solution of a second-order differential equation. Some simplifications (such as the approximation of $\sin\theta$ by $\theta$) are usually made for solving the equation quickly. These simplifications are not always valid and can be violated (e.g., the approximation of $\sin\theta$ by $\theta$ is not valid for large $\theta$ i.e., for large displacements). A correct solution requires the use of special numerical methods (which are computationally intensive). Moreover, a solution of the equations to balance the pole is not easily possible as the solution point is unstable with respect to the system's initial conditions. The solution is also sensitive to various parameters such as mass of the bob, length of the shaft, and strength of the motor.

### Fuzzy rules for balancing an inverted pendulum

Accurate and robust control of such a system can be obtained by using a set of fuzzy rules of the form:

    IF Angular_displacement is small AND Angular_velocity is small

        THEN Force_applied is small

Figure 8.10 depicts a set of 11 rules which can be used to control a simple inverted pendulum[18]. Theta and Dtheta are used to represent the angular displacement and the angular velocity of the pendulum respectively. It is also assumed that an electric motor is used to apply necessary force to balance the inverted pendulum. NM, NS, Z, PS and PM are used as acronyms for the fuzzy sets negative_medium, negative_small, zero, positive_small, and positive_medium respectively. The shapes of these fuzzy sets are as shown in Figure 8.11 (not drawn to scale).

Note that the input values of Theta and Dtheta are crisp. Also, a crisp value has to be given to the motor as the recommended value of current to balance the inverted pendulum. The inference procedure with crisp input values is similar to that for fuzzy input values (as

# Case studies of fuzzy logic applications 249

| IF | Theta | is NM | AND | Dtheta | is Z  | THEN | Current | is PM |
| IF | Theta | is NS | AND | Dtheta | is Z  | THEN | Current | is PS |
| IF | Theta | is Z  | AND | Dtheta | is Z  | THEN | Current | is Z  |
| IF | Theta | is PS | AND | Dtheta | is Z  | THEN | Current | is NS |
| IF | Theta | is PM | AND | Dtheta | is Z  | THEN | Current | is NM |
| IF | Theta | is Z  | AND | Dtheta | is NM | THEN | Current | is PM |
| IF | Theta | is Z  | AND | Dtheta | is NS | THEN | Current | is PS |
| IF | Theta | is Z  | AND | Dtheta | is Z  | THEN | Current | is Z  |
| IF | Theta | is Z  | AND | Dtheta | is PS | THEN | Current | is NS |
| IF | Theta | is Z  | AND | Dtheta | is PM | THEN | Current | is NM |
| IF | Theta | is PS | AND | Dtheta | is Z  | THEN | Current | is Z  |
| IF | Theta | is NS | AND | Dtheta | is PS | THEN | Current | is Z  |

**Figure 8.10** Fuzzy rules used to control an inverted pendulum

fuzzy sets are generalizations of classical sets) and is depicted in Figure 8.12. Two fuzzy rules from Figure 8.10 are shown in Figure 8.12. Note that now there are two premise clauses in the rules. The input values of Theta and Dtheta are 0 and an arbitrary value u respectively. The highest degree of match between the input values of Theta and Dtheta and the premises of rule 1 are given by r11(=1) and r12 (a number around 0.5 as shown in Figure 8.12). Note that r11=1 as the input value of Theta can be considered as a fuzzy set of one element, 0, with a degree of membership of 1 for that element. The contribution of the rule conclusion to the output is the portion below the minimum of the two degrees of match, r11 and r12. Note that there is no contribution from rule 2 to the output in Figure 8.12 for the shown input as r21 = 0 (the minimum of r21 and r22 is 0). The rest of the inference procedure is the same as shown in Figure 8.7.

Note that in Figure 8.12, even though crisp values are used as inputs, the output of the fuzzy rules is a fuzzy set. However for specifying the current for the motor, the output fuzzy set has to be defuzzified i.e., converted into a crisp number that can be specified as the desired value of the current. The center of mass defuzzification technique (of Figure 8.8) is used in Figure 8.12. Thus the value v (which is close to zero) in Figure 8.12 is the final output crisp value for the current (assuming that only the two rules shown in Figure 8.12 contribute to the output).

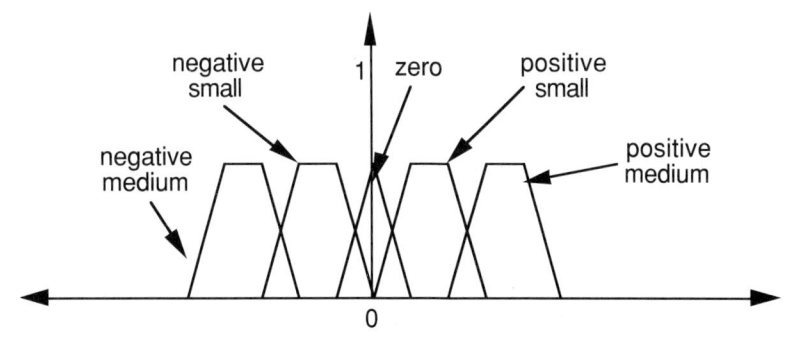

**Figure 8.11** Fuzzy set shapes for the inverted pendulum

## 250 Approximate reasoning using fuzzy logic

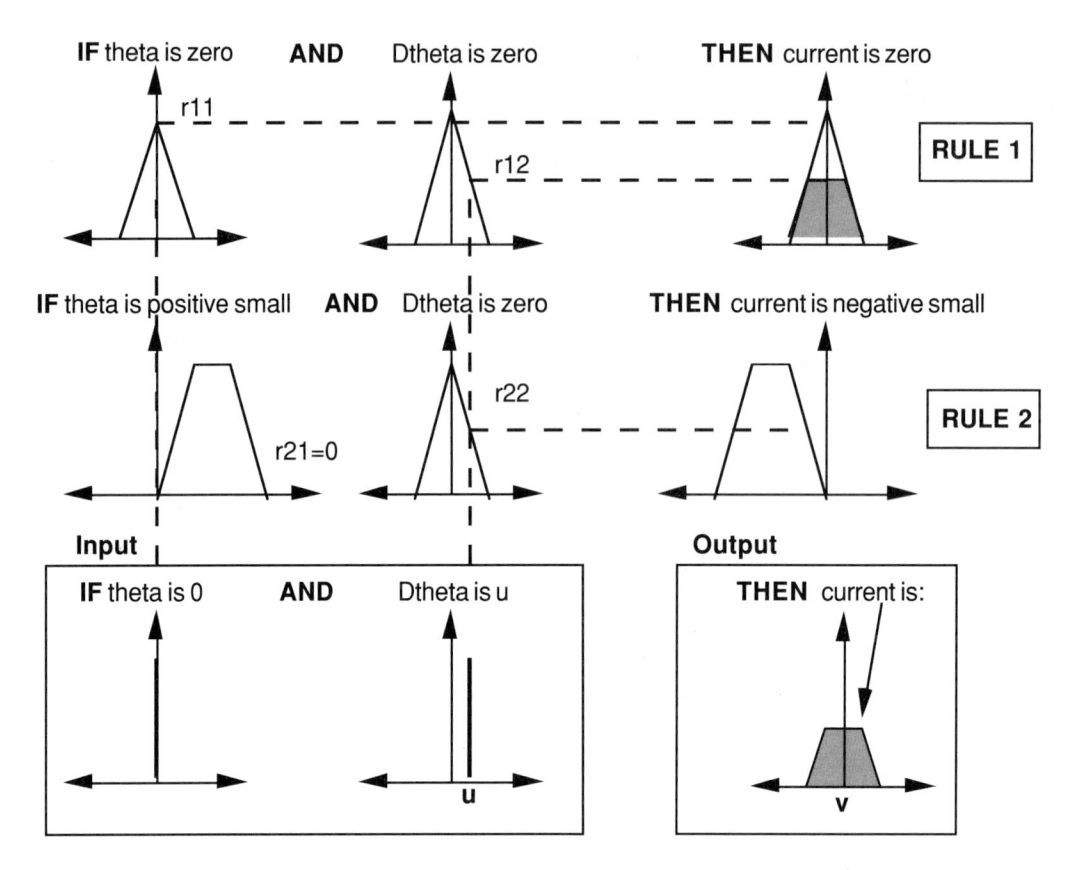

**Figure 8.12** Fuzzy inference in the inverted pendulum

### Properties of fuzzy control

The fuzzy rules used for controlling the inverted pendulum (Figure 8.10) just use as inputs the angular position and the angular velocity of the bob. Thus even if the mass of the bob or the motor strength is varied dynamically, the same 11 rules can be used successfully for balancing the inverted pendulum. This is in contrast to conventional control methods which are very sensitive to changes in these parameters. Obtaining the correct fuzzy rules requires more of experience and engineering skills than sophisticated mathematics. It has been observed that performance of the system is not very sensitive to precise definitions of the various fuzzy distributions used. This makes the task much easier from an engineering viewpoint. Also, the system is very robust to noise and breakdowns. Even if some rules in Figure 8.10 are disabled (for example, by a hardware error), the remaining active fuzzy rules are still able to control the inverted pendulum, albeit not as steadily as before. This graceful degradation is one of the attractive properties of fuzzy control.

Note how the inverted pendulum system is modelled not by a mathematical model but by a set of heuristic rules. These rules use linguistic variables defined on the input and output domains under consideration. The rules used in other FL applications (such as the Yamaichi trading program) are analogous to these fuzzy rules in structure and function.

### Complex inverted pendulum systems

Several variations on the basic inverted pendulum (Figure 8.9) are possible, including:

- a pendulum with a soft, pliable rod. The pendulum of Figure 8.9 assumes that the connecting rod is rigid. Without this assumption, the system becomes enormously more complex to model and solve precisely.

- a pendulum with 2 or 3 stages i.e., in which the (rigid) rod holding the pendulum bob consists of one or two joints. Such a system can be modelled accurately, but the control equations are complex enough to demand the use of supercomputers to solve them in real time.

It is nearly impossible to build a real-time controller (with current hardware) to control the above 'complex' variations of an inverted pendulum. However, researchers from Apt Computers (a San José-based company started by a group of Chinese FL researchers) and other companies in Japan have successfully used FL to successfully control these complex inverted-pendulum structures. The fuzzy rules used are similar to those shown in Figure 8.10. The success of FL in controlling such complex systems (where conventional control techniques have failed) has endeared it to engineers who find it an extremely practical and reliable tool for controlling complex processes.

### Sendai subway control[19]

A conventional automatic train operation (ATO) system is usually based on PID (proportional, integrated and differential) control. PID control is a popular conventional control procedure used in many industrial control systems. Its essence consists of taking the difference of the desired and the actual values (of a certain variable), aggregating it over time, and generating a proportional feedback corrective signal. Variations in the train speed with the use of an ATO system is depicted in Figure 8.13[20]. There is usually a preset target speed (below the maximum speed limit) which the train ATO system tries to reach by generating appropriate powering and braking commands. In actual practice there are many changes in the running conditions, such as the gradient of track and the braking force of rolling stock. To follow the target speed, it then becomes necessary to send control commands frequently for acceleration and brake application. As a result, the smooth operation of the train becomes difficult and riding comfort degrades. Though PID control is very popular, one of its major limitations is that it works best for linear systems i.e., systems in which the output variables vary as some linear combination of the input variables. A train is a complex non-linear system (note that even the simple inverted-pendulum system described earlier is an example of a non-linear system), and all ATO systems use simplified linear representations (of the train's operations) to apply PID control. Needless to say, it is very difficult to construct linear models of a train which are also fairly accurate.

Though a careful manipulation of numerical parameters can let the train follow the target speed limits fairly closely, the requirements on automatic train operations have diversified recently to include other factors such as energy savings and improved riding comfort. Satisfying these additional requirements with the use of conventional techniques

## 252 Approximate reasoning using fuzzy logic

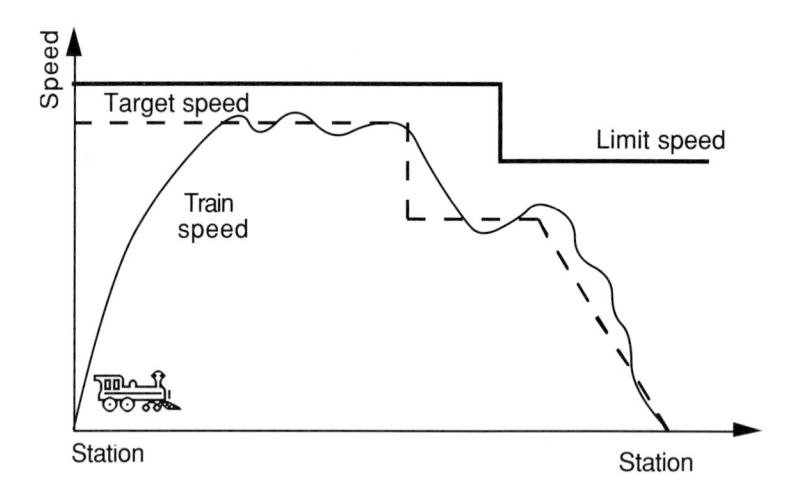

**Figure 8.13** Automatic train operation by conventional control

is a very difficult task. This was realized by Hitachi engineers working on the Sendai subway line, who spent many years trying to improve in vain the existing PID control systems to meet the newer performance requirements. Towards the early 1980s, they started investigating the use of fuzzy control for automatic train operation on the Sendai subway system. The results have been a dramatic success.

The fuzzy control procedures used in the Sendai subway system consist of a set of fuzzy rules quite similar in structure and function to those used for the control of the inverted pendulum. These rules attempt to emulate reasoning and control decisions made by an experienced subway driver as he maneuvers the train down a certain track. The control rules not only attempt to minimize the difference between the desired speed and the actual speed, but also satisfy other goals such as 'good riding comfort' and 'accurate stopping'. For example, consider the choice of an optimum 'notch' for the traction and/or braking. To enhance riding comfort, it would be desirable to minimize the changes in the selected notch. The fuzzy control rules also take into account factors like predicted speed at some later time, time elapsed after the previous change in notch, and judged coasting point. Figure 8.14[21] gives a qualitative feel for the fuzzy sets for some of the input variables used in the fuzzy control system.

It has been observed that the use of fuzzy control results in about three times less changes in the notch settings as compared to PID control. The enhanced results obtained using fuzzy control are depicted in Figure 8.15[22]. The use of fuzzy control in the Sendai subway system has also resulted in energy savings of about 10% and better stop accuracy i.e., the accuracy with which the door markers on the station are followed. It has been seen that the standard deviation of the errors in stopping are also about three times less than that with PID control.

## Commercial activities in fuzzy logic 253

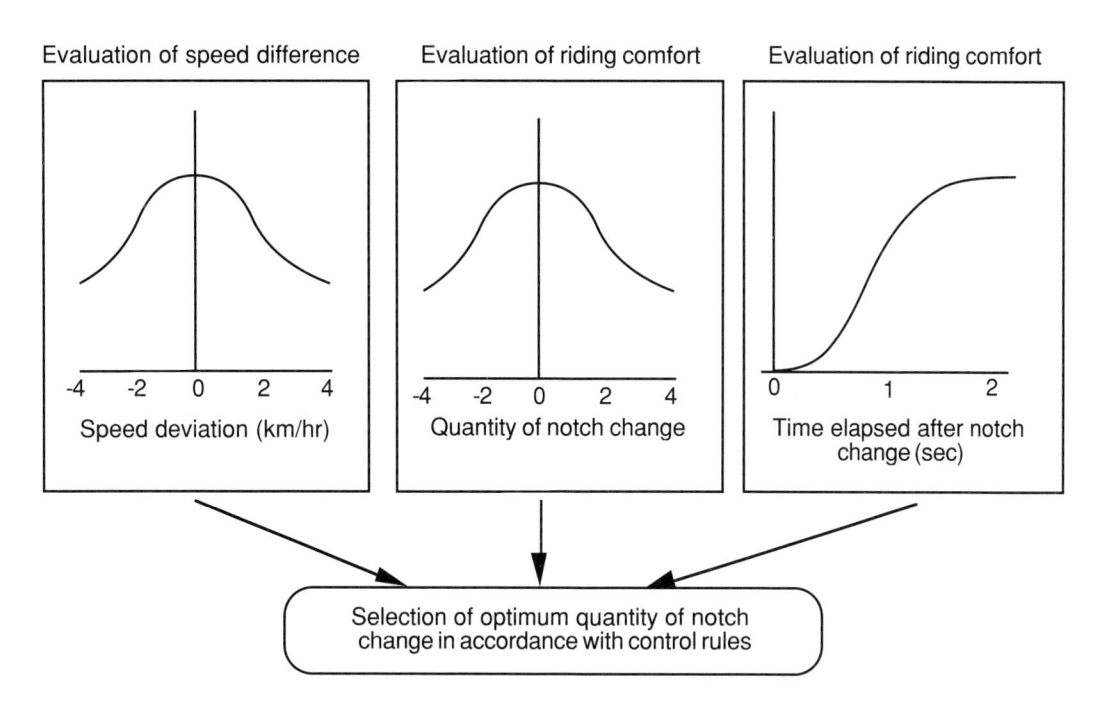

**Figure 8.14** An example of a fuzzy rule in automatic train operation

### Commercial activities in fuzzy logic

FL is one of the fastest growing sectors of applied AI technology. According to experts, FL is forecasted to become a two-to-three billion dollar business within a decade[23]. Already, there are several hundred successful applications of FL. In Japan alone, there are more than 2000 FL patents. The success rates of FL applications have been phenomenally high. According to Professor Sugeno, an expert on AI and FL, success rates of FL projects (in Japan) has been around 80%[24].

There are two broad categories of commercial applications of FL:

● industrial process control — FL is being used successfully for modelling and controlling complex industrial systems/processes. Examples of such applications are the controls of the Sendai subway system, and the cement kiln controllers marketed by F. L. Smidth of Copenhagen.

● modelling human intelligence — the coupling of FL and KBS technology has lead to the development of fuzzy KBSs, which are adept at modelling the imprecise reasoning processes of human experts, and in dealing with an uncertain environment. Examples of such applications are the trading program of Yamaichi securities and the fuzzy expert chef chip in Toshiba cookers.

**254** Approximate reasoning using fuzzy logic

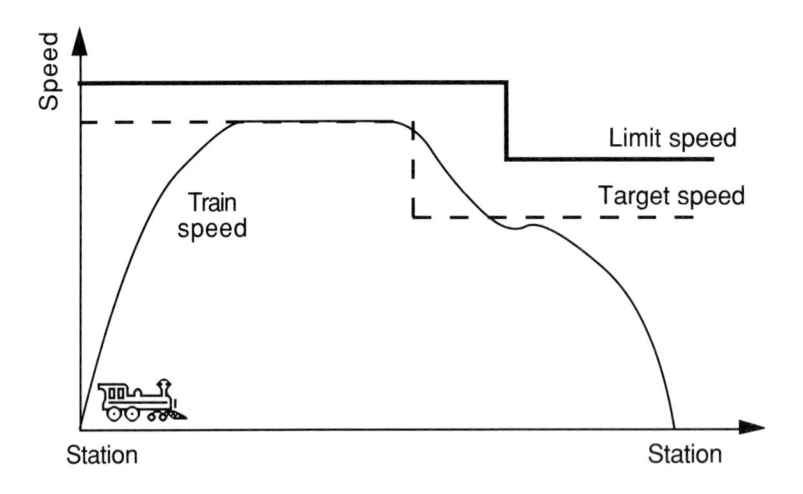

**Figure 8.15** Automatic train operation with fuzzy control

Though the theoretical foundations of FL have largely been developed in the USA, Japan has monopolized the commercialization of the technology. Most important Japanese companies are investing actively in FL applications and almost all show-case applications of FL are from Japan. The reasons for this lop-sided adoption and development of the technology are not entirely clear. Even within American academic circles acceptance of FL and its successes has been slow, and there has been much debate about the benefits and limitations of FL[25]. Others ascribe the cool US reception to FL to the name fuzzy logic, which tends to give naive readers a fuzzy, uneasy, and confused feeling. Bart Kosko, an ardent advocate of FL, compares the name fuzzy logic to a boy named Sue[26]. Yet others ascribe it to deeper cultural factors[27]. They argue that Asian cultures, and in particular the Japanese, have shown little resistance to adoption of new approaches espoused by FL because their cultures are not so deeply rooted in scientific rationalism (in contrast with Western cultures).

## Asia

The two most important players within Asia are China and Japan, with India and Singapore playing minor rôles. China boasts of the largest collection of researchers (over 10,000) working on FL, and Japan has played the dominant rôle in commercialization of the technology. All major Japanese companies are actively involved in the application of FL. According to sources within Mitsubishi, all their products can potentially use FL to improve their performances[28]. FL has proven to be an useful alternative methodology for industrial process control. However, the capability to embed knowledge cheaply and effectively inside each individual product with a fuzzy chip has been the primary catalyst in the large scale commercialization of FL. Today, virtually all Japanese makers of home

# Asia

appliances have either already applied FL in many of their products, or are planning to do so in the near future. Some representative examples from the wide range of current applications of FL applications are given in Table 8.2.

Omron, a $2.6 billion Kyoto-based manufacturer, is perhaps the most active Japanese company in the development and sale of fuzzy products. Since early 1989, Omron has been selling fuzzy processor chips for control and simple pattern recognition tasks. It also sells a fuzzy software tool designed to create and run fuzzy rules on the IBM PC and has

| Company | Application domain |
| --- | --- |
| Hitachi | Automatic control for subway trains (in Sendai) yielding a smoother, more efficient ride with a higher stopping precision |
| Hitachi | Control of container cranes in Moji Harbor, Kitakyushu, to increase precision in loading/unloading |
| Nippon Electric | Control of temperatures in glass fusion at the Notogawa and Takatsuki factories |
| Canon | Stepper alignment in semiconductor production |
| Mitsubishi | Regulation of surface temperatures in ethylene cracking furnaces at the Mizushima plant. |
| Nissan | Anti-skid brake systems and automatic transmissions for cars |
| Subaru | Automatic transmissions for cars |
| Canon Ricoh Minolta | Auto-focusing in cameras by choosing the right subject in the picture frame to focus |
| Panasonic | Jitter removal in video camcorders by distinguishing between jitters and actual movement of subjects |
| Sanyo | Iris control in video camcorders by helping to react subtly and automatically to changes in light conditions |
| Matshushita Toshiba Sanyo Hitachi | Vacuum cleaners that use sensors to gather information about floor and dirt conditions then use a fuzzy KBS to choose the right program |
| Sanyo Toshiba | Ovens and cooking ranges which incorporate the culinary expertise of chefs |
| Matshushita | Air conditioners that make judgements based on factors such as number of persons in room and optimum degree of comfort |
| Yamaichi | Computerized trading programs which mimic approximate reasoning processes of experienced fund managers |
| Sony | Handwriting recognition in palmtop computers |

Table 8.2 Representative commercial applications of fuzzy logic

developed hardware boards which can be plugged into the expansion slot of an IBM PC to enable faster execution of fuzzy rules. Omron has recently announced the development of a fuzzy computer, although it is not yet sold commercially. It has also developed the first industrial temperature controller using FL. It projects sales of $750 million, or nearly 20% of total revenues by 1994 from the sale of fuzzy hardware, and hopes to include fuzzy functions in 20% of its manufactured end-products (which range from ticket-vending machines to healthcare diagnostic products). Omron has filed about 600 FL patents in Japan. In August 1991 Omron created a strategic alliance with NEC, the world's largest micro-controller supplier, for the development and marketing of FL micro-controller chips. The commercial importance of this development can be understood by noting that the current world market for micro-controller chips is over $5.2 billions[29].

The strongest endorsement for FL and its successes has come from Japan's Ministry of International Trade and Industry (MITI) which is now actively stimulating the rapid development of FL in Japan. It has set up a consortium of 48 top Japanese companies to develop fuzzy systems with a five year initial life-span (till 1994). The consortium is called the Laboratory for International Fuzzy Engineering (LIFE) and has a $70 million budget coming from member companies such as Canon, Fuji, Fujitsu, Nissan, Honda, Minolta, NEC and Omron. LIFE is intended to be the world's premier center for FL development. Its efforts are focused in three areas: (a) fuzzy control of industrial processes (b) fuzzy information processing (c) fuzzy computer systems (hardware and software). The ultimate aim of LIFE is to build more 'human' computers, ones based on fuzzy rather than binary logic and which can execute programs resembling human reasoning more closely.

## America

Though FL technology was invented in the USA it has, until recently, been largely ignored by the US industry. Today, partly as a result of the increasing competitive pressure of Japanese products, American companies are taking a serious look at the technology to judge its usefulness and applicability.

The first US patents in FL have been awarded to Nissan for its fuzzy transmission and anti-braking systems. NASA has recently announced the first successful application of FL technology in outer space. FL was used in the Commercial Refrigerator Incubation Module (CRIM) aboard the space shuttle Endeavor, STS-49, which was launched on May 7, 1992. The CRIM provides a regulated thermal environment for experiments such as the growth of protein crystals. NASA has other FL applications in the prototype stages. One of the most advanced projects is a controller for maneuvering the space shuttle to keep it in position with respect to another object in space. In response to competitive pressures created by FL elevators marketed by Hitachi and Mitsubishi, Otis Elevators is now using FL controls to help elevators respond rapidly to changing demands. Southwestern Bell has used FL to build a sophisticated information retrieval system which reduces the problem of calling up unwanted citations. General Electric is considering using FL to regulate jet engines, save water in home appliances, and drive 200-ton rollers in steel mills[30]. Allen-Bradley (Milwaukee) plans to introduce FL controllers to replace its line of conventional PID control systems.

Similar to the alliance between Omron and NEC, Motorola has created (in February

92) a strategic alliance with Aptronix, a small San José-based company specializing in FL products. Steven C. Marsh the director of strategic operations at Motorola's microcontroller division estimates that, by 1995, about half of all Motorola micro-controllers will incorporate FL[31]. In another major development, MCC of Austin, Texas, has recently added FL as its fifth major research area (in addition to artificial intelligence, natural language, neural networks, and database technology) and has plans to spin off a new company, Pavillion Technologies, to exploit the commercial potential of FL. Note that MCC is an industry consortium set up in the USA in response to the Japanese fifth generation project with leading US companies as members including Control Data, DEC, Kodak, and NCR.

Two US companies actively selling FL hardware and software are Togai Infralogic of Irvine and Aptronix of San José. The founder of Togai Infralogic, M. Togai, was the co-designer of the first fuzzy chip at Bell Laboratories. Togai Infralogic markets fuzzy chips and a variety of software packages. For example, the TilShell is object-oriented software which allows the creation of stand-alone FL expert systems or the integration of FL inference capabilities into existing expert systems. Aptronix markets fuzzy chips and the Fuzzy Inference Development Environment (FIDE), a general-purpose fuzzy software development environment. It has recently entered into a potentially important strategic alliance with Motorola.

Fuzzy chips are also manufactured by the Microelectronics Center of North Carolina, a non-profit research consortium in Research Triangle Park, NC. These chips have the distinction of being among the fastest today on the fuzzy chip market — being able to perform about 580,000 fuzzy inferences per second. A variety of KBS vendors (such as Micro Data Base Systems of Lafayette, Indiana and Knowledge-based Technologies of White Plains, NY) are also beginning to incorporate FL inference capabilities in their KBS development packages.

# Europe

France and Germany are the two leading European countries in FL research and applications. Major FL research centers in France include IRIT (University Paul Sabatier, Toulouse), LAFORIA (University of Paris 6, Paris), NEURINFO (Institut Mediterraneen de Technologie, Marseille), CRAN-LEA (Vandoeuvre) and the University of Valenciennes. In September 1991, the club Logique Floue (supported by French academics and industry) was created with the encouragement of the French government to stimulate research in FL theory and applications. Also, in 1991, the European Laboratory for Intelligent Techniques Engineering (ELITE) was started in Aachen, Germany. The goal of ELITE is to coordinate and integrate scientific activities on a pan-European basis in different intelligent technologies including FL, neural networks and KBSs. Strong FL research interest groups also exist in most other (both Western and Eastern) European countries.

While some of the earliest industrial applications of FL occurred in Europe, European industry is far behind the Japanese in exploiting the commercial potential of FL. One of the very first commercial applications of FL in France was in 1989, and it involved control of the furnace in a cement factory in Rochefort (Jura). The group PSA (Peugeot-Citroen) is using FL for automatic braking in its vehicles equipped with the Interactive Road Sign System (ISIS). Researchers at the University of Valenciennes are researching the application of FL to the Paris metro. Dassault is considering using FL for guidance in its flight simulators. Moulinex plans to use FL in its next line of ovens and vacuum cleaners. Usinor Sacilor is using FL in its high temperature furnaces. SGS Thompson announced in August 1991 that it is investing $30 million over the next five years to develop FL hardware and micro-controllers. Two French companies, ITMI and Tekelec, are actively working in the domain of fuzzy hardware and applications. Omron has also recently established a subsidiary in Paris to sell fuzzy products to French and other European companies.

Similar FL applications and products can be found in other European countries also. A German company INFORM sells a variety of state-of-the-art fuzzy hardware and software products. These include FuzzyTech, a graphical fuzzy software development environment, and a fuzzy chip (developed in collaboration with Siemens). Various research prototypes of FL applications have been developed at the RWTH University of Aachen. Different German companies such as Siemens-Nixdorf, Volkswagen, and Software are considering using FL in their products.

## The business impacts of fuzzy logic applications

FL is proving to be an important source of competitive advantage in business. The competitive impact of FL applications can be analyzed along several dimensions. The simplest of these is that it is enhancing KBS technology by introducing new representational and modelling techniques. Of a more fundamental nature is the impact it is having on changing the granularity of intelligence. With the help of a fuzzy chip, it is possible to transplant a KBS into individual products. Also very important is its rôle in transforming industrial process control and enabling new product development strategies.

### Enhancing knowledge-based technologies
Conventional rules are limited in their abilities to handle vague data and model imprecise reasoning procedures. The integration of FL and KBS technology can led to a more robust modelling of uncertainty and imprecision, as demonstrated by the introductory examples of the Sendai subway controls and Yamaichi's computerized trading program.

Conventional KBSs are usually 'brittle'. They contain detailed knowledge about a narrow domain, and are usually unable to effectively deal with inputs which are minor variations of the expected or planned inputs. This is partly because the rules in a KBS are based on Boolean logic, and require a perfect match with the inputs. FL allows rules to have a partial match with the inputs and produce meaningful answers under a broader range of input variations.

Conventional KBSs have also been plagued by their dependence on a few critical rules. As the rules fire sequentially, a missing match on a critical rule can lead to a breakdown in the inference process. In contrast, fuzzy rules are robust and can continue to function in the absence of a few rules. An useful analogy here is with autocracies and democracies. A conventional KBS can be compared to an autocracy, where all decisions rest with a single person, the autocrat (the critical rule). Taking the autocrat out of the system can lead to a breakdown of the decision process. On the other hand, a fuzzy expert system can be compared to a democracy, where all members (rules) participate in the decision process. The process still functions (albeit, not equally effectively) with one or more members missing.

### Embedded intelligence

FL has changed the granularity of intelligence. The invention of the fuzzy chip is doing for AI what the microprocessor did for computing. The invention of the microprocessor spawned a whole generation of computerized products by making it possible to insert a small computer (on a chip) inside individual products. In a similar manner, the fuzzy chip has enabled the distribution of intelligence at the ultimate granularity — inside every individual product.

It is now possible not only to computerize products, but to do it smartly. Such embedded intelligence makes products easier to use, and more efficient. It is not surprising to note that these new 'intelligent' appliances are meeting with huge commercial successes. Distribution of intelligence at such a fine granularity is not possible with conventional KBS technology. With this ability to embed intelligence, daring and innovative products will enter the market in the future. Plans for the future include products with small diagnostic fuzzy KBSs for trouble-shooting and trouble-free maintenance. The ability to distribute the expertise and knowledge of experienced technicians inside products will have far-ranging impacts on the quality of products marketed.

### Intelligent process control

The earliest commercial application of FL was for industrial process control. Today, it continues to be one of the most important application areas for FL. Most industrial systems are complex and non-linear. Conventional control theory is most developed for controlling relatively simple, linear systems. The traditional approach to industrial process control has been to develop a linear model of the system to be controlled, and then apply conventional control approaches. Such an approach has not always provided the desired solution.

FL has given rise to a new form of process control. The essence of this new approach is the modelling of the complex non-linear relationships between the various parameters in the system by a set of fuzzy rules. Such an approach has proven to be very successful in practice. The use of rules for process control also allows integration of the expertise of skilled personnel into the control procedures, as in the example of the Sendai subway control system. Though not as visibly as in home appliances with embedded intelligence, FL is playing an important rôle in reshaping industrial process control systems.

### New product development strategies

FL saves time and money. Omron, Japan's leading maker of factory controllers, claims to have slashed development time by 75% by using FL in a system (designed for Komatsu) to check machine tools for worn-out gears or dirty oil filters. Similar experiences have been reported by other Japanese companies also. The reasons for this are as follows. Precision is in general very expensive. While a mandatory requirement for many situations, it is often not desired for many engineering problems. Consider for example, the problem of programming an automated vehicle to park itself within a certain marked slot. In principle, it is possible to park the vehicle with a fine tolerance of a few hundredths of an inch within the allocated space. But such an vehicle would not only be very difficult to build, it would also be very expensive to program and operate. It turns out that satisfactory performance can be obtained using FL but minus the high cost of precision[32]. The solution is simpler to operate and easier to build. This tolerance for imprecision is very common in humans. We rarely try to park cars with all four wheels perfectly aligned and equidistant from the curb.

By not requiring that certain modelling choices be made (e.g., threshold temperatures or heights), FL builds into the heuristic modelling process a greater tolerance for imprecision. By directly representing heuristic relationships between important input and output parameters, fuzzy modelling avoids dependencies on a variety of intermediate system parameters which complicate the modelling process. For example, note that fuzzy rules of Figure 8.10 used to control the pendulum of Figure 8.9 are independent of several parameters such as the mass of the bob and the length of the rod. Thus the same 12 rules of Figure 8.10 can be used to control pendulums with different bob masses and rod lengths. Such flexibility is not easily achievable with conventional modelling approaches.

The precise modelling of real-world situations is usually very difficult and expensive. FL has proven to be a handy tool for modelling real-world complexity. The developed models are usually simpler and give more accurate results, as shown by the experience of the Rockwell engineers. The fact that the use of FL can give better products while saving both time and money has important implications for product design and development procedures. Few companies can afford to ignore a technology which holds the potential to cut product development costs and times.

## Summary

Though FL was invented nearly three decades ago, it has evolved into a commercially mature technology only over the past few years. Today, FL is rapidly becoming one of the most commercially successful sub-fields of AI. FL offers a powerful mechanism for representing and reasoning with imprecise knowledge. The inherent tolerance to imprecision in FL is an important factor for the commercial success of FL systems. Important issues discussed in this chapter include the following:

● FL directly represents imprecision by using fuzzy sets. In a fuzzy set, each member is assigned a degree of membership in the range, 0 to 1. This is in contrast to conventional sets in which the membership of an element can be either 0 or 1 only.

● Linguistic variables can assume both linguistic labels and numbers as values. Linguistic labels (such as tall, short, and average height) can be represented with the help of fuzzy sets.

● The combination of FL and rule-based reasoning is the basis for the commercial success of FL technology.

● Fuzzy rules allow linguistic variables and adopt a special inference procedure. The primary differences between fuzzy rule-based inference and conventional rule-based processing (Chapters 2 and 3) are (1) fuzzy rules allow partial matches between the data and rule premises, and (2) fuzzy inferencing is inherently a parallel procedure. The benefits of fuzzy rule-based inferencing are (1) greater tolerance to input variations (2) robustness (3) graceful degradation, and (4) greater tolerance to errors in rule specifications.

● FL can be used effectively to control complex systems by specifying heuristic relationships between input and output parameters of the system with the help of fuzzy rules. Such an approach to the modelling and control of systems has several important advantages (which are not attainable with conventional approaches).

● There are two broad categories of commercial applications of FL (1) modelling and control of complex industrial systems, and (2) modelling of imprecise reasoning processes.

● Japan is leader in the commercial exploitation of the technology. All major Japanese companies are using FL in their products and services. American and European companies are yet to match their Japanese counterparts in the commercial exploitation of FL technology.

● The major business impacts of FL technology are (1) enhancing conventional knowledge-based technologies (2) allowing embedding of intelligence inside individual products (3) providing a new heuristic basis for the control of industrial processes, and (4) enabling new product development strategies (which save time and money).

It is important to note that FL applications, like other KBSs, need to be linked to the strategic needs of the organization. Thus concepts described in Chapter 5 are also applicable for FL applications in organizations.

## Bibliography and suggested readings

Zadeh's original papers on fuzzy set theory (Zadeh 65), (Zadeh 88), and (Zadeh 84), are the best references on the technology of FL. A recent book (Yager et al 87) contains all important papers by Zadeh related to FL. Other overview descriptions of FL technology can be found in books by Dubois and Prade (Dubois & Prade 80), and Zimmerman (Zimmerman 87). Reference (Sugeno 85) describes several applications of FL to industrial process control. Good non-technical overviews of FL technology and its applications are contained in references (Elmer-Dewitt 89), (Newsweek 90), (Forbes 91), and (Business week 92).

Business week, *Software that can Dethrone 'Computer Tyranny'*, April 6, pp. 70–71, 1992.

Dubois D. and H. Prade, *Fuzzy sets and systems: Theory and applications*, Academic Press, New York, 1980.

Elmer-Dewitt, P., *Time for some fuzzy thinking*, Time, Sep. 25, 1989.

Forbes, *Why Fuzzy Logic is Good Business*, May 13, 1991.

Newsweek, *The Future Looks 'Fuzzy'*, pp. 46–47, May 28, 1990.

Sugeno, M., Editor, *Industrial applications of fuzzy control*, Elsevier Science Publishers BV, the Netherlands, 1985.

Yager, R. R., S. Ovchinnikov, R. M. Tong, and H. T. Nguyen, (Eds.), *Fuzzy Sets and Applications: Selected Papers by L. A. Zadeh*, John Wiley, 1987.

Zadeh, L. A., *Fuzzy logic*, Computer, IEEE, pp. 83–93, April 1988.

Zadeh, L. A., *Fuzzy Sets*, Information Control, Vol. 8, pp. 338–353, 1965.

Zadeh, L. A., *Making computers think like people*, IEEE Spectrum, 26–32, Aug. 1984.

Zimmerman, H. J., *Fuzzy Sets, Decision Making and Expert Systems*, Kluwer Academic, 1987.

# Notes

1 *Fuzzy control ensures a smooth ride*, Age of Tomorrow, Hitachi Ltd., pp. 12–19, 1987.

2 *Fuzzy control ensures a smooth ride*, Age of Tomorrow, Hitachi Ltd., pp. 12–19, 1987.

3 *The Future Looks 'Fuzzy'*, Newsweek, pp. 46–47, May 28, 1990.

4 The Toronto Globe and Mail, October 11, 1989.

5 The Toronto Globe and Mail, October 11, 1989.

6 *Why Fuzzy Logic is Good Business*, Forbes, May 13, 1991.

7 *Why Fuzzy Logic is Good Business*, Forbes, May 13, 1991.

8 Zadeh, L. A. *Fuzzy Sets*, Information Control, Vol. 8, pp. 338–353, 1965.

9 Mamdani, E. H. and S. Assilian, *A Case Study on the Application of Fuzzy Set Theory to Automatic Control*, in the Proceedings of IFAC Stochastic Control Symposium, Budapest, 1974.

10 Holmblad, L. P. and J. J. Ostergaard, *Fuzzy logic control: Operator experience applied in automatic process control*, FLS Review, 45, F. L. Smidth, Copenhagen, 1981.

11 Togai, M. and H. Watanabe, *A VLSI implementation of a fuzzy inference engine: Towards an expert system on a chip*, Information Science, 38, 147–163, 1986.

12 Johnson, R. C., *New LIFE for Fuzzy Logic*, Electronic Engineering Times, pp. 39–42, Sep. 18, 1989.

13 Readers interested in a more rigorous and mathematical description of fuzzy logic should consult references listed in the bibliography for this chapter.

14 Zadeh, L. A., *A Theory of Approximate Reasoning*, in *Machine Intelligence*, J, Hayes, D. Michie and L. I. Mikulich (Eds.), Vol. 9, pp. 149–194, Halstead Press, New York, 1979.

15 Zadeh, L. A., *The Concept of a Linguistic Variable and its Application to Approximate Reasoning*, Parts I, II, Information Sciences, 8, 1975; Part III, 9, 1976.

16 Kerre, E. E., R. B. R. C. Zenner and R. M. M. DeCaluwe, *The use of fuzzy set theory in information retrieval and databases: A survey*, Journal of the American Society for Information Science, 37(5), 341–345, 1986.

17 See for example: (a) Dubois D. and H. Prade, *Fuzzy sets and systems: Theory and applications*, Academic Press, New York, 1980; and (b) Zimmerman, H. J., *Fuzzy set theory and its applications*, Kluwer Academic, 1991.

18 Fuzzy-C Inverted Pendulum, demonstration software distributed by Togai Infralogic Inc., Irvine, CA.

19 Additional information can be found in (a) *Fuzzy control ensures a smooth ride*, Age of Tomorrow, Hitachi Ltd., pp. 12–19, 1987; and (b) Automatic train operation system based on fuzzy control, Railway Systems and Components, Japanese Railway Information, 36, Feb. 1988.

20 Figure adapted from: *Automatic train operation system based on fuzzy control*, Railway Systems and Components, Japanese Railway Information, 36, Feb. 1988.

21 Figure adapted from: *Automatic train operation system based on fuzzy control*, Railway Systems and Components, Japanese Railway Information, 36, Feb. 1988.

22 Figure adapted from: *Automatic train operation system based on fuzzy control*, Railway Systems and Components, Japanese Railway Information, 36, Feb. 1988.

23 *The Future Looks 'Fuzzy'*, Newsweek, pp. 46–47, May 28, 1990.

24 Johnson, R. C., *New LIFE for Fuzzy Logic*, Electronic Engineering Times, pp. 39–42, Sep. 18, 1989.

25 See for example: (a) Cheeseman, P. C., *In defense of probability*, in Proceedings of the 9th International Joint Conference on Artificial Intelligence, Los Angeles, pp. 1002–1009, Aug. 1985; (b) Haack, S., *Do we need fuzzy logic*, International Journal of Man-Machine Studies, 11, pp. 437–445, 1979; and (c) Stallings, W., *Fuzzy set theory verses Bayesian statistics*, IEEE Transactions on Systems, Man, and Cybernetics, pp. 216–219, March 1977.

26 *Company Hopes Its Fuzzy Thinking Pays Off*, Los Angeles Times, Oct. 1989.

27 Elmer-Dewitt, P., *Time for some fuzzy thinking*, Time, Sep. 25, 1989.

28 *Fuzzy Logic Improves High-Tech Gadgetry*, Tokyo Business Today, March 1991.

29 Johnson, R. C., and T. Costlow, *Moto's Fuzzy Future comes into Focus*, Electronic Engineering Times, Jan. 27, 1992.

30 Armstrong, L., *Software that can Dethrone "Computer Tyranny"*, Business Week, pp. 90–91, April 6, 1992.

31 Armstrong, L., *Software that can Dethrone "Computer Tyranny"*, Business Week, pp. 90–91, April 6, 1992.

32 Preprints of the Second Congress of the International Fuzzy Systems Association, Tokyo, Japan, 1987.

# Chapter 9
# *Connectionist modelling of intelligence*

Much of the work in artificial intelligence (AI) has been based on the symbolic paradigm. The fundamental concept of this paradigm is that manipulation of symbols is central to cognition. Symbols are abstract entities which derive semantics (meaning) by representing certain external phenomenon. Symbols can be stored and retrieved in a computer, and rules can be specified for determining how to combine and transform symbols. The most familiar example of a symbolic approach to computation is common arithmetic, in which there are symbols (such as: 1,2,...,9,0,+,-,/,*,...), and rules for manipulation of the symbols (e.g., rules about how to add two numbers). In a symbolic system, it is possible to reassign interpretations for the symbols without affecting the results of the symbolic computation. For example the result, 2+3 = 5, holds irrespective of the semantics (such as apples, or oranges, or shoes) given to the symbols 2 and 3.

Logical systems also are based on symbol manipulation. For example in propositional logic, symbols (such as AND and OR) represent various propositions and operators, and rules specify the manipulation of these symbols (e.g., how to take the AND of two propositions). Conventional rule-based systems are based on deductive logic, and are thus also symbol manipulation systems. The idea that all intelligence involves logical manipulation of symbols dates back to the work of philosophers such as Descartes and Leibniz. AI has largely embraced this idea, and advocated the use of computers to design symbol manipulation systems which exhibit 'intelligent' behavior. A computer can be viewed as a formal symbol manipulation system in which the computer program is a sequence of symbols determining the operations that a computer performs on them (these operations do not change with the semantics associated with the program). This view has been supported by Newell and Simon (generally considered as the fathers of the field of AI) who note[1] that a 'physical symbol system[2] has the necessary and sufficient means for general intelligent action'.

## The connectionist approach

A new alternative paradigm of intelligent computation known as connectionism has been gaining in importance and popularity since the mid-1980s. The connectionist paradigm differs from the symbolic paradigm by discarding the belief that cognition is entirely based on symbol manipulation, and instead attempting to directly model the processes in the human brain. Our knowledge of neuro-biology tells us that the human brain consists of a networked mesh of (about $10^{11}$) independent units called neurons. The degree of inter-connectivity of these neurons is very high: the average neuron has many junctions with other neurons. On receiving a stimulus, these neurons either excite or inhibit adjacent neurons in spreading waves of activation which stop only when a stable state is achieved. Computation in the connectionist paradigm thus focuses on processes by which an inter-networked mesh of independent units inhibit or excite each other. No symbols are stored (unlike the computer program in a conventional digital computer), and it is necessary to assign an interpretation to the input stimuli (the input problem) to make sense of the resulting stable state (the output answer). Neural networks (NNs) and parallel distributed models are alternative names for connectionist models.

## History of connectionism

The origins of connectionism can be traced back to a paper published by Warren McCulloch and Walter Pitts during the 1940s[3] in which they demonstrated how networks of simple binary state units could perform the logical operations of AND, OR, and NOT by passing excitatory and inhibitory impulses to each other. McCulloch and Pitts termed these units as neurons, and modelled them by simplifying the then-known knowledge about the transmission of electrical signals in neurons in the brain. In subsequent research, they attempted to use their neuronal model for simple pattern-recognition tasks by taking inspiration from the known processes of pattern-recognition in the human brain.

Other researchers such as Frank Rosenblatt, Oliver Selfridge, Donald Hebb, and David Marr continued to build on the ideas of McCulloch and Pitts over the next few decades. Rosenblatt renamed the neurons of McCulloch and Pitts as perceptrons, and supplemented them by making the connections between units continuous as opposed to binary, and allowing later layers to send excitatory or inhibitory signals back to lower layers. Rosenblatt also demonstrated the important perceptron convergence theorem which demonstrated that a controlled feedback of error signals (the difference between the desired and the actual states of the perceptrons) to the earlier layer could result in a stable network within a finite number of iterations. Like McCulloch and Pitts, Rosenblatt only considered networks with two layers. Hebb made the important suggestion that when two neurons in the brain were jointly active, the strength of their connection was increased. This insight played a critical rôle in the design of effective learning algorithms which enhanced the popularity and usefulness of neural networks. Marr made detailed studies of the human brain and showed how various parts of the brain (such as the cerebellum, the hippocampus, and the neocortex) could be modelled by such network models. These studies were useful for clarifying the relations between the human brain and connectionist models.

Though research in connectionist models had been progressing at a fairly even pace till the 1960s, a major obstacle came with the publishing of the book Perceptrons[4] by Marvin Minsky and Seymour Papert in 1969. In their influential critique of connectionist models, Minsky and Papert looked at the kinds of computations capable of being performed by existing network models, and demonstrated that some simple mathematical functions (such as the XOR[5] logical function) could not be performed by the perceptron model. While recognizing that the XOR function could be performed with a three-layer network, they noted that there then existed no convergence model (analogous to the Rosenblatt's perceptron convergence result) for three-layered networks. Based on this, and other doubts about the applicability of network models for large-scale real-life problems, Minsky and Papert concluded that connectionist models had a bleak future. Such a judgement from two influential academic figures sounded the death knell for research in connectionist models by diverting most governmental research funding (in the USA) to symbolic approaches over the next decade.

Towards the early 1980s, several new and important research results were announced by a few dedicated connectionist researchers (such as Steven Grossberg, Geoffrey Hinton, and J. A. Anderson). Among these were new NN architectures, convergence theorems for three-layered networks, and improved mathematical sophistication in describing dynamic non-linear systems. At the same time, there was a growing awareness of the limitations of rule-based symbolic approaches. Rule-based systems were brittle (i.e., broke down if the provided input was some variation of the 'regular' input), inflexible, could not effectively solve pattern recognition problems, seemed unable to learn, and were often inefficient. Neural networks seemed to provide some hope to overcome these limitations. These factors have led to a dramatic revival of the field since the mid-1980s.

### Governmental support

Connectionist modelling has lately been receiving strong governmental support in most industrialized countries. Major governmental agencies in the USA[6] are actively funding NN research. Japan is focusing its post-fifth-generation computer project towards NNs in a government-sponsored program called real world computing[7]. Work on NNs is continuing in Europe within ESPRIT II, a five-year project involving eight countries. A strong emphasis on commercialization of the technology has been laid with the announcement of a new program, ANNIE (the Application of Neural Networks for the Industry in Europe)[8]. Strong country-wide efforts are also underway in individual European countries. Germany has sanctioned a NN research budget of about $ 250 million[9], and the British have a NN project funded at about $ 470 million. The Scandinavian countries have a coordinated four year $ 12 million program. Various NN projects are also being funded in France[10].


### Neural networks

A NN consists of an interconnected network of simple processing units termed as neurons. A key distinguishing feature of NNs is that the various units operate independently, and in parallel. Instead of sequentially executing a series of program instructions (as is the case for traditional computers), they evaluate many competing hypotheses simultaneously. Thus, they are useful for the recognition of patterns from large amounts of noisy data (as

## 268 Connectionist modelling of intelligence

in speech and image recognition) because these tasks require high computation rates and the ability to pursue several hypotheses in parallel. Despite the simplicity in the structures of individual units, the entire network can as a whole demonstrate some remarkable and subtle properties, such as an ability to dynamically adapt to a changing environment.

## Problem types tackled by neural networks

Prior to the application of a NN, it has to be trained to recognize patterns from the problem domain. The training phase of NNs can be either supervised (when the training phase presents both the input pattern and the correct classification of the input), or unsupervised (when the training phase presents the input patterns without the corresponding labels). In unsupervised learning schemes, the network self-organizes itself into clusters using competition, or cooperation, or both. In competitive learning schemes, special connections among clusters of neurons encourage 'competition' between the clusters to recognize different patterns. In cooperative learning schemes, clusters of neurons work together in 'cooperation' to recognize a particular pattern. Supervised learning is more popular, and better understood than unsupervised learning.

### Classification

Figure 9.1 depicts supervised training where the (input, output_label) pairs, (I1, O1), (I2, O2),...,(In, On), are used for training the network, and the trained network is tested with the input Ij (1≤i≤n) corrupted by noise. The trained NN is expected to reproduce the output Oj corresponding to Ij, in spite of the presence of noise. Such a task has been termed as the classification or the recognition problem (as in shape and speech recognition). The behavior of the NN under these conditions is similar to that of an associate memory: the network 'learns' a set of patterns during training, and is able to retrieve the correct output pattern label when presented with a partial (or noisy) input pattern.

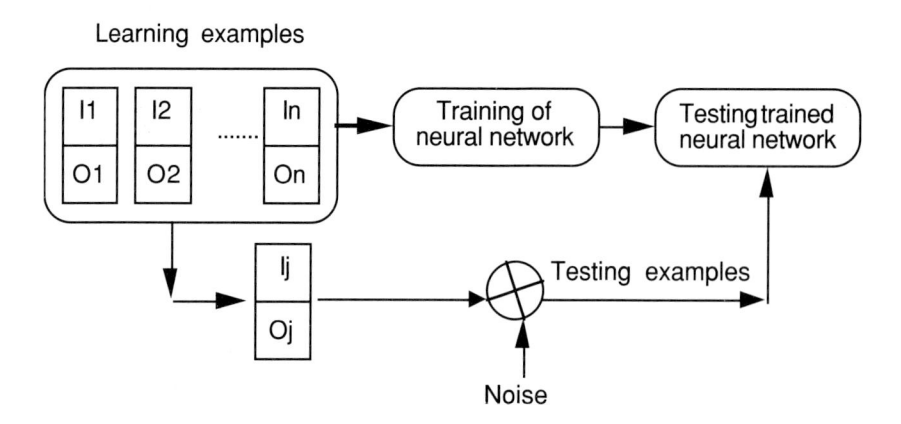

**Figure 9.1** Recognition or classification problem

## Generalization

A variant of the recognition problem is the generalization problem depicted in Figure 9.2. The training phases of the recognition and generalization problems are similar. However, in generalization problems the trained network is tested with input In+1, which is distinct from the inputs I1, I2,..., In used for training the network. The network is expected to correctly predict the output On+1 for the (previously unseen) input In+1 from the model of the domain it has learned from the training input-output pairs. An example of a generalization problem is the prediction of future trends in the economy[11]. NNs used for generalization problem-solving have also been termed as expert networks as they are able to respond to unseen inputs, and thus can be viewed as displaying some 'expertise' about the domain under consideration.

## Clustering

Another important task solved by NNs is the clustering of a set of input data into distinct clusters. Such applications of NNs are common in image and speech transmissions. In contrast to the recognition and generalization problems, there are no labels attached to input data. The network clusters the data autonomously using unsupervised learning schemes.

## Types of neural networks

Different NN architectures have been defined, each having its own operating procedures and unique characteristics. A taxonomy of important NN architectures is given in Figure 9.3[12]. Networks trained with supervision (such as the Hopfield net and perceptrons) are usually used for solving recognition and generalization problems, while networks trained without supervision (such as Kohonen's feature maps) are used for clustering a set of input data.

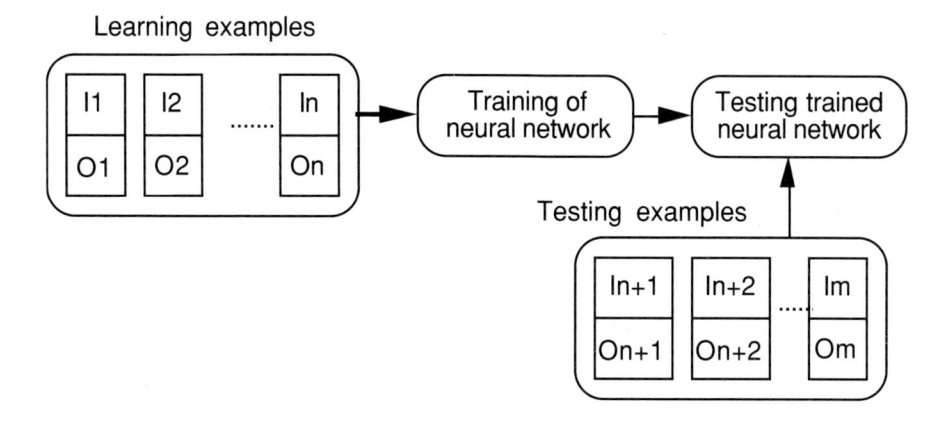

**Figure 9.2** Generalization problem

## 270 Connectionist modelling of intelligence

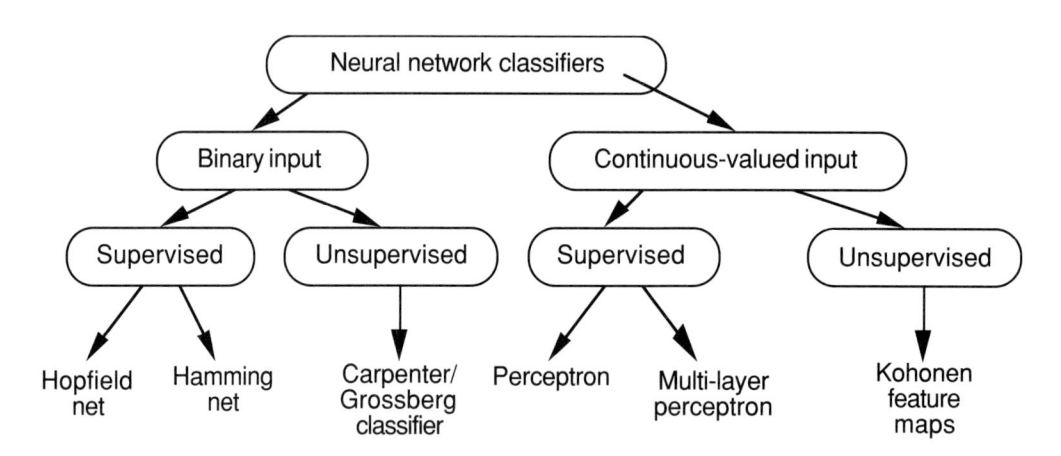

**Figure 9.3** Different types of neural networks

NNs can also be differentiated as being either feedforward or feedback networks. In feedforward networks, the output of a neuron is never dependent on any of its prior values. The transmission of signals is uni-directional, with the output of any neuron being dependent only on the inputs coming into the neuron. In feedback networks, the output of a neuron is connected via some path to its input. Thus the output of neurons is made dependent on its prior values. Perceptrons are examples of feedforward networks, and Hopfield networks are examples of feedback networks. Computational considerations make feedforward architectures more popular than feedback networks. It can be calculated[13] that 20,000 neurons (with 200,000,000 unique connections) are required to store 100 distinct patterns in a (feedback) Hopfield network. In contrast, feedforward networks with about 300 neurons and 20,000 connections have succeeded in learning the correct pronunciations for about 1000 words, or about 7000 letter-to-sound associations. Feedforward networks are also faster during execution as there are no feedback loops involved. In contrast, feedback networks have to cycle through many times (for each input pattern) to arrive at a stable output answer.

## Selected neural network architectures

To understand the structure and function of NNs, consider one of the most popular NN architectures — the multi-layer perceptron network.

### Multi-layer perceptrons

Figure 9.4 depicts a simple multi-layered perceptron. There are three layers in the network. The first layer is the input layer of four neurons. Four (continuous) input signals, I1-I4, come into these four neurons. The output of each of the neurons in the input layer is fed as input to each of the neurons in the next layer, the hidden layer[14]. The outputs of each of the neurons in the hidden layer are in turn fed as input to the two neurons in the highest layer, the output layer. There are two continuous output signals (O1 and O2) from

## Selected neural network architectures 271

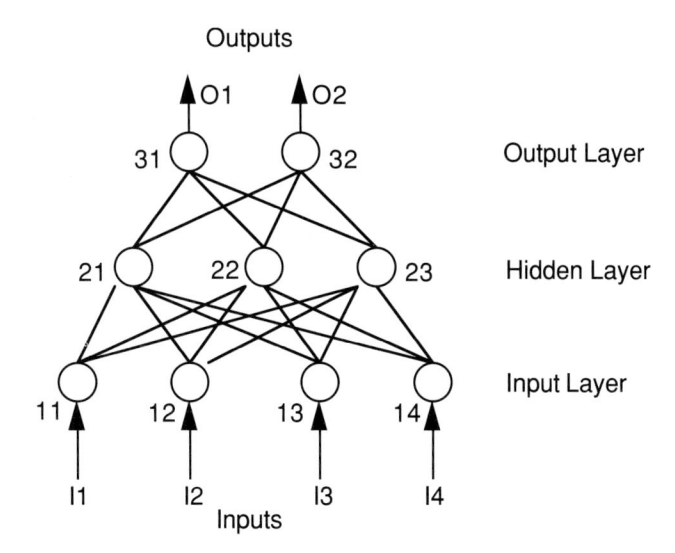

**Figure 9.4** A simple three-layered perceptron

the network. Observe that all interconnections are between neurons in different layers (sometimes in special cases, neurons within the same layer may be interconnected). Note also that there are more inter-neuron connections than neurons. The neurons in the various layers are numbered for ease of reference. Though not shown in Figure 9.4, each connection between two neurons has an associated numerical number, called the weight of the connection. For conceptual simplicity, they can be thought of as indicating the strengths of the connections between two neurons. During the training of the network, these weights are varied according to some learning procedures.

### Structure of neurons

Figure 9.5 gives a schematic representation of the processing occurring within an arbitrarily selected neuron, #22 of Figure 9.4. There are four inputs (O11-O14) to the neuron, which are the outputs from each of the four neurons in the input layer. There is one output from the neuron, O22 which is fed as input to the two neurons in the output layer. There are weights on the connections entering and leaving the neuron. The notation adopted to represent these weights is as follows: xxWyy represents the weight on the connection (emanating) from neuron #xx and ending on neuron #yy. Note that (for clarity) all weights are not shown on the connections in Figure 9.5. There are two basic computation processes occurring within the neuron. First, a weighted sum, Y22, is computed using the incoming input signals and the corresponding connection weights. In the case of neuron #22, this is given by:

$$Y22 = (O11)(11W22) + (O12)(12W22) + (O13)(13W22) + (O14)(14W22)$$

This weighted sum is then passed through a transfer function to produce the neuronal output O22. Different kinds of transfer functions have been defined in related literature, and each results in different properties for the network. The simplest transfer function is a linear function in which the output is obtained by multiplying the weighted sum by a

## 272 Connectionist modelling of intelligence

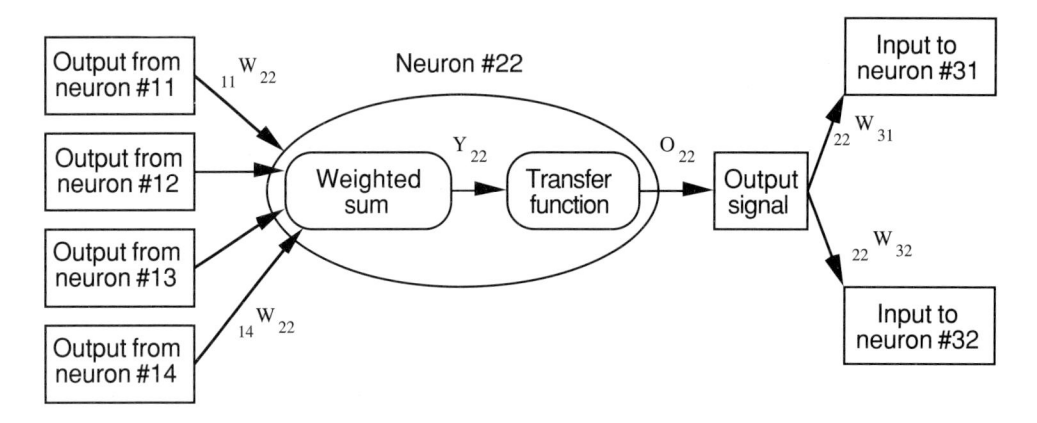

**Figure 9.5** A schematic representation of processing within a neuron

constant value (and possibly adding another constant value to it). Linear transfer functions do not result in very interesting network properties, and are almost never used.

Non-linear transfer functions (Figure 9.6) exhibit more desirable properties and are commonly used. Figure 9.6 (a) depicts a step transfer function in which the output is limited to two possible values. Below a certain threshold (point T in Figure 9.6 (a)) the output is always low, while above the threshold it is always high. The discontinuity in the function makes it non-linear (but also mathematically unwieldy as the derivative does not exist at the discontinuity). This transfer function was used in many early NNs.

However, the most popular transfer function for multi-layered perceptrons is the S-shaped sigmoid transfer function shown in Figure 9.6 (b). The output is a continuous monotonic function of the input. Both the function and its derivatives are continuous everywhere. This facilitates the derivation of sound mathematical properties for networks with such transfer functions.

### Training

Training in perceptrons is supervised (Figure 9.3). The training set consists of various 'input-output' example pairs (Figures 9.1 and 9.2). To learn the exemplar patterns, the network has to execute a particular algorithm. Different training algorithms are available

(a) Step transfer function

(b) Sigmoid transfer function

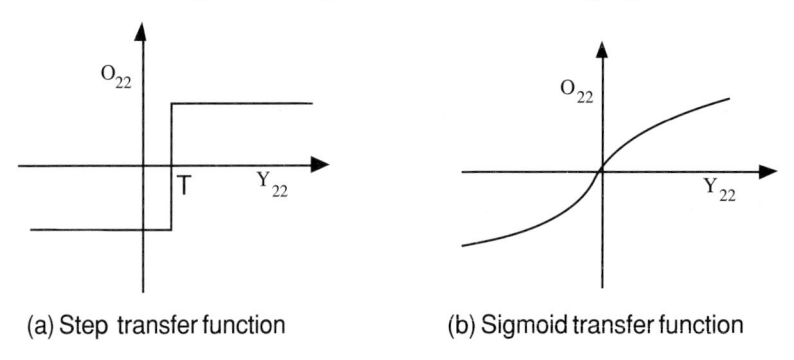

**Figure 9.6** Examples of non-linear transfer functions

# Selected neural network architectures 273

in related literature. The back-propagation algorithm is perhaps the most popular training algorithm. Back-propagation is an iterative gradient descent algorithm designed to minimize the mean square error between the actual output of a multi-layer perceptron and the desired output. It requires that the transfer functions used in the neurons be continuously differentiable non-linearities. Thus sigmoid transfer functions (Figure 9.6 (b)) are commonly used in perceptrons using the back-propagation training algorithm. The basic steps of the back-propagation algorithm are:

- step 1 — assign small and random weights to the various inter-neuron connections in the network
- step 2 — feed a set of inputs from an input-output training example to the input layer of the network
- step 3 — compute the output of the network given the current connection weights and the inputs of step 2. The computation inside each individual neuron occurs as depicted in Figure 9.5
- step 4 — compare the output of the network (step 3) with the desired output (from the input-output example of step 2) and compute the error
- step 5 — use a recursive algorithm starting at the output nodes and working backwards to the input layer nodes, to adjust the weights on the various connections in a manner so as to reduce the error (of step 4)
- step 6 — repeat steps 2–5 with the input-output pairs from the training set till all (input, output) pairs in the training set are passed through the network
- step 7 — repeat steps 2–6 till no changes are required in the weights on the various connections (step 5) for any example input-output pair. Thus, the algorithm cycles through the entire training set repeatedly till the weights on the various connections converge to a stable value.

The mathematical details of back-propagation are dependent on actual implementation of the neuron transfer functions, and are omitted here[15]. Note that due to the repeated cycling (steps 6 and 7) through the training set, back-propagation is computationally expensive and can consume a lot of processing time (of the order of dozens of hours of CPU time[16] for large networks). It is however a popular choice for learning in multi-layer perceptrons because it has yielded good results in a number of different domains such as speech recognition, speech synthesis, and bond rating.

### Testing
Once a network has been trained, it can be used on actual data. As explained in Figures 9.1 and 9.2, the inputs during the testing phase can either be the training input patterns corrupted by noise, or new (previously unseen) input data. In the former case, the network should reproduce the 'closest' pattern, and in the latter case it should output the 'correct' pattern.

### Learning
Note that all 'learning' occurs within the network by the manipulation of weights. This is in contrast to rule-based systems where learning occurs by addition or modification of rules. The weights determine the overall characteristic of the network, and changes in the

weights change the nature of the responses of the system. The back-propagation algorithm determines the changes in the weights without the intervention of an external agent (all changes are made dependent on local internal information).

A trained network can adapt and change its weights over time. Given a new input, any error in the output can be observed and the network can rerun the back-propagation algorithm by including the (new_input, correct_output) pair in the training set. This feature allows the network to learn from its mistakes and dynamically modify its set of (connection) weights to adapt to changes in the external environment.

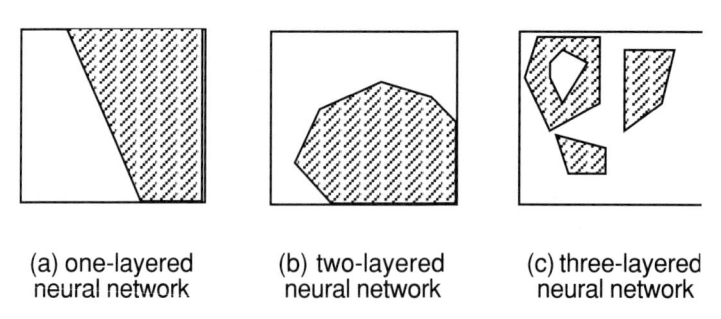

### Decision regions solved by perceptrons[17]

The problem-solving capabilities of NNs vary with the number of layers in the network[18]. The most general decision region solvable by a one layer perceptron (consisting of a single neuron) is a half-plane bounded by a hyper-plane (Figure 9.7 (a)). This is not very interesting, and thus one layer perceptrons are rarely used.

Two layer perceptrons (in which the input nodes are directly connected to the output nodes) can solve a closed or open convex[19] region (Figure 9.7 (b)). An intuitive understanding of the shape of this decision region can be obtained by observing that the convex region can be thought of being composed of the intersection of the half-plane decision regions (Figure 9.7 (a)) of each node in the input layer. The number of sides of the convex region is limited by the number of nodes in the input layer.

Rumelhart[20] has indicated that a two-layered network is inadequate when the similarity structures of the input and output patterns are very different. In such cases a three-layered network is required. Three-layered networks (with one hidden layer) are more powerful, and are able to solve arbitrarily-shaped decision regions (Figure 9.7 (c)). There is a recoding of the input patterns in the hidden units of a three-layered network such that the network can support any required mapping from the input to the output units. Hornik et al[21] have demonstrated that perceptron models with a hidden layer have the 'universal approximation' property i.e., the network can provide an approximation to any function (mapping the input vectors onto the output vectors) likely to be encountered, provided the number of hidden units is large enough.

The classification power of multi-layer perceptrons arises from the non-linear transfer functions used within the nodes. If the nodes are linear elements, a single-layer network with appropriately chosen weights can exactly duplicate the capabilities of a multi-layer network.

(a) one-layered neural network

(b) two-layered neural network

(c) three-layered neural network

**Figure 9.7** Decision regions solved by perceptrons

## The Hopfield net

The Hopfield net is a popular network choice for solving many optimization problems. A simple Hopfield net[22] is shown in Figure 9.8. There are three nodes, each with a non-linear step transfer function (Figure 9.6 (a)). Both the inputs and outputs of the network are binary valued (either -1 or +1). The output of each node is fed back to every other node. For training, the weights are set using a fixed formula which depends on the number of nodes in the network and the descriptions of the patterns to be learnt. For testing, an unknown pattern is imposed on the network by forcing the nodes of the network to match the unknown pattern. Then the network iterates through an algorithm (different from back-propagation) till the outputs no longer change in successive iterations. The pattern specified by the stable node outputs (shown at the top of Figure 9.8) is the net output. When Hopfield networks are used as associative memories, the stable net output gives the complete stored pattern. When they are used as a classifier, the output after convergence is compared to the different exemplar patterns to determine a possible match.

## Kohonen's self-organizing feature maps

Kohonen's self-organizing feature maps are interesting because they exhibit unsupervised learning. Kohonen's network attempts to produce a self-organizing feature map by drawing inspiration from biological evidence suggesting some similar self-organization among (brain) neurons during learning. Structurally, Kohonen's network consists of a grid of output nodes which are densely interconnected and a set of input nodes. Each input node is connected to all output nodes. Figure 9.9 illustrates a simple network. Note that the dark lines depict connections between the output nodes in the network. Continuous valued inputs are presented sequentially in time to the network. Over time, the weights on the connections between the output nodes change (according to a specific algorithm which is executed as each input is presented to the network) to form clusters such that topologi-

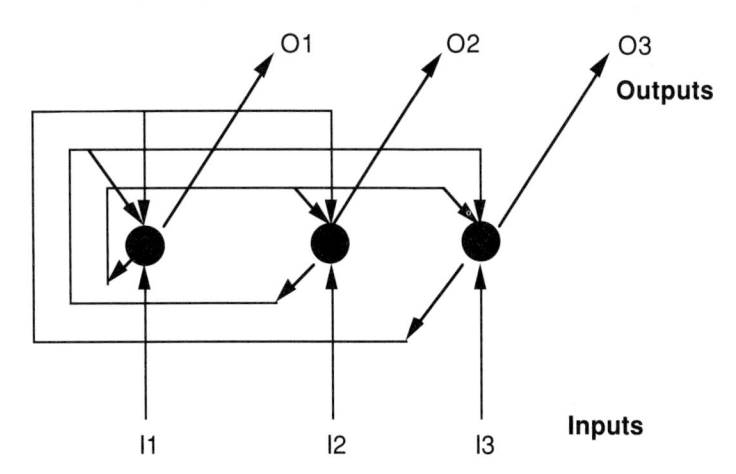

**Figure 9.8** A simple Hopfield network

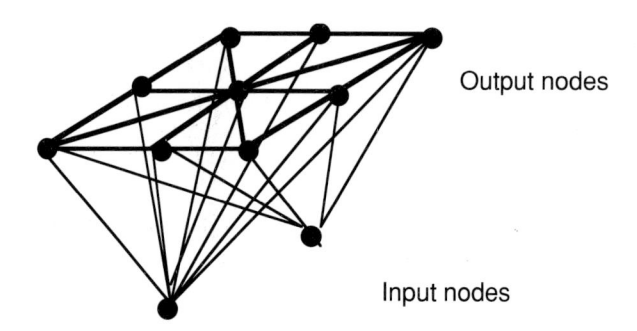

**Figure 9.9** Kohonen's self-organizing feature maps

cally close nodes are sensitive to similar inputs. Note that the learning in Kohonen's network is unsupervised as there is no specification of the desired output while presenting the various inputs. Such networks are useful for speech processing.

## Designing applications using neural networks

There are four important phases in designing applications with NNs:

● suitability — the compatibility of domain and problem characteristics with a NN solution has to be determined

● design — an appropriate NN has to designed

● training — suitable data has to be collected for training the NN.

● deployment — the completed NN application has to be deployed, and appropriate arrangements made for its maintenance and integration (into the information systems architecture of the deployment environment).

Note that many of the organizational and strategic aspects of the process of implementing knowledge-based systems (Chapter 5) also apply to the construction of successful NN applications. The following description of the above-mentioned four stages in NN application development focuses only on details specific to NNs.

## Domain and problem characteristics

Problems involving pattern-recognition or statistical mapping are most suitable for NN applications. Bailey and Thompson[23] note that successful NN application domains usually have one or more of the following attributes:

● applications are data-intensive and depend on multiple interacting criteria

● problem area is rich in historical data or examples

● data set is incomplete, noisy, and contains errors

● the function to determine solutions is unknown, or expensive to discover.

These characteristics are usually shared by existing NN application domains such as speech recognition and synthesis, forecasting, process monitoring, and image processing. Bailey and Thompson also note that the following characteristics favor the use of NNs for application development:

● alternative computer solution techniques do not yield satisfactory results

● conventional analyses of problem are difficult (and perhaps not possible)

● the data available is intrinsically noisy and multi-variate

● project development time is relatively short.

Application domains which are not suitable for a NN approach usually have one or more of the following characteristics:

● mathematically correct and computationally feasible techniques are available for problem solution (which if accurate, will probably yield better results)

● historical data are not available (this makes training of the network difficult or impossible)

● a high degree of mathematical precision is required in the answers (NNs are not good at high precision symbolic computations)

● problem solution requires high-level deductive reasoning such as forward or backward chaining (a limitation for current NNs).

A careful analysis of the problem and domain characteristics can determine the suitability of a NN solution. NNs alone can rarely provide a complete solution to real-life problems. Rather, they are often useful in conjunction with other solution techniques (either mathematical models or conventional rules). Thus, attention should be paid to isolate those aspects of the problem which are amenable to a NN solution.

## Designing the network

This stage includes selection of the type of NN to use (Figure 9. 3), and design of the structure of the chosen NN type. The selection of the correct network type depends on the following parameters:

● inputs — some networks accept binary-valued inputs while others accept continuous-valued inputs. Domain characteristics make it more natural to use either binary- or continuous-valued inputs

● learning — learning in NNs can be either supervised or unsupervised. Supervised learning is possible if appropriate output labels can be associated with the input training patterns. For some problems, this may not be possible (or be undesired), in which case NNs with unsupervised learning have to be used

● problem domain — some network types have been found to be more successful than others in certain domains. For example, Hopfield networks have been quite successful at solving optimization problems. But Hopfield nets sometimes miss finding the global maxima or minima. A Hamming network is a variant of the Hopfield network that avoids this limitation, but its training procedure is usually very slow. The multi-layer perceptron model with back-propagation has been successful in a wide range of domains, and is often a good choice for developing NN applications.

There are no strict guidelines about the network type best suited for a particular problem. Some experimentation with different network types is often necessary for effective problem solution. Once a network type has been chosen, it has to be structured i.e., decisions have to be made about (a) the number of layers (b) the number of nodes in each layer (c) the pattern of connections between various nodes, and (d) other parameters of the system, such as the transfer function used.

Most of the above decisions are dependent upon the chosen network type. As an example, consider the multi-layer perceptron network. The number of layers is decided by the decision region required for problem solution (Figure 9.7). In situations where knowledge about the decision region required for problem solution is lacking, it is necessary to experiment with different layers in the network. It is not desirable to use a network with more layers than required for two reasons. First, the training of larger networks is more expensive (in time and computational requirements). Second, for a given set of input data, large networks can lead to 'over-fitting', and consequently poor generalization. Figure 9.10 depicts over-fitting graphically. The graph on the left in Figure 9.10 shows a good fit to noisy data. The graph on the right shows over-fitting on the same data. Using a larger network requires the setting of more weights (parameters) and can lead to such over-fitting. The resulting network will be good for the training data, but will generalize poorly with new test data (i.e., generalize inadequately).

There is usually a natural correspondence between the number of nodes in the input layer and the number of parameters of the input data. As an example, for the input pixel image of Figure 9.11, a NN with 36 input nodes (each node corresponding to one pixel intensity) is appropriate. Similarly, the number of distinct desired outputs determines the number of nodes in the output layer. Assume that the network shown in Figure 9.11 is trained to recognize patterns corresponding to the numbers 0, 1, ..., 9. As there are 10 possible different output labels, it is again natural to design the network to have 10 nodes in the output layer, each node corresponding to one of the 10 numbers.

A good fit      Over-fitting

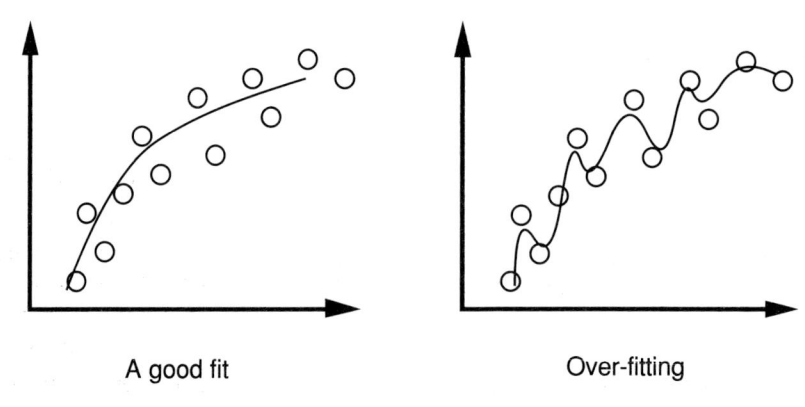

**Figure 9.10** Over-fitting to data

# Designing the network

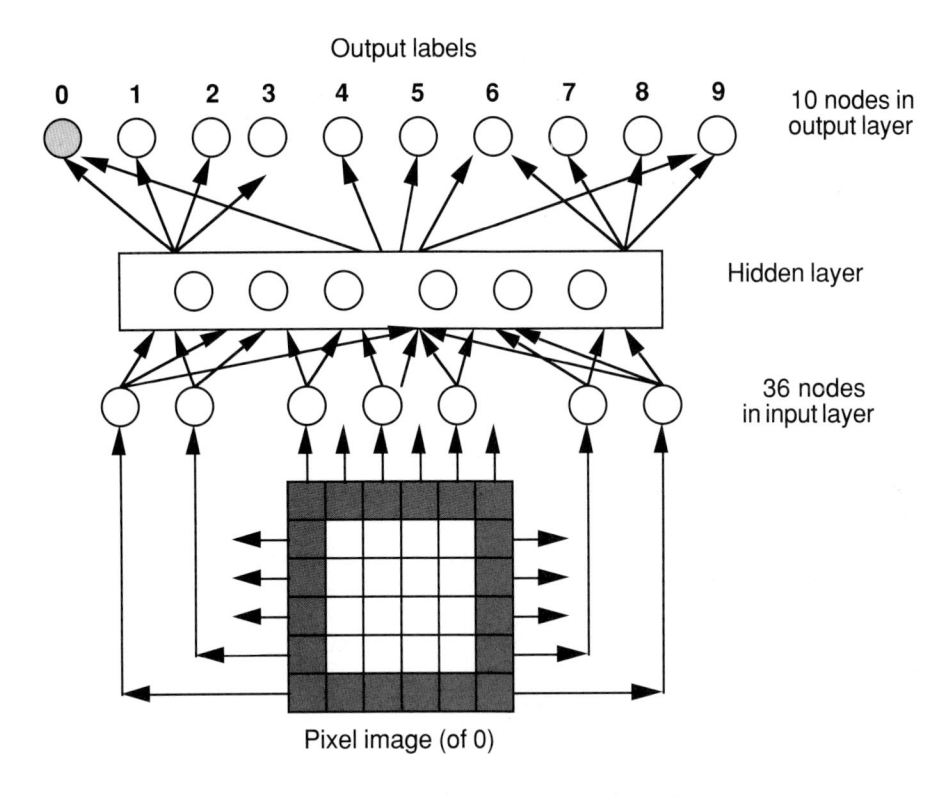

**Figure 9.11** Input and output nodes in a neural network

A rough heuristic for determining the number of nodes in the hidden layer (of a three-layered network) is to choose three times as many as the number of nodes in the input layer[24]. Too few nodes in the network may prevent the network from learning all the training patterns, and too many nodes may prevent the learning algorithm from learning the weights on all connections. Usually, there are several other network dependent parameters which can also be adjusted. Note that there are no formal guidelines for structuring a network. There are some heuristics, but no strict procedures. The process of structuring a network is part art, and part science.

## Training and testing the network

Four important tasks need to be accomplished during this stage: (a) a training algorithm has to be chosen (b) an appropriate training data set has to be collected (c) the network has to be trained, and (d) the trained network has to be tested.

The choice of the training algorithm to be used is limited by the network type chosen in the previous step. For any particular network type, there is a relatively small subset of possible training algorithms, and they are often all variants of one basic algorithm. Most commercial NN software support a single training algorithm per network type. For multi-layer perceptrons, the back-propagation algorithm is used most often. Factors affecting the attractiveness of a particular learning algorithm are:

- compatibility between the kind of data required by the algorithm and the data available in the problem domain
- computational efficiency of the algorithm (some training procedures take a lot of time)
- prior experiences of using the algorithm in other similar domains (some algorithms are more effective than others for certain applications).

Gathering an appropriate training data set is of critical importance for the success of NN applications. This is because NNs learn to solve the problem from the training data set. If the training data set is erroneous or incomplete, the problem solution capabilities of the NN will be affected. The following features are desirable in the training data set:

- the data set is complete i.e., it contains examples of all patterns to be learnt by the network. Besides, it should also contain routine, unusual, and boundary condition examples
- the data set is neither very ambiguous, nor completely random, nor so error-ridden so as to be incomprehensible
- there are no internal conflicts in the training data
- the data has been suitably pre-processed (if possible). For example, it may be useful to feed ratios directly to a network rather than feed them as separate inputs if domain knowledge indicates the ratios are more meaningful for the problem to be solved
- any known important properties of the domain (such as relations between certain inputs) have been conveyed to the network through appropriate examples
- large volumes of data may not be desirable as it may increase training time significantly. It is usually better to focus on the quality of training data (defined by the above points), as opposed to its quantity.

The actual process of training the NN requires the setting of a number of parameters which are dependent on the network type and the training method employed. Most commercial NN software packages provide default values for these parameters, so that even naive users can run ordinary applications. However, some complex manipulations of the training data set (such as injecting some noise), or a specific resetting of parameters may be necessary at times to get good results. Commercial packages also provide access to information about the behavior of individual nodes in the network (allowing the experienced NN developer to fine-tune performance of the network).

Aim of testing a NN is to verify accuracy of the patterns learnt from the training data. As shown in Figures 9.1 and 9.2, a trained NN can be tested with the following two general techniques:

- corrupt some of the training data with noise, and observe the responses of the system after feeding this corrupted data to the trained network. If the network is able to reproduce the correct output labels, it can be assumed to have been trained well. The testing data sample should also contain routine, unusual, and boundary condition examples. Such testing is common when the network is used as an associative memory, or for solving recognition or classification problems.

## Training and testing the network

- prepare a new (unseen by the network) batch of data (input, output_label) pairs, and observe how closely the output of the network matches the known correct output when fed with the corresponding input data. The network can be assumed to have been trained well if the network output matches the correct output for a large proportion of the test data. Such a form of testing is usually used for generalization problems where the NN is expected to have learnt the underlying domain model from the training data.

Other sophisticated methods for testing a trained NN are given in the literature. These include analyzing the weights on the connections between the neurons (to determine whether to change the structure of the network), and doing a sensitivity analysis of the network by observing changes in the outputs with specific variations in the inputs. If the testing phase indicates a poor performance of the network, one or more of the steps described in the preceding sub-sections may have to be revisited. As there are no formal guidelines for structuring and training networks, some experimentation with different structures, different training data sets, and variations of learning algorithms may be necessary till desirable performance is achieved.

### Maintaining and integrating applications

Upon deployment, a trained NN needs to be periodically tested to check its accuracy. This is because changes in the external environment can cause the network performance accuracy to decrease over time. Depending upon the degree of degradation in performance, it may be necessary to periodically retrain the network, and possibly even restructure the network. Guidelines similar to those given for steps 1 through 3 will have to be followed for restructuring and retraining the NN. Note that while it is possible to retrain a NN continuously (with each new data input), it is often not feasible due to the computational requirements of training NNs.

Many current NN applications have been developed as standalone systems with little integration with other information systems. However, the need and importance of more integrated NN applications is evident. Figure 9.12 depicts how a NN can be integrated with a conventional rule-based system. Such an architecture leverages the benefits of both NNs and symbolic rule-based systems. The NN is used to classify the pattern data and

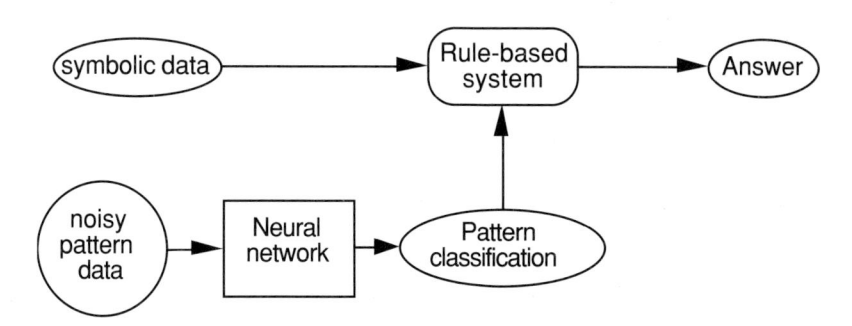

Figure 9.12 A neural network front-end for a rule-based system

## 282 Connectionist modelling of intelligence

feed its answer (the pattern classification label) to the rule-based system. Figure 9.13 illustrates how a NN can be coupled with a database. A NN can help in finding patterns in the data stored in a database. Other more complex integration architectures are possible, such as using a NN as a knowledge source in a blackboard system (Figure 3.19).

### Commercial tools

A variety of tools, both software and hardware, are available commercially for developing NN applications. A recent survey[25] found that more than 30 major NN products were being sold commercially in the USA in 1991. Table 9.1 lists selected NN tool vendors and their products.

Most NN tools are software packages simulating the operation of a NN. They are similar in principle to shell tools for knowledge-based systems, and offer the possibility of rapidly building NN applications with minimal programming. This is particularly true for tools such as ExploreNet, which allow the user to 'program' a NN graphically by filling in a few windows and charts. Most tools also support many different types of networks. This increases the range of problems and domains to which the tool can be applied, and gives the user or developer more freedom in experimenting to find the best NN solution.

Due to the importance of data (both training and learning) for the operation of NNs, all tools offer data-bridges and links to common spreadsheet and database packages. Most tools run on popular hardware platforms such as IBM or Macintosh personal computers, and SUN engineering workstations. To respond to the demanding computational requirements of training NNs, many vendors offer dedicated coprocessors which can speed up network performances significantly. Dedicated neurocomputers (with specialized hardware) are also available, but they are used in specialized applications only.

### Case study: using neural networks for bond rating[26]

The process of developing a NN application for the prediction of corporate bond ratings is described now. The default risks of bonds are rated by various independent organizations, such as Standard and Poor's (S&P) and Moody's (in the USA). Table 9.2 summarizes some of the ratings given by S&P and Moody's. The purpose of these ratings[27] is to

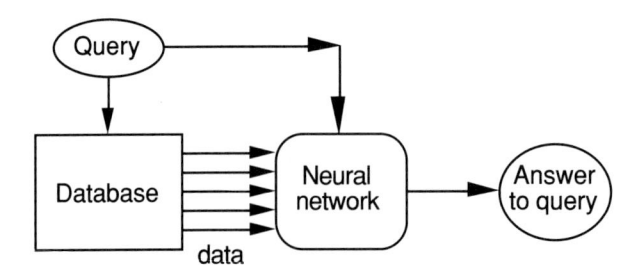

Figure 9.13 Coupling neural networks with databases

| Vendor name | Product name | Product description | Product price |
|---|---|---|---|
| Adaptive Solutions Beaverton, Ore, USA | CNAPS Server | A stand-alone dedicated neurocomputer with specialized hardware for NNs | $ 50,000 |
| | CNAPS CodeNet | An integrated software tool-kit for the development of NN applications on the CNAPS Server | $ 10,000 |
| California Scientific Software, Grass Valley CA, USA | Brainmaker | A simple to use software tool for NN application development. In professional and introductory versions | $ 800(prof ver) |
| HNC, San Diego CA, USA | ExploreNet | An icon-based (Windows-compatible) NN development software tool-kit. Support for many NN types | $ 1500 |
| | Balboa 860 | A NN coprocessor for DOS and Sun 3/4 | $ 11,000 |
| Nestor Providence, R.I., USA | NDS 1000 | A software environment for development of NN applications | $ 25,000 |
| NeuralWare | NeuralWorks | A complete and flexible NN development and deployment tool. Different NN types are supported. It is also possible to convert designed NNs into C source code | $ 2000 to $ 5000 |

**Table 9.1** Selected vendors of commercial neural network products

provide the investor with a simple system of gradation by which the relative investment qualities of bonds may be noted. These ratings are often used to define allowable bond purchases by certain investors. For example, the Comptroller of Currency (in the USA) has stated that bank investments must be of investment grade (i.e., in the top four rankings). Institutional portfolio managers also use these ratings as a metric to reflect the risk of their investments in bonds.

## The problem of bond rating

To evaluate a bond's potential for default, rating agencies rely upon a committee analysis of the issuer's ability to repay, willingness to repay, and protective provisions for an issue. It is not known what model, if any, do these rating agencies use for rating the various bond issues. Aspects analyzed by the ratings committee are not known completely, and some features such as willingness to repay are affected by a number of variables which are difficult to characterize precisely. Thus, it is difficult to define an accurate mathematical model for rating the bonds. It is difficult to develop a knowledge-based system for rating bonds because few experts are available, and most knowledge about the process of ratings is confidential. Developing a model for rating corporate bonds is important as it enables an independent assessment of the default risk of bond investments.

The task of assigning ratings to the bond issues of companies is an example of the classification problem. Each bond instance can be described by a set of features which represents important financial information about the company issuing the bond. The various bond ratings (AA, B, and so on) form the set of possible classes to which the input bonds can belong. The problem then consists of assigning the correct output label (bond rating) to the corresponding input (financial) information.

| Moody's | Standard & Poor's | Definition* |
|---------|-------------------|-------------|
| Aaa | AAA | The highest rating assigned. Capacity to pay interest and principal very strong |
| Aa | AA | Very strong capacity to pay interest and principal. Minor differences from highest rated issue |
| A | A | Strong economic capacity to repay interest and principal, but may be susceptible to adverse changes in economic conditions |
| Baa of B | BBB B | Adequate protection to repay interest and principal but more likely to have weakened capacity in periods adverse economic conditions Moderate default risk |

* Adapted from S&P's Bond Guide and Moody's Bond Record

Table 9.2 Definitions of bond ratings

## The problem of bond rating

The above domain and problem characteristics indicate that NNs may potentially be useful for solving the bond rating problem.

### Use of statistical models for bond rating

Finance researchers have built several complex statistical models for bond rating[28]. They usually take coded bond ratings as an independent variable and regress on a set of quantifiable financial variables. The success rates of prediction (of bond ratings) with these models have been in the range of 60–65%.

### Decision region required for bond rating

The decision region of the problem of bond rating consists of many closed regions (corresponding to the different possible ratings) in the multi-dimensional space of the input variables. Figure 9.14 depicts the different decision regions assuming only two input features F1 and F2. Linear regression models are inadequate for solving the problem accurately as a hyper-plane cannot discriminate among the decision regions of the various ratings. However, if the decision problem is posed as recognizing only a single bond rating, a linear regression model may be adequate. For example in Figure 9.14, a linear regression model (or a one-layer perceptron model) can be devised to generate the lightly shaded planar decision region (which discriminates between AAA bonds and other ratings).

The decision region generated by a two-layer NN is an open or closed convex region (Figure 9.7). Thus two-layer NNs are also inadequate for the general problem of bond rating (i.e., for discriminating among all the ratings). But they can be used correctly when the decision problem is posed as recognizing a single bond rating. There are similarities in the decision regions generated by certain non-linear regression models and two-layered perceptron models. It can be seen from Figure 9.14 that two-layer NNs can yield a better model than linear regression as the decision region can 'encapsulate' any one rating decision region (e.g, rating A in Figure 9.14). Three-layer neural networks are capable of generating arbitrary decision regions (Figure 9.7), and thus can be used for the general problem of bond rating.

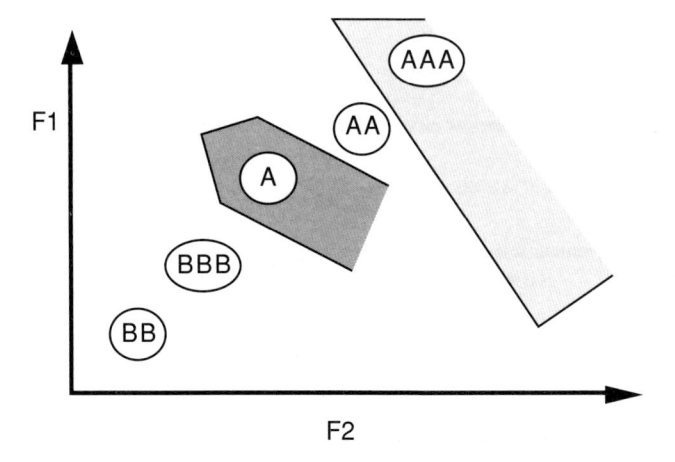

**Figure 9.14** Decision regions in the bond rating problem

### Selection of variables
Table 9.3 lists the 10 financial variables used as inputs to determine the bond ratings. The influence of the variables on bond rating (as evident from prior research in finance) and the ease of availability of data were the primary factors guiding the selection of the variables.

### Data collection
Values of the input variables listed in Table 9.3 were collected from the April 1986 issues of the Valueline Index and the S&P Bond Guide. Bond issues of 47 companies were selected at random. Thirty companies were arbitrarily selected to be used as the training sample. The other 17 companies were used as the testing sample. All selected bonds had approximately the same maturity date (1998–2003).

For the purposes of the application, the symbolic ratings of bonds were converted into numerical values as shown in Table 9.4. For enhancing discrimination in the output, similar ratings (such as AA+, AA, and AA-) were mapped onto the same numerical value (0.9).

### Neural network
To enable an easy comparison of the performance of a NN with a regression model, the problem posed to the NN was simplified from distinguishing between all possible ratings to recognizing the class of all bonds with a AA rating. Such a formulation of the decision region enables a reasonably fair comparison of regression and NN models (Figure 9.14).

| Var. # | Definition | Var. # | Definition |
|---|---|---|---|
| 1 | Liability/(cash + assets) | 2 | (Total funded debt)/(net property) |
| 3 | Sales/net worth | 4 | Profit/sales |
| 5 | Financial strength of company as given in the Valueline Index | 6 | Number of times available earnings cover fixed charges |
| 7 | Past five year revenue growth rate | 8 | Next five year projected revenue growth rate |
| 9 | Working capital/sales | 10 | Subjective prospects of company (from Valueline) |

Table 9.3 Financial variables used to predict bond ratings

| Bond rating | Numerical value | Bond rating | Numerical value |
|---|---|---|---|
| AAA | 0.95 | BBB+, BBB, BBB- | 0.5 |
| AA+, AA, AA- | 0.9 | BB+, BB, BB- | 0.35 |
| A+, A, A- | 0.7 | B+, B, B- | 0.25 |

Table 9.4 Conversion of bond ratings to numerical values

A multi-layer perceptron with the back-propagation learning algorithm was selected because such networks have been successfully used in a variety of different domains. The NN had 10 input nodes (corresponding to the 10 variables of Table 9.3) and one output node (to give the numerical equivalent of the bond rating). Different network configurations (two-layered, three-layered, different number of hidden nodes in three-layered neural networks, and so on) were experimented with (as there are no firm guidelines about the 'correct' NN structure for the best performance).

### Regression

A statistical package was used for performing a multi-variate linear regression analysis on the training sample data. The regression coefficients were then used to predict the ratings of both the learning sample (to see how well the regression model fitted the learning sample), and the testing sample of new bond issues (to test how well the regression coefficients predicted the ratings of the test bonds). A non-linear regression model was not used due to a lack of knowledge about the correct functional form to use for obtaining the regression coefficients.

### Results

The results of the application are shown in Tables 9.5 and 9.6. Tables 9.5 and 9.6 summarize the results of the learning and testing phases respectively. The % entries in Tables 9.5 and 9.6 represent the % of correct prediction of the two models (regression and NN). The absolute error for each model is also listed to give an idea of goodness of fit. The entry labelled 'tot_sq_err' gives the sum of the squares of the errors in prediction.

| Neural network | | Regression |
|---|---|---|
| two-layered | three-layered | |
| 80% | 92.4% | 66.7% |
| tot_sq_err = 0.224 | tot_sq_err = 0.054 | tot_sq_err = 0.924 |

Table 9.5  Results from the learning phase

| Neural network | | Regression |
|---|---|---|
| two-layered | three-layered | |
| 88.3% | 82.4% | 64.7% |
| tot_sq_err = 0.164 | tot_sq_err = 0.228 | tot_sq_err = 1.643 |

Table 9.6  Results from the testing phase

It can be observed that NNs consistently outperform the regression model in predicting bond ratings from the given set of financial variables. Both in the training and learning phases, the total squared errors for regression analyses are about an order of magnitude higher than that for NNs. Also, the success rates of prediction for NNs are considerably higher than that for regression analyses e.g., the success rate during the testing phase for the two-layered NN is 88.3% as compared to 64.7% for the regression model. A better fit (with respect to the training sample) can be obtained using a larger number of layers in the NN but the additional layer does not seem to add to its predictive power as evidenced during the testing phase. This is due to over-fitting (Figure 9.10).

## Applications of neural networks

Due to the late resurgence of interest in connectionist models, the commercial market for NNs is not as well-developed as that for knowledge-based systems. The commercialization of NNs has started during the late 1980s, and analysts predict a string of powerful applications during the 1990s. According to some estimates[29], revenues from this technology should total about $5 billion by the end of the decade. More than 40 companies specializing in NNs arose during 1987–88[30]. Most large US companies and industrial research laboratories also have active NN research and development programs.

Neural networks are now being applied in a variety of industries including manufacturing, defense, finance, and medicine. Table 9.7 provides a partial list of industries using neural networks and the type of functions being performed by neural networks. Appendix 3 lists some representative commercial applications of NNs. Details of some successful NN applications follow.

| Industry | Function served |
|---|---|
| Manufacturing | Process control |
| | Fault diagnosis |
| | Quality control |
| Defense | Signal recognition |
| Space | Scheduling |
| Airline | Traffic control |
| Healthcare | Diagnosis and treatment prescription |
| | Resource management |
| | Performance monitoring |
| Financial services | Credit and insurance policy approval |
| | Fraud detection |
| | Bond rating |
| | Portfolio selection |
| | Interest rate and security price forecasting |
| Consumer products | Customer segmentation |

**Table 9.7** Applications types of neural networks in industry

## NETtalk[31]

The NETtalk system was designed by Sejnowski and Rosenberg to read English text. In NETtalk, text (either separate words or connected discourse) is presented in groups of seven consecutive letters as input to the NN via a moving window that gradually scans the text. The network is expected to produce as output the phoneme code (Chapter 7) corresponding to the central letter in the seven-letter input string. The output phoneme code is fed to a speech generator. Figure 9.15 depicts a simplified setup of the NETtalk system. In one simulation, the network was exposed to a learning sample of 1024 words. After each word had been presented to the network about 50 times, the network could achieve an accuracy of 95% in correctly predicting the phoneme corresponding to the central letter in the input window. When tested with another (test) body of 439 words which had not been seen by the network, a 78% success rate was achieved.

The performance of the NETtalk system is comparable, but inferior to that of commercially-available speech systems such as DEC-talk. DEC-talk is based on linguistic knowledge and represents a symbolic approach. However, this comparison is not entirely fair as DEC-talk represents about 10 years of developmental work by many linguists. In contrast, the NETtalk system was designed and trained using only examples and without any linguistic knowledge. Also, NETtalk is not a commercial application and thus lacks adequate developmental investment. However, this example illustrates the potential of neural networks for domains in which domain knowledge is missing. Symbolic approaches usually yield good results when domain knowledge is easily available.

## Determining the secondary structure of proteins[32]

A protein has associated with it three structures — primary, secondary, and tertiary. The primary structure consists of a linear sequence of amino acids (out of 20 different possibilities). The secondary structure involves the local configuration of the primary structure.

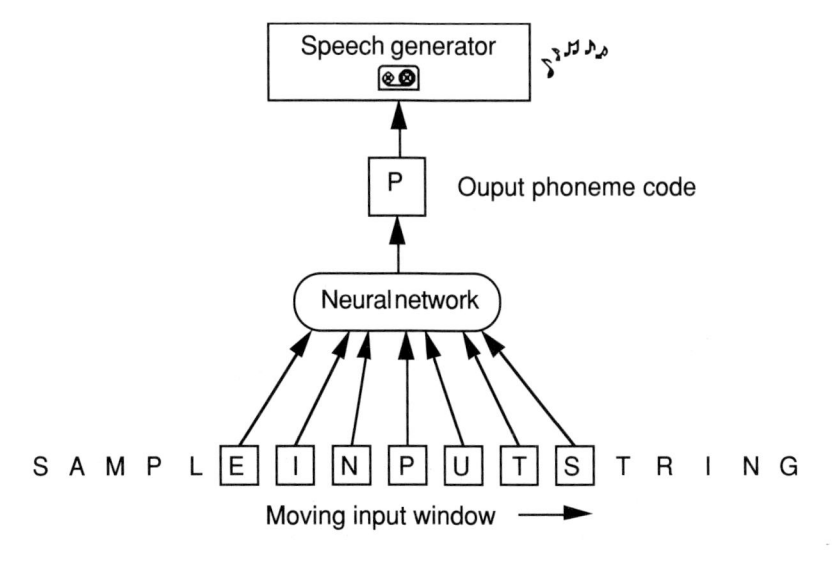

**Figure 9.15** NETtalk system architecture

The most common of these local configurations are the α-helix and the β-sheet. There are similarities between the problem of determining the secondary structure of proteins (from the primary structures) and that solved by the NETtalk architecture. Qian and Sejnowski[33] achieved a success rate of 62% in using a NN to predict the secondary structure of proteins (given the primary structure as inputs). This is currently the best solution method for this problem as the next best alternative yields a success rate of 53%.

### Car navigation[34]

Pomerleau has built the Alvinn system, which uses a NN for controlling a car on a winding road. The inputs to the NN consist of a 30 by 32 pixel image from a video camera mounted on top of the car, and a 8 by 32 pixel image from a range finder coding distances in a gray-scale. The output of the network indicates the degree to which the car should either 'go straight ahead', or 'go towards the left', or 'go towards the right'. Alvinn learns 'how to drive' by observing a human driver do it for about five minutes. Currently it 'knows' about a dozen different road types (such as two-lane highways and dirt roads). In summer 1991 Alvinn could cruise suburban Pittsburgh, correctly stopping at stoplights and changing directions to avoid obstacles. In fall 1991 it was transplanted to an army ambulance, and set an autonomous-land-vehicle speed record of more than 55 mph, while covering a distance of 21 miles[35]. Though far from perfect (for example, it tends to exit at every off-ramp on a highway), it offers the best possibility today for building autonomous vehicles.

### Backgammon[36]

The game of backgammon requires each player to roll two dice and then choose one of typically 20 different moves consistent with the outcome of the dice. Neurogammon is a NN that was trained to choose the best move given the particular dice outcome. The input to the network consists of the current position, the dice values, a possible move, and some precomputed features (specific to backgammon) such as pip count and degree of trapping. The output of the network is a rating on a scale of -100 (worst move) to +100 (best move). This program won the gold medal at the computer olympiad in London (1989) by defeating all other programs (five commercial and two non-commercial). Reportedly[37] the network exhibited a great deal of 'common sense,' almost invariably choosing the best moves in situations that were transparent or intuitively clear to a human player. However, it lost to a human expert by a score of 2–7.

### Diagnosis and treatment prescription for hypertension[38]

Researchers at the University of Florence have designed a NN for diagnosis and prescription of treatment of patients suffering from hypertension. Traditionally, diagnosis and treatment are done by a doctor who considers a range of information to decide whether the patient is suffering from hypertension and, if so, the drugs required to correct the condition. A classical knowledge-based system was found to be inappropriate because the knowledge required for the decisions cannot be easily coded in a frame or rule-based system.

A NN was trained using data consisting of blood pressure time series for approximately 300 clinically healthy individuals and for 85 suspected hypertension sufferers. One module of the system was designed to learn to recognize the hypertension condition by comparing with the learning data, another module to identify allowable drugs for a given individual, and a final module to prescribe the most appropriate compatible drug when hypertension is diagnosed. In tests, the system correctly diagnosed 33 out 35 subjects, prescribing correct or acceptable treatment in 9 out of 11 correctly-diagnosed hypertension cases.

## Strengths and limitations of connectionist models

Connectionist models have several strengths and several weaknesses. Strengths are:

- a similarity to neural processes — the brain has several strengths which would be desirable in AI systems; (a) it is a dynamic system which changes and adapts over time to the external environment (b) it is robust in that nerve cells die regularly without affecting performance significantly (c) it is capable of dealing with information that is fuzzy, noisy, and inconsistent, and (d) it is highly parallel (all stimuli passes between nerve cells in parallel).

Since its inception, the connectionist approach has taken its inspiration from the human brain. McCulloch and Pitts termed the independent units in their network as neurons because they could be either on or off (corresponding to neurons in the brain being either in resting or firing states). The propagation of activation (excitatory or inhibitory) within a NN is also based on the physiological processes occurring within neurons. Of course, NNs do not capture the complexity of the structure of the brain in detail. At best, they provide a coarse approximation to the architecture of the brain. This is consistent with the approach (within AI) to view neural networks as simulators of the cognitive tasks performed by the brain, and not of its biological functions. Advances in neuro-biology have served as an important source of ideas for new developments in connectionist models. These similarities to neural processes are an attractive feature of NNs

- pattern-recognition — pattern-recognition is a fundamental component of human cognition. It is fairly well-developed even in infants and children. However, rule-based systems have limited capabilities for performing pattern recognition due to the hard constraints inherent in their structure. A rule is deterministic in nature. If the antecedent of a particular rule is activated, it fires and triggers an additional set of rules. The constraints built into the firing of rules is hard. Systems based on hard constraints do not adapt well to pattern recognition tasks. For example, consider the different ways in which persons write a particular number or letter. Writing rules (hard constraints) to recognize all possible variations is a formidable task (which does not yield very good results).

NNs have proven to be good at pattern recognition tasks, partly because the constraints within the system can be thought of as soft. Within a network, each neuron is connected to and receives signals from several different neurons. Each connection can be viewed as a constraint on the neuron (much like the inter-connection of rules in a rule-based system). The signals received from each connection can be different (some excitatory and others inhibitory), and the individual neuron selects the best output response so as to satisfy all these multiple constraints (and not any one constraint alone). Thus the constraints imposed by the connections on the neuron are termed as soft. NNs can be viewed as performing pattern recognition by recognizing some basic features which are common to all variations (of a particular pattern), and then allowing for some variability (soft constraints) on how a particular input pattern can differ from these basic features

● graceful degradation — conventional rule-based systems are brittle i.e., they often break down abruptly when faced with a slight variation of the planned inputs. NNs are more tolerant to variations in the inputs. The soft constraint satisfaction within network models allows them to deal with unseen patterns and exceptions. If the new pattern has similarities with prior seen patterns, the NN will point it out and give its best response.

Also, the performance of rule-based systems is often dependent on a few critical rules. System performance can be seriously affected if one or more of these critical rules malfunction (possibly due to a software bug). In contrast, performances of connectionist models tend to degrade more gracefully. This feature can be understood by noting that connectionist models are based on networks of interconnected neurons. If some neurons or neuronal connections malfunction, the performance of the system degrades, but does not terminate abruptly

● a capacity to learn — rule-based systems are typically static systems, with no autonomous capabilities to learn and adapt to changes in a dynamic environment. All changes in the system structure and rules have to be done by explicit programming.

In contrast, learning is an integral part of the design and use of NNs. Most NNs go through a period of training or learning in which they are presented with examples of patterns to recognize. Subsequent to this initial training phase, a trained network can be used to recognize test data. With each new test data item, the NN can learn from its mistakes and autonomously reassign the strengths of connections between neurons to provide the best response to changes in the external environment. Thus, NNs are also known as self-adapting dynamical systems. This ability to learn from experience is one of the most attractive features of NNs. It is also similar to certain learning processes occurring in the human brain where the strengths of connections between neurons are modified over time in response to changing stimuli from the environment.

● function as a content-addressable memory — a library can be thought of as a content-addressable memory. The indices (author, title, and so on) in the library database aid in searching for a particular book. The information given in the index (author and title) is actually part of the information given in the book i.e., the book is addressed by its partial contents. This ability is very important for organizing large amounts of information. Connectionist models have a natural tendency to function as a content-addressable memory. When provided with a partial pattern (i.e., incomplete information about the desired content in memory), the soft constraints in a connectionist system fill in unknown details to provide the answer which best matches the specified input (partial) information. Such a feature is difficult to replicate in conventional rule-based systems

● rapid application development — it is possible for non-programmers to develop NN applications rapidly, and with minimal programming. NN software packages (such as ExploreNet) offer user friendly graphical interfaces and ready-to-run network packages which can cut application development times dramatically.

## Limitations

Despite the above attractive features, neural networks have some important limitations:

● NNs are not very good at performing symbolic computations. They cannot be used (effectively) for rule-based reasoning, and arithmetic operations

● NNs have poor explanation facilities. There are no facilities for justifying answers, and responding to what or how questions (as is typical in rule-based systems). This also leads to problems in detecting errors in the network as the errors are diffused over multiple neurons and inter-neuronal connections

● there are no well-accepted or formal guidelines for the design and implementation of NNs. Application development is part science and part art, and a substantial amount of experience is needed for engineering connectionist applications

● accuracy of a NN's performance is dependent to a large extent upon the quality of the training examples. Finding a complete and accurate set of training examples is difficult in some real-life domains.

## The future of symbolic and connectionist approaches

The roots of symbolic approaches to modelling intelligence go back many centuries (Chapter 1). More recently, influential researchers such as Newell and Simon[39] have strongly endorsed symbolic means for modelling general intelligent action. Others such as Fodor and Pylyshyn[40] contend that while the structure of the human brain may indeed be like a network, this fact by itself is irrelevant for modelling cognition. They maintain that cognition occurs at a higher level, at which only symbolic processing (typified by rules) is important.

Proponents of the connectionist approaches have their own rebuttals, which can be classified[41] into the following two categories — approximationist, and compatibilist. The approximationist response (advocated by connectionist pioneers such as Rumelhart and McClelland) turns around the arguments of Fodor and Pylyshyn to claim that a symbolic approach cannot be better than a connectionist model, because it is simply a coarse approximation of some regularities in cognition. In such a view, connectionist approaches are inherently superior because they model cognition at the true granularity of detail. This, it is claimed, is supported by the variability, flexibility, and subtlety of connectionist models, features notably missing or difficult to replicate in rule-based systems. The compatibilist response adopts a middle-ground, and notes that symbolic approaches can co-exist with connectionist approaches. Some tasks (e.g., high-level reasoning) are better suited for symbolic rule-based approaches, while others (e.g., pattern-recognition) are better handled by connectionist networks. Researchers supporting the compatibilist response have been actively trying to simulate rule-based reasoning processes in NNs.

Current attempts in introducing the advantages (such as enhanced pattern-recognition abilities) of connectionist approaches in rule-based systems, and those of symbolic reasoning (such as high-level reasoning) into connectionist networks have not met with great success. Though future success in these attempts cannot be ruled out, pragmatic scientists and engineers are already applying the powers of both approaches by adopting integrative architectures (Figure 9.12).

## Summary

Connectionism is a radical departure from the usual emphasis on symbolic techniques within applied AI. The popularity of connectionist approaches stems from their powerful capabilities for pattern recognition and autonomous learning. Connectionist systems and their properties are being actively investigated today in universities and industry. Though several commercial applications of NNs already exist (see Appendix 3 also), connectionist technology is yet to mature for widespread commercial use. However, it is an important technology for the near future. The primary issues of this chapter can be summarized as follows:

- Much of the work in applied AI has been based on the symbolic paradigm. The new alternative paradigm of connectionism is different in disregarding logical information processing and in directly emulating the structure and processes of the human brain.

- Connectionism started around 1940, but suffered serious setbacks during the period 1960–1980. It has made a dramatic comeback since the mid-1980s.

- Neural networks and parallel distributed models are alternative names for connectionism.

- A NN consists of an interconnected network of simple processing units (neurons) which operate independently and in parallel. A NN has to be trained (with example patterns) prior to application. The training of a NN can be either supervised or unsupervised. Back-propagation is a popular supervised training algorithm.

- Problems tackled by NNs can be classified into the following three categories — classification (associating labels with input patterns), generalization (predicting labels for new patterns), and clustering (grouping similar patterns).

- Different types of NNs have been proposed. Distinction is commonly made between feedforward and feedback networks. Computational considerations make feedforward NNs more popular. The multi-layer perceptron is a feed-forward NN which is commonly used in connectionist applications. The Hopfield net and Kohonen's self-organizing feature maps are examples of other NN architectures.

- The problem-solving capabilities of NNs vary with the number of layers in the network. In general, a three-layered NN is powerful enough to solve for arbitrarily complex decision regions.

- There are four important phases in designing NN applications — determining the suitability of a NN solution, designing an appropriate NN, training the NN, and deploying the NN application.

- NNs provide a good solution technique in data-intensive domains lacking adequate domain knowledge. There are no formal techniques for designing NN applications. Therefore suitable experiments have to be conducted to determine the best NN architecture and design. The data used for training and testing the NN are crucial. It is possible to design NN applications to be autonomously updated (to reflect changes in the application environment) upon deployment.

- There are several NN products (running on personal computers) which are sold commercially by vendors.

● The strengths of connectionist models are — a similarity to neural processes, powerful pattern-recognition capabilities, graceful degradation, a capacity for autonomous learning, function as a content-addressable memory, and rapid application deployment.

● Limitations of NNs include the following — poor performance of symbolic computations, inadequate explanation facilities, dependence upon training data, and a lack of design guidelines.

● Both symbolic and connectionist approaches have their relative advantages. Many current systems attempt to integrate the two techniques.

## Bibliography and suggested readings

There are several recent books on NNs which provide good overviews of the subject. Technical descriptions can be found in references (Rumelhart et al 86), (McClelland & Rumelhart 88), (Anderson & Rosenfield 88), (Hecht-Nielsen 89), (Wasserman 89), and (Hertz et al 91). An easy to read description of NNs with a practical emphasis is given in a book by McCord and Illingworth (McCord and Illingworth 91). A fascinating discussion of connectionism from a cognitive perspective is available in reference (Bechtel & Abrahamsen 91). Good overview articles on NNs are references (Lippman 87) and (Hecht-Nielsen 88). Industry magazines such as AI Expert (AI Expert 88) and Electronic Engineering Times regularly provide good articles and updates on recent developments in NNs.

AI Expert, Vol. 3, No. 8, August 1988.

Anderson, J. A., and E. Rosenfield, (Eds.), *Neurocomputing: Foundations of Research*, MIT Press, Cambridge, 1988.

Bechtel, W., and A. Abrahamsen, *Connectionism and the Mind*, Blackwell, 1991.

Hecht-Nielsen, R., *Neurocomputing*, Addison Wesley, 1989.

Hecht-Nielsen, R., *Neurocomputing: Picking the Human Brain*, IEEE Spectrum, Vol. 25, No. 3, pp. 36–41, March 1988.

Hertz, J., A. Krogh, and R. G. Palmer, *Introduction to the theory of neural computation*, Addison Wesley, 1991.

Lippman, R. P., *An Introduction to Computing with Neural Networks*, IEEE ASSP Magazine, April 1987.

McClelland, J. L., and D. E. Rumelhart, *Explorations in Parallel Distributed Processing*, MIT Press, Cambridge, MA, 1988.

McCord Nelson, M., and W. T. Illingworth, *A Practical Guide to Neural Networks*, Addison Wesley, 1991.

Rumelhart, K., J. McClelland and the PDP Research Group, *Parallel Distributed Processing: Explorations in the Microstructure of Cognition*, Bradford Books, Cambridge, MA, 1986.

Wasserman, P. D., *Neural Computing: Theory and Practice*, Van Nostrand Reinhold, New York, 1989.

## Notes

1 Newell, A. and H. Simon, *Computer Science as an Empirical Enquiry*, in J. Haugeland (Eds.) Mind Design, Montgomery, VT, Bradford Books, 1981.

2 Newell and Simon define a physical symbol system to consist of symbols (physical patterns), expressions (symbol structures obtained by placing symbol tokens in a physical relation such as adjacency), and processes that operate on expressions.

3 McCulloch, W. S. and W. Pitts, *A Logical Calculus of the Ideas Immanent in Nervous Activity*, Bulletin of Mathematical Biophysics, 5, pp. 115–133, 1943. Reprinted in: Anderson, J. A., and E. Rosenfeld, (Eds.), *Neurocomputing: Foundations of Research*, MIT Press, Cambridge, 1988.

4 Minsky, M. A. and S. Papert, *Perceptrons*, MIT Press, Cambridge, MA, 1969.

5 The logical statement A XOR B is defined as true only if either A or B is true, but not both. It is false under all other conditions.

6 Colin Johnson, R. and T. J. Schwartz, *DARPA backs neural nets*, Electronic Engineering Times, 498, Aug. 8, pp. 1, 96, 1988.

7 Gross, N., *A Japanese "Flop" that became a Launching Pad*, Business Week, pp. 75, June 8, 1992.

8 Newquist III, H. P., *Parle-Vous Intelligence Artificielle?*, AI Expert, Vol. 4, No. 9, pp. 60, Sep. 1989.

9 Colin Johnson, R., *DARPA Neural awards stress practical use*, Electronic Engineering Times, 558, pp. 22, October 2, 1989.

10 Colin Johnson, R., *French Research: Vive le Neuron*, Electronic Engineering Times, 492, June 27, pp. 57, 1988.

11 White, H., *Economic prediction using neural networks: The case of IBM Daily stock returns*, in the Proceedings of the IEEE International Conference on Neural Networks, San Diego, July 1988.

12 Figure adapted from: Lippman, R.P., *An Introduction to Computing with Neural Networks*, IEEE ASSP Magazine, pp. 4–22, April 1987.

13 Brainmaker users manual, California Scientific Software, Sierra Madre, CA.

14 The name 'hidden layer' refers to the fact that the neurons in this layer are sandwiched between the input and output layers, and are thus 'hidden' from the outputs and inputs.

15 It is given in most references on neural networks such as: Lippman, R. P., *An Introduction to Computing with Neural Networks*, IEEE ASSP Magazine, pp. 4–22, April 1987.

16 CPU time refers to the actual computation time taken by the central processing unit of a computer. This is a common measure of the amount of computational complexity of programs.

17 The discussion of the decision regions solved by perceptrons (two- and three-layered) is strictly valid only for perceptrons with one output node and with the neurons using a step-type of transfer function (Figure 9.6 (a)). The behavior of perceptrons with multiple output nodes and sigmoidal transfer functions is similar in character, though more complex.

18 Lippman, R. P., *An Introduction to Computing with Neural Networks*, IEEE ASSP Magazine, pp. 4–22, April 1987.

19 Here the term *convex* means that any line joining points on the boundaries of the region will lie within the interior of the region.

20 Rumelhart, K., J. McClelland and the PDP Research Group., *Parallel Distributed Processing: Explorations in the Microstructure of Cognition*, Bradford Books, Cambridge, MA, 1986.

21 Hornik, K., M. Stinchcombe and H. White, *Multi-layer Feedforward Networks are Universal Approximators*, Neural Networks 2, 1992.

22 Figure adapted from Lippman, R. P., *An Introduction to Computing with Neural Networks*, IEEE ASSP Magazine, pp. 7, April 1987.

23 Bailey, D. and D. Thompson, *How to Develop Neural-Network Applications*, AI Expert, June 1990.

24 Lippman, R. P., *An Introduction to Computing with Neural Networks*, IEEE ASSP Magazine, April 1987.

25 Enrado, P., *Neural-Net Resource Guide*, AI Expert, pp. 60–70, July 1991.

26 For more details on this application see Dutta, S. and S. Shekhar, *Bond-Rating: A Non-conservative application of neural networks*, in the Proceedings of the IEEE International Conference on Neural Networks, July 1988.

27 Moody's Bond Record, Moody's Corporation, NY.

28 See for example (a) Horrigan, J. O., *The Determination of Long Term Credit Standing with Financial Ratios*, Empirical Research in Accounting: Selected Studies, Journal of Accounting Research, 1966; (b) Pinches, G. E. and K. A. Mingo, *A Multivariate Analysis of Industrial Bond Ratings*, Journal of Finance, March 1977; and (c) Pinches, G. E. and K. A. Mingo, *A Multivariate Analysis of Industrial Bond Ratings*, Journal of Finance, March 1977.

29 AI Expert, pp. 71, June 1990.

30 McCord, M., and W. T. Illingworth, *A Practical Guide to Neural Networks*, Addison-Wesley, pp. 22, 1991.

31 Sejnowski, T. J. and C. R. Rosenberg, *Parallel networks that learn to pronounce English text*, Complex Systems, 1, 145–68, 1987.

32 Hertz, J., A. Krogh, and R. G. Palmer, *Introduction to the theory of neural computation*, Addison Wesley, pp.134, 1991.

33 Qian, N. and T. J. Sejnowski, *Predicting the secondary structure of globular proteins using neural network models*, Journal of Molecular Biology, 202, 865–884, 1988.

34 Pomerleau, D. A., *ALVINN: An autonomous land vehicle in a neural network*, in *Advances in Neural Information Processing Systems I* (Denver 1988), Ed., D. S. Touretzky, 306–313, Morgan Kaufmann, San Mateo, 1989.

35 Schwartz, E. I., and J. B. Treece, *Smart Programs go to Work*, Business Week, March 2, pp. 48–49, 1992.

36 Tesauro, G., *Neurogammon wins computer olympiad*, Neural Computation, 1, 321–323, 1990.

37 Hertz, J., A. Krogh, and R. G. Palmer, *Introduction to the theory of neural computation*, Addison Wesley, pp.137, 1991.

38 Poli, R., S. Cagnoni, R. Livi, G. Coppini, and G. Valli, *A Neural Network Expert System for Diagnosing and Treating Hypertension*, IEEE Computer, pp. 64–71, March 1991.

39 Newell, A., and H. Simon, *Computer Science as an Empirical Enquiry*, in J. Haugeland (eds.) Mind Design, Montgomery, VT, Bradford Books, 1981.

40 Fodor, J. A., and Z. W. Pylyshyn, *Connectionism and cognitive architecture: A critical analysis*, Cognition, 28, pp. 3–71, 1988.

41 Bechtel, W., and A. Abrahamsen, *Connectionism and the Mind*, Blackwell, 1991.

# Appendix 1
# Commercial applications of knowledge-based systems

This appendix describes selected commercial applications of knowledge-based systems (KBSs). The emphasis in the following description is not on trying to list all KBS applications in business and industry (a futile task today, given the large number of successful KBS applications), but rather to present brief descriptions of selected commercial KBS applications.

The following three criteria have been used to select the KBS applications listed in this appendix:

- first, the KBS application should demonstrate the use of KBS technology to some useful task in organizations. Attempts have been made to include KBS applications from a variety of domains
- second, the KBS application should be in actual commercial use (and not limited to a research prototype)
- finally, a reasonably complete description of the system should be available.

Each of the following descriptions of KBSs consist of four parts: a short introduction listing the primary application characteristics (see Chapter 5) of the KBS, a description of the domain to provide the context for the KBS application, some details about the technical architecture and the development process of the KBS and, finally, the organizational benefits and issues related to the KBS application. Actual details and figures are provided when available. Note that KBS applications described in earlier chapters (such as those described in Chapter 2) are not included in the following list.

## Expert auditing of airline passenger tickets[1]

The passenger revenue accounting (PRA) system at Northwest Airlines audits approximately 60,000 tickets daily, and uses a KBS to compare each item on the ticket against the complex set of rules governing airline fares, and commission programs to detect any discrepancies.

| | |
|---|---|
| Task type: | monitoring |
| User support type: | front-end interface |
| System type: | standalone — linked |
| Activity type: | enhanced knowledge processing within audit activity, and enhanced information flow to the marketing activity |

### Domain
The activity of auditing airline tickets consists of two parts — a fare audit, and a commission audit. The aim of the fare audit is to ensure that the correct fare has been collected on the tickets. This process is complicated by a large number of complex restrictions on airline fares such as advance purchase restrictions, and combinability restrictions (conditions under which fares of different types can be combined on the same ticket). Northwest often changes restrictions on about 10,000 fares in a single day. The commission audit checks whether the ticketing agents have been awarded the correct commissions on the airline tickets sold by them. The task of commission audit is complicated by the large number of tickets sold per day and the different commission programs (about 40,000) between Northwest and its travel agents. Agents typically do not explicitly state the specific type of commission program under which they are claiming the commission. An accurate commission audit allows Northwest to check accuracy of the claimed commissions, and to verify the results of its marketing efforts.

### System structure and development
To mirror the real-life domain knowledge, the audit KBS has two distinct knowledge-bases: a fare audit knowledge-base, and a commission audit knowledge-base. The fare audit knowledge-base has two inputs: data about ticket sales from clearing houses located worldwide, and the fare database which is obtained from daily transmissions from the Airline Tariff Publishing Company (which provides historical information on fares of all airlines). There are about 250 rules for auditing fares. In case an error is found, a textual message describing the error is printed out. The commission audit knowledge-base also has two sources of input — the data about ticket sales, and data from the marketing contract database (which contains details of all marketing contracts between Northwest and its travel agents). The conditions of the commission programs are more complex than those of fares, and it is not possible to write a rule for each different possible combination. The compromise solution adopted was to divide conditions into generic categories, and then to write rules for each category. There are about 350 rules in the commission audit knowledge-base. Any fare or commission discrepancies found by the system are flagged, and brought to the notice of a revenue-accounting staff member. Commission programs which are found to be unprofitable to Northwest are detected more easily by the marketing department.

The KBS was implemented using a high-end shell tool (ART, marketed by Inference of California). The full-time efforts of three knowledge engineers for one year was required to develop the system. The KBS was implemented as a production release on May 21, 1990. One knowledge engineer is devoted on a full-time basis to maintenance of the KBS.

### Benefits and issues

A complete audit of airline tickets had never been attempted at Northwest Airlines, due to the sheer volume and complexity of the task. The audit KBS has made it possible for Northwest to regularly and completely audit its tickets. Northwest estimates a benefit of about $10–30 million annually from the use of the KBS. These savings arise from elimination of unprofitable commission programs, fewer errors in the auditing process, and the overall automation of the audit process. The KBS has provided Northwest with a greater degree of flexibility in its auditing process, and has also helped to enhance its marketing efforts.

## Inspector: monitoring foreign exchange trading[2]

Inspector is an expert system installed by Manufacturers Hanover Trust (MHT) in 1989 to monitor, on a global basis, trading activities in foreign exchange. Worldwide trading activity data is centralized in a relational database in New York, and at the end of each day, the Inspector KBS is used to verify every transaction, and to look for possible irregularities. The system runs during the night, and is able to produce all relevant reports for action by the start of the next day.

| | |
|---|---|
| Task type: | monitoring |
| User support type: | replacement |
| System type: | standalone — linked |
| Activity type: | enhanced knowledge processing in monitoring activity |

### Domain

About two dozen different international MHT locations conduct deals (each deal varying from $5–10 million in size) in foreign exchange trading totalling several billion dollars every day. Due to the nature of foreign exchange trading, dealers are allowed to make decisions about large sums of money with a high degree of independence. The risk of dealers becoming over-enthusiastic and overstepping the risk-management policies of the company is high. In addition, as both the volume of transactions per day and the dollar amount of transactions are very high, the environment is conducive to fraud. It would be ideal if a bank could verify the accuracy of every transaction. However, this requires a person to have the extensive knowledge of foreign exchange trading procedures, operational control and accounting practices, and the patience to go through thousands of transactions every day to gain the satisfaction of locating a few suspicious deals. This is, to say the least, highly inefficient and unrealistic. Yet the potential payoff is high. A single unauthorized or fraudulent trade can damage the institution's profitability and its reputation.

Traditionally, financial institutions have relied on dealer self-discipline, risk-management limits, back-office verification, senior management experience, and periodic internal and external audit-checks to minimize such problems. Despite these safeguards, losses due to irregular practices are not uncommon, and are very often in the range of millions of dollars annually.

### System architecture and development
The Inspector KBS is a standalone system with strong linkages to the centralized relational database for accessing transactional data. For any suspicious deal, it checks with the database to see if any other similar deals were flagged (because fraudulent deals rarely appear suspicious at first glance). Based on this historical query, it decides whether to perform additional analyses, or to file the transaction in an alert log in the database. The knowledge base is based on current risk-management policies and controls, augmented by the practical knowledge and experience of traders, chief dealers, seniors managers, controllers, and auditors. Trader fraud can happen in many imaginable, as well as unimaginable ways. To capture the unimaginable, the experts had to consider situations that have never, and should never occur, but were they to occur would cause alarm. MHT has built a network of telecommunication links between branches and head office to centralize the transaction information into the relational database. The Inspector KBS operates on top of the relational database, and is dependent on conventional technologies (databases and networking) for its success.

The development team for the Inspector KBS consisted of four persons: a foreign exchange expert, a knowledge engineer, and two programmers. The development process was started in January 1989, and the first deployment was done in September 1989.

### Benefits and issues
The following benefits have resulted from the application of the KBS:

● full inspection and fast turnaround — the system inspects every transaction and produces reports to management within twenty four hours of the time of booking the transaction. To obtain this audit benefit, senior management at MHT specially assigned an experienced foreign exchange person to review the daily reports of Inspector, and to investigate alerts, when necessary

● knowledge retention — the system draws on the practical experience of chief dealers, senior managers, controllers, and auditors. Such knowledge about irregular practices may not be used very often, and can be difficult to retrieve when in need. The KBS helps to maintain this type of knowledge for use in times of need

● prevention — such a system acts as a deterrent to would-be rule-breakers. Centralizing the knowledge processing serves to magnify this 'big brother' effect

● management reports — creating the centralized database of daily transactions was necessary to implement the Inspector KBS, but this database has proven to be a rich source of timely and precise management reports. This is leading to the growth of a sophisticated management information system within MHT.

There is no doubt that the project has added value to MHT. However, within the domain of monitoring foreign exchange activities, certain issues of concern are:

- **system maintenance** — with continuous advances in banking technology, and the technology of foreign exchange trading, new techniques for fraud are bound to arise. The knowledge that the system is 'frozen' on the current technology may become an invitation to innovation frauds
- **division of responsibility** — although monitoring activities are now centralized, this does not mean that local management is relieved of all responsibility in this regard. The audit centralization may put the local management in a difficult situation, and force them to set informal local rules which are more stringent than head office rules so as to be on the safe side.

## Nynex Max: troubleshooting telephones[3]

The Max KBS is used by Nynex (a regional Bell operating company in the USA) to help diagnose faults in (currently residential) phone lines.

| | |
|---|---|
| Task type: | diagnosis |
| User support type: | partial replacement |
| System type: | standalone — linked |
| Activity type: | enhanced knowledge processing within maintenance activity |

### Domain
Diagnosing and maintaining customer-reported telephone faults is an important problem for telephone companies. This diagnosis task has been recently complicated by the proliferation of new types of customer premise equipment (such as sophisticated answering machines), and non-standard equipment (not envisaged in the current diagnosis systems). The goals of improved maintenance are: reduced time to diagnose and repair, a reduction in repeat complaints (from the same customer about the same problem), a reduction in false dispatches (i.e., sending out a technician when the actual problem is in the customer premise equipment), and a reduction in double dispatches (i.e., sending the repair technician to the customer's home when the problem is in the cable, or in the central office).

### System structure and development
The existing diagnosis procedure consists of customers calling a centralized number, where maintenance administrators diagnose the fault, and dispatch technicians. There is an automated facility called the MLT system which performs many routine checks on the customer's line, and reports the results to the maintenance administrator to assist in the diagnosis task. The Max KBS is designed to emulate the behavior and function of the maintenance administrator.

The core of the Max system is a knowledge-base consisting of about 75 rules. The diagnosis procedure is based on five categories of information: the MLT electrical signature (such as voltages and resistances on the faulty line), the type of switching equipment (to which the customer is attached), the class of customer's service, the weather, and the number of stages of cable facilities in the customer's line. A forward chaining process is used to reach possible diagnoses from the available data. Under certain conditions, Max can decide that the available MLT data is inconclusive, and ask for fresh electrical tests.

The output of the Max system is presented in the form of abbreviated English sentences. An important problem in constructing the knowledge base was the fact that, even existing maintenance administrators within Nynex did not have a deep knowledge of the tests performed by the MLT system. Thus the company had to go to seasoned veterans who worked before the installation of the MLT system to determine the true nature and significance of the tests performed by the MLT facility.

The entire Max system was programmed by three people and took a period of 2.5 years to develop, from conception to deployment. During the implementation phase, many minor alterations had to be made to adjust to local regulations. This was achieved by introducing additional parameters in the knowledge base which could be tuned to reflect regional differences. The Expert Systems Lab within Nynex Science and Technology has assumed responsibility for the maintenance of Max. Currently, Max is being expanded to include the more complex problem of diagnosing faulty equipment in large businesses.

### Benefits and issues

Max is running in 42 maintenance centers in New York and New England regions (for virtually all residence-oriented maintenance centers). It screens 38% of all troubles i.e., about 10,400 complaints per day. A comparison of Max's diagnoses with that of a human expert found 96% agreement. In an evaluation study (done over a seven-week period for two years — one without Max, and the other using Max — in the same maintenance center), the Max KBS was found to reduce the number of false dispatches from 9.39% to 8.76% (i.e., nearly a 1000 saved dispatches over the seven-week period). The Max KBS is saving Nynex around $ 6 million per year[4]. Other benefits are improved decision-making, and higher efficiency at the maintenance centers of Nynex.

Max has caused some reassignment of jobs within the maintenance administrators, and has caused fears of layoffs within some sectors of the company's staff. In particular, clerical and craft workers tend to see it as having a destabilizing effect on their work environment. This problem had to be managed effectively by managers. Currently, the Max KBS operates in 42 different locations independently. There is some concern about having knowledge about a critical task being stored in so many different locations, and some managers would like to see all the different Max KBSs consolidated into one large maintenance center. However, others argue for the decentralized strategy by citing the importance of staying tuned to regional differences. Thus there is a debate between centralization and decentralization, which is yet to be resolved.

## Lending advisor: credit analysis[5]

The task of credit analysis is repetitive, and many heuristics are involved in the decision process. The Lending Advisor is a skeletal KBS for the task of credit analysis. It is designed and marketed by Syntelligence of Sunnyvale, California.

| | |
|---|---|
| Task type: | diagnosis |
| User support type: | assistant |
| System type: | standalone — linked |
| Activity type: | enhanced knowledge processing in credit analysis activity |

## Domain

The credit analysis process involves evaluating the credit-worthiness of a customer based on a variety of criteria, and determining a credit limit. This is possible on the premise that past experience can be used as a guide in predicting the credit-worthiness of future customers, or of existing customers in the future. Analysis of the credit-worthiness of customers can be synthesized, for example, in terms of five broad categories of attributes as shown in Table A1.1[6]. A KBS is appropriate for this task because of the repetitive nature of the task, and the extensive use of heuristics for problem solution.

A KBS application in this domain will need two sources of information: a customer database, and a knowledge base. The customer database will contain all available data pertaining to the bank's customers. The knowledge base will consist of two parts, one containing heuristic knowledge that reflects the expert's knowledge and expertise for assessing the credit-worthiness of customers, and the other containing a model to support the determination of credit limit. This reflects the need to evaluate a customer according to the five attribute categories of Table A1.1, and to use judgement to integrate the conclusions of the results of the evaluation.

## System architecture and development

The Lending Advisor is a skeletal KBS containing generic knowledge about credit analysis. Syntelligence adapts and tunes the Lending Advisor to meet the needs of different customers. The design of the Lending Advisor is based on the following four elements

| Categories | Attributes |
|---|---|
| Financial strength | Audited or unaudited statements |
|  | Proforma or actual statements |
|  | Profitability |
|  | Debt management |
|  | Liquidity |
|  | Intangibles |
| Customer background | Number of years in business |
|  | Number of years of relationship with bank |
|  | Perceived management quality |
|  | Recent filing of bankruptcy/liquidation |
|  | Nature of bank references |
| Payment record | Past payment record (with bank) |
|  | Past payment record (trade) |
|  | Internal or cash flow problems |
| Business potential and frequency | Growth potential |
|  | Customer's market position |
|  | Market for firm's other products |
|  | Order frequency |
| Geographical location | Perceived economic climate in customer location |
|  | Prior experience in customer location |

Table A1.1 Categories and attributes for credit-worthiness analysis

of collective credit experience, which determine how a bank manages and obtains its portfolio:

- analytical credit methodology — this makes the decision process more consistent and thorough. The questions asked are the following. What types of analyses are required? What outside information is needed? How do the analyses fit into the structure of the credit memorandum?

- credit analysis and approval processes — this streamlines the decision process. It also ensures that stated policies have been met e.g., if the bank's policy requires that loans for a disk drive manufacturer be approved by the technology sub-committee, then the system would give that instruction. It examines the following aspects. Who is responsible for completing each aspect of the analysis methodology? What are the steps to follow? What are the relevant limits and requirements?

- institutional preferences — this makes such preferences explicit, and easily understood by loan analysts. The preference set can be subdivided into: analytical preferences (such as the relative emphases to place on cash flow, traditional ratios, and liquidity in the preliminary assessment of the borrower's strength), approach preferences (such as hands-on operating quality analyses, solvency analyses, and management character analyses), and attitude (by focusing on the balance between aggressive marketing and good asset quality, and by ensuring that the bank's strategic goals are considered).

The Lending Advisor KBS maintains a predetermined balance between risk and reward in portfolio volume, asset quality, profitability, and customer quality. It integrates all the above factors from the perspective of the bank's strategic goals. The system also alerts the loan officers when a credit deteriorates significantly. It could be designed to suggest solutions to the problems, or simply raise an alert for the loan analyst's attention. The Lending Advisor is a mainframe IBM-based system, and fits into the traditional hardware environment of most banks. Developing the Lending Advisor has taken over 50 man years of technical efforts. The Lending Advisor is used by many banks including First Wachovia, Wells Fargo, and Bank One in USA[7].

### Benefits and issues
It should be emphasized that different banks may adopt similar credit analyses and approval processes, but the preferences and attitudes vary widely. It is possible to tailor the Lending Advisor to suit each bank's own credit culture. Thus, the Lending Advisor skeletal KBS is applicable to many banks and financial institutions. It not only evaluates loan applications, but can also be designed to predict loan requirements of existing customers as it is integrated with the existing database. This is particularly useful for determining marketing strategies and campaigns. Benefits are also obtained from the knowledge acquisition process. While tailoring the system, senior officers are forced to improve their credit analyses by making them more consistent and thorough.

In such a KBS application, questions are frequently asked about the accountability of the bank officers vis-à-vis the system. It is generally up to the bank to determine the level of accountability. Invariably, most banks take the view that officers should be accountable instead of the KBS, and emphasize such accountability, and the need to overrule the system's assessment (when necessary), during training.

# Agatha: diagnosing personal computer boards[8]

Agatha is a KBS used by Hewlett Packard (HP) to test and diagnose complex computer boards.

| | |
|---|---|
| Task type: | diagnosis |
| User support type: | assistant |
| System type: | (integrated) backend |
| Activity type: | enhanced knowledge processing in diagnostic activity and improving effectiveness of other manufacturing activities. |

## Domain

Implementations of HP's new reduced instruction set architecture (RISC) have produced some of the most complex computer boards ever manufactured by HP. Each RISC computer board can contain upto eight very large scale integrated (VLSI) chips, several high-speed memory chips, one or more buses with over 100 lines, and several other components. Besides the complexity of boards, the diagnosis task is also influenced by the facts that technicians have to remember many special-case failure modes, diagnostic procedures often produce volumes of data which are difficult to analyze and manipulate, and there is considerable uncertainty in test results.

Due to these reasons, technicians were experiencing problems in efficiently diagnosing faulty computer boards. This was resulting in a backlog of undiagnosed boards accumulating at a rate of 10% per month. To save time, technicians were often taking shortcuts, but these actions sometimes lead to replacement of incorrect parts, thus causing further repair cycles.

A KBS solution was deemed as appropriate in this context because expertise was available, but in short supply, and the process of training of technicians was expensive and slow. The diagnosis procedure was becoming a bottleneck in the entire manufacturing process, and significant gains could be expected by removing this bottleneck.

## System structure and development

Due to the functional diversity of the components on the computer board, a blackboard-type architecture was used. Agatha is made of several slices. Each slice is like a small KBS (a knowledge source[9]), which is responsible for analyzing the results of a particular set of diagnostic tests. All slices cooperate with each other, and communicate with the help of the diagnose manager. The diagnose manager has overall responsibility for coordinating the entire test procedure, invoking separate slices at specific moments, and interfacing with the user. The blackboard-type architecture has facilitated the maintenance of the system, because new board types and components can be accommodated by adding new slices to the architecture.

Agatha is completely integrated as a backend to the existing board testing equipment, PRISM (which can perform specific tests on computer boards). Computer boards are passed through PRISM, and Agatha diagnoses boards found faulty by PRISM. Agatha produces its output as a list of parts recommended for repair. Agatha is coded almost entirely in Prolog, and is the result of joint efforts between HP's divisions in Bristol,

England, and Colorado, USA. Agatha has been in routine use since January 1990 at three sites within HP (two manufacturing facilities and one field-repair service center). A manufacturing facility uses Agatha 24 hours a day. The Integrated Circuit Business Division in Colorado, the primary user of Agatha, is responsible for its maintenance.

### Benefits and issues

There have been several observed benefits from the Agatha system. First, it has helped to reduce a bottleneck in the manufacturing process, and eliminated the backlog in the diagnosis procedure. Second, Agatha saves time and costs in the diagnostic activity. Third, it provides a more thorough and consistent level of diagnosis on a continuous basis. Though it is difficult to quantify the full effect of Agatha within HP, diagnostic times have generally been reduced significantly — by around 40% (in some cases, by as much as 80%). Agatha has also had an impact on training of technicians and has, at one production site, caused a 25% reduction in technician training time, and a dramatic improvement in the ramp-up time for new technicians. It has also resulted in greater user-satisfaction due to a friendlier interface to the diagnostic equipment.

## Qdes: quality design for steel products[10]

Meeting customer demands for higher quality is a major business focus at Nippon Steel Corporation (NSC), the largest supplier of steel in the world. Qdes is a KBS used by NSC to solve problems in the quality design of steel products.

| | |
|---|---|
| Task type: | structured design |
| User support type: | assistant |
| System type: | standalone — linked |
| Activity type: | enhanced knowledge processing in design activity with an important impact on manufacturing |

### Domain

Customer requests for new steel products (for example, sections of different sizes) have become more complex recently, with an accompanying increase of emphasis on quality. NSC employs quality design experts, whose job is to determine whether production of a desired product is possible, and to design the product. The normal process of quality design at NSC consists of two phases: a macro design phase at head office, and a micro design phase at the manufacturing plant. Experts at head office typically design the macro production and operating conditions. For both types of conditions, experts rely on their knowledge of similar prior requests, and use parameters from previous requests for their macro designs in the current case. For new materials, or dramatically new requests, the experts have to use a considerable amount of intuition. The experts at the manufacturing plant perform a detailed design of the production and operating conditions for the customer's request. Knowledge of the production and operating conditions of prior similar requests are again used significantly by the experts. Considerable intuition is also required to determine production stability, and the feasibility of production.

A KBS solution is appropriate for this domain because quality design experts are scarce, and difficult to train or recruit. At the same time, there is considerable pressure on NSC to decrease the time required to perform the design process.

## System architecture and development

The Qdes system consists of two interconnected KBSs, one at head office, and another at the manufacturing plant. The head office component of Qdes performs a macro design of the product, and passes control to the manufacturing plant component of Qdes when it judges that a detailed design is necessary. Taken as a whole, the Qdes system first assesses whether a specific customer's request can be produced, and if deemed feasible, it creates a plan for the design, including operating conditions and cost figures. Because of the special nature of the domain knowledge, Qdes integrates a variety of special knowledge representation and inferencing techniques:

● case-based reasoning[11] — Qdes has an extensive database of prior product designs, and it searches this database for the most similar previous request to use as a starting point in its design procedure. It includes many rules both for selecting the most appropriate prior request, and for adapting the prior request solution to the current problem. Case-based reasoning is the primary mode of knowledge representation and reasoning within Qdes

● neural networks — a three-layered network with the back-propagation learning algorithm is used to help experts make rough intuitive judgements about feasibility of production of new products. There are three types of input conditions — tensile conditions, thickness conditions, and temperature conditions. The output specifies whether the product design is feasible, or unfeasible, or partially feasible

● fuzzy logic — this is used to represent imprecise classifications of test results, and uncertainty in the domain. For example, changes in temperature can be small, or rather small, or medium, or big where each of these is a label for an appropriate fuzzy set. The use of fuzzy logic is useful for effective reasoning with imprecise rules.

To support case-based reasoning, Qdes includes a maintenance component which stores solutions of current requests into the database of prior cases, so that it can be used sometime in the future. Thus Qdes has a capability for self-maintaining its knowledge base. The entire Qdes system has 3,000 rules, and about 500,000 lines of code. It is implemented using the Art KBS shell tool, and is integrated with the Unify database management system. It runs on Sun engineering workstations. About 18 months of time, and 350 man-months of effort were needed for developing the Qdes KBS. Qdes has been in use since May 1990.

## Benefits and issues

NSC receives about 20 customer requests each month for shaped-steel products, and all of these requests are currently handled by Qdes. Qdes has reduced the design cycle time by 85%, and has improved the accuracy of the design procedure by about 30%. The cumulative knowledge of Qdes (in the form of stored prior cases) improves automatically over time due to its internal case accumulation capabilities. Qdes has allowed NSC to save approximately $200,000 annually. Qdes is being expanded in two directions: it is being transferred to other NSC plants, and its knowledge is being extended to accommodate the design of new types of products.

## OHCS: hydraulic circuit design[1,2]

Most manufacturing industries use oil hydraulic systems (which transmit and control power through the use of pressurized oil within an enclosed circuit) extensively. OHCS is a KBS, designed and implemented at Kayaba Industry Company, for hydraulic design.

Task type: structured design
User support type: assistant
System type: standalone — linked
Activity type: enhanced knowledge processing within design activity

### Domain
The design of hydraulic circuits can be seen as being composed of four phases: circuit design (a graphical representation of the hydraulic circuit is obtained), component selection (during which the designer selects commercial hydraulic machine components), static and dynamic analyses of circuits (which consist of simulation analyses, both quantitative and qualitative in nature, to determine the behavior of the circuit), and inspection of completed drawings (a primarily qualitative process, which includes checks to ensure that the functions of each circuit correspond to specifications). Each of the above phases is typically done by a separate expert. A major problem in this approach is that when the final inspection reveals a discrepancy between the functions and the specifications of the circuit, much of the previous design and analyses have to be redone — causing great productivity losses in the process. There are also communication barriers, and lags between the different experts, which make the entire design process tedious and slow. A KBS seems to be appropriate for this domain as it would enable the knowledge of all experts to be aggregated, and brought to bear on the design problem simultaneously.

### System architecture and development
The OHCS KBS integrates the knowledge of all experts involved in the design of hydraulic circuits. The system has five major components:

● generation of circuit diagrams — OHCS is able to generate (using the acquired knowledge of circuit designers) computer-aided drawings (CAD) which meet desired specifications. A rich object-oriented interface allows the user to click graphical items from a menu, and rapidly configure circuits

● component selection — OHCS contains an object-oriented database with descriptions of about 1500 commercial hydraulic components, and suggests the best components from its database for the generated circuit diagram

● analytical models — the KBS automatically generates appropriate analytical models for the hydraulic circuit. Static and dynamic simulations can be carried out with these models

● quantitative simulation — OHCS performs a numeric simulation of the hydraulic model with the help of the generated analytical models. Prior to OHCS, the simulation component was completely separated from the circuit design stages. OHCS also makes it possible to repeat simulations till certain circuit parameters are satisfied

● diagram inspection — the system incorporates the qualitative knowledge required for inspection of the circuit to see that it meets specifications.

Three forms of knowledge representation techniques are used in OHCS:

(1) declarative knowledge (such as knowledge about components)

(2) IF..THEN.. rules (to express various heuristics)

(3) algorithmic knowledge and models (often expressed as functions).

To respond to the needs of the domain, OHCS also provides for a tight coupling between qualitative and quantitative modes of reasoning.

It took five persons about 18 months to develop the OHCS system. It has been deployed since 1988. It uses the Art KBS shell tool, and runs on a Symbolics Lisp workstation. There are about 700 rules within OHCS.

### Benefits and issues

The OHCS system has reduced the time for hydraulic circuit design by more than 50%. The overall quality of the produced circuits has also increased dramatically. Kayaba Industry Company is now looking into the use of KBS technology for other stages of the design operation, namely the layout design, and the generation of the quality assurance sheet.


## MOCA: airline maintenance scheduling[13]

Federal Aviation Administration regulations in the USA require all planes to stop over at a regional maintenance center at least once every 60 hours of flying time. Scheduling airline maintenance for an airline of the size of American Airlines (AA) is a formidable task. Until recently, this was a manual task performed by the Maintenance Operations Center controllers at AA. Today AA uses MOCA, a KBS, to automate the process of maintenance scheduling, and to provide intelligent assistance to the maintenance controllers.

| | |
|---|---|
| Task type: | planning and scheduling |
| User support type: | assistant |
| System type: | standalone — linked |
| Activity type: | enhanced knowledge processing in maintenance scheduling activity |

### Domain

AA operates more than 550 planes, and flies over 2200 scheduled flights a day to over 160 destinations worldwide. Besides the sheer size of AA's fleet, maintenance planning is complicated by the dynamic constraints in the domain. An aircraft changes routing every 2–3 days, and unanticipated events such as weather, crew restrictions, and unforeseen maintenance demands can also change the routing of aircrafts with little advance notice. Ensuring that all aircrafts in AA's fleet are maintained regularly in such a dynamic environment, is a time-consuming and challenging task. Maintenance controllers are required to plan new routings for planes, react to dynamic and unforeseen events, and replan all affected maintenance routings. It is not uncommon to havemore than 50% of AA's entire fleet on some sort of maintenance routing. Prior to MOCA, each controller typically routed (manually) 60–100 aircrafts on a normal day. Besides being slow and inefficient, the entire maintenance problem was burdened by paperwork (such as station sheets, which list all current aircraft routings by fleet type for all flights flown in a single day), and unwieldy documents (such as manuals listing all maintenance requirements for a particular aircraft). The maintenance controllers at AA also have to communicate with other AA centers, such as the Systems Operations Center (which is responsible for the daily operation of the airline) for scheduling maintenance.

The importance of automating the maintenance scheduling problem had long been realized at AA. Several automation attempts using traditional operational research methods failed to produce satisfactory results due to the complexity of the domain, and the dynamic nature of the constraints. This led to the exploration of the utility of KBS technology for this task. A quick prototype built during the three-month period, December 1987 to February 1988, convinced AA of the suitability of KBS technology. Besides, it was seen that a KBS could provide a user-friendly, reliable, and interactive intelligent aid to the maintenance controllers to automate routine aspects of their jobs.

### System architecture and development

The MOCA system consists of a set of modules, with each module being responsible for providing a particular functionality. The six important modules are (1) a communication module to provide access to the real-time flight operations system (FOS), which stores all information pertinent to daily operations of AA (2) a planning module for the resolution of all planning goals (3) a dynamic changes module to deal with special unforeseen events (4) an impact analysis module to compare solutions and provide explanations for differences (5) a plan generation module for generating daily plans, and (6) an interface module for interfacing with the user.

MOCA is developed on Texas Instrument's Micro Explorer workstation using the Art KBS shell tool. The entire system has more than 5000 rules. One of the most challenging aspects of the implementation of MOCA was to interface the Micro Explorer to the large transactions-processing system, FOS. When first started, MOCA loads seven days of flight data from FOS. During operation, MOCA receives updates about modifications in FOS at intervals of five minutes. The user interface is specially designed to provide maximum flexibility to the maintenance controllers. A heuristic search procedure is used by the planning module to generate the best maintenance schedules under the current conditions. This allows MOCA to explore more alternative solutions in a shorter period of time. The user can either accept MOCA's first answer, or can ask the system to produce alternative answers.

MOCA was deployed in a phased manner over a period of several months. Particular emphasis was paid to training, as the maintenance controllers were, by and large, not computer literate. MOCA is now used by the controllers 24 hours a day, 7 days a week.

### Benefits and issues

The system has been widely accepted by the maintenance controllers because it is 99% reliable, produces solutions of high quality (about 95% of its first answers are accepted) in a timely manner, and is easy to use. MOCA has dramatically increased the degree of access that controllers have to information. This has, in turn, enriched their jobs significantly. At the company level, the most important benefit of MOCA has been that it has allowed AA to grow in size, and yet allowed its maintenance controllers to perform their task effectively. Besides eliminating virtually all paperwork associated with maintenance scheduling, MOCA has reduced the number of flight breaks (which occur when an aircraft has to deviate from its normal operating schedule to satisfy some external constraints), has increased the average number of hours an aircraft flies between regular maintenance checks, and has allowed an increase in the capacity of flights handled by the Maintenance Operations Center without an increase in the number of staff members (a significant savings in training and salary costs to AA). It is estimated[14] that MOCA saves AA at least $500,000 annually.

## Ecapp: intelligent process planning[15]

As product life cycles shrink and pressures mount for reducing time to market, it is critical for a computer manufacturing company such as Digital to be able to quickly and correctly produce routings for manufacturing products. Ecapp is a KBS in use within Digital since March 1989, which integrates expert process-engineering knowledge, capabilities of specific manufacturing plants, and product information to generate the best route for a product through a factory.

> Task type: planning
> User support type: assistant
> System type: standalone — linked
> Activity type: enhanced knowledge processing in the process planning activity, and enhanced knowledge transfers between the design and planning activities

### Domain
Specially in the computer industry, the number and complexity of new products is increasing rapidly. Due to the high capital costs of the automatic assembly equipment used to manufacture these products, the insertion patterns for driving these machines used to be manually developed by the process engineers in the manufacturing plant. This task was time-consuming (typically between 8–16 hours each), tedious, error-prone, and made the assembly machine unavailable for regular work during that period. A certain amount of process flexibility is desired to account for dynamic constraints, such as product mix changes, and unanticipated events (e.g., machine failures). Due to communication gaps between process engineers and the design engineers, products designed by the design engineers did not make efficient use of the assembly machines. The normal time required to introduce a new product into production by a manufacturing engineer was about 1–2 days. Conventional attempts at automation failed because in each case, the manufacturing engineer was still required to make decisions regarding the best route for the product (which required a considerable effort from the part of the engineer).

### System architecture and development
Ecapp has been designed to meet the following goals: (a) reduce time to market (b) improve consistency in generated process plans (c) reduce machine setup times, (d) improve productivity of process engineers (e) adjust to daily changes in manufacturing

plant's operations, and (f) create and preserve a process-planning knowledge base. The knowledge base of Ecapp contains four mini-knowledge bases: an equipment knowledge base (giving descriptions of assembly machines in the plant), a process knowledge base (describing process operations in the plant), a product database (containing knowledge about product features), and a manufacturing engineering knowledge base (containing heuristics used by process engineers for route selection, and ease-of-manufacture checking). As output, Ecapp generates all feasible routes for the product through the plant, setup reports for each assembly machine's configuration, process sheets (detailing steps required to assemble the product), product time standards, and the actual insertion patterns which are used to drive the assembly machines. The user interface is object-oriented, user-friendly, and provides numerous flexible features to process engineers (such as the ability to explore or compare alternative process routes).

Ecapp is implemented in Vax Lisp and the Knowledge Craft KBS shell tool. It runs on the Vax family of minicomputers and workstations. Ecapp was developed and implemented during a period of 2.5 years. It was put into actual production use in July 1989 in the Augusta plant of Digital.

### Benefits and issues

Ecapp is currently being used on all new products introduced at the Augusta plant, and for the older products which can be transferred on the new automatic assembly equipment (for which Ecapp is designed). The following benefits have been observed from the use of Ecapp within Digital: (a) a reduction in product introduction times, (b) consistent generation of high quality process plans (c) reduction of lost time on automatic assembly machines (d) facilitation of communication with design engineers (who can use Ecapp to design products for manufacturability), and (e) enhanced ability to react to dynamic environmental changes.

## Bibliography and suggested readings

The best sources for descriptions of commercial applications of KBSs are the proceedings, (Schorr & Rappaport 89), (Rappaport & Smith 90), and (Smith & Scott 91), of a series of conferences on the Innovative Applications of Artificial Intelligence, organized by the American Association for Artificial Intelligence (AAAI). The descriptions of most of the KBS applications in this appendix have been taken from papers presented at these conferences. These conferences are held annually during the summer. Descriptions of commercial applications of KBSs can also be found in the proceedings of the IEEE Conferences on Artificial Intelligence Applications (published by IEEE Computer Society Press), and other conferences on artificial intelligence topics. An excellent, non-technical description of how companies are actually using KBSs for gaining a competitive advantage is available in reference (Feigenbaum et al 88). A fairly large catalogue of KBSs applications is given in books by Harmon et al (Harmon et al 88) and Rauch-Hindin (Rauch-Hindin 88). Reference (Chorafas & Stenmann 91) provides an excellent overview of KBS applications in banking and finance. A recent article in Business Week (Schwartz & Treece 92) presents an useful summary of recent trends in AI applications.

Chorafas, D. N., and H. Steinmann, *Expert Systems in Banking*, MacMillan, London, 1991.

Feigenbaum, E., P. McCorduck, and H. Penny Nii, *The Rise of the Expert Company*, Times Books, 1988.

Harmon, P., R. Maus, and W. Morrissey, *Expert Systems: Tools and Applications*, John Wiley, 1988.

Rappaport, A, and R. Smith, (Eds.), *Innovative Applications of Artificial Intelligence 2*, AAAI Press/MIT Press, 1991.

Rauch-Hindin, W. B., *A Guide to Commercial Artificial Intelligence*, Prentice-Hall, 1988.

Schorr, H. and A. Rappaport, (Eds.), *Innovative Applications of Artificial Intelligence*, AAAI Press/MIT Press, 1989.

Schwartz, E. I., and J. B. Treece, *Smart Programs go to Work*, Business Week, pp. 47–51, March 2, 1992.

Smith, R., and C. Scott, (Eds.), *Innovative Applications of Artificial Intelligence 3*, AAAI Press/MIT Press, 1991.

## Notes

1  Valles, A. J., and J. A. Van Loy, *An Expert Auditing System for Airline Passenger Tickets*, in *Innovative Applications of Artificial Intelligence*, Vol. 3, R. Smith and C. Scott (Eds.), pp. 3–9, AAAI/MIT Press, 1991

2  Byrnes, E., T. Campfield, N. Henry, and S. Waldman, *Inspector: An Expert System for Monitoring Worldwide Trading Activities in Foreign Exchange*, in *Innovative Applications of Artificial Intelligence*, Vol. 2, A. Rappaport and R. Smith (Eds.), AAAI/MIT Press, 1991.

3  Rabinowitz, H., J. Flamholz, E. Wolin and J. Euchner, *Nynex Max: A Telephone Trouble Screening Expert*, in *Innovative Applications of Artificial Intelligence*, Vol. 3, R. Smith and C. Scott (Eds.), pp. 213–230, AAAI/MIT Press, 1991.

4  Schwartz, E. I., and J. B. Treece, *Smart Programs go to Work*, Business Week, pp. 47–51, March 2, 1992.

5  Descriptions of products marketed by Syntelligence can be found in: (a) Duda, R.O., P.E. Hart, R. Reboh, J. Reiter, and T. Risch, *Syntel:Using a Functional Language for Financial Risk Assessment*, IEEE Expert, 2(3), pp. 18–31, 1987; and (b) Hart, P.E., *Syntel: An Architecture for Financial Applications*, in *Innovative Applications of Artificial Intelligence*, H. Schorr and A. Rappaport (Eds.), pp. 63–70, AAAI/MIT Press, 1989.

6  Srinivasan, V., and Y. H. Kim, *Developing Expert Financial Systems: A Case Study of Corporate Credit Management*, Financial Management, Vol. 17, No. 3, pp. 32–44, Autumn 1988.

7  BancA Corporation has developed Power A, a similar loan tracking and evaluation KBS, that is being used at Citibank, Mellon Bank, and the Canadian Imperial Bank of Commerce. Loan evaluation and advisory KBS are also being used by several international banks e.g. Caisse d'Epargne in France, the Cera Spaarbank in Belgium, Union Bank, Credit Suisse in Switzerland, and others.

8  Allred, D., Y. Lichtenstein, C. Priest, M. Bennett and A. Gupta, *Agatha: An Integrated Expert System to Test and Diagnose Complex Personal Computer Boards*, in *Innovative Applications of Artificial Intelligence*, Vol. 3, R. Smith and C. Scott (Eds.), pp. 87–103, AAAI/MIT Press, 1991

9  See description of blackboard systems in Chapter 3.

10 Iwata, Y., and N. Obama, *Qdes: Quality-Design Expert System for Steel Products*, in *Innovative Applications of Artificial Intelligence*, Vol. 3, R. Smith and C. Scott (Eds.), pp. 177–191, AAAI/MIT Press, 1991

11 Case-based reasoning is described in Chapter 3.

12 Nakashima, Y., and T. Baba, *OHCS: Hydraulic Circuit Design Assistant*, in *Innovative Applications of Artificial Intelligence*, Vol. 1, H. Schorr and A. Rappaport (Eds.), pp. 225–236, AAAI/MIT Press, 1989

13 S. Smits and D. Pracht, *MOCA — A Knowledge-Based System for Airline Maintenance Scheduling*, in *Innovative Applications of Artificial Intelligence*, Vol. 3, R. Smith and C. Scott (Eds.), pp. 21–37, AAAI/MIT Press, 1991

14 Schwartz, E. I., and J. B. Treece, *Smart Programs go to Work*, Business Week, pp. 48, March 2, 1992.

15 A. Fraser, H. Sloate, and M. Tseng, *Ecapp: A Process Planning Tool using Artificial Intelligence*, in *Innovative Applications of Artificial Intelligence*, Vol. 2, A. Rappaport and R. Smith (Eds.), pp. 117–130, AAAI/MIT Press, 1991.

# Appendix 2
## Commercial vendors of knowledge-based products

Brief descriptions of selected vendors of commercial knowledge-based system (KBS) products are given here. This appendix is the result of a survey[1] conducted partly by INSEAD MBA student Michel Grunspan. There is a strong bias towards European companies (or the European subsidiaries or distributors of American companies) in the following sample. This makes the following vendor list interesting, because most other such lists focus primarily on the North American market. The following vendor list is neither exhaustive, nor complete. It has the modest aim of providing the reader with a relatively broad perspective on the diversity of KBS vendors and commercial products. It is recommended that this appendix be used in conjunction with the observations made in Chapter 4 about the market for commercial KBS products.

The entry for each vendor consists of the following items of information[2]: name, address, contact person, and brief descriptive features and prices of major products. If available, the revenues earned from KBS products and services are mentioned within brackets below the name of each vendor.

### AICORP
(KBS revenues: $2.4 million)
Address: 138 Technology drive, Waltham, MA 02254, USA
Phone: 1 617 891 6500          Fax: 1 617 893 8919
Contact person: Kristine Copley, Corporate sales representative

1st Class: a KBS tool designed for the easy development and deployment of powerful knowledge-based applications. It uses a spreadsheet or a decision tree for entering knowledge ($2495 on DOS).

KBMS (Knowledge Base Management System): KBMS was originally an IBM mainframe development tool (implemented in C) providing backward and forward chaining and object-oriented knowledge representation. It is today a full function KBS development tool for DOS, OS/2, VAX, and other environments. It can be used in a cooperative processing mode, allows the distribution of applications across multiple platforms, and the access of data stored on remote processors (From $90,000 to $250,000).

### AION Corporation
(KBS revenues: $10 million)
Address: 101 University avenue, Palo Alto, CA 94301, USA
Phone: 1 415 328 9595          Fax: 1 415 321 7728
Contact person: Vaughn G. Hysinger, VP International Operations

ADS (Aion Development System): a comprehensive development workbench for building complex KBSs. ADS combines backward and forward chaining, procedural processing, frames, and object-oriented programming with an extended environment to provide a complete object processing system. It provides support for transaction processing and for database code. A high performance pre-compiler is also available. (From $7,000 on PC to $60-100,000 on MVS).

### Arity Corporation
(KBS revenues: $1.8 million)
Address: Damonville, Concord, MA 01742, USA
Phone: 1 508 371 1243          Fax: 1 508 371 1487
Contact person: Meredith Bartlett, VP Marketing and Sales

Prolog: a compiler and interpreter for Prolog ($650)

Expert development package: a set of development tools running on top of Arity Prolog. It includes frame and rule-based knowledge representation, and backward chaining inference. It is targeted at developers wanting to embed KBSs in applications ($295).

## Blackboard Technology Group
Address: PO box 44, 401 Main Street, Amherst, MA 01002, USA
Phone: 1 413 256 8990        Fax: 1 413 256 3179
Contact person: Daniel D. Corkill, President

GBB Version 2.0: a common LISP programming framework for constructing high-performance blackboard-based KBS applications. GBB supplies the blackboard infrastructure technology, allowing developers to concentrate on domain-specific applications. GBB provides the benefits of blackboard technology — modular and independent knowledge sources, multilevel problem representations, incremental solution development, and flexible and opportunistic control capabilities ($5000 on Mac).

## Bull S A
(KBS revenues: FF9 million)
Address: 68 route de Versailles 78430 Louveciennes, France
Phone: 33 1 39 02 4211        Fax: 33 1 39 02 4744
Contact person: Sylvie le Bars, Promotions and Communications Manager, CEDIAG

KOOL 4WD: a KBS generator with objects and rules. It supports classes and meta-classes, attributes and attribute descriptors, inheritance, daemons, and methods. (From FF75,000 on PC to FF120,000 on workstations).

CHARME: a KBS tool based upon a constraint propagation mechanism.

SESAME: a KBS tool based upon a translator which analyses, understands, and translates a natural language request into SQL.

EDEN (Expert Diagnostic Environment): an application-specific KBS for industrial applications.

## Cambridge Consultants
(KBS revenues: £1.5 million)
Address: Science park, Milton Road, Cambridge CB4 4DW, UK
Phone: 44 223 420024        Fax: 44 223 423373
Contact person: Ron Smith, Software technology group

MUSE: a toolkit for development of real-time KBS applications. It consists of a package of knowledge representation languages coupled with a set of supporting tools for creating, testing, and delivering advanced KBS applications (including forward and backward chaining systems). (£15000 on a single SUN 3/4 workstation).

CORNELIUS: a KBS tool designed for building applications for diagnosing faults. It allows a maintenance specialist to build the KBS. Cornelius is based on the notions of function, component, behavioral link, and test. No knowledge of the concepts of rule-based systems, or object-oriented programming is required for using the tool.

# 324 Commercial vendors of knowledge-based products

## C2V
Address: 38 rue Mauconseil, 75001 Paris, France
Phone: 33 1 40 08 07 07     Fax: 33 1 43 87 35 99
Contact person: Benoit Hap, Research Director

GENESE: a KBS product which allows an expert to create decision-making aids by producing a visual presentation of knowledge. This program allows non-computer-experts to develop KBSs.

## Cimflex Teknowledge
(KBS revenues: $16 million)
Address: 1810 Embarcadero Road, PO box 10119, Palo Alto, CA 94303, USA
Phone: 1 415 424 0500     Fax: 1 415 493 2645
Contact person: Richard S. Brooks, Program/Product Manager

M1: a knowledge engineering tool for building KBSs. It was originally written in Prolog, and later ported to C. It provides a rule-based programming language including procedural and object-oriented extensions. ($5000 on PC)

COPERNICUS: a software tool for developing and fielding high-performance KBSs. Systems built with Copernicus can stand alone, be embedded, or be integrated with existing data processing applications. ($30,000 on SUN 3, Apollo, or Vax/VMS)

## Cisi Ingenierie
Address: 3 rue Le Corbusier SILIC 232, 94528 Rungis Cedex, France
Phone: 33 1 49 79 46 90     Fax: 33 1 46 87 69 89
Contact person: Nguyen Thuc Diem, Marketing Manager

KOD Station: Knowledge Oriented Design tool for assisting cognitive engineers and KBS developers throughout the entire knowledge engineering process, starting from the acquisition of human expertise through to the organization of machine-based knowledge. KOD-Station guarantees that the knowledge base is internally coherent.

## Computas Expert Systems
(KBS revenues: NOK10.2 million)
Address: PO Box 410, N 1322 Hovik, Norway
Phone: 47 67 57 5822     Fax: 47 67 57 8029
Contact person: Roar Fjellheim, Technical Manager

G2: a real-time KBS for process control applications (from Gensym)

CX MEK: a multi-processing extension kit for Smalltalk/V ($100)

## Creative Logic
(KBS revenues: £220,000)
Address: Brunel Science Park, Kingston lane, Uxbridge, Middlesex UB8 3PQ, UK
Phone: 44 895 74468          Fax: 44 895 70244
Contact person: Mark Lewis, Sales and Marketing Director

LEONARDO: a KBS shell tool offering knowledge representation for casual knowledge, using production rules, objects, frames and inheritance, and procedural or algorithmic knowledge. (from £1000 on PC to £12,000 on Vax 8800)

## Cril
Address: 146 boulevard de Valmy, 92707 Colombes Cedex, France
Phone: 33 1 47 69 53 49      Fax: 33 1 47 69 53 99
Contact person: Pascale del Hierro, Product Manager

SPIRAL: a KBS shell tool written in C, and based on a logic programming language. It supports an object-oriented representation of knowledge.

OBJECTIVE C: an object-oriented superset of Ansi C allowing object data types, messages, and class definitions.

## Cybernetix
Address: 36 Blvd des Oceans, BP 87, 13274 Marseille Cedex 9, France
Phone: 33 91 25 25 00      Fax: 33 91 73 78 54
Contact person: Frederic Gonon, Expert Systems Manager

X-SYS: a KBS shell specially geared to aid construction of KBSs by persons with weak computer knowledge.

Nat: a natural language applications generator. Nat is composed of a set of software modules intended for the construction of natural language interfaces.

## Decibac
Address: 2 rue Lebouteux, 75017 Paris, France
Phone: 33 1 42 27 22 36      Fax: 33 1 42 27 48 44
Contact person: Emmanuel Lehman, Technical Manager

DECIBAC: a hybrid KBS development tool allowing object hierarchies with multiple inheritance. Dynamic rules, and objects loading and unloading are a set of new concepts in the tool. (FF30,000 on PC-DOS).

## Delphi Spa
(KBS revenues: LIT600 million)
Address: Via della vetraia 11, 55049 Viareggio, Italy
Phone: 39 584 395225      Fax: 39 584 9472676
Contact person: Sabrina Russell, Marketing and Sales Aid

Delphi Common LISP: complete implementation of Common LISP. It is based on Kyoto Common LISP, but with additional features such as support for graphical editing. ($3,700 on Sun Sparc 1)

## 326 Commercial vendors of knowledge-based products

### Epsilon
(KBS revenues: DM1.2 million)
Address: Kurfüstendamm 188/189, D 1000 Berlin 15, Germany
Phone: 49 30 8826991          Fax: 49 30 8823594
Contact person: Bernhard Boehringer

TWAICE: developed by Nixdorf Computer Ag, Twaice is a hybrid KBS shell based on Prolog. It is oriented towards diagnostic, classification, and planning tasks. It combines multiple knowledge representation and inferencing techniques, a friendly and expandable user-interface, efficient knowledge engineering tools, and a high degree of connectivity to other software systems. It is ported and supported by Epsilon on various hardware platforms. (From DM18,000 on PC to DM56,800 on VAX 8800 for the development system)

MProlog: a Prolog implementation for professional logic programming on PCs, workstations and mainframes. It is compatible with Clocksin and Mellish Prolog, and includes special development tools such as a window-based user interface. (DM1,750 for development system on PC 386, DM3,500 for production system on PC 386)

### ERDA
(KBS revenues: SEK8.5 million)
Address: St Larsgaten 12, S 58224 Linköping, Sweden
Phone: 46 13 11 4075          Fax: 46 13 12 8521
Contact person: Jürgen Smith, Product Manager

Epitool: a KBS tool providing an environment for development and delivery of industrial and commercial KBSs. Epitool is a hybrid system allowing objects, rules, and procedural knowledge. The tool is designed to be used easily by software engineers inexperienced in building KBSs. It integrates a functional language within the tool itself, rather than relying on procedural attachments, or calls to other programming languages.

### Euristic Systemes
Address: 3 bis rue Pierre Baudry, 92140 Clamart, France
Phone: 33 1 46 38 07 14          Fax: 33 1 46 38 88 19
Contact person: Dominique Villain, CEO

CHRONOS: a development tool for real-time KBSs, designed specially to handle temporal reasoning, and to manage the continuous acquisition of data. (FF60,000 on PC, FF120,000 on UNIX and Vax/VMS).

## Expertech
(KBS revenues: £1.7 million)
Address: Expertech House, 163 Bestobell Road, Slough, Berkshire SL1 4TY, UK
Phone: 44 753 696321        Fax: 44 753 696734
Contact person: J Binns, Technical Director

XI plus: a comprehensive tool for building KBS applications on a PC.

XI rule: a rule induction tool for XI plus. It provides an automatic method for discovering the rules applying to a set of decisions.

Egeria: a KBS development tool for interactive, embedded, and real-time KBS applications. It is intended to compete with hybrid toolkits such as KEE and ART. Egeria is object-oriented, and is based on compiler technology for fast performance. It allows representation of knowledge from simple facts to complex inference networks, and contains a comprehensive procedural language to control inferencing and interfacing. (From £400–3,000 on PC to £5,000–12,000 on Vax VMS).

Egeria rule: a rule induction tool for Egeria.

## Expertelligence
Address: 203 Chapela Street, Santa Barbara, CA 93101, USA
Phone: 1 805 962 2558        Fax: 1 805 962 5188

Action!: a development environment composed of a Smart editor and an expert object code ($1,995).

Spoke: an object-oriented language providing a dynamic environment, an advanced garbage collector, an incremental compiler, and an interpreter for rapid development.

## Franz
(KBS revenues: $2 million)
Address: 1995 University Avenue, Berkeley, CA 94704, CA, USA
Phone: 1 510 548 3600        Fax: 1 510 548 8253
Contact person: Hanoch Eiron, Director of Product Marketing

Allegro CL: a complete implementation of Common LISP. Additional features provided include debugging tools, object-oriented extensions, Common windows, and interfaces for C and Fortran routines.

Franz LISP: originally designed and implemented as part of Berkeley Unix, but now has some Common LISP capabilities ($1,500 on PC, $5,000 on workstations, and up to $30,000 on mainframes).

Allegro Composer: a Common LISP program development environment.

### Gensym
Address: 125 Cambridge Park Drive, Cambridge, MA 02140, USA
Phone: 1 617 547 9606          Fax: 1 617 547 1962
Contact person: R. Haarstick, Sales Director

G2: G2 is a real-time KBS tool designed for large applications where hundreds of variables are concurrently monitored. The G2 simulator allows models to supply data, with the inference engine giving analyses and explanations just as it would in an actual on-line situation. Explanations of the reasoning showing the rules and trend graphs, help the professional to trace the reasoning process and improve the knowledge base. The object- and frame-based representation of knowledge in G2 is augmented by a representation of deep structure, object interactions, and models of behavior. Objects may interact either through connectivity or proximity.

### Gold Hill Computers
(KBS revenues: $12 million)
Address: 26 Landsdowne Str, Cambridge MA 02139, USA
Phone: 1 617 621 3300          Fax: 1 617 621 0656
Contact person: Francis P. Maggio, Manager International Marketing

Goldworks II: a knowledge-based hybrid KBS development environment providing frames with multiple inheritance, rules for backward and forward chaining, object-oriented programming, and a graphical interface. (from $4,900 on Mac to $9,900 on Sun workstations).

Golden Common LISP: a LISP version for PCs. It is a subset of Common LISP. ($1,995 for the developer version )

### Graphael — Euriware
(KBS revenues: FF15 million)
Address: 3 rue Stephenson, 78182 St Quentin en Yvelines, France
Phone: 33 1 30 14 5424          Fax: 33 1 30 14 5410
Contact person: Camille Fromion-Hebard, PR manager

G-Base: G-base is an object-oriented database management system integrated with LISP (FF100,000 on TI Explorer, and FF150,000 on Sun workstations).

### Gsi Tecsi
(KBS revenues: FF25 million)
Address: 1 place des Marseillais, 94227 Charenton le Pont Cedex, France
Phone: 33 1 47 78 6767          Fax: 33 1 47 78 6768
Contact person: Christelle Boy, Sales Representative

IS II: a rule-based KBS shell using forward and backward chaining with a user-friendly interface. (FF35,000)

IS*LIB: a database query language to access the knowledge bases generated by IS II. (FF7,000)

### Harlequin

Address: Barrington Hall, Barrington Cambridge, CB2 5RG, UK
Phone: 44 223 872522          Fax: 44 223 872519
Contact person: Niels Dench, Product Manager

LispWorks: a complete programming environment to develop applications in Common LISP.

KnowledgeWorks: a high-performance toolkit to develop large KBSs.

DataWorks: a package for developing graphical and object-oriented interfaces to relational databases.

### Ilog

(KBS revenues: $4 million)
Address: 2 Avenue Gallieni BP 85, 94253 Gentilly Cedex, France
Phone: 33 1 46 63 66 66          Fax: 33 1 46 63 15 82
Contact person: Edouard Efira, Sales Director

SMECI: a complete KBS development environment using an object-based representation scheme. The KBS designer can mix declarative and procedural programming styles to suit requirements of the application.

Classic: Classic is a user-friendly KBS shell. It is useful both as a KBS prototyping tool, and for constructing complex industrial applications.

MASAI: This is a WYSIWYG[3] editor allowing the knowledge engineer to instantly verify and test the interface during the development of KBSs.

### Information Builders

Address: 1250 Broadway, New York, NY 10001, USA
Phone: 212 736 4433          Fax: 212 643 8105
Contact person: Brian McLaughlin, International Marketing Director

LEVEL5: a KBS tool which is embedded in the FOCUS fourth generation language. ($685 on PC, $5,000 on workstations, and $45,000 on mainframes)

LEVEL5 Object: an object-oriented KBS development environment.

### Inrets

Address: 2 Avenue du General Malleret-Joinville, BP 34, 94114 Arcueil Cedex, France
Phone: 33 1 47 40 71 27          Fax: 33 1 45 47 56 06
Contact person: Bernard Schnetzler, Research Engineer

AIDA: a declarative language for real-time applications using production rules (in second-order logic), semi-unification mechanisms, and contexts.

### Integral Solutions

Address: 3 Campbell Court, Bramley, Basingstoke, Hants RG26 5EG, UK
Phone: 44 256 882028          Fax: 44 256 882182
Contact person: Colin Shearer, Sales Director

Poplog: Poplog was originally developed at the University of Sussex. It is a KBS development environment allowing developers to combine several high-level languages and programming paradigms to effectively tackle complex problems. The Poplog languages (Prolog, Common LISP, and POP11) can be mixed as required, and can interface to software written in any compiled language. (From £7,000 on workstations to £18,000 on mainframes)

Poplog Neural: a neural network development toolkit running on UNIX and VAX/VMS systems. Users can take advantage of virtual memory and specialized hardware to increase the speed of learning. A graphical user interface allows display of multiple networks on the screen.

Poplog Flex: Flex combines the power and elegance of Prolog with the high-level support required to develop sophisticated large-scale KBSs rapidly and efficiently. It provides a frame-based data representation, integrated forward and backward chaining inference mechanisms, and an English-like knowledge specification language (KSL).

RULES: RULES applies advanced data analysis techniques to generate effective classification rules which can be integrated in both KBS systems and conventional programs. RULES also provides an interactive training environment in which users can experiment with prototype rules, and refine them by evaluating their performances on new test cases.

Keris: This is a toolkit designed for knowledge engineers and developers of other advanced software. Keris provides a comprehensive set of proven paradigms including object-oriented and rule-based programming, supported by a high-productivity environment incorporating a set of graphical debugging and development tools.

## Intellicorp
(KBS revenues: $22 million)
Address: 10 Jewry Street, Winchester, Hampshire SO23 8RZ, UK
Phone: 44 344 305305          Fax: 44 962 344 305100
Contact person: Russell Prince-Wright, Manager UK Operations

KEE (Knowledge Engineering Environment): this is the flagship product of Intellicorp. It provides an object-oriented, frame-based representation language. It also offers advanced functionalities for building models, reasoning about and analyzing these models, and communicating with external systems (From $10,000 on PC to $50,000 on workstations).

SIMKIT: a set of knowledge-based simulation and modelling tools in KEE designed for library developers and model builders. It adds discrete event-simulation capabilities to KEE for applications using time-dependent models ($21,000 on Sun workstations).

KAPPA-PC: a high performance object-oriented software environment for developing and delivering powerful PC-based business applications under Microsoft Windows ($3000 on PC).

PRO KAPPA: a powerful general-purpose application development and deployment environment for Unix and X-Windows workstations targeted at professional application programmers.

## Intelmark
Address: Parc d'innovation Bretagne Sud, PIBS CP 27, 56038 Vannes Cedex, France
Phone: 33 16 97 427590          Fax: 33 16 97 424367
Contact person: Jean Michel Grand, President

DESCRIPTOR: a decision-model generator that is based on the concepts of analytical hierarchies and fuzzy logic.

## Interface Computer
(KBS revenues: DM6 million)
Address: Garmischer str. 4/V, D 8000 Munchen 2, Germany
Phone: 49 89 510860          Fax: 49 89 5108628
Contact person: Annette Kolb, AI Product Manager

IF/Prolog: a portable version of Prolog. It is coded in C, and includes interfaces to a variety of systems (operating systems, GKS, RDBMS, and so on) and a window-based debugger (DM3,000 for PC 386).

TABLO: an interactive system for development and processing of decision tables based on IF/Prolog.

### Isoft
Address: Chemin du Moulon, 91190, GIF-sur-Yvelle, France
Phone: 33 1 69 41 27 77   Fax: 33 1 69 41 25 32
Contact person: Perdrix, President

Kate (Knowledge Acquisition Toolbox for Expert Systems): Kate's frame-based language is used to represent training data for the induction of rules, handle hierarchies of classes and descriptors with multiple inheritance, model physical constraints that exist in the application domain, and define procedural calls which deduce descriptor values (in forward or backward chaining). In Kate, objects are a unifying factor because representation, deductive reasoning, induction, graphics, editing tools, access to external programming languages, and database management systems are all object-oriented. (FF300,000 on TI Explorer, FF65,000 on Mac)

### Knowledge-based Silicon
Address: AT&T building, 1201 Main Str suite 2000, Columbia SC 29201- 3200, USA
Phone: 1 803 779 2504   Fax: 1 803 779 2505

REX board: a microprocessor-based inference engine ($1,450).

CAKE (Computer Aided Knowledge Engineer): a KBS development tool including an expert guide, a frame editor, a rule editor, a rule linker, a rule translator, and a screen editor ($2,950).

### Lithp Systems
(KBS revenues: DFL1 million)
Address: PO Box 553, 1440 AN Purmerend, Holland
Phone: 31 2 990 38153   Fax: 31 2 990 37449
Contact person: Hans Thomas, PR Manager

ACQUAINT: a frame-based KBS shell tool written in muLisp, and incorporating both backward and forward chaining ($7,000 on PC).

### Logic Programming
(KBS revenues: £350 k)
Address: Studio 4, Royal Victoria Patriotic Building, Trinity Road, London SW18 3SX, UK
Phone: 44 81 871 2016   Fax: 44 81 874 0449
Contact person: Clive Spenser, Marketing Director

FLEX: a hybrid KBS toolkit integrating frame-based programming, data-driven programming, and rule-based programming within a logic programming environment. This is supplemented with the additional functionality of a declarative AI language to provide a powerful and versatile KBS development toolkit (£2,000 on PC or Mac).

## Lysia
Address: Crown House, 2 Crown Dale, Upper Norwood, London SE19 3NQ, UK
Phone: 44 81 670 7163         Fax: 44 81 670 4541
Contact person: Ms A. C. Beerel, Managing Director,

This company offers a broad range of strategic application-oriented KBSs such as the following: Mergers & Acquisitions Model (MAC), Business Strategy Review for Financial Institutions (BSR), Business Strategy Review for Manufacturing Institutions (BSRM), Marketing Audit (MAUD), Investment Risk Assessment Model (IRAM), Investment Analyst Advisor (IVOR), Corporate Risk Assessment Model (CRAM), Client Portfolio Management System (CPS), Interest Rate Risk Management Advisor (INTRAM), Advertising Compliance Tutor (TACT), General Business Plan Expert System (GBP), Strategic Market Planner (SMARTPLAN), Product Portfolio Audit Manager, (PPAM), Document Efficiency Review System (DRS), General Business Audit (GBA), and Manufacturing New Product Introduction Decision Support System (NFI).

## MDBS (Micro Data Base Systems)
(KBS revenues: $6.4 million)
Address: 2 Executive drive, PO box 248, Lafayette IN 47902-0248, USA
Phone: 1 317 463 2581         Fax: 1 317 448 6428
Contact person: Gary Rush, Chief Operating Officer

Guru: Guru combines KBS development and information management tools in a single software environment. It includes backward and forward chaining, multiple rule-firing during consultations, integration of rules with information management tools, case saving, consultation replaying, visual representation of rule-goal-variable relationships, and rule-set nesting ($6,500 on PC, $17,000 on workstations, $34-60,000 on mini/mainframes).

Guru First Step: This contains the essential components for building basic KBSs.

Guru Solver: This tool is designed for non-computer professionals, and provides a ready-to-use, systematic approach to diagnosing problems, and building specialized KBSs.

## Mind Soft
(KBS revenues: FF5 million)
Address: 3 rue de l'arrivée BP 63 75749 Paris Cedex 15, France
Phone: 33 1 45 38 70 12         Fax: 33 1 45 38 68 73
Contact person: Mouangue Essoukan, Technical Manager

Nexus: a hybrid KBS building tool composed of predicates, variables and actions, a MODULA-2 like language, and an intelligent interactive rule editor. It includes graphical representation of rule structures, and supports procedural and non-procedural functions. The rule base in Nexus can support up to 5000 rules in 10 knowledge base segments (£4,800 on PC).

IEP (Instant Expert Plus): a generator of graphical KBSs. It is rule-based, and includes natural language processing and graphics capabilities. (£499 on PC or Mac).

## 334 Commercial vendors of knowledge-based products

**Neuron Data**
(KBS revenues: $8 million)
Addresses: 444 High Street, Palo Alto, CA 94301 and 23 rue Vernet 75008 Paris, France
Phone: 33 1 40 70 04 21     Fax: 33 1 47 23 71 43
Contact person: Brian Robins, Marketing Manager

NEXPERT OBJECT: a C-based KBS shell, integrating rules and objects, a graphical user interface, and an open architecture (from $5,000 for PC and Mac to $8,000 for workstations).

NEXTRA: a high-end knowledge acquisition and transfer tool, which structures intangible knowledge into clusters of logical relationships, then uses that knowledge to automatically generate rules and objects usable in Nexpert ($4,000).

**Odyss'ia**
Address: Aeropol 3, 5 Avenue Albert Durand, 31700 Blagnac, France
Phone: 33 16 61 30 06 09     Fax: 33 16 61 300684
Contact person: Jean Paul Patacq, Managing Director

Easybreeder: an application-specific KBS for the design of cross-breeding of plants.

Ramses: an application-specific KBS for the automatic routing of banking messages.

**Olivetti**
Address: 20300 Stevens Creek Blvd., Cupertino, CA 95014, USA
Phone: 1 408 996 3867     Fax: 1 408 996 3053
Contact person: Piero Scaruffi, Manager AI Center

AIE (Artificial Intelligence Environment): an object-oriented development system with logic programming capabilities.

ESS (Expert System Shell): a tool for development of practical KBSs on PCs and workstations. ESS features both rule-based and frame-based knowledge representation, multiple hierarchical knowledge bases, traditional variables, procedural attachments, and sub-goal caching for faster processing. Its integrated inference procedures provides both backward and forward chaining with support for probabilities and non-monotonic truth maintenance.

**PA Consulting Group**
(KBS revenues: £1 million)
Address: 123 Buckingham Palace Road, London SWIW 9SR, UK
Phone: 44 71 730 9000     Fax: 44 71 333 5050
Contact person: Paul Sachs, Manager Intelligent Systems

ISSUE (Intelligent Spread Sheet Utility Environment): a KBS shell tool enabling experts to express their knowledge clearly and precisely. It handles multiple cases simultaneously, combines numeric and judgmental data, provides 'what if' explorations, lets the user drive the dialog, deals with missing or uncertain data, and enables rapid prototyping.

ESCORT (Expert System for Complex Operations in Real Time): an application-specific shell tool to assist in management of plant operations.

## Paperback Software
(KBS revenues: $1.1 million)
Address: 2830 Ninth St Berkeley, CA 94710, USA
Phone: 1 510 644 2116    Fax: 1 510 644 8241

VP EXPERT: a rule-based KBS development language with a built-in text editor, and supporting backward and forward chaining ($249 with SQL functionality).

## Procyon Research
(KBS revenues: £180,000)
Address: St John's Innovation Centre, Cowley Road, Cambridge CB4 4WS, UK
Phone: 44 223 421 221    Fax: 44 223 421 218
Contact person: Richard Barber, Managing Director

Procyon Common LISP: a European implementation of Common LISP. It includes a Common Graphics portable graphics and windowing system, and a programming environment (£1,595).

ESB 96: a graphical KBS construction toolkit that makes the advantages of object-oriented LISP available to non-LISP application developers.

## Prolog Ia
(KBS revenues: FF4.6 million)
Address: Luminy, Case 919, 13288 Marseille Cedex 9, France
Phone: 33 16 91 268636    Fax: 33 16 91 419637
Contact person: Sylvie Alleaume, Sales Manager

OURSE: a KBS shell tool allowing representation of negative facts, and containing facilities for knowledge coherence, precise knowledge deduction, and access to Prolog II. It is suited to diagnostic tasks, and control of complex processes (FF23,000 on Mac and PC, FF45,000 on Sun workstations).

PROLOG II+: an alternative to Clocksin & Mellish Prolog. It is very portable because it is written in a language which translates into Pascal (from FF3,500 to FF50,000).

PROLOG III: a constraint logic programming language.

BEST (Banking Expert System Tool): an application-specific KBS shell for banking applications. It provides decision support for granting loans to individuals.

### Quinary Spa
(KBS revenues: $1 million)
Address: Via Crivelli 15/1, 20122 Milano, Italy
Phone: 39 2 58302712          Fax: 39 2 58305374
Contact person: Massimo Massironi, Managing Director

QSL: an object-oriented KBS development architecture which is fully embedded in Common LISP. It is suitable for professional knowledge systems developers ($16,000 on workstations and Vax/VMS).

PECUNIA: an application-specific KBS for advising about investment portfolios.

FIDUCIA: an application-specific KBS for evaluating loan risks.

### SIG (Systemes Informatiques de Gestion)
Address: 4 bis rue de la liberation, 78350 Jouy en Josas, France
Phone: 33 1 39 56 14 55          Fax: 33 1 39 56 57 42
Contact person: Michel Klein, R&D Manager

OPTRANS: software for developing decision support systems with KBS functionalities.

FINSIM: a KBS to support financial analysis and planning.

### Steria
Address: ave Joseph Wybranlaan 40, Erasmus Tech. Center, B 1070 Brussels, Belgium
Phone: 32 2 520 9640          Fax: 32 2 520 6617
Contact person: Mr. Canon, Technical Director

Gecosys' operational products integrate natural language processing, KBSs, and optical character recognition. These technologies enable Gecosys' products to process free-form text (even in conversational mode). Message processing systems automate all tasks related to the handling of messages in the telecommunications and payment departments of organizations. The SCARBO system automatically processes paper forms intended for internal applications or transmission on external data networks.

### Sun Microsystems France
Address: 13 avenue Morane Saulnier, 78140 Velizy-Villacoublay, France
Phone: 33 1 30 67 52 05          Fax: 33 1 30 67 53 04
Contact person: Eric Mahe, AI Marketing Manager

SCL (Sun Common LISP): Common lisp running on Sun workstations.

SPE (Symbolic Programming Environment): a complete symbolic programming environment for the development of KBSs. It integrates Sun Common LISP with object-oriented programming, graphics, and a sophisticated windowing system.

Sun C++: an object-oriented version of C specially suited for execution on Sun workstations.

## Symbolics
Address: St John's Court, Easton Street, High Wycombe, Bucks HP11 IJX, UK
Phone: 44 494 443711          Fax: 44 494 23939
Contact person: Mike Morrisey, Marketing Communications Manager

Genera: a LISP-based software development environment.

Joshua: a programming language and development environment, built on Genera, for building and delivering KBSs ($15,000 on workstations).

Statice: an object-oriented database system with persistence, sharing, and multiple inheritance.

## Syntelligence
(KBS revenues: $9 million)
Address: 1000 Hamlin Court, Sunnyvale CA 94089, USA
Phone: 1 408 745 6666          Fax: 1 408 744 1342
Contact person: Michelle Wilson, Marketing Communication Director

SYNCORE: Domain-specific KBS development technology targeting the financial services industry. It is designed to provide risk assessment expertise, guidance, and assistance.

## Yard
(KBS revenues: £600,000)
Address: 1 Atlantic Team, Broonyelew, Glasgow G2 8JE, Scotland
Phone: 44 41 204 2737          Fax: 44 41 3216 4135
Contact person: Chris Edmonds, Manager AI & System Studies Group

Symtactics: Symtactics is a special-purpose military simulation toolkit which enables rapid development of high fidelity, flexible land, sea, and air battle simulations. It is written in a combination of LISP and KEE.

Y3: a toolbox for building KBSs. It is composed of an object-oriented language Yafool, an inference engine Yaflog, and a graphical interface Yafen. Y3 is implemented using Le_Lisp and interfaces with X-Windows.

# 338 Commercial vendors of knowledge-based products

## Bibliography and suggested readings

An excellent description of commercial KBS tools is available in the book by Harmon et al (Harmon et al 88). Vendor lists are also provided in (Harmon et al 88), and most other books on KBSs mentioned in the bibliographies of earlier chapters. Detailed vendor profiles can be obtained from the reports of consulting companies such as (Ovum 88). Other useful sources of information on KBS products are references (Gevarter 87) and (Rauch-Hindin 88).

Gevarter, W. B., *The Nature and Evaluation of Commercial Expert System Building Tools*, IEEE Computer, pp. 24–41, May 1987.

Harmon, P., Maus, R., and W. Morrissey, *Expert Systems: Tools and Applications*, John Wiley, 1988.

Ovum, *Expert Systems in Europe*, Management report prepared by Ovum Consultants, London, UK, 1988.

Rauch-Hindin, W. B., *A Guide to Commercial Artificial Intelligence: Fundamentals and Real-World Applications*, Chapters 9, 10, 25, & 26, Prentice Hall, 1988.

## Notes

1  The survey results are based on a questionnaire mailed to over 150 KBS vendors (about 80 responses were received), company literature about their marketed products, and results of prior surveys available in literature (such as books and reports by consulting companies).

2  It should be mentioned that much of the data (such as revenue figures, prices, contact persons, and so on) date to 1990–91 and some of it will have changed since then. However, they should provide the reader with an approximate idea of the profiles of different KBS vendors.

3  What You See Is What You Get

# Appendix 3
# *Commercial applications of neural networks*

This appendix contains brief descriptions of selected commercial applications of neural networks (NNs). Like many other artificial intelligence applications, details about these applications are hard to obtain because they are seldom reported. It is likely that more details will become available as commercialization of NNs increases. The following list of applications, while sketchy in parts, does outline the commercial applications of NNs in different domains. The description of each of the following applications consists of a short statement of the function of the application, the company of deployment, and a brief outline of the implementation.

## Airline

Function: air-traffic control
Company: US Federal Aviation Administration[1]

Description: the US Federal Aviation Administration (FAA) has developed NNs to perform a range of air-traffic control activities. Two systems developed for the FAA by the San Diego firm Neurologic are:

● simulation training controllers — Neurologic used TRACON, an air-traffic control simulation program to build a multi-network system. The system comprises local networks for each monitored aircraft, each of which contains information about the other local networks (monitored aircraft). By extrapolating current velocities and positions, the system avoids collisions, and issues warning messages and instructions for avoiding conflicts. These responses can be compared with those of a human trainee

● real-time decision aid — Neurologic's air-traffic control Field Interaction Network is designed to keep every aircraft on the screen on a good flight path, based on given objectives. The system maintains a constant distance between aircraft using a heuristic algorithm based on 'attraction' (movement towards destination) and 'repulsion' (avoidance of collisions). In addition, the system can instruct aircraft to change altitude or speed.

At present, a human controller is still responsible for monitoring the air traffic in a sector of air-space to achieve safety and efficiency, subject to the constraints of traffic in other sectors. The benefit of a NN would be in automating some air-traffic control functions, relieving the stress of controllers, and improving the efficiency of air-space usage.

## Defence

Function: signal recognition
Company: Lockheed Missiles and Space Company[2]

Description: the Lockheed Missiles and Space Company has successfully applied NNs to the problem of classifying sonar signals as either 'submarine' or 'surface noise'. The NN was trained on a data set of 1767 examples of submarine noise, and 4326 examples of surface noise (comprising ship noise and wave noise). In tests, the network performed well (Table 3.1) on samples of noise similar to those in the training data (test 1 and 2), and on samples of submarine data very different from the training data (test 3).

| Percent correct classification |         |
|---|---|
| Test 1: | 93.75% |
| Test 2: | 100.00% |
| Test 3: | 95.44% |

**Table A3.1** Test results of Lockheed's NN application

## Financial services

Function: mortgage insurance
Company: unspecified firm of mortgage underwriters[3]

Description: Nestor of Providence, RI, has developed a NN to decide about mortgage insurance applications for potential mortgage applicants who need the insurance to cover any of the usual required down-payment they are unable to raise. Before the NN, expert mortgage insurance underwriters had to analyze the inputs to reach a decision. As cases vary significantly, a high degree of judgement was required and disagreements among experts on a given case was common. Thus, the domain does not lend itself to a rule-based system.

The NN uses about 25 inputs describing the applicants' financial and cultural background, and details of the mortgage. The network is organized in three levels of three sub-networks, which mimic a series of three decision-making committees. The process starts at the lowest level 'committee' and moves up to the next level if the three networks cannot agree on a decision. The process stops as soon as a unanimous decision is reached at one level. If there is no unanimity in the third level also, then the system delivers a 'can't decide' verdict. The NN was developed from a database of 5000 loan applications, equally distributed between accepted and rejected applications.

Nestor's network made decisions which agreed with the original underwriter in 82% of cases. Although the problem is one of forecasting which applicants will not default over the whole term of the loan, three years on it is claimed that the network would seem, on the whole, to have given better business judgements in tests than the original human underwriters, in cases of disagreement.

Function: share price movement prediction
Company: Daiwa Securities[4]

Description: running on an NEC supercomputer, Daiwa's NN scans share prices to look for patterns known as flags, pennants, and wedges that often presage an imminent sharp rise or fall. A prototype version analyzing price movements of 16 stocks spotted the triangular patterns with 80% accuracy. Daiwa is in the process of employing a system capable of tracking hundreds of shares with greater accuracy. (A NN is also used by Shearson Lehman Brothers for the similar task of recognizing patterns in market activity[5].)

Function: credit approval of personal loans
Company: an unspecified financial services company[6]

Description: a NN was developed by for the purpose of approving personal loans. The NN used a database of 17,000 completed loans, with about 100 input variables from the loan applications. The trained network was tested on 7,000 new examples. There already existed computer models to assist humans in credit scoring i.e., assigning a score based on a number of (financial and other) characteristics of the loan application, which was used to either accept or reject an application. On the basis of the test, it would seem that the NN could increase the profitability of personal loans by 27%, compared with the existing credit scoring model.

Function: bond rating and portfolio selection
Company: G. R. Pugh, Cranford, New Jersey[7]

Description: the problem tackled is that of determining whether existing ratings of corporate bonds (given by independent agencies like S&P and Moody's in the USA) reflect the true investment value of the bonds[8]. The NN produced a rating forecast from 23 financial inputs with a 95% accuracy. The NN was developed using California Scientific Software's BrainMaker. Training the network took four hours on a PC XT.

## Government

Function: detection of bombs
Company: Federal Aviation Administration (FAA), USA[9]

Description: since August 1989, a bomb detector system (called SNOOPE) employing NNs has been in use at New York's JF Kennedy International Airport. SNOOPE identifies explosives by identifying the characteristic patterns of gamma-ray emissions. It is sensitive enough to differentiate between emissions from nitrogen in a bomb, and nitrogen in edible materials. About 2.5 pounds of explosives are required to trigger SNOOPE. About 10 pieces of baggage can be passed through the system per minute.

SNOOPE was developed by Science Applications International Corporation at a cost of about $1.1 million. The FAA plans to install similar systems in more airports gradually.

Function: recognizing hand-written ZIP codes
Company: US Mail[10]

Description: the US Mail has developed a NN application to develop hand-written ZIP codes. The input to the network is a 16 by 16 pixel image of a particular handwritten digit, scaled to a standard size. Location of the handwritten digit on the envelope is done by another system. The network is fairly large, using four layers and 1256 neurons. The network was trained on 7300 digits and tested with another 2000. The error rate was 1% for the training sample and 5% for the testing sample.

## Healthcare

Function: resource-management and performance monitoring
Company: Anderson Memorial Hospital, South Carolina[11]

Description: Anderson Memorial Hospital uses NNs to provide a profile of the 'average physician' to enable doctors to compare their own performance relative to their peers. The system goal is to derive length of hospital stay as a function of seven different variables: diagnosis, complications, relevant body symptoms (respiratory, cardiovascular, and so on), surgical and non-surgical procedures, patient demographics, general health indicators, and admission category.

The system was trained to predict diagnosis severity using data from 80,000 cases and 473 diagnoses, providing 400–1000 examples of each diagnosis considered. The data came from the hospital mainframe database and was downloaded to a PC for the NN application. Two additional NNs were built to predict the required resource allocation and the type of hospital discharge for each diagnosis. These additional NNs used 26 inputs variables. Training took four hours on a 386 PC.

The system predicts diagnosis severity with a 95% accuracy. In addition, the system (with the help of an expert system module) provides physicians with profiles of their own practice compared with that of the 'average physician' and the hospital as a whole, in the form of one-page summaries with supporting graphs. The system allows Anderson Memorial to manage its resources based on the comparative resource requirements of each diagnosis. It is claimed that the system led to substantial cost savings in its second year of operation. By increasing awareness of resource use and encouraging doctors to improve their weaknesses, the system helps to shorten hospital stays and reduce mortality.

## Marketing

Function: direct mail
Company: Spiegel, Oak Brook, Illinois[12]

Description: Spiegel mails about 200 million brochures and catalogs to its customers each year. It uses a NN (developed by Neuralware) to separate one-time buyers from repeat buyers. Data (such as age, income, family make-up, and home ownership) about existing customers of Spiegel and their buying patterns were used for training the NN. The NN discards about 60% of one-time buyers and retains about 90% of repeat buyers. Spiegel expects to use this application to save over $1 million annually, and execute a more focused marketing campaign.

## Manufacturing

Function: process control
Company: Texaco[13] — Puget Sound Refinery

Description: refinery engineers at Puget have integrated NNs into the plant's process-control strategies. One NN was applied to a de-butanizer which separates and condenses hydrocarbons according to molecular weight. The process requires careful monitoring of temperatures, pressures, and flows. A 17-hour batch cycle subjects the process to constant instability. The NN ensures product quality during flux.

The application was built on a PC with the NeuroShell NN software from Ward Systems Group, and ported to Data General MV10000s for implementation. The NN uses 1,440 data sets of seven inputs (control and disturbance variables). It usually corrects errors in the control parameters before they appear. A feedback mechanism eliminates unexpected errors that do occur. The NN appears to be in control 80% of the time, and even more often during unstable processing.

Function: manufacturing fault diagnosis
Company: CTS Electronics, Brownville, Texas[14]

Description: the Metamoros plant of CTS Electronics produces several million loudspeakers per year. Audible defects in the produced speakers had previously been detected by human operators, a process which had considerable subjectivity and error. CTS had also tried to use a PC-based audio-test system with statistical pass/fail limits to detect defects. However this system was unable to classify defects — a task necessary for effective process control.

A NN application now successfully classifies defects into four output categories. Ten input nodes represent distortion at ten discrete frequency points. Four output nodes denote the loudspeaker defect classes. Forty minutes of training are sufficient before the network parameters can be incorporated into the audio-test software. The trained network correctly classified loudspeakers under laboratory conditions. In the next phase, CTS plans a pilot production run to help define procedures for workers to train and maintain the network in practice.

Function: manufacturing quality control
Company: an unspecified chemical plant in Cleveland, Ohio[15]

Description: the task is to check that products contain the correct proportions of chemical components, and that no contaminants are present. Before the NN, expert quality control engineers were required to interpret the spectroscope data because the data only indicates the result of the interaction of chemicals and not the presence of the individual components causing the interaction. Any misinterpretation by the engineers can result in a contaminated product.

The NN analyzes infrared spectroscopy data to validate the product or to advise technicians. The NN is trained for each product with the spectroscopic data of a known set of contaminants. The NN then learns how the individual components interact, and how these interactions are reflected in the spectroscopic data of the contaminated product. The NN allows effective product quality by technicians who are not trained in analyzing spectroscopic data. The NN application was developed using software provided by AI Ware of Cleveland, Ohio.

Function: checking noisy blower motors
Company: Siemens, Germany[16]

Description: manual detection of noisy blower motors (made by Siemens for Ford car heaters) is a tiresome chore as it involves listening to each blower. Engineers at Siemens have designed a NN to check for noisy blower motors. The NN has an accuracy of over 90%.

Function: speech instructions to manufacturing processes
Company: Intel[17]

Description: Intel has used NNs to build a successful speech recognition system by limiting the system to one speaker, and the vocabulary to about a hundred isolated words and phrases. The system has an accuracy of over 99%, and is being used for giving manual instructions to various manufacturing processes.

## Space

Function: scheduling the Hubble Space Telescope
Company: Space Telescope Science Institute, USA[18]

Description: the Hubble Space Telescope is designed to make 30,000 exposures of 3,000 celestial sites per year. A NN has been implemented to schedule the telescope subject to the constraints of mission preference, orbital viewing occulations, propulsion, and communication limitations. Schedules must have the flexibility to accommodate spacecraft problems and the occurrence of significant astronomical events.

The network can be thought of as a matrix of time segments (columns) and scheduling clusters (rows). Each neuron represents the possible commitment of a cluster to a segment, a solution being reached once commitment is achieved. A Hopfield NN is used to produce several 'good' solutions rather than one optimal solution.

## Bibliography and suggested readings

The best sources for updates on recent commercial applications of NNs are industry magazines, such as AI Expert and Electronic Engineering Times. However, the descriptions of applications in such sources are usually sketchy, and lack details. More details on NN applications are available in the proceedings of major conferences on NNs, such as the IEEE Conference on Neural Networks (whose proceedings are published by the IEEE Computer Society Press). Descriptions of some commercial NN applications are also available in some books on NNs, such as references (Anderson 88), (DARPA 88), and (Nelson & Illingworth 91). However, details of NN applications are only slowly appearing. This reflects the relatively immature state of the commercialization of the technology.

Anderson, J. A., *What Neural Nets Can Do*, Video Companion Manual, Lawrence Erlbaum Associates, Hillsdale, NJ, 1988.

*DARPA Neural Network Study*, AFCEA International Press, Fairfax, VA, 1988.

McCord Nelson, M. and W. T. Illingworth, *A Practical Guide to Neural Networks*, Addison Wesley, 1991.

# Notes

1 *AI Expert*, pp. 71, December 1990.

2 Publicity materials from Hecht-Nielsen Neurocomputers, San Diego.

3 Reilly, D. L., C. Collins, C. Scofield and S. Ghosh, *Risk Assessment of Mortgage Applications with a Neural-network System: An Update as the Test Portfolio Ages*, Proceedings of the International Joint Conference on Neural Networks, Vol. 2, Washington DC, pp. 479–482, 1990.

4 *Japan's answer to human fund managers is a computer with 'fuzzy' trading logic*, The Toronto Globe and Mail, October 11, 1989.

5 Schwartz, E. I., and J. B. Treece, *Smart Programs go to work*, Business Week, pp. 47–51, March 2, 1992.

6 Publicity materials from Hecht-Nielsen Neurocomputers, San Diego.

7 *AI Expert*, pp. 71, June 1990.

8 See Chapter 9 for more details on the bond rating problem and the use of neural networks for the prediction of corporate bond ratings.

9 R. Colin Johnson, *Neural nose to sniff out explosives at JFK Airport*, Electronic Engineering Times, 536, May 1, 1989.

10 Y. LeCun, B. Boser, J. S. Denker, D. Henderson, R. E. Howard, W. Hubbard and L. D. Jackel, *Back-propagation applied to handwritten zip code recognition*, Neural Computation, 1, 541–551.

11 *AI Expert*, pp. 71, Feb. 1991.

12 Schwartz, E. I., and J. B. Treece, *Smart Programs go to work*, Business Week, pp. 47–51, March 2, 1992.

13 *AI Expert*, pp. 71, June 1990.

14 *AI Expert*, pp. 71, June 1990.

15 *AI Expert*, pp. 71, October 1990.

16 O'Reilly, B., *Computers that think like people*, Fortune, Vol. 119, No. 5, Feb 27, pp, 90–93, 1989.

17 *DARPA neural network study*, AFCEA International Press, Fairfax, VA., pp. 417–420, Appendix E, Nov. 1988.

18 *AI Expert*, pp. 72, June 1990.

# Index

Artificial intelligence, 5, 7–13
    applied, 15
    birth, 7
    commercial market, 19–20
    commercialisation, 17–19
    computing roots, 9–10
    development, 10–11
    governmental funding, 13–14
    knowledge processing, 16–17
    mathematical roots, 8–9
    philosophical roots, 7–8
    sub-fields 11–13

Blackboard systems, 84–85, 309–310

Case–based reasoning, 12, 86–87, 310–311
Church-Turing hypothesis, 8
Computer vision, see Image processing
Computing,
    evolution, 4–5
    parallel, 9–10
    progress, 3–4
Connectionism, see Neural networks

Decision support systems, 5
Development of knowledge–based systems, 95–115, 145–158
    corporate strategies, 146–150
    database interfaces, 114–115
    deployment and maintenance, 155–158
    feasibility of applications, 152–153
    hybrid systems, 104–115
    identification of applications, 150–152
    management of development, 153–155
    rule-based systems, 95–103
    stages in organizations, 145–146
    tools, 116–120, 321–337
    user-interface, 111–114

Epistemology, 38–39

Expert system, 11

Frames
    behaviour, 80–81
    communication between, 82
    comparison with rules, 82–84
    development of systems, 104–115
    hierarchies 76–82
    structure, 77–80
Fuzzy logic, 12, 235–260
    applications, 235–238, 247–253, 255, 311
    benefits of fuzzy rules, 246–247
    business impact, 258–260
    commercial activities, 253–258
    development, 238–239
    fuzzy control, 247–250
    fuzzy rules, 242–246, 248–250
    linguistic variables, 241–242
    representational concepts, 239–242

Image processing, 197–221
    ambiguity, 200–202
    applications, 212–221
    biological roots, 198–199
    business impact, 227
    computational requirements, 199–200
    computer vision, 12, 198
    digitizing and sampling, 204
    edge detection, 207–208
    image understanding, 210–212
    labelling, 208, 210
    segmentation, 208–209
    smoothing, 207
    stages of, 203
    thresholding, 205–206
Inference
    backward chaining, 62–64
    engine, 34–36
    forward chaining, 60–64

Intelligence,
   links to understanding, 168–169
   nature of, 14–15

Knowledge
   common-sense, 11, 41
   declarative, 41
   deep, 40–41
   definition, 39
   dimensions, 40–42
   domain, 11
   explicit, 40–41
   in computer configuration task, 39–40
   in organizations, 129–134
   meta-knowledge, 42
   procedural, 41–42
   stages of, 42–43
   surface, 40–41
   tacit, 40–41
Knowledge acquisition, 36, 44–51
   automated tools, 48–51
   knowledge engineer guided, 45–46
   process, 46–48
Knowledge-base, 34–36
Knowledge-based systems, 5, 11, 31–34
   and expert systems, 37–38
   and organizational knowledge, 132–135
   application types, 135–141
   applications, 32–34, 303–318
   corporate strategies for development, 146–150
   definition, 31
   deployment and maintenance, 155–158
   development, 36–37, 95–115, 145–158
   epistemology, 38–39
   examples, 32–34
   feasibility of applications, 152–153
   identification of applications, 150–152
   impact on industry structure, 144–145
   management of development, 153–155
   organizational benefits, 141–143
   organizational hazards, 143–144
   organizational issues in development, 145–158
   shell tools, 35–37, 321–337
   structure, 34–35
Knowledge engineering, 37
Knowledge processing,
   birth, 5–7
   moving from data processing, 20–21
Knowledge representation, 50, 57–87
   alternative approaches, 84–87
   frame hierarchies, 76–82
   hybrid, 95
   networked, 74–82
   semantic networks, 75
   using rules, 58–73

Learning,
   inductive, 49–50
   machine, 12

Machine translation, 11, 180–184
   application, 166–167
   commercial, 183–184
   knowledge-based, 182–183
   pattern-based, 180–181
   syntactic and semantic, 181–182

Natural language processing, 11, 165–190
   ambiguity in, 169–170, 179
   applications, 165–166, 186–189
   approaches to, 170–179
   business impact, 190
   interfaces, 184–185
   keyword matching, 170–173
   knowledge-based, 176–178
   multiple sentences and dialogs, 179
   semantic analyses, 175–176
   syntactic analyses, 173–176
   tools, 185–186

Neural networks, 12, 265–293
  applications, 282–291, 311, 341–347
  commercial tools, 282
  decision regions, 274
  developing applications, 276–282
  governmental support, 267
  history, 265–267
  Hopfield net, 275
  Kohonen's self-organizing feature map, 275–276
  learning, 273–274
  maintaining and integrating applications, 281–282
  network types, 269–271, 277–279
  perceptrons, 267–274
  relation to symbolic approaches, 265–266, 293
  strengths and limitations, 291–293
  structure of perceptrons, 270–272
  suitable problem types, 267–269, 266–277
  training and testing, 272–273, 279–281

Organizational knowledge, 129–134
  and knowledge-based systems, 132–135
  levels, 130
  management, 130–132

Prolog, 67–73, 170–171

Rules, 34–35, 58–73
  benefits, 73
  comparison with frame hierarchies, 82–84
  complex, 59–60
  development of systems, 96–103
  fuzzy rules, 242–246, 248–250
  in Prolog, 67–73
  inference procedures, 60–64
  limitations, 73
  meta-knowledge, 64
  reasoning under uncertainty, 65–66
  simple, 59–60
  structured, 59–60, 102–103

Semantic networks, 75
Speech processing, 11, 199
  ambiguity, 221–223
  business impact, 227
  morphological analysis, 226
  phonetic analysis, 225–226
  phonological analysis, 226
  recognition, 11, 223–224
  signal processing, 225
  understanding, 224–226

Tools for developing knowledge-based systems, 116–120
  commercial vendors, 120–122, 321–337
  hardware platforms, 118–119, 321–337
  selection guidelines, 119–120
  shell tools, 35–37, 117–120
  trends, 121–122
  types, 116–117, 321–337
Turing machine, 8–9